THE
DIVERSITY
ADVANTAGE

THE
DIVERSITY
ADVANTAGE

MULTICULTURAL IDENTITY IN

THE NEW WORLD ECONOMY

G. PASCAL ZACHARY

Westview
PRESS

A Member of the Perseus Books Group

Copyright © 2003 by G. Pascal Zachary

Westview Press books are available at special discounts for bulk purchases in the United States by corporations, institutions, and other organizations. For more information, please contact the Special Markets Department at the Perseus Books Group, 11 Cambridge Center, Cambridge MA 02142, or call (617) 252–5298, (800) 255-1514 or email j.mccrary@perseusbooks.com.

Published in 2003 in the United States of America by Westview Press, 5500 Central Avenue, Boulder, Colorado 80301–2877.

Find us on the World Wide Web at www.westviewpress.com

A Cataloging-in-Publication data record for this book is available from the Library of Congress.

ISBN 0–8133-4050-0

The paper used in this publication meets the requirements of the American National Standard for Permanence of Paper for Printed Library Materials Z39.48–1984.

10   9   8   7   6   5   4   3   2   1

FOR LIAM AND OONA

CONTENTS

PREFACE

SEPTEMBER 11, THE WORLD ECONOMIC RECESSION AND THE POLITICAL ECONOMY OF MULTICULTURAL IDENTITY

A Preface to the Paperback Edition

This book was originally written and published before September 11, 2001—before the attack on the World Trade Center towers and the Pentagon and the launch of a wide-ranging "war on terrorism." Before 9/11, the movement toward greater ethnic, racial and religious mixing seemed unstoppable around the world. After 9/11, separatism has reared its head in many quarters. The scholar Samuel P. Huntington and many other popular thinkers have seen in the new horrors of terrorism fresh evidence of a deepening "clash of civilizations." While the attacks exposed American complacency about domestic security and an innocence about the reach of terrorism, the awful events of that day did not end the global movement of social mingling—rather, it highlighted the tensions between diverse peoples in new ways.

All societies are in constant "clash" because conflict —moral, military, cultural, political and economic—is inherent in all societies. Conflict is the engine of change, the motor of history, and the way conflict is managed is the test of a good society. Conflict exists because conflicting demands and values contend in every societies. The question can never be how to create a world without conflict but rather how to manage the clash of values and ways of life that spring from the still-astonishing diversity within nations and across the globe. One way to manage the clash between peoples of the world would be to erect new fences, to build new walls: to return to a vanished era when all Americans (or Germans or Mexicans or Indians) were expected to hold the same set of values, at their core. Although it is still early, 9/11 may yet trigger a new era of conformity in the United States and across the globe. But as I write, there is scant evidence of a new separatism. Instead, the commitment to respect and tolerance for diverse groups and peoples remains strong. The social forces I originally chronicled in this book—the rise in mobility and intermarriage, the rise of multicultural forms of identity and the economic advantages accruing to open societies that draw frankly on immigrant energies—remain in full force. In the United States, enthusiasm for diversity persists. Moreover, there have been relatively few abuses recorded against immigrants, even those of Arab origin. Significantly, President George W. Bush refrained from blaming the Muslim religion for the terrorist attacks and even went to a mosque after the carnage as a show of support for the many "good" American Muslims.

Immigrants, while coming under new scrutiny, remain a potent force within American society. Rather than repudiate the value of immigration since 9/11, many Americans have concluded only that the country needs to be more choosy about the strangers it accepts. Justifiable blame has fallen on the Immigration and Naturalization Service (INS) for its ineptitude in granting visas to so many of the 9/11 hijackers—and for generally botching the job of managing the flow of visitors into and out of the United States. The failure on the part of the FBI and the CIA to mount a strong defense against terrorism also has contributed to a vague sense that the 9/11 attacks against the United States were preventable and, even if they were not, that the American embrace of immigrants and diversity is not to blame for the carnage. Quite the opposite. Americans cite their diverse backgrounds and affiliations as a source of national strength and, challenged by terrorists, see ways to bridge traditional enmities. In New York City, for instance, race relations have markedly improved, polls say, since 9/11. In one poll, conducted by the New York Times and CBS News in June 2002, for the first time in fourteen years more than half of the white, black and Hispanic respondents described "race relations" as "generally good."

To be sure, the attacks of 9/11 and the ongoing "war on terrorism" raise doubts in general about the ideal of an open society and its survivability in a world in which anxieties over security and strangers match enthusiasms for diversity and the exotic. Because these are difficult times for advocates of openness, it is worth recalling what forms of openness are generally believed to promote happiness and prosperity—for those ought to be the forms of openness that good societies encourage. Societies are open when they allow diverse races, ethnic groups and national identities to mix and match as they see fit, forming new associations even as they retain—to one degree or another—ancestral ties. Societies are open when they show respect for dissenting views, even dissenting views about ethno-racial categories that have been embraced as a bulwark of official attitudes toward diversity and tolerance. Societies are open when they construct procedures for resolving disputes over the values, tactics and goals of their differing groups and members. Societies are open when they realize that justice cannot be applied mechanically, without concern for the aspirations and sensitivities of contending groups and that majority rule cannot trump all. The word "diversity" is often misunderstood. The large question facing most countries in the world—and all of the wealthy countries—is what kind of diversity they wish to have, not whether they will have diversity. Mixing is now the norm, so that residents of a country cannot merely tolerate the newcomer but must allow the newcomer, the immigrant, the stranger to influence them in something approaching equal measure. In successful diverse societies, the natives and the newcomers borrow from one another. The content of political and economic debate in the successfully diverse country turns on the basis on which the exchange between native and newcomer occurs.

If there is a political economy of diversity, it arises out of the collision between natives and newcomers. In successfully diverse societies, the dominant group refrains from imposing a rigid style and set of values not only on the outsider but also on its own members. Rather than embracing one answer for the complexity of life, an open society allows many answers to flourish, with the confidence that the "clash of civilizations" in one society will produce a stronger and more vibrant, economically productive society. While successfully diverse societies encourage the emergence of fluid national, ethnic and racial identities, societies that struggle with diversity usually do so because a dominant group imposes a fixed set of identities and values on all of a nation's residents.

There is a difference, of course, between promoting tolerance and encouraging diverse residents to erase their ethnic, racial or cultural affiliations in favor of a homogeneous identity. Certainly xenophobia, bigotry and racism still exist in America. But conditions favor tolerance even in these worrisome times—not simply because of the official encouragement given to different ethnic or cultural groups but also because individuals have the freedom to withdraw from the groups they were born into. In the United States, people have a positive freedom to alter their inherited identity, but they also have a negative freedom to stick with their own kind. While successful diverse societies promote mixing, they also permit residents to retreat into ancestral communities or imagined communities, even allowing these people to wall themselves off from modernity. The United States is the world's foremost collection of hybridized peoples, yet the Amish, an immigrant group from the colonial era, has maintained its separate way of life with the support of U. S. law. When considering the one-fifth of voters in France who prefer the politics of Le Pen—a politics of exclusion and intolerance of difference—consider the possibility that the rise of Le Pen results from the failure of the French state to appropriately support conditions for a negative freedom—a freedom to retreat from a multiethnic society—that quells the anxieties of natives who wish to hold on to their traditions, as they understand them.

Successful diverse societies must appreciate that freedom from is as important as freedom to. Individuals and groups have wings, which carry them to new places and spaces, but they also have roots. A group should not prevent its members from withdrawing, rebelling or freely mingling with outsiders. Traditionalists should not hold hostage dissenting members of their group or tribe. Traditionalists are entitled to reject the new and to recoil from change. But they can only carry along the true believers. Members of tribes and traditions who harbor doubts—who want to explore other traditions, to participate in other tribes—ought to be free to do so. Discussions about group identity often concentrate on the basis for inclusion. But groups ought to pay equal attention to the means of exit; members who wish to mongrelize must have a clear path to adopting other traditions, other affiliations, even and especially while maintaining their own. Group authorities ought not to wall off their members from the rest of the world. All nations are of course only partially open. Limits against outsiders—whether conscious or unconscious, formal or informal—exist in every society. Certainly such limits exist in America. The question is never whether to allow an unrestricted flow of outsiders—and their ideas and practices—into a society. Limits are necessary in order to achieve a balance between roots and wings. Although some commentators believe that the United States has been torn apart by contending ethnic, racial and subnational groups, the "disuniting of America" is overstated. American unity is higher today than it has been at many other times in the nation's history. The United States is governed by laws, on which the diverse peoples of America have relatively little influence. American society imposes on its members a commercial and popular culture that, while respectful of diversity, exalts a sterile homogeneity and an ideal of happiness built on the relentless pursuit of consumable goods and experiences. And American leaders promote the use of English, whether in schools, government, the media or private life.

In the main, the forces that bring together those who live in America—the law, commercialism, language—are fair and reasonable. They could be fairer; they could better reflect the aspirations of the diverse peoples living in the United States. The insistence on English everywhere, for instance, has drawn criticism from many quarters, including foreign countries that exist, happily, with multiple official languages. The predictable manner in which immigrants to the U.S. lose their native tongue suggests to many outsiders that U.S. ethnic identities are a sham and that the experience of Americanization, even in an era of high levels of immigration and an official embrace of diversity, actually diminishes diversity. In this radical critique of American diversity, usually mounted by Europeans and Canadians with plural linguistic traditions, expressions of "ethnic pride" in America are seen as hollow, an ode to a vanished diversity rather than evidence of real difference. This cri-

tique ignores the complexity of American society and the paradoxical struggle to affirm traditional identities and to transcend them at once. To quote
the writer Richard Rodriguez, "Americans are gathering together and splitting apart simultaneously." The new combinations give rise to new identities
and revive traditional ethnicities at the same time—all for the pursuit of happiness. Yet after 9/11 I am more sober than before about the strengths of the
U.S. and, while still sanguine about the American model of diversity, I believe we should pay close to attention to the country's critics, yet American
omnipotence, while a useful bogeyman for many foreign demagogues, remains more fiction than fact.

In the following pages, I argue that the diversity of the U.S. population—
ethnic, social, racial and national—makes the country more economically
competitive than Germany, Japan and other leading national economies that
rely heavily, or even exclusively, on a culturally uniform labor force. I argue
that although U.S. macroeconomic polices and the size of the country's domestic market are important determinants of American economic success,
the critical reason for the global dominance of many U.S. industries—and
the U.S. economy as a whole—is the country's diverse workforce. Out of the
collision of these diverse talents, I argue, comes creativity, adaptability and
innovation.

If the U.S. economy is so competitive, one might ask, why as I write, is
the stock marketing falling steadily, the dollar losing value for the first time
in many years and many U.S. companies filing for bankruptcy? Moreover,
the dot.com sector has imploded, financial scandal has exposed the failures
of U.S. corporate accounting and the telecommunications industry has suffered from large losses and layoffs. These developments raise doubts about
the health of the U.S. economy and whether American industry can remain
the global business pacesetter. Is the diversity of the American workforce, in
the face of recent economic setbacks, still such a decisive asset? To critics of
American power, the collapse of U.S. stocks, the dollar's slide and the bust in
high-tech are welcome news. U.S. arrogance about an unending boom was
exposed as wishful thinking. To be sure, the downturn reveals the perils of
too much money chasing too few opportunities. Investors sank $880 billion
in telecommunications from 1997 through mid-2002 and an estimated one-
half of the value of this investment has been lost. Dozens of companies have
failed and the industry has shed half a million jobs. The pain is widespread.
But the telecommunications collapse in the United States doesn't signal the
sunset of American leadership in innovation industries. "Thumped . . . but
don't write off American capitalism just yet" is how The Economist head-
lined a lead editorial in July 2002. The British weekly went on to write:

"The American economy is the most creative and enterprising and productive system ever devised," George Bush told a Wall Street audience this week, before moving on to acknowledge some recent embarrassments. He was right about this, of course. The anguish of some American commentators over the spate of corporate scandals and about what these reveal about the supposedly rotten core of American capitalism is about as exaggerated—and in many cases as downright phony—as the corresponding delight of their European counterparts. An intelligent response to the Enrons and WorldComs needs to begin by acknowledging the strengths of America's basic model and the dangers of attempting to fix what is not broken.

Another reason for caution in evaluating the American economy is that Japan and Western Europe aren't faring any better. Leading telecommunications companies in these parts of the world also are writing off bad investments and scaling back plans. In short, the crisis in the American economy isn't the result—as in the 1980s—of an ascendant national rival. Rather Germany, France and Japan—the three national economies whose industries are the most competitive against the significant U.S. industries—are not resurgent. Neither is the fifteen-nation European Union. Japan and the EU face a huge task of modernizing their managerial and technical ranks—merely to draw even with the United States. And despite the crisis of confidence, American industry still snatches much of the best talent from all over the world. German and Japanese rivals, by comparison, remain constrained by the social or political pressures that put natives at the head of job queues even when foreigners present stronger resumes. German and Japanese companies not only don't get the cream of the crop from India, China or Russia—three talent hot spots dominated by U.S. corporations—they don't get their fair share of their own country's talent. A significant number of top students and younger entrepreneurs in Germany and Japan move permanently to the United States. Yet few Americans relocate to Japan or Germany for work.

A brief story highlights the way in which the talented people of the world view the United States as the ultimate destination—and thus create continuing difficulties for Germany and Japan in their economic competition with the United States. Erik Masing, a Berlin software entrepreneur who I will write more about later, cofounded a company in Germany with a Russian scientist. Such transnational pairings are routine in the United States, but they remain unusual in Germany. Masing favors a wider opening for foreign talent in his country, where he is frustrated by his inability to find risk-taking computer code writers. After I published the first edition of this book, I spoke with him about a technical alliance he sought to forge with a company in Boston. Masing figured that he needed a tie into the U.S. in order to help his company stay sharp. He visited Boston expecting to meet some "cowboy" Americans or perhaps some Asian immigrants. But when he toured the offices of the company, he heard a familiar sound coming from the cubicles where the code writers worked: German. Everyone was speaking German.

Masing unwittingly had stumbled on a group of top German code writers who had left home together for the Boston area, where Harvard University and the Massachusetts Institute of Technology nourish the innovation scene. So through an odd twist, Masing found in America the very Germans he sought unsuccessfully in his own land.

As long as the Masings of the world have such encounters, American industrial leadership will be hard to rival.

The state of American industry, of course, is no measure of the health of world capitalism. Capitalism is defined by its crises and by the way capitalists adapt to crises. The current global crisis—of overproduction, deflation, deepening inequality and hyperspeculation followed by depreciation of corporate assets—has not run its course. But a few things are clear. Neoliberal economic managers, of the sort produced by the International Monetary Fund, the World Trade Organization and the U.S. Treasury Department, have suffered gravely over the past five years. The rigid belief in the ameliorative effects of open markets has been exposed as naive and, worse, destructive. While the spread of diversity around the world paralleled the triumph of neoliberal capitalism in the 1990s, these two forces travel on different tracks. The mongrelization of the world's population is an independent historical force. Mongrelization, in its simplest form of global migration, is one of the three engines of globalization, along with capitalism and advanced technology. Mongrelization, or high levels of ethno-racial mixing, predate the onset of capitalism and the rise of nationalism. Even in a period of relative economic decline, high-levels of immigration are likely to continue in western Europe because European nation-states are short of people and must import them simply to maintain the current size of their economies. The same is true of Japan. Thus, the breakdown of national identity and race—as fixed social categories—is a separate movement, coincident with contemporary capitalism but not a consequence of it. The ascent of hybridity is unhinged from economic ideology and will continue in any economic environment. Even during a period of more active government regulation of industry and capital markets and of more nationalistic economic policies, migration and mixing will continue apace.

For the paperback edition of this book, I have revised and updated the text, chiefly to take account of the events of September 11 and to introduce a few more relevant profiles. In updating the book, I chose a new title, The Diversity Advantage. I believe the new title more clearly conveys the central argument of the book, which is that ethnically and racially mixed societies are more successful than homogeneous societies or those that try to impose a single ethnoracial or religious pattern on all residents. The book's original title, The Global Me: New Cosmopolitans and the Competitive Edge, reflected one of the important subthemes of the book, regarding the diverse ways in which individuals personally respond to the growing diversity of their native countries and the radical increase in mixing and mobility. Individuals still lie at the core of the book, providing vivid examples of the "identity took kit" available to people on all rungs of the social ladder. Since I argue that group identities—whether racial, religious, ethnic, national or subnational—can no longer fully define the social-economic reality of individuals, "the global me" remains a useful and accurate label for a new kind of transnational personality who possesses both roots and wings. But the phrase, "the global me" obscures my argument about the future of nation-states and the ingredients of national success. Much of the book is devoted to answering the question of why nations succeed or fail, and most of my answers to this question can be explained by the phrase "the diversity advantage."

One Friday, a few weeks after the September 11 attacks, I stood in front of a tall, whitewashed mosque set back from a busy commercial street that cut through a densely populated valley in northern California. Friday is the holiest day of the Islamic week, what Saturday is for Jews and Sunday is for Christians. As I watched nearby, five rows of Afghan men prayed in the hot midday sun. They mourned the death of an old friend in the suburban town of Hayward, across the bay from San Francisco. Hayward is home to the greatest concentration of Afghans in the United States. Until 9/11, they lived in relative anonymity. Now they are no longer alone.

On the day of my visit, an American flag flew in front of the mosque. The flag went up after 9/11. Before that, Afghans felt no need to advertise their loyalty to America. Things have changed. The flag, atop of 50-foot pole, can be seen from a distance.

Afghans, whether devout Muslims or not, suddenly have something to prove. At the time, the U.S. government was at war with the Taliban government of Afghanistan—and Afghans in California understandably don't wish to be considered disloyal. Along with other immigrants in the United States, whose loyalty may also be questioned, they want to show sensitivity to an America at risk.

The task is complicated by the cumulative effect of twenty years of high levels of immigration into the United States; roughly one million a year for two decades. The 2000 census put the number of foreign-born people in the United States at 56 million. One-quarter of the residents in California, the largest state, are foreign born. In New York City, which suffered the most from the September 11 attacks, 43 percent of the residents are foreign born and another 9.2 percent are the children of two foreign-born parents. The numbers suggest a radical shift in American sensibilities. If there was once a single criterion of what it means to be an American, there no longer is. As ethnoracial fragmentation rises in the United States, no "group" commands enough of a following to impose its model on the others. The pressure on subcultures to conform to a single ideal of what counts as Americanness is perhaps less than it has ever been. In World War II, law-abiding citizens of Japanese descent were jailed as a precaution. In late 2001, Afghans freely criticized the U.S. bombing of their country, and some even complained that Islamic extremists have reason to resent America. President Bush, although elected on the strength of his fervent Christianity, visited a mosque and pointedly said that he has no argument with genuine Muslims, only with the phony ones who endorse or defend terrorism.

As the Afghan men dispersed on the holy Friday, their prayers done, three volunteers from a San Francisco civil rights group passed out leaflets, explaining to the Afghans that they should not speak to any agents of the FBI without the presence of an attorney, which the group they represent would provide free of charge. The volunteers also told the Afghans that they should report any "hate crimes" they experience.

One of the volunteers, Nadia Olmedo, is the child of immigrants. She is a social worker whose parents hail from South America. "People in this country should feel solidarity with Afghans, not fear them," she said.

Her words echo an American motto: e pluribus unum, "out of one, many." The phrase is deceptively simple. Just how does America create unity out of diverse peoples—and in a time of war?

The United States once imposed uniformity on its people through legal means, such as segregated schools, or by actively discouraging newcomers from maintaining ties with their homelands and encouraging them to abandon their native languages in favor of English. Other countries in the world, including Germany, adopted a practice of forced assimilation. One of the great outcomes of the civil rights movement of the 1960s was to discredit assimilationist policies, not only those imposed on African Americans but also on the so-called white ethnics. The landmark immigration act of 1965 shifted the emphasis of immigration towards people from poorer developing countries as opposed to Europe, the historic source of America's population. Immigrants from developing countries were generally brown—people from Asia and Mexico. These newcomers took advantage of the civil rights transformation, benefiting from laws and programs originally designed to assist African Americans. Immigrant lifestyles and values flourished. Newcomers still made accommodations to mainstream "white" America, but they were more assertive about their ethnic or national loyalties. By the early 1990s, tolerance of immigrant cultures was so engrained in U.S. law and social practice that many conservatives and even some liberals complained about "the unraveling of America."

Some unraveling is inevitable, of course, and attractive. Newcomers have energized the United States, helping its economy, giving its population a younger, more dynamic cast. But their large numbers have carried costs as well as benefits. If there was once a prescription for a typical American, there is no more. The differences among Americans, in short, probably are as great today as they were during the last great wave of immigration at the turn of the twentieth century. These differences seem more likely to endure, as immigrants use the Internet, the telephone and easier modes of travel to maintain connections with their native lands—and to cultivate their differences.

To be sure, there is something wonderful about the new America, borne of immigration and radical mixing of peoples. At a Catholic church not far from the Hayward mosque, the congregation consists of people from Brazil, Nigeria, the Philippines, Mexico and yes, the United States. Masses are held in Mandarin Chinese, Spanish and Portuguese. Not only are immigrants welcome to worship at St. John the Baptist Church, but also the priest says that the parish's survival depends on them.

Father John Maxwell, the parish priest, walks his talk too. One Sunday, some weeks after 9/11, the church gymnasium filled with hundreds of immigrants from the West African country of Nigeria. They came to celebrate their country's fall harvest festival, serving palm wine, roasted chicken and rice. Father Maxwell donned a native Nigerian costume and even danced to Nigeria's frenetic hi-life music.

Such scenes are a staple of U.S. life. Even the country's armed forces, which include tens of thousands of immigrant soldiers, celebrate diversity. The insistence on tolerance, meanwhile, is so routine as to become a cliché. A public-service television advertisement aired after 9/11 depicted dozens of people from different ethnic and racial backgrounds, including Arab-looking men and women. Each person said proudly, "I am an American." The ad, designed by an industry group, sends a clear message: e pluribus unum.

But what can the phrase "out of one, many" mean in a country honeycombed with ethnic, racial and national diversity? America is a world society, so that the ritual of invoking a mythical unity is a hollow one. In the wake of September 11, the United States remains a divided but cohesive nation. These divisions don't flow from differences over how to respond to terror. Most Americans are convinced that military attacks on Afghanistan and other sponsors of terrorism are justified. But coordinating the response to the threat of terrorism, especially the domestic responses, poses difficulties for a U.S. society accustomed to duplication, overlaps and bureaucratic failures. America, at its best and worst, is a disordered place. The very breadth of its diversity brings great innovations but also makes coordination and crisis management more difficult. It is a testimony to America's status as a world society that hundreds of people from scores of nations died in the attacks on the World Trade Center. But the same senseless violence may also have killed a simplistic notion about American unity. Differences among those who live in the United States are too profound, too stubborn, to erase. The genius of America is that it affords its people the opportunity to reinvent themselves and their communities time after time. America's diversity advantage, in short, is a way of life. No manner of social monitoring and suspension of individual rights, prompted by wartime anxieties, will revive assimilationist policies.

President Bush has tried to smooth away the rough edges of America's diversity advantage by elevating the importance of citizenship. Great diversity can be tolerated among citizens, perhaps, but not noncitizens. So goes the argument, which is Bush's justification for trying some noncitizens in secret in military courts. Many members of Congress similarly are placing more importance on the distinction between citizens and noncitizens. They have required, for instance, that federal airport security workers hold U.S. citizenship. Yet contradictions abound. Members of the armed forces—the very soldiers fighting the war on terrorism—need not be citizens of the U.S.

Citizenship was never intended to be the apotheosis of American identity; after all, immigrants are welcomed to this country in the first place precisely because they are not citizens. They are welcomed because they are strangers, aliens, others, different, not one of us. Their very differences benefits the United States economically, socially and culturally. Immigrant energies are the soil from which American power springs. The American genius is the reflexive grasp of the diversity advantage.

This stubborn truth will always shatter utopian fantasies of unity—or dystopian visions of backlash against diversity and multiculturalism. In the illusion of a unified America, in the myth of e pluribus unum, the triumph of American multiculturalism is paradoxically ratified anew. The inescapable truth is that American security is built on a hybrid foundation and a frank recognition of the nation's diversity advantage.

G. Pascal Zachary
October 2002
Berkeley, California and Accra, Ghana

INTRODUCTION

THE NEW COSMOPOLITANS

Of every hue and caste am I.
I resist anything better than my own diversity.
—WALT WHITMAN[1]

We have needed the new peoples . . .
to save us from our own stagnation.
—RANDOLPH BOURNE[2]

Diversity defines the health and wealth of nations in a new century. Mighty is the mongrel. The mixing of races, ethnic groups and nationalities—at home and abroad—is at a record level. The hybrid is hip. In a world of deepening connections, individuals, corporations and entire nations draw strength and personality from as near as their local neighborhood and as far away as a distant continent. The impure, the mélange, the adulterated, the blemished, the rough, the black-and-blue, the mix-and-match—these people are inheriting the earth. Mixing is the new norm.

This is no passing fashion but a deep change. Say good-bye to the pure, the straight, the smooth. Forget the original, the primordial, the one. They are old news, Humpty-Dumpties, shattered when the walls fell down. No one can put them back together again. The apostles of purity are doomed. Resistance is futile.

Nativists and skinheads, rage. Nationalists, wave your flags and sing your anthems. Your storms and anxieties only signal the calm ahead. History betrays you. Mixing trumps isolation. It spawns creativity, nourishes the human spirit, spurs economic growth and empowers nations. Racial, ethnic and national categories no longer impose fixed barriers and unbending traditions. These categories do not vanish either, but join the many pieces inside a kaleidoscope, which presents a different image from one instant to the next.

And there are many pieces indeed: as many as 5,000 ethnic groups and 600 living languages.[3] The combinations of these groups are breathtaking; so are the combinations of those combinations. Far from creating a deadening sameness, mongrelization breeds greater diversity. And this hardy diversity will defend and sustain itself.

The mania for mongrels is overdue. They are everywhere, after all, lacking only a song, a logo, a credo. They need to announce themselves to the world. This is their moment. No more apologies. No more choosing between one race or another, one ethnicity or another, one self or another. No more thinking that rootlessness is the opposite of rooted. Cheer thy mongrel selves. Cheer thy manifold attachments. Mongrels are not accidents, unavoidable collisions of the unnatural, but the flowering of fine humanity. Whole societies, moreover, can possess roots and wings. Nothing can stop the rise of mongrel nations, mocking the very idea that union requires homogeneity and victory depends on smothering dissent in a blanket of uniformity.

Rich nations will go mongrel because it is right and good. They will go mongrel because it is the only antidote to stagnation, the only durable source of innovation, the one viable way to preserve their traditions while embracing change.

For the world's wealthy countries, the question is not whether to embrace diversity but how.

RADICAL MIXING

The virtues of diversity and multiculturalism are familiar to many Americans, especially those living in the immigration-rich East and West coasts. Throughout the United States, racial and ethnic mixing is commonplace, and hybridity is well established. Flexible identities are proliferating. As many as 30 percent of all Hispanics and Asians marry outside their ethnic group, and in the nation's most polyglot cities interethnic marriage is the norm. Significantly, mixing breeds more mixing: intermarriage rates are highest among people who report that their own roots are mixed. People are awakening to the primacy of impurity. Soledad O'Brien, a journalist for NBC, has a mother who is Cuban and black and a father who is Australian and Irish. "When I get on the subway in New York today," she says, "most of the people look like me—they're a mix of some kind."[4]

This sort of mixing is winning wide acceptance in the United States, but even its fans lack a vocabulary to describe, defend or even celebrate it. Americans are trapped in outmoded ways of thinking about ethnic and racial mixture. That diversity is a big plus for U.S. global competitiveness isn't widely appreciated. The nation's power—political, economic and cultural—depends heavily on diversity. This ought to reassure Americans who worry that mongrelization weakens national unity. People abroad envy the American capacity for converting the tensions spawned by intermingling of different peoples into a creative force. But they fail to understand how the United States achieves this and are bewildered at the thought of doing it themselves.

Americans are bewildered too. The traditional way of thinking about ethnic and racial pride, born of the 1960s civil rights movement, makes less and less sense. America is no longer a noisy street fair in which every ethnic group gets a booth in which to peddle its foods, clothes, music and rituals. In the streets of this fading multicultural America, each group received respect and dignity, but no one questioned group boundaries. Members couldn't jump them at will; their authentic identities were permanently written on them by biology or history.

The new multicultural American transcends these hyphenated identities of a generation ago. New Americans live both within and beyond the traditional boundaries of ethnoracial identities. The old constellation of hyphenated Americans still imposes its grid on society, presenting a view of America as a kind of United Nations, when actually these metaphorical nations have bled into one another. Or rather, hybrid identities are increasingly the preferred way of showing allegiance to these groups. People live through layers of affiliation, putting on another layer or taking one off, depending on the setting. "They're not just sharing; they're creating entirely new intercultural mixes," says one observer. "They're not denying who they are, or trying to be something they're not. They're genuinely and authentically adopting something from another culture, not based on a sense of inferiority, but because hey, I like that; that's cool."

Accepted categories can't describe this new reality. Not only is ethnicity losing its traditional meaning; race is too. Consider the suburb of Walnut, home to 32,000 people in southern California. At the town's high school, ethnic consciousness is prominent, but students claim a piece of ethnicities that they weren't born into. Asian students named a black to be president of their Asian club. The Black Students Union chose a white faculty adviser. A Chinese American who speaks fluent Spanish is one of the most popular members of the Latin Alliance. One student—whose parents hail from Egypt and the Philippines—explains why the school's diversity is so popular. "We're going to be better people when we graduate because we already learned how to get along," she says. "We have an advantage."

This isn't just talk. At Walnut's junior prom, Thai-born "Sara Vichit, luminous in a shimmering gown, is slow-dancing with a black senior, Chris Matthews, whose tuxedoed elegance hints at the adult world he is graduating into. There's Jesse Waites, who is white, moving in sync to a hip-hop beat with his African American date, Tiffany Palmer, and a Latino friend, Steven Casado." As one observer of Walnut notes, "Forget the increasingly anomalous all-white world on prime-time TV. . . . Here, diversity is commonplace, comfortable—and cool."[5]

The new American is actively, creatively, sincerely and positively *mongrel*.

Freedom lies at the core of his or her being: the freedom to pick and choose among a vast array of human traits. Ethnic pride is a necessary condition for such flexibility, but it is not sufficient. These new Americans are ethnic-plus. They have roots *and* wings. They are proud of their backgrounds but unafraid of *adding* to their identities because they realize that doesn't *subtract* from who they are. For them, mongrelization means taking ethnic pride to a new level—by drawing on the whole scene. They are realizing, in a fresh way, an old American ideal. "You cannot spill a drop of American blood," Herman Melville wrote in 1849, "without spilling the blood of the whole world."[6] More than ever, Melville's declaration applies not only to America but to all nations.

MONGREL CAPITALISM

Mongrelization suits this economic and technologic age. Diversity pencils out. Money follows the mongrel. Innovation favors the mixed. The adept handling of diversity is the secret of economic competitiveness and national vitality.

This contradicts conventional wisdom. Many political leaders, economists and social critics believe that homogeneity boosts a nation's economic competitiveness and wealth so that it is a worthy aim on strictly pragmatic grounds. The decade of the 1980s, when the world's two great monocultures, Germany and Japan, vied with the United States for global economic leadership, reinforced the view that monolithic societies outperform diverse ones. Scholars and policymakers—not to mention ordinary Japanese and Germans—boasted that drawing on "purity" was more efficient than drawing on diverse social and cultural sources and that the United States, "saddled" with diversity, faced an inherent disadvantage in competition with Germany and Japan. If those two countries needed to learn from outsiders, meanwhile, they could directly import know-how. They could separate the people from the skills, so to speak, and thus retain their monocultural advantages.[7]

After a decade of relative stagnation in Germany and Japan, this argument has lost force. In Germany, leading corporations and government officials are quietly searching for ways to begin importing large numbers of skilled and professional workers—a frank, if still veiled, recognition of the failures of their brand of monoculturalism. This shift is accompanied by a renewed effort in Germany to raise the status of ethnic minorities and redefine the terms of assimilation. In Japan, the picture is different. The Japanese remain uneasy even with the idea of absorbing outsiders into the mainstream. In contrast to Germany, in Japan no major corporation nor civic leader promotes the goal of an ethnically diverse country. Yet tellingly, Japan's influential Economic Planning Agency urges that the country accept more foreign professionals and other trained workers to revitalize Japan's economy. And a special commission of the prime minister calls for shifts in Japanese society that would make the country more appealing to outsiders willing to move there. Both bodies advocate making it easier for talented foreigners to obtain Japanese citizenship, a benefit today denied even some native-born Japanese of foreign descent. These calls for change hardly mean Japan will go mongrel. But at least they suggest a growing awareness of the folly of trying to maintain national purity.[8]

To be sure, the economic fortunes of nations rise and fall. The performance of Japan and Germany, relative to the United States, could reverse in a decade. But if it does, it will happen because those countries learned the requirements of success in a new century—that paradoxically, national success is now based on the embrace of a radically new kind of mixing. Every rich country—and for that matter, each individual, community and corporation—faces the same central question: How do you protect your identity, or inherited affiliations of race, religion and ethnicity, and yet allow yourself to be porous, to acquire additional attachments and then somehow strike a balance among these contending, overlapping ties?

HYBRID TALK

Much confusion about diversity stems from loose talk, people saying the same words but meaning something different. We need new terms to get the job done.

Words like "diversity," "pluralism" and "multiculturalism" are too broad. They don't stand for anything. They have been emptied of meaning in debates over levels of immigration, degrees of assimilation and just how much ground the dominant social and cultural styles should cede to newcomers. While popular, the terms "diversity," "pluralism" and "multiculturalism" obscure more than they reveal. Consider probably the most entrenched of these terms, multiculturalism. This refers to the idea that ethnic communities, while maintaining the languages and cultures distinct from those of the mainstream society, are legitimate and consistent with citizenship in the United States or other diverse nations. "Multiculturalism also means recognition of the need for special laws, institutions and social policies to overcome barriers to full participation of various ethnic groups in society."[9]

This is all well and good, but only a starting point. The term "multiculturalism" begs many important questions. What type of multiculturalism? On whose terms? Which laws promote assimilation into mainstream society without undercutting minority identities? Which laws go too far in "protecting" ethnic or racial groups so that their members become resentful, stigmatized and less likely to participate in mainstream society? How do multiculturalists view the blurring of borders between ethnicities that were once seen as static? Do they see border jumpers as turning their backs on their own "people"? If the guardians of multiculturalism seek to protect the integrity of different groups, do they defend the freedom of individuals to acquire multiple ethnoracial ties?

Because of the looseness of the term "multiculturalism," nearly everyone can claim it. In Germany, multiculturalism still lets the government dismiss a female teacher for wearing a chador, or religious head scarf, in school or to deport (to Turkey) a fourteen-year-old boy, born and raised in Germany of Turkish-born parents.[10] In Canada, multiculturalism deters a French parent from allowing her children to do their schoolwork in English, even though she wants the child to do so. In the United States, multiculturalists are liberals and conservatives, who favor old-fashioned assimilation or promote separation of groups. Under the banner of multiculturalism, they may support—or oppose—the decision by the U.S. Census to allow (in the year 2000) respondents to essentially create their own racial and ethnic categories. Some multiculturalists see this infidelity as eradicating traditional cultures, whereas others see it as an inevitable step toward their ideal of a single "race" based on massive mixing.

The possibility that Americans can simultaneously maintain both traditional and newfangled identities escapes many multiculturalists. Yet they no longer accept the phrase (found on the back of American coins) *e pluribus unum*, "out of many, one." Multiculturalists are comfortable with difference—that there is no American melting pot but rather an always shifting alliance between individuals and groups. They still lack a language to describe how a person can blend into the crowd in one place, stick out with a traditional identity in another and display an eclectic mix of attachments in a third setting. Because they lack this language, many multiculturalists, who should be sympathetic to boundary-jumping Americans, are frightened by them and don't recognize their value to the United States.

To describe these category busters, we need new terms. This seems to be one of those cases where—to paraphrase the historian David Hollinger—it is "better to struggle to redefine an old word than to develop and popularize a new one."[11]

The old words I prefer are "mongrel," "hybrid" and "cosmopolitan." Each has problems, but when a new twist is added to their meaning, each can do the job.

Let's begin with "mongrel," a much maligned word that suggests "half-breed," "mutt" and "bastard." The newest edition of the *Concise Oxford Dictionary* describes the word as "offensive" and traces its origins to medieval

Germany. The dictionary offers two definitions: "a dog of no definable type or breed" and "a person of mixed descent." These meanings of mongrel are common. Other dictionaries further suggest that the mixing is "indiscriminate," so that mongrelization seems random and without purpose.[12]

"Mongrel" must take on a new meaning that conveys the idea of positive, purposeful mixing—a mixing that expands freedom while honoring the origins and preferences of those who mix. "Mongrel" also should not convey deracination, but the possibility of a rich specificity—too rich to fit existing categories. Thus, the mongrel is the category breaker and the source of innovation, daring and toleration. "Mongrel" is a defiant, unapologetic label. It signals a declaration of solidarity with all outsiders; with all those who intermarry, migrate to another country; learn another language; adopt a new religion; display a new public persona while maintaining former ones. By calling oneself a mongrel, one sides with the shunned, the neglected, the overlooked, the underdog. In this sense, mongrels are heroic. They have more perspective than the one-dimensional person and are more willing to rebel against tradition or question habitual ways of thinking and doing. Creativity, in the broadest sense, is part of the human condition. But in a world where tribes are increasingly in collision, mongrels can be more creative than supposed pure breeds. And as a result, mongrels aren't underdogs anymore.

I am not alone in seeking to transform "mongrel" from a slur into a postmulticultural ideal. No less a literary titan than Salman Rushdie also gives "mongrel" a positive spin, using the word to celebrate the intermingling of different cultures and to rebuke those who insist that mixing will inevitably kill off their own roots. Rushdie "celebrates hybridity, impurity, intermingling, the transformation that comes of new and unexpected combinations of human beings, cultures, ideas, politics, movies, songs." He "rejoices in mongrelization," insisting that "melange, hotchpotch, a bit of this and a bit of that is how newness enters the world." He embraces "change-by-fusion, change-by-conjoining," singing what he calls "a love song to our mongrel selves."[13]

The mongrel doesn't suggest a universal self, or a global soul formed out of an amalgamation of humanity. That's because there is no common set of values, practices and perspectives for all of humanity, or even big swatches of it. It is troubling that some intelligent people think otherwise; that they mistake the rise of an international culture for the demise of local cultures and the need for every educated, moral person on the planet to join hands in some great "circle of we." The classic cosmopolitan ideal—of a humanity defined by species-wide values and styles—is neither possible nor desirable. Instead, we have the diversity advantage: local people who are neither limited to their particularities nor doomed to an empty we-are-the-world universalism.

TWO OTHER TERMS help describe the realities of mixing. The first is "hybrid," which sounds more neutral than "mongrel." Many scholars use the term to refer to what sociologist Robin Cohen calls "the evolution of new, dynamic, mixed cultures." To be sure, the literal meaning of hybridity carries a different sense. "As plant breeders know," Cohen writes, "hybrids have marked tendencies toward sterility and uniformity, precisely the opposite meaning those who used the term 'hybridization' intended to convey." But Cohen concedes that "misnomers are common in the English language" and eventually acquire their given meaning through the sheer weight of repetition. He predicts the same for hybridity.[14]

I am less certain. "Hybridity" has a clinical feel to it. Who will want to call themselves a new hybrid? Genetic engineering has far to go before that term will be biologically accurate. "Mongrel" sounds much hipper and insurgent but fails to convey the positive sense in which all of humanity share the same boat. The word "cosmopolitan" does this, while still getting across that an individual isn't bound by his inherited race or ethnicity. "Cosmopolitan" suggests the freedom to break with tradition in order to adapt to new conditions or promote happiness. The word is more neutral than "mongrel" and sexier than "hybrid" (though perhaps only for the reason that feminist Helen Gurley Brown named her magazine *Cosmopolitan*, spawning the moniker "Cosmo Girl").

But "cosmopolitan" has shortcomings. Early in the twentieth century, some disparaged the term, largely out of disillusionment with efforts to achieve international peace and lay the groundwork for "world citizenship." The failure of the League of Nations (in the 1920s) to halt the drift toward a second world war surely undermined the cosmopolitan ideal. Then the inability of the United Nations to prevent the Cold War—and the cynical ways in which both the Soviet Union and the United States sought to mobilize world opinion—further hurt proponents of cosmopolitanism and world government.

When in the 1960s and 1970s a passion for ethnic "roots" emerged in the United States, cosmopolitanism took another blow. Then in the 1990s, more than twenty new nation-states—largely based on a dominant ethnic community—emerged, making it no longer possible to imagine ethnic and national identities disappearing or even fading. The term "cosmopolitan" can be reinvented, however. A new cosmopolitanism is consistent with a passion for roots and nourished by it. In the twenty-first century, a cosmopolitan revival will appeal to people who want international solidarity but not at the cost of local affiliations; people who want to tackle global problems but not by bypassing national and local governments or civic society.

I am not alone in wanting to revive the cosmopolitan label. Anthony

Appiah, a Harvard University professor born in the west African nation of Ghana, favors the term "rooted cosmopolitan" because he believes there's no point in roots if you can't take them with you. In his view, two seeming opposites—roots and wings—can be reconciled. He imagines "a world in which *everyone* is a rooted cosmopolitan, attached to a home of his or her own, with its own cultural particularities, but taking pleasure from the presence of other, different, places that are home to other, different people."

In *The Diversity Advantage*, I will use "mongrel," "hybrid," and "cosmopolitan" interchangeably to argue for a life of roots and wings, certainty and surprise. These divergent forces need not tear people apart but can knit them together, ensuring prosperity at the same time. As Appiah writes: "We do not have to deal decently with people from other cultures and traditions in spite of our differences; we can treat others decently, humanely, through our differences. The humanist requires us to put our differences aside; the cosmopolitan insists that sometimes it is the differences we bring to the table that make it rewarding to interact at all."[15]

THE FORMULA

With clearer terms, this book's overriding idea is easier to grasp: Hybrid societies trump monocultures in a climate of social cohesion. High levels of cohesion are not the result of an absence of conflict, but arise from creative conflict. High levels of cohesion arise from the recognition that a conflict-free society is an impossibility and that the best results come from treating unavoidable conflicts between different groups as potentially beneficial, not destructive. In a cohesive society, hybrid individuals and groups increase a nation's power by strengthening economic competitiveness and "social capital," the intangible resources (such as trust, initiative and problem solving capacity) of a society that contributes to economic success.

Since hybridity brings innovation and homogeneity brings stagnation, the wealthy nations of the world face three related challenges: First, they must choose which kind of diversity they want. Second, they must create a new basis for social harmony within their country. Third, they must promote and achieve hybridity among individuals and groups without jeopardizing social cohesion.

HYBRIDITY + SOCIAL COHESION = NATIONAL POWER

These challenges must be faced because greater diversity seems inescapable. Demographic shifts alone make this so. More mixing won't occur because people suddenly love the stranger (though some clearly will), but because they have a pressing need. They need the stranger because of a startling demographics shift—most pronounced in Europe and in Japan—that is only starting to hit home. All rich nations face population stagnation or even outright decline. Low birthrates and an aging citizenry are clear threats to their vitality. One in five Japanese, Germans and Italians will be over age sixty-five in 2010. The proportion of elderly will be nearly as high in France, Britain and Spain. The percentage of elderly in the United States, Canada and Australia, while significantly lower, will still rise sharply over the next ten years. But the United States, Canada and Australia have effectively defused the demographic bomb by accepting high levels of immigrants, who are younger and have larger families. Europe and Japan still hear the demographic bomb ticking and, despite opposition to more immigration, may indeed accept that mixing through immigration is preferable to the erosion of their national cultures through infertility.

Besides demographic factors, rich nations will be more open to mixing from beyond their borders because of trends in technology, intermarriage, work, leisure and personal identity. The coming collisions between ethnic groups, races and nationalities make the achievement of social harmony more important than ever. Nations that learn how to resolve conflicts between majorities and minorities, natives and newcomers, will increase their chances to create wealth and happiness for all. They will not do this alone. Individuals, corporations and nongovernmental organizations (or activist groups) must also respond to rising diversity in novel and courageous ways. Their various responses to the challenge of diversity suggest that only by supporting hybrid forms of individual and group identity can societies manage the inherent conflict between diversity and harmony.

This tension is reshaping every part of human life. Virtually ignored by analysts of national power, hybridity explains much about change *within* rich nations and competition *between* them. While hybridity explains some dimensions of developing countries, it goes to the heart of what makes wealthy nations vital or stagnant, winners or losers.

An analysis of rich nations comprises the core of this book. The world's twenty-six richest nations are home to nearly one billion people, or about one-sixth of humanity. As a bloc, these nations account for roughly 85 percent of the world's output, 80 percent of its trade, 70 percent of its direct investment, 90 percent of its research and development, three-quarters of its telephone lines and nine-tenths of its Internet usage. These nations cover parts of Asia (Japan, Korea, Taiwan, Singapore, Australia and New Zealand); North America (Canada and the United States); and Western Europe (including Britain, Denmark, Germany, France, Iceland, Ireland, Italy, Sweden).[16]

Rich nations are the only ones in which the power of hybridity can be fully realized. They are the only nations that have the capacity to deliver the security and the rights that are the foundation of cosmopolitan communities and mongrel lives. As the Canadian writer Michael Ignatieff has observed, "a postnational consciousness" is only possible "for those cosmopolitans who are lucky enough to live in the wealthy West."[17] The five billion people living in the world's poorer nations possess dazzling diversity, but they cannot reap the benefits of it without first achieving a threshold of social, economic and political stability.

GLOBAL ME

I started chasing hybrids many years ago, before I'd even heard of the term. Beginning in the mid-1980s, I spent a decade reporting on Silicon Valley, one of the global hotspots for encountering the future. Most people think the valley is all about technology: whizbang gadgets and engineering speak. As time went on I came to realize it wasn't that simple. The valley was also about how new ways of being human and new human communities were growing in the shadows of older forms. By the early 1990s, I was more interested in the people of the valley than the machines. It seemed to me that the big story wasn't about which companies won and lost or which technologies conquered global markets, but rather how a new breed of talented people were redefining national identity and global competitiveness. No one knew how to categorize them. I was struck by how they came from everywhere and how their original nationality—whether American or not—gave an incomplete sense of who they really were and their effect on the world. I decided to follow the story abroad.

During my international travels for *The Wall Street Journal,* I found many hybrids who shared my frustration that they were misunderstood, especially by policymakers who had no clue about the importance of hybrids in the intensifying global competition for trade and technology, wealth and jobs. Emboldened, I met with experts on identity, diversity and multicultural politics, searching for a new vocabulary and perspective that might do justice to radical mixing. I devoted much of my time to observing ordinary people close to the ground. When I spoke to government officials, leading pundits, and tycoons—people who live at 30,000 feet—they seemed surprised by what I was finding. To them, the future was straightforward. At the famous annual Davos conference in Switzerland, which I attended in 1997, the best and the brightest were convinced that an international elite was taking over and that it was pointless to defend local identities, which were doomed anyway. I knew in my gut they had it all wrong.

The Diversity Advantage is a response to this poverty of imagination, an outgrowth of my instinct that I could grasp forces sweeping through all rich nations and, possibly, through many poor ones too by studying lots of ordinary people and a handful of significant countries. By comparing these people and countries, I began realizing that almost everything people think they know about identity, diversity and the competitive advantage of nations is wrong. So convinced are people that nations are in terminal decline that they fail to see that a new kind of nationalism is arising that will be diversity's best friend. So convinced are people that ethnic hatred will define future social relations that they fail to see the many small ways in which even nations with no tradition of tolerance are going mongrel. So convinced are people that global capitalism is relentlessly opposed to local cultures and diverse identities that they fail to realize that among the most vigorous proponents of mongrelization are the world's biggest, richest, most profit-hungry corporations.

In the pages ahead, I explain how this can be so. The first two chapters examine new forms of identity that enable people to possess both roots and wings, strong ethnoracial affiliations and an openness to new ties. Chapter 3 looks at the relationship among diversity, creativity and economic strength. The fourth chapter, in which I largely draw on the American experience, explores the relationship between diversity and national unity. In Chapter 5, I recount the fitful evolution of Germany from monoculture to mongrel nation. In Chapter 6, I analyze the cases of Ireland, a historically isolated and monolithic country that is pragmatically diversifying its society, and of Japan, another island-nation that risks stagnation because it isn't doing so. In Chapter 7, I examine the role of multinational corporations in fostering hybridity. Chapter 8 looks at what political and civic leaders can do to promote hybridity. In the final chapter, I review pitfalls and limitations of the diversity advantage.

Those who favor protecting local identities and national economies by excluding outsiders and enforcing assimilation to a fixed model may find *The Diversity Advantage* disturbing. I hope you do. Those who wish to sacrifice individuality and enterprise on the altar of national unity will be sorely disappointed in the years ahead. A society of hybrids will be more inclusive, soul-satisfying and fair-minded than the tribes of today. The ability to "take one's roots with you," to paraphrase Appiah, seems a metaphor for civilization in a world turned upside down by change. Indeed, hybrids are a new breed. Just as the French writer Crèvecoeur in the late eighteenth century called the American "this new man" forged out of a "strange mixture of blood," the hybrid is a new creature. But he isn't a homogenized "global soul" or a "globo" sapiens. Hybrids are richly particular people adept at fitting into many places precisely because their portable roots give them so much to offer.

To be sure, hybridity poses risks. A hybrid person may lose himself in a jumble of affiliations. A hybrid nation may botch the process of reinvention. Still, the price of these errors seems less than the cost of circling the ethnic wagons and either shutting out outsiders or forcing them to become "one of us." Never before have so many people married across racial and ethnic lines. Never before have so many left their homelands for work or pleasure. Never before have so many people touched and tasted the clothes, foods, music and ideas of cultures not present in their youth. These people are not becoming phantoms or dilettantes. Rather they are part of an outpouring of human creativity fired by radical mixing.

This mixing will occur with or without the blessing of political and cultural elites; it will occur whether it is welcomed or regretted, understood or misunderstood. The only uncertainty is whether mongrelization will be seen as a grand success or terrible failure.

In a world where the pure is still synonymous with authenticity, I can't imagine a more necessary act than to resoundingly defend multiplicity. This book is my defense: Hooray for the hybrid. Hip-hip for the mongrel. Hallelujah for the global me.

A LIVERPOOLIAN SINGS CANTO-POP... IN HONG KONG

MANCHESTER, ENGLAND—At a Christmas party for Chinese immigrants here, a group of elderly women sigh when they spot the star of the show. He's a tall, lean and good-looking twenty-one-year-old singer whose entire act is in Cantonese, the language of their youth in Hong Kong.

One woman calls out to him in Cantonese. "What are you going to sing tonight?" she asks. He smiles. "Wait and see," he says. The woman—old enough to be his grandmother—gives him a thumbs up, then hugs him and says in English, "You go to Hong Kong someday—be big star."

In the seat next to her, the woman's husband studies Barry Cox. "His father must be Chinese," he says.

He is kidding of course. Cox's father was English—and as white as Prince Charles. Cox is himself unmistakably Anglo-Saxon: He eats meat pies, speaks with the accent of his native Liverpool and likes cricket. Yet through an act of self-creation that amazes and mystifies his friends and family, he can speak, read and write in Cantonese. His friends are mainly Chinese. He has a Chinese name (Gok Pak-wing, which means "long life"). He works full-time in a Chinese grocery store. He even dates a British-born Chinese girl and talks with her Shanghai-born parents about how she can't speak Chinese.

Incredibly, none of this gets people really going. What really gets people going is this: Cox wants to be a Chinese pop star.

"My goal is to make it big in Hong Kong," he says. But even if he can't crack the elite ranks of the city's so-called Canto-pop scene, he may settle for just being Chinese. "He lives, breathes and sleeps Chinese," says his mother Valerie. "I think he'd actually be Chinese if he could."

Judging from his performance later that night, Cox may be as close as he can get to passing. Surrounded by a dozen female dancers, he strides onto the stage of a local nightclub and belts out a dozen

Canto-pop songs with such titles as "Kiss Under the Moon," "Love Once More" and "Ten Words of an Angel."

One listener, a twenty-something woman from Hong Kong named Sofun Leung, sits near the stage and mouths the words as Cox sings. "I've got a crush on him," she admits.

Nearly everyone does. He sings, for instance, in the various distinct tones that make Cantonese among the most difficult of Chinese dialects. Yet his Canto-pop "covers" are so convincing that during a pause between songs the Chinese emcee puts her arm around him and asks, "Are you English or Chinese?"

As if on cue, he retorts, "I'm English—look at my skin!" The audience roars in laughter.

The Chinese are laughing with Cox, whose performance suggests that, in a globalizing world, people can wear an identity like a mask or pair of clothes, putting it on and off depending on circumstances. Most important, he shows that the menu of options for people seeking to revamp their identities have expanded. Even though he's a working-class kid from Liverpool, he can adopt an exotic guise. He's unusual but not just a freak show.

Cox realizes, of course, that he can take his Chineseness only so far. Still, he wants to push the limits. "If I didn't mix with Chinese and speak Chinese and sing Chinese, what would I be doing now?" he wonders. "I'd just be a normal person, nothing special about me. Although I know I'm not Chinese, I'm trying to put myself into a Chinese body." He doesn't mean this literally, but he says that at times on stage, before a roaring Chinese audience, "I get carried away. I feel more inside them, closer to their community."

The sudden death of Cox's father, a year ago, has sharpened his desire for connecting with others. But his fascination with the Chinese runs deep. In high school, he experimented with martial arts and fell in love with the soundtracks to Jackie Chan movies. Hanging around fish-and-chip shops, after graduating in 1994, he met scores of Liverpool's Chinese immigrants, many of whom own and run the local "chippies."

Frustrated that he could not understand those Chinese who spoke no English, Cox did the unexpected. He decided to study Cantonese, the dominant language among the Chinese there. He took a class at Liverpool's "Pagoda" center. Improbably, he had a flair for the language and, more important, for getting on with Chinese people. He quit his job as a salesman in an electrical store, going to work as a waiter in a Chinese restaurant so he could hone his language skills. A year later, one of his Chinese friends invited him to spend a summer with relatives in Hong Kong. His parents worried about him; he'd only been to London twice. But the experience left him hungrier than ever for Hong Kong and a Chinese identity of his own.

Returning to Liverpool, he began performing at Chinese gatherings, usually for free. He spends about a week studying the words for each new song, reviewing them with a friend, a Chinese linguist from Hong Kong, who makes sure he understands the full meaning of the lyrics so he can sing them with the proper feeling. His vocalizations are accurate, but the linguist, Poling Lo, is even more impressed by Cox's grasp of Chinese calligraphy. "His Chinese writing is very beautiful—better than a lot of Chinese people," she says.

It is from singing, however, that Cox hopes to make his name, and a living. As improbable as it may sound, China-watchers think he has a shot at making it in Asia—if only because Chinese will delight in watching a Westerner imitating them. Canto-pop is itself an imitation of Western pop and emerged when Chinese singers tried to put their own cultural stamp on a foreign idiom. What's especially intriguing about Cox is how he represents the paradox of an Oriental art form, inspired by the West, in turn being imitated by Westerners in the West.

Such lofty theorizing is lost on Cox's fans, nearly all of whom are Chinese. They know it is rare for a Westerner to imitate them, especially in pop culture, and even rarer still for a working-class British boy to do so. To his credit, Cox takes Canto-pop seriously and refuses to present himself as a novelty act.

His sincerity is persuasive, and he is committed to appearing authentic. He even refuses to sing in English, fearing it may harm his Chinese elocution. "I can't sing in English," he says.

The Chinese, famously hardworking, appreciate Cox's determination. "People accept Barry as one of their own family. They respect what he's done," says Lo, who's lived in Liverpool for twenty years.

Cox is indeed treated as a local celebrity. He is applauded almost everywhere he goes in the tight-knit Chinese community of Liverpool and nearby Manchester, where Chinese immigrants number about 50,000.

One winter evening, he visits a music store in Manchester's sprightly Chinatown. He peruses the latest CD releases from Hong Kong and picks the newest album from Leon Lai, his favorite singer and a big name in China. As he waits at the checkout counter, the cashier, David Lau, recognizes him.

"I have your autograph," he says, having gotten it following Cox's last performance here. "I was amazed," he tells his mother next to him. "Because he is so good. Despite what his nationality is."

CHAPTER 1

THE IDENTITY TOOLBOX

No identity is stable in today's wild, recombinant mix of culture, blood, and ideas. Things fall apart; they make themselves anew. Every race carries within it the seeds of its own destruction.

—ERIC LIU[1]

The diversity feeds on itself, driving itself forward.

—STUART KAUFFMAN[2]

Protean patterns best reveal themselves over the course of entire lives.

—ROBERT JAY LIFTON[3]

ROOTS NOURISH. They define a person's life. Roots are an anchor: deep, firm, fundamental, established, the everlasting source of pride, strength, meaning and identity. They embody family, ethnic or cultural origins that explain a person's emotional attachment to a place or community.

Roots are sunk. The deeper, the better. They represent tradition, the past, forebears, ancestors, wisdom, beginnings. Who would lack roots? Rootlessness is bad. The rootless are unstable, artificial, fake, impermanent, transient, unproductive, restless, itinerant. They have no tribe, no family beyond their own. They lack a place, a space, a race of one's own.

Doesn't everybody have roots? Who would cut them on purpose? Isn't that suicide? Can they grow back? If people don't like their roots, can they get new ones? Can they grow more roots without threatening their old ones?

People obsess over their roots even as they bristle at paying the price for them. Roots are expensive. They exclude. Roots can limit the pool of marriage partners, dictate one's religious faith and where one lives, and how one earns a living. Roots can determine who to stay away from, what not to do or say or think. As a result, many people can't live on roots alone. And the world won't let them anyhow. Once, nations or ethnic groups provided almost everyone's main form of collective identification. National and ethnic affiliation, though only one source of identity, trumped all the others. Being French meant more than being a doctor. Being Korean overshadowed being raised in a small town in Japan. Being black in Boston meant more than being friendly. Being Mexican took precedence over being born in California.

This is rapidly changing. Nations and ethnic groups no longer impose a common identity on all their people. Now identity depends more on what they've studied; where they've traveled; with whom they are friends; what they do for a living; whom they marry; and perhaps even what music they enjoy, restaurants they eat in, style of dancing they prefer or books they read. The global spread of technology, trade, mobility and culture are revolutionizing individual identity. No statistics exist to document this shift, but that itself tells an interesting story. People don't measure what they don't classify. Many governments do not even track the ethnic affiliations held by citizens in its borders; some don't even count the different racial groups. A country as large as Britain, for instance, until the year 2000 never counted the number of Irish people, or their descendants, living in Britain, even though the Irish-British are believed to number in the millions. Germany has no hyphenated category, so that the child of a German father and a Turkish mother must be either-or, not both. Until the year 2000 census, the United States classified people according to four main racial groups, essentially ignoring those who saw themselves as mixed race. Statistically, hybridity doesn't exist. This is logical. If people don't ask the right questions, they won't get the right answers. Statistics mislead, and they are plenty misleading in the case of ethnic and racial mixing.[4]

Confusion over statistics, however, can't hide the truth: A fixed sense of identity, based on a rigid definition of national belonging and ethnic traits, is on the decline. The world may not be borderless, but a lot more alien stuff is getting through. Once, people's attachments were defined by their parents: the language they spoke, the food they ate, how they expressed emotion (or didn't), the clothes they wore and their habits of mind. Now people increasingly construct themselves, piecing their identity together from diverse experiences, relying on not only their own kind but also their knowledge of the wider world, their tastes and inclinations and their belief in what works for them.

Out of this mongrel process arises the global me.

The fluidity of affiliations is surprising, since people are urged every day to preserve their roots and honor their heritage. They are told: "Be true to yourself! Proudly display your roots!" These exhortations grow more shrill even as it appears likely that a person can fit the whole panorama of human society—or at least a healthy slice of it—under their sombrero. Like Barry Cox, they can be British in the morning and Chinese in the evening. German on Wednesday, Puerto Rican on Friday and maybe American in between.

Are these people chameleons? Are they starving their roots? Won't they fail to cement new ties and yet lose old identities, ending up as a "nowhere man," a homogenized McPerson?

These questions are reasonable, but they confuse the process of forging new ties with the loss of the failure to establish a consistent underlying identity. People want more attachments, not fewer. Their goal is ethnic-pride plus, national-pride plus; in short, hybridity. They want freedom to augment their sense of self, not diminish it. They don't want to be limited by their bloodlines.

They see their attachments not as inert but as dynamic and defined by over-lapping loyalties and idiosyncratic self-definitions. They no longer receive their identities; they take them and remake them. And they passionately con-nect with not just one ethnic or national culture but many. When people have mixed ethnic or national commitments, they can still have stable identities. Many people, having made over their ethnic profile from a menu of options, become positively dedicated to this menu. And having forged various com-mitments does not mean they will keep on adding more and more, only that they consider a life defined by a single, inherited identity inconceivable.

Listen to the novelist Amin Maalouf talk about his own hybrid identity:

> How many times since I left Lebanon in 1976 to live in France, have people asked me, with the best intentions in the world, whether I felt "more French" or "more Lebanese"? And I always give the same answer: "Both!" I say that not in the interests of fairness or balance, but because any other anwer would be a lie.
>
> What makes me myself rather than anyone else is the very fact that I am poised between two countries, two or three languages and several cultural traditions. It is precisely this that defines my identity. Would I exist more authentically if I cut off part of myself?
>
> To those who ask the question, I patiently explain that I was born in Lebanon and lived there until I was 27; that Arabic is my mother tongue; that it was in Arabic translation that I first read Dumas and Dickens and *Gulliver's Travels*; and that it was in my native village, the village of my ances-tors, that I experienced the pleasures of childhood and heard some of the stories that were later to inspire my novels. How could I forget all that? How could I cast it aside? On the other hand, I have lived 22 years on the soil of France; I drink her water and wine; every day my hands touch her ancient stones; I write my books in her language; never again will she be a foreign country to me.
>
> So am I half French and half Lebanese? Of course not. Identity can't be compartmentalized. You can't divide it up into halves or thirds or any other separate segments. I haven't got several identites: I've got just one, made up of many components in a mixture that is unique to me, just as other people's identity is unique to them as individuals.

So how does one build a hybrid self, where multiple affiliations don't spin out endlessly and where a stable identity emerges from the welter of possibilities?

Meet a woman named Chiori Santiago. She's fortyish, a mother of two, active in her community, a teacher, a writer and anything but typical. She's a power-hybrid who has spent a lifetime acquiring a taste for gumbo. She didn't have to find hybridity; it found her. Now she's learned how to show off her mongrel selves with wisdom and grace.

Chiori lives in Berkeley, California. She's attractive, stylish, well-spoken, genial but highly opinionated. She speaks English and Spanish fluently, and writes well in both. Her lifestyle pegs her as neo-hippie California earth-person, but physically she's hard to place. Her looks are familiar, but not the whole package. Her dark hair and thick eyebrows make her seem Latina. Her brownish skin suggests Mexico or maybe Asia somewhere. She is large-boned, which maybe means Anglo. Yet she's so swarthy that Iraq wouldn't be a wild guess. But then she's got freckles, which could mean she's Irish.

The mystery is only partly explained by her parents. Her mother, Yoshiko, was born in 1926 and grew up in Los Angeles, a member of an active Japanese-American family whose roots in Japan can be traced back more than a thousand years. One of Yoshiko's brothers was the American correspondent for a big Tokyo newspaper during World War II. Of the family, he alone escaped internment. After the war, he served as founding editor of the *Pacific Citizen*, the newspaper of a leading Japanese-American advocacy group. Another brother founded a magazine that he later sold to Hugh Hefner of *Playboy* fame. A third brother, Shinkichi, joined the U.S. Army from his internment camp and fought in the liberation of Europe. He returned to the United States briefly, then moved to Europe where he became a well-known sculptor.

Chiori's father was born in Oregon, the descendant of settlers who arrived in the Northwest in the nineteenth century. An all-purpose WASP, Chester Fuller Roberts Jr. is six feet, two inches tall with blue eyes and black, curly hair. He was a journalist who worked first for a Seattle newspaper and then for *Stars & Stripes* in Tokyo during the American occupation after the war. He met Yoshiko in the newsroom. A bilingual speaker, she was an editor and Chester's boss. After working late together too many nights in a row, Yoshiko and Chester began dating, fell in love and married.

It was the late 1940s, and Yoshiko was in no rush to return to the West Coast of America. Too many bad memories. When she and Chester finally left Japan, it was for Chicago, where he completed a master's degree at the University of Chicago. The couple moved to San Francisco when the Asia Foundation hired Chester as a researcher. When Chiori was four, the foundation sent her father to Singapore, where her brother was born, and then to Karachi, Pakistan.

Chiori's earliest memories are of Pakistan. A servant followed her around all day, and she lived in a compound large enough to house the help in a separate building. She learned Urdu, the local patter, and attended a British-run private school, where she learned to curtsy and take tea and speak the Queen's English.

For whatever reason, Karachi was Chester's last stop with the Asia Foundation. In 1959, he was faced with returning to the United States. He and Yoshiko chose Berkeley because they thought that an interracial couple would have a better chance fitting in there.

Chiori's transition was rocky. Though nearly eight years old, she was placed in a kindergarten class and treated as an immigrant. "It was America, 1959," Chiori says. In the anti-immigrant 1950s, "Anyone from a foreign country must be stupid."

She wasn't. She read all the books in the classroom in her first five days and then sat at her desk, terrified, with nothing to do. "Here my classmates were playing with blocks," she recalls. "I'm thinking Americans are so stupid."

And of course, there were no servants.

Actually, her parents had fallen on hard times. Her dad wasn't working, and her mom got a job in a factory. For some months, she even brought work home with her. Piecework. Chiori recalls gluing cheap toys together with her younger brother.

Under the circumstances, Chiori's nostalgia for Pakistan made sense. "I kept expecting that this was temporary. That another year or two we'd go back to Pakistan and everything would be fine. But we were stuck here."

She laughs when she says this. Indeed, her recollections are punctuated with smiles and chuckles. She bears no trace of bitterness. Toughness, yes, but no anger.

It was during her father's period of idleness that she got to know him. Her father had a daughter from a previous marriage and the two children with Yoshiko, of course, but this was the first time he'd spent time with a child. "It was great for me because my dad was home," Chiori says. "This is significant because a big part of my identity is as a white male. I very much liked and identified with my father."

She still sees herself in him: organized, rational, even her mannerisms suggest him. "That's why I get so enraged about racism because I feel as a white male I should get better treatment. So what if I don't look like a white guy?" Or even a guy.

It was clear to her, from a young age, that few took her for white. Maybe a year after arriving in Berkeley, she was walking to the library when an old lady began speaking Spanish to her. "I knew it was Spanish but not what she was saying. So I was staring at her, shaking my head and she started cursing me out, hysterical. Still in Spanish. I could tell she was angry I wasn't responding to her. I thought I better learn Spanish."

Another time, when her father was working, she went with him to his office. She was trailing him, running to keep up, but he went through the door of the building and the doorman shut it fast. She tried to convince him to let her in, but he wouldn't. By then, her father had doubled back from the elevator. "Open the door, that's my daughter," he said.

"Well the doorman's jaw dropped. He was polite, but I could tell he was shocked. He couldn't imagine that this little brown girl was his daughter. I always expected the doorman to open the door for me like they did for my dad. Because I am his daughter."

It was the outside world that frustrated Chiori. "No matter where we went, no one could figure out what race we were," she says. "Most people thought we were Mexican American. The black and Latino kids would hang out with us. The white kids maybe. And the Asian kids, forget about it." Her mother's people shunned her. "The Japanese were very into purity," she says. "They didn't like mixing. I was a half-breed to them."

She recalls scary moments outside a Buddhist temple, where she attended a weekly class on Japanese heritage and language. "Every week we'd have to run for our lives from kids who wanted to beat us up," she says.

In high school, Chiori discovered hybridity. "I decided I can't change anybody's attitudes," she recalls. "They're going to think what they'll think. So I'm just going to blow their minds."

Her mother advised her simply to tell people that she was "Eurasian," but she never did. She started telling people she was Peruvian or Hawaiian. Once, she even said Eskimo. The more she experimented, the more she realized that "people were looking to figure out what race I am so that then you're going to know how to deal with me."

This insight wasn't always a happy one. Chiori was an excellent student and expected to apply for admission to the University of California at Berkeley, the state's flagship public university. She was in advanced classes and had the grades to gain entry, but inexplicably her high school guidance counselor, convinced she was the child of Mexican immigrants, urged her to select an easier school.

It was 1969. "He looked at my face and said Mexicans don't have what it takes," she says. "He said if you work very hard I can get you a job cleaning floors at the children's hospital."

By then, Chiori actually did think of herself as Hispanic. Many of her friends were minorities. And her mother now lived with a black man whose singular feature was being an albino. He was ivory-colored and had blue eyes. "We learned from him that color and race don't go together," Chiori says. "Talk about mixed. He's living in the house. So I'm living with a 'white' black man."

She knew her counselor had no idea who she was, but still his remarks stung. "I did feel hurt because I thought of myself as Mexican. I thought, Is he right? Maybe he knows something?"

In the end, she decided he didn't. She attended Cal and graduated. But a hard lesson stuck with her. "We are judged by how we appear and nothing's going to change that."

Still, what matters most is how Chiori views herself, and her self-conception is varied, slippery, and imprecise. She's been married twice, both times to men of Puerto Rican parents. The first time her first husband visited her apartment, he asked nonchalantly where "all her Japanese stuff is." Chiori told him dryly, "I'm not that Japanese."

Yet her husband had a practical point. It was the mid-1970s and ethnic pride had zoomed in the United States. Not just blacks but everybody seemed to be lining up with his or her ethnic group.

"I didn't line up with anybody," Chiori says. "I wanted to line up with everybody. But people didn't like that." She couldn't hold out. As she learned more about the mixed heritage of Puerto Rico, she decided it at least mirrored her own mixed background. Now she began checking the Puerto Rican box on forms.

She has a son from her first husband and a son from her second. As the times changed in the United States, the outlines of her public selves softened. Especially in the 1990s, when mixed-race people began calling for more recognition and a blurring of ethnoracial lines, she began more frequently displaying her Anglo-Asian roots.

Her hybridity brings wisdom to polarized situations. She is no self-righteous wannabe, hiding from an identity she won't defend. "White people don't have a monopoly on racism," she says. "Asians are, black people are. You've got to understand that first before you can go beyond it. So let's just cop to it. I'm racist. I do my own judging. Let's just say so. Then we can talk."

ROOT CAUSES

Chiori Santiago and Barry Cox aren't exceptions. They are the future. They are able to succeed, not only because they are driven to do so but also because six sweeping forces are promoting ethnic, national and racial mixing on an unprecedented scale. People are responding to these six forces by creatively constructing multiethnic identities, or portable roots.

Intermarriages   Intermarriages are rising across races and ethnic groups. In the United States, marriages across the standard ethnoracial spectrum (black/white/Asian/Hispanic) have increased dramatically. Since 1970, they have more than quadrupled. Viewed across generations, the shift is more dramatic. Of third-generation immigrants, nearly two-thirds of all Hispanics and 41 percent of all Asians marry across group lines. And although black-white intermarriages are occurring at a far lower rate, they are still at record highs.[5]

Intermarriages don't occur only between people living in the United States, of course. Americans increasingly find their mates abroad. "We're not just living in the Global Village, we're playing the Global Dating Game," exults one advocate of international marriages. From 1979 to 1994, 2.3 million Americans married a foreigner and settled in the United States. Annually, about 200,000 international marriages involving Americans are consummated (American men marrying foreign women make up two-thirds of the total). For those who can't or won't search on their own, international matchmakers offer to help. More than 200 international matchmaking organizations operated in the United States alone in 1998. The Immigration and Naturalization Service (INS) estimates that they bring together about 4,000 to 6,000 couples yearly who marry and petition for immigration of the female spouse to the United States. Most of the women come from the Philippines or from the newly independent states of the former Soviet Union, the INS believes.[6]

Some Americans condemn marriage across ethnic and racial boundaries, of course. But interestingly these boundaries shift over time. "What were once 'mixed marriages' involving Irish, Jewish, Polish and other 'European-American' ethnic groups are no longer so regarded, whereas marriages across the standard color lines continue to invite this label." And yet despite the label, marriages across color lines are rising and gaining more acceptance with Americans.[7]

The United States isn't alone in posting rising intermarriages. Virtually every industrialized nation, from Singapore to Sweden, is seeing steady growth in marriage across ethnic and racial groups. In cosmopolitan havens, such as Berlin and Singapore, one in every four matches involves a foreigner and a native. In the most diverse U.S. cities, like New York, rates of intermarriage are even higher.

Category Breakdown The second trend highlighting the decline of fixed identities is the growing dissatisfaction with the standard ethnoracial categories. The conventional white/black/Asian/Hispanic grid is too narrow to satisfy Americans any longer, and no less so to describe their highly varied ethnic and racial characteristics. (Europeans show even less fidelity to this grid.)

Hispanics, for instance, are now widely viewed as neither a race nor an ethnicity but "a disparate collection" of perhaps as many as seventy different nationalities "descended from Europeans, African slaves and American Indians."[8] Asians are an even more polyglot category. Culturally, the differences between Cambodians and Koreans, South Indians and Tibetans, Filipinos and Malaysians are breathtaking. So are their physical differences. Some Hispanics claim whiteness and others don't; South Indians are similarly selective, or perhaps confused. Even blacks are debating the viability of racial categories, with some critics calling the uniform black-white divide "blatantly" inadequate.[9] A 1995 poll found that a third of all African Americans rejected the concept of a single race for blacks.

All this questioning has given people the opportunity to redefine themselves, even in contradiction to racial and ethnic labels they thought were permanent. The freedom of self-definition extends to race. To be sure, the black-white divide is perhaps the single greatest barrier between people. In the United States, intermarriages involving blacks occur much less frequently than those between other groups, while people with even some African heritage are generally labeled as black. But there is a growing appreciation, among blacks and whites, that "racial identities are social inventions" and thus can be reinvented, says Peter Morrison, a demographer at Rand Corporation.

A small but growing number of people of color are choosing to call themselves "mixed race" instead of black. Perhaps the most notable example is Tiger Woods, the American golfer whose father is African American and mother is from Thailand. "Rather than fit into a mold, people want to distinguish themselves, so they're more likely to point out their multiracial background," says Jorge del Pinal, an analyst with the U.S. Census Bureau.

The emphasis on mongrel roots challenges African-American identity, especially since many blacks have ancestors who were white, Latino or Native American. Historically, the common obstacle of racism fueled black solidarity. While discrimination remains, "we are more and more able to define ourselves rather than succumb to the pressure of how others have defined us," says Toi Derricotte, a poet in New Orleans who has written eloquently about the arbitrariness of racial boundaries. So light-skinned that she can "pass" for white, Derricotte grew up feeling culturally black but increasingly sees "shades" of nonwhiteness. "Everybody is trying to nail down everyone's identity in terms of race," she adds. "I'm saying let there be a space for people not to know, and for people to dwell in that place and for that to be all right."

This questioning of once rock-solid racial categories underscores the way traditional categories are breaking down and why growing numbers of people feel compelled to redefine themselves in the light of the realities of hybridity.

Many Strangers Familiarity need not breed contempt. By the time a child in Los Angeles leaves school, he's met so many people from different backgrounds that diversity seems natural to him. The ubiquity of foreigners in the United States partly explains why many Americans seem both parochial and international at the same time: They may feel they don't need to show much interest in certain foreign countries when some of the best, brightest and hardest-working people from those countries live around the block. On the minus side, intimacy with immigrant communities—Cubans in Miami, Filipinos in San Francisco, Dominicans in New York, Tunisians in Minneapolis—gives Americans a false sense of knowledge about the countries of origin and the wider world. But at the same time, this contact educates them about differences, giving rise to a new kind of cultural literacy. Ubiquity is one key to achieving this literacy. In most big U.S. cities, there are so many foreigners, and so many well-educated ones, that positive relationships between natives and newcomers are more likely.

This is why small numbers of immigrants paradoxically make it harder for dominant natives to cope with diversity. Natives, after all, typically face one of two situations: They live in a country where everyone else acts like them (or is supposed to act like them), in some obvious ways (such as in the language they speak or their religion). Or they are part of a distinct group that contends for power with another distinct group. Such polar situations are common throughout rich nations: Catholics and Protestants in Northern Ireland; French speakers and Flemish speakers in Belgium; French speakers and English speakers in Canada; Finns and Swedes in Finland; French, Germans and Italians in Switzerland. When in a single country there are two or three distinct groups, each with a sizable share of the population, resistance to diverse newcomers is far stiffer than in a country where ethnicity, race and religion are highly fragmented so that no single group dominates. What's surprising, though, is that countries with distinct and fixed groups are prone to conflict more than are countries that are highly fragmented. The evidence for this is rather strong. Paul Collier, the chief development economist at the World Bank, draws on this evidence to advance the intriguing thesis that diversity in a country inversely correlates with peace and harmony. In other words, the less diversity, the greater chances of violent social conflict. The more diversity, the more likely that differences will be resolved peacefully.

This conclusion seems so counterintuitive that it warrants some elaboration. In studying the economic causes of civil wars and the breakdown of order in developing nations, Collier examined scores of countries over the period from 1960 to 1995. He found that what he calls "ethnic and religious fractionalization"—or, simply, significant numbers of people from a large number of groups—"significantly reduces the risk of conflict." Holding other factors constant, he argues that "highly fractionalized societies are safer than homogenous societies." Because of the more diverse population, he concludes, it is "much harder," for any group in such a society to mount a violent challenge against other groups. In short, a country where conflicts can't be portrayed as "us against them"—because there are too many "thems"—is likely to be more peaceful and prosperous than a country where two or three groups are constantly jockeying for power, waiting to seize an advantage. Heterogeneity, then, strengthens, not weakens, social cohesion.[10]

Now, this reading of the experience of developing countries ought to provide a wake-up call to the many Europeans and Americans who presume that by sharply restricting the pool of aliens they allow into their countries that they are at the same time reducing the likelihood of social tensions. Just the opposite. Absorption actually becomes harder; the logic of us versus them seems more appealing; the chances for social explosion grow. Small numbers of newcomers are easily marginalized. Large numbers may seem more threatening at first but become easier to assimilate (or hybridize) in the long run. It's a matter of numbers: Past a certain threshold of diversity, a nation can achieve the diversification of diversity, and reap the consequent boon of greater social cohesion. This process can be seen clearly through individual immigrant groups. When the size of an immigrant group reaches a critical mass—when its community is large enough that its internal diversity can emerge—members of this community begin to see themselves in new ways. Think about the dynamics of, say, Salvadorans in San Francisco, California. If there were relatively few Salvadorans in San Francisco, they would tend to reinforce their similarities, defensively turning inward; and at the same time, they might become invisible, disappearing into the larger Latino community. However, an entirely different scenario unfolds when there are larger numbers of Salvadorans in San Francisco. A larger group is less likely to be monolithic than a smaller one; it is more likely both to come to terms with the dominant culture of the society and to retain the edge of its distinct subculture. Individual freedom will be more on display as Salvadorans are more likely to affirm the differences among themselves, accentuating regional and local identities that may hold more meaning in their home country. Secure in their ties to other group members, this larger Salvadoran community will be freer to explore new American identities too.

The value of achieving the diversification of diversity—or a threshold size for a number of minority communities—is clear. Rather than seek to perpetuate ethnic enclaves, these larger communities consistently express the wish to adopt most, if not all, of the core values and characteristics of the dominant group in the nation. This desire for acceptance makes sense because with size comes political clout and with political clout comes a stake in the values, the culture, the system, of the dominant society. It is only when the dominant group seeks to keep immigrant communities small—and cut off from their homeland through tight limits on further immigration—that the benefits of diversity are sharply reduced.

Invention of Tradition   People are more aware than ever that their supposedly primordial ethnic or national identities are actually often of recent origin, constructed to meet the requirements of ethnic solidarity or nation building. If they were constructed in the first place, they can be reconstructed to better suit changed circumstances.

Recent scholarship documents that racial, ethnic and national traits are made, not an ancient inheritance. In the 1980s, historians, sociologists, anthropologists and artists rebelled against the habit of treating traits—skin color, ethnicity, nationality, even gender—as irreducible. The British historian Eric Hobsbawm popularized the term "invented traditions" to refer to the array of practices and beliefs—presumed ancient and durable, yet actually of recent birth—that set groups apart. National languages, for instance, far from being "mother" tongues, were usually only standardized after the birth of a nation.[11]

Other scholars asserted that the ties between the people of a nation were constructed, making them "imagined communities," in the words of Benedict Anderson, a historian at Cornell University. Having been invented, nations could thus be "reinvented" in response to shifts in population, values or leaders. This approach applied to other sources of identity too. Ethnicities went the way of nations as academics showed that they also arose chiefly from social forces rather than inheritance. "Ethnic groups are typically imagined as if they were natural, real, external, stable and static units," when in fact, writes Werner Sollors, "ethnicity is not so much an ancient and deep-seated force surviving from the historical past, but rather . . . an acquired modern sense of belonging."[12] While ethnic tensions were no less real because they were based on an invention, a cultural construction, scholars routinely undercut the moral claims that often went along with associated campaigns to insulate ethnic categories from change. In a typical paper, two scholars demolished the idea of a "primordial" ethnicity, dismissing the concept as "bankrupt." They concluded: "If primordial is to mean 'from the beginning,' a priori, ineffable, and coercive—which it must if it is to be genuinely primordial—then the evidence suggests conclusively that the term is only inappropriately assigned to most of the ethnic phenomena of our day."[13]

Even "whiteness" can be viewed as a construction, reflecting choices about how to classify people rather than describing an underlying reality of skin color. Underscoring this new awareness, one scholar described the manner in which Irish immigrants to America came to be accepted as part of the white fraternity after initially being compared unfavorably with blacks. Surveying this literature, David Hollinger summarized the new understanding as "racism is real, but races are not."[14]

Global Village   Even if you don't go anywhere or meet any foreigners, you can draw on an array of "alien" styles and traits. And if you're in a strange place, rather than being cut off from your roots, you can carry them with you—thus making it easier for you to retain your roots while you add to your affiliations. This frees you to feel that you can take on new identities without jeopardizing your old ones and thus emboldens you to do so with less hesitation.

Consider the effect of the spead of telephony in poor countries in recent years on the ability of migrants to maintain links with their home turf. "International communications traffic has increased dramatically, driven largely by the voice and data demands of international business," Peter Stalker writes in his valuable survey, *International Migration*, "international migrants have been able to take full advantage of this to keep in close touch with the home communities." Stalker adds:

And in the emigrants' countries the telephone has taken on a new significance. In many towns in El Salvador, for example, the main locus of social activity is no longer the church or the plaza, but the office of the local telephone company, Antel. In one town of 3,000 people, the operator places around 400 collect calls per month to the U. S. The Mexican telephone company, Telmex, has made things even easier by opening branches in California that will allow migrants to pay the telephone bills of their families back home. . . . The possibilities for calling home have increased dramatically with the availability of mobile telephones, which in rural areas of many developing countries have overnight put some of the remotest places in touch with the outside world. . . . While most of the outgoing calls are local, the majority of the incoming calls are international.

A quarter century after Marshall McLuhan popularized the idea of a single media net, ensnaring all the world's people, the species remains far from interconnected. Half of the world's population has never used a telephone.[15] That's three billion people who not only don't have an e-mail account or a Web browser; they don't have a dial tone.

This situation puts into context the claim that a homogeneous global culture is sweeping the world, steamrolling local cultures in order to satisfy the needs of entertainment empires. Besides, the same electronic media that deliver a single image throughout the world can also provide people with powerful tools to preserve and expand their particular identities and local cultures. The Internet has transformed the way people learn about their roots, making extensive family trees readily available for the first time, and then offering an inexpensive means—in the form of Web pages—for small, dispersed groups to maintain a common set of beliefs and information. Radio stations from all over the world now broadcast over the Web, giving far-flung ethnics a chance to hear their favorite stations live. Many foreign newspapers also publish on the Web or are sent electronically to printing presses in other countries. Satellite broadcasts make television programming borderless.

It seems likely, for instance, that emigrants will increasingly consume the media of their native lands without leaving their new homes. Sixty percent of Germany's Turks had satellite television connections in 1998 in order to receive a half dozen Turkish channels. One Turkish newspaper had daily sales in Germany of 110,000 copies. Such practices are likely to spread. From a distance, anyone will be able to root for local politicians, sports teams and entertainment personalities—of another country. With the spread of electronic commerce, they may even shop at their favorite foreign stores by hitting their keyboard. All this, of course, will make their visits to their "home" easier and more satisfying (and they will get home more often because of lower fares— it costs as little as $125 to fly roundtrip from points in Germany to Istanbul). Using the same technology, a Jamaican living in New York can stay current with his home via Jamaican newspapers, radio and television. And when he visits Jamaica, he can keep in touch with New York. Media move both ways.[16]

Those who talk about the specter of a monolithic world also fail to recognize the degree to which pop culture—peddled by multinational corporations— upsets traditional identities: from sex roles to what it means to be happy or a decent person. This subversive effect can be seen in the passions of a teenage

Dublin girl. Sinead[17]—sixteen, freckle-faced and looking like a tomboy in her track suit—has lived her whole life in Ireland, attends Catholic school, scores well on her exams and aspires to attend a university. She doesn't smoke, drink or cuss, and she certainly doesn't have a boyfriend—which is why the posters on the walls of her bedroom are striking. One is of Will Smith, the African-American actor. The other is of a black British football star. Sinead explains that she finds Will Smith "cool, handsome and funny." Though she neither has any black friends nor has ever even spoken to a black person, she admits that she finds black men "physically attractive," and not just the stars either. She can imagine herself dating a black man, she says.

Sinead's parents are well aware of the posters. "She likes these black men because they are handsome, famous, exciting," says her mother, a nurse. "It has nothing to do with them being black."

Even if the mother is right, her child's ideal of attractiveness is clearly being shaped by global media. To be sure, the worship of film and sports stars narrows cultural options, but it can broaden them too, by exposing an Irish teenager to a positive image of blacks. Would those who think that actors and athletes are trite role models be happier if the inner lives of Irish girls were still ruled by the Church and government censors? The materials out of which young people construct their identities are expanding. This is the good news. Not all these materials are uplifting, of course, but they may yet give individuals a means to escape restrictive tribes and borders. In the process, people don't lose themselves, but find new attachments. This leads to greater variety than before. Far from a global soul, the result is the diversification of diversity.[18]

Science and Technology   Innovations are giving people the power to make over their identities, and they are using them. To what extent people can figuratively and literally reinvent themselves through a combination of computer simulation, computer-human merger, biomechanics, bioelectronics and genetic re-engineering is more a matter of speculation than reasoned debate. But one thing is clear already: Genetic engineering also casts a shadow over the future of the individual. Some fear that gene manipulation will permit another Hitler to spawn a breed of blond, blue-eyed pseudo-Aryans. Think again. It is equally possible that this technology will reinforce the mongrelization of humanity. Why not a nation of men who reflect the qualities of Michael Jordan and Carl Sagan or of women who embody the blending of Meryl Streep and Toni Morrison?

More immediate a concern than genetic engineering is the prospect of the re-engineering of visible, physical characteristics. Altering facial features, skin color or body type could become routine in the years ahead. Again, rather than buoying the ranks of racialists and purists, re-engineering should boost the case for cosmopolitanism by further shredding ethnoracial categorizations. It will also give people the freedom to look the way they feel. Or to change looks to reflect shifting self-conceptions, or the multiplicity of their affiliations. Maybe Barry Cox wants to look Chinese, if not always, then some days of the week.

Walk the streets of any major city and you're apt to see a Chinese woman who has dyed her hair blond, an African American wearing contact lenses that make her eyes green and a white teenager with dreadlocks and Middle Eastern henna tattoos on her hands. The floodgates are opening.

WHOSE ROOTS?

Not everyone is as successful as Chiori or Barry Cox in building and managing a hybrid life. Self-creation is subject to manipulation and error. Fabricated lives can seem phony. I am not talking about garden-variety dissembling. Everyone lies. Not everyone is a hybrid. There are people who genuinely want a hybrid identity but can't carry it off. They don't put in the time or the effort, the sweat and the pain that make a Chiori Santiago. They are wannabes. They are looking for quick cover for the loss of their roots. They are the pseudo-cosmopolitans, the smug, self-satisfied "nowhere man," as Pico Iyer calls those who spend their lives making cell-phone calls from airport lounges to voicemail machines in offices that they never visit. "If all the world is alien to us, all the world is home," Iyer adds, as if declaring an anthem for his friends.

This is nonsense. Not even global marketeers brag anymore about the virtues of rootlessness. Iyer, of course, is too smugly ironic to believe that anyone can achieve more than faux roots. Mistaking being part of a frequent-flier plan for real living, he writes, "I have a wardrobe of selves from which to choose." But he finds none compelling. To be sure, there is something admirable about the willingness of Iyer and other jet-setters to take "the whole globe as our playpen." But just what does he bring to the party? As he concedes, rather sadly, "We are masters of the aerial perspective, but touching down becomes more difficult." Why? Because he lacks commitment. "What are the issues that we would die for? What are the passions that we would live for?" Dissent and disagreement, which are the soil out of which true identities spring, offend him. "Conflict itself seems inexplicable to us, simply because partisanship is."

Yet taking sides is what identity is about. Barry Cox doesn't just love Cantopop. He loves Cantonese and the people who speak this Chinese dialect. Barry is drawn to his new persona not because it drains him of tension, but because it creates tension between his adopted and inherited identities. Chiori isn't internally conflicted. Like Iyer, Barry and Chiori have a wardrobe of selves, but unlike him they seem as if they belong, acting with a purpose. Barry is the sort of person Iyer would run from in an airport lounge. Chiori would make his stomach turn. Their passion would mystify him, indeed frighten him. As he concedes, his soulless universal man fears only one thing: "passionate people with beliefs."

IYER AT LEAST IS HONEST about the hollowness at the core of his stylized hybridity. Others dissemble about their constructed selves, and in their denial do violence to themselves and their traditions. Often, this dissembling is understandable. Cosmopolitanism sometimes arises from the pain of roots, the traumas of affiliation. The case of Madeleine Albright illustrates this. She arrived in the United States at the age of eleven, in 1948, the Catholic daughter of a Czech intellectual. She graduated in 1959 from Wellesley, a bastion of the Establishment, and three days later wed Joseph Albright, a wealthy member of a newspapering dynasty. She converted to Episcopalianism, the faith of the 1950s American elite. She rapidly blended into the elite of New York and later Washington, D.C. In the 1980s, she left a life dominated by family and motherhood for the swirl of Democratic Party politics, eventually being named by President Bill Clinton as the first female secretary of state.

Yet Albright's life, in crucial respects, was fabricated. Her father and mother were actually Jews who, following the trauma of Nazi persecution, hid their pasts from their daughter. As late as 1997, when Albright was sixty years old, she claimed not to know that three of her grandparents were killed in Nazi death camps. She also claimed ignorance of her Jewish background, explaining lamely that her Czech father had raised her in ignorance. It was only after a reporter dug up her family history that, she claims, she knew of her ties to Judaism and the Holocaust.[19]

Albright's tale is implausible on its face and invites a charge of deracination. That she sought out surviving Jewish relatives from Prague, apparently as early as 1967, suggests that Albright never accepted her father's fictions. In the end, Albright could not escape her past; having chopped off her roots, she lived to see them come charging after her. The lesson is painfully obvious, yet the mistake is nonetheless poignant.

The Albright affair points to one danger of hybridity: deracination, the humiliating, even destructive abandonment of roots in favor of acceptance by the dominant group. The other danger of hybridity is more common, if less dramatic: not enough roots to begin with. Examine the situation facing Jessica Snyder. Like lots of seventeen-year-old schoolgirls, she wants to attend college in the United States. She studies hard, gets good grades, runs track, works on a farm over summers. She ought to win admission to many top schools. Only Jessica has a worry. She's never lived in America. What if she doesn't fit in?

Jessica's dad is an Ohio-born attorney for General Electric, who has spent nearly two decades living abroad. He is a can-do type who shows an American open-mindedness toward difference. Her mother hails from the Bordeaux region of France. Her parents met in the United States and, after having Jessica and her brother, lived in France, the Netherlands and Belgium. They now live in London. They speak both French and English; so do their children. They visit France more often, but each year travel to Toledo, where Jessica's father grew up.

Jessica is a petite blond who dresses casually and is polite but informal. She attends an international high school and appears more American than French, but her friends are mainly from Europe and Latin America, and "when you scratch the surface," her dad says, "she's more French-European."

That's her mother's doing. Danielle grew up on a French farm amid fruit and wine, and still visits her home region often. "As much as my kids don't have roots, I do," she says. Partly to compensate, she and her husband recently bought a villa in Bordeaux. "I realize the importance of roots, and I wanted my kids to have a place to go," Danielle says. This isn't backward thinking on her part but the frank recognition that people who are best at acquiring a taste for gumbo—for overlaying new affiliations, for achieving hybridity—are people who have stronger roots to begin with. And, as I will explain in the next chapter, it is the very strength of these original roots that allows new roots to sink deep because the new ones are no threat.

So far, Jessica is a creature of her parents' divergent tendencies. She switches on and off, now drawing on her dad and then emulating her mom. If not a substitute for roots, this shows her adaptability. "If you don't learn to adapt, you're always a tourist or a stranger," she says. As for her identity, she exhibits chameleonlike qualities. "When I'm in the United States, I'm American, and I'm the French girl in France. I am both."

Jessica's answer is too pat and obscures the real identity challenges that lie in her future. Will she forge a hybrid identity, drawing on sources now beyond her imagination and experience as well her parental endowments? Or is she too rootless, as her mother fears, so that her best option is to strengthen her ties to a distinct nationality, at least at this stage in her life?

In either case, the perils of fabrication are clear, but so are its enticements. "You do have the ability to define your own world," Chiori says. And with that ability comes an evolution: the uncertainty and excitement of watching and waiting to see what unfolds.

AUTHENTICITY

How can we know our constructed identities are legitimate? How can we avoid the charge of phoniness? The old way of thinking about identity—you are as you were born—doesn't help here. We need a new way of thinking about authenticity, in which people legitimize their affiliations through hard work and sincerity. Albert Camus, the French journalist and philosopher, understood this as well as anyone. In the 1940s, he presented a new vision of identity in which an individual brings authenticity to his constructed self by dint of commitment.

The importance of Camus's insight wasn't readily apparent because he tied his reformulation of identity to a frank acceptance of the proposition that life was meaningless. "Whatever meanings there may be, we have put them there," writes Robert Solomon, a historian of philosophy, "but knowing that they are only our projections is sufficient for Camus to conclude that they cannot be real or significant." Camus's response is to find "all values in life . . . futile and illusory: it is only life itself that is of ultimate value."[20] Thus a person like Barry Cox earns his legitimacy through a convincing performance, and the objection of whether he is "really" Cantonese vanishes.

Camus's rejection of the possibility of meaning need not be shared in order to grasp his justification of authenticity. Born in French Algeria and a member of the French Resistance during World War II, Camus battled his way through life, ultimately dying in a car accident at the age of forty-seven. He accepted a stark existential vision of life as "divested of illusions and lights," where a man "feels an alien, a stranger." He felt that man's rational hopes of justice and satisfaction were met with "the indifference of the universe." This "absurd" condition certainly described the helplessness of Holocaust victims and even those less punished by the pity of war. The absurd was at bottom rational for Camus, who admired man's ceaseless drive to make sense of himself and his environment.

Other postwar thinkers also recognized the absurdity of existence, but notably Camus viewed the absurd as grounds for hope. In his 1942 book *The Myth of Sisyphus*, he asserted that even the immortal Sisyphus, consigned to push his rock endlessly up the hill, must hold fast to hope. "The absurd does not liberate; it binds," he writes. Hope must arise from persistence, even absent results.

This hope can only be understood in parallel with Camus's sense of a retooled self. Whereas a rigid self requires a fixed morality in order to ensure a measure of integrity, the flexible self is built on the presumption that a person's values and affiliations will shift over time so that integrity, or authenticity, must be justified in a new way. Ordinary people, not just elites, do this retooling all the time, chiefly through action. For Camus, the self is a series of social roles, which aren't arbitrary but not easily ranked by status either. "A sub-clerk in the post-office is the equal of a conqueror if consciousness is common to them," Camus writes. This parity translates into a refreshing open-mindedness about the authenticity of mongrel identities. When a Japanese woman immerses herself in French society, how authentic is her Frenchness? Camus might say that the issue isn't the mix but rather the spirit in which she undertakes her effort. More critical than the role she plays is her method. For Camus, the method is persistence—hope in the face of a loss of a rigid identity. There is no restoring a "pure" self merely to achieve meaning and authenticity. Impurity is its own reward.

Today many extol the virtues of adaptation in the spirit of Camus. They accept that hybrids are not fakes, but respond genuinely to the high levels of mixing and the breakdown of ethnoracial categories, forces that prod people to craft new senses of belonging in the first place. The real issue is how well a person handles his various ties—how he juggles it all. But the impulse to juggle is psychologically healthy. People draw from a bigger identity menu in such a way as to link "elements and subselves not normally associated with one another," notes psychologist Robert Lifton. "The new combinations may take one in unexpected directions and provide one with equally unexpected capacities." Hybridity is an act of sanity; mongrelization is natural.[21]

It is these capacities—speaking a new language; working productively in a diverse team; raising a multicultural child—that give lie to the claim that a hybrid's multiple affiliations are somehow random or arbitrary. People don't wear identities as casually as clothes, but they are free to discard elements or to select new ones. A striving for authenticity separates dilettantism from a legitimate desire to expand one's persona portfolio. In the view of the Canadian philosopher Charles Taylor, this process of self-legitimization always occurs against the backdrop of assorted inherited identities, such as the ones derived from biological parents or from teachers. Even if a person succeeds in forging a multiethnic identity, Taylor thinks this new identity always exists in a dialectic with his original identities; indeed, "always in dialogue with, [and] sometimes in struggle against, the things our significant others want to see in us." Taylor adds: "Even after we outgrow some of these others—our parents, for instance—and they disappear from our lives, the conversation with them continues with us as long as we live."[22]

This inner conversation—this persistence that Camus saw as his existential method—binds together the mongrel, lifts hybridity to the level of authenticity and makes it the equal of the primordial, the original, the pure. And, as we shall see, real hybrids will win in the twenty-first century.

AN AFRICAN PLAYWRIGHT
GOES NATIVE...IN
BELGIUM

LOUVAIN-LA-NEUVE, BELGIUM—The letter from a friend in Burundi contained news that Marie-Louise Sibazuri could use: A court in the central African country had sentenced a man to prison for raping a female employee in his office, after protests forced police to make an arrest.

So Sibazuri had a fresh scenario for her radio drama, *Our Neighbors Are Our Family,* which airs three times a week in Burundi. Fact-based fiction, the show is a cross between *60 Minutes* and *Ally McBeal,* broadcast in Kurundi, Burundi's native language. The show is so popular in Burundi that the Army once asked the show to be rescheduled so on-duty soldiers wouldn't miss it.

The episodes are gritty. One portrayed a well-known priest who fathered a child, then bribed the mother to stay silent. Another, inspired by the plight of a farmer wrongly jailed for a mass murder, exposed police blunders and got the man released. A doctor jailed for performing an abortion was also freed after his case was dramatized.

Such is the power of Sibazuri's pen. In a violence-torn country, where ordinary people, for fear of reprisal, can't effectively lodge complaints, she forcefully promotes fairness and the redress of error. A major theme of her real-life drama in the former Belgian colony is to show that it is possible to overcome the mistrust that prevails between the minority Tutsi and the majority Hutu tribes.

One thing that makes *Our Neighbors* unusual is that Sibazuri writes and directs it from a suburb of Brussels, 4,000 miles away from her audience, actors and home. She moved here with her four children in late 1998 to join her husband, Melchior, a political exile—and to escape a seven-year civil war in Burundi that has taken at least 200,000 lives. She left behind a group of actors, led by her brother, who continue their work under her remote guidance. She is able to stay in the thick of Burundian life, without touching ground there, by simple technologies and her diaspora community to bridge time and reduce distance.

The show, launched in 1998 and partly funded by a U.S. foreign-aid program, is still taped in Burundi's capital of Bujumbura. Each weekend, Sibazuri's veteran cast rehearses, then records the latest batch of her scripts. The actors rarely speak with her now. Telephone calls are too expensive—and too emotional. Sibazuri broke into tears the last time she spoke to one of the actresses. She prefers staying in touch through letters and faxes. She doesn't use electronic mail (she writes her scripts in longhand and doesn't use a computer). Few of her friends in Burundi have e-mail either.

She does miss hearing the show. She doesn't get Burundian radio and can't afford to have tapes sent to her. Her husband is unemployed, and she makes a little money from teaching and writing. Belgian aid covers the rest of the family's needs. Burundi's state-run radio station, which airs her drama, gets the show free of charge. Search for Common Ground, a private, nonprofit group in Washington, D.C., pays her and the actors a small stipend and covers the cost of production.

The long-distance relationship with her cast troubles Sibazuri, but she has only to stroll through her neighborhood on the outskirts of a French-speaking university here to gain a sense of her homeland. Out of more than 100 compatriots living nearby, she has assembled a "virtual Burundi." Walking down the street, she greets one countryman after another: an officer currently serving in Burundi's army; a woman in a dance group that she's organized; a childhood friend.

One recent afternoon, she sits in a ground-floor room with nine others, all men from Africa and most from Burundi. Sibazuri, who is lively and take-charge around African women, sits quietly, letting the men have their say. The group supports reconciliation between Hutus and Tutsis, here and in Burundi, and a newcomer is making a pitch for a new project. But he sounds vague about what he wants to do and, after the men question him, Sibazuri breaks in.

"I want to add something," she says. "When you speak about peace, you have to speak by example. You have to show the example. You can't tell people, please make peace, let's all be friends, be nice to one another." She then throws her arm around the man seated next to her, smiling and swaying. "The most important thing is to be credible," she adds. "You can't always make a show for peace. You have to live what you think and not just say it. If we pretend being friends, the audience will follow the example and pretend to be friends too."

Sibazuri's existential philosophy helps her tackle the web of fear, mistrust and retribution that ensnares the Tutsis and the Hutus. In Rwanda, next door to Burundi, Hutus slaughtered an estimated 800,000 in the summer of 1994, using the radio to whip up hatred and even to direct the killing. In Burundi, the killing hasn't reached such a horrific level, but violence between Hutus and Tutsis is routine, and repeated efforts to end the violence, which dates back a half century, have failed.

Our Neighbors has sought to prove that radio, which had fomented trouble, could also bring people together. The show's premise is that answers to one person's problems can be delivered by someone on the other side, that working together is essential. The show's original characters, still Sibazuri's favorites, are two peasant families from the countryside. The husband of one family has been murdered, and his widow—struggling to get by—relies on a married couple from the "other" group for help.

Sibazuri never makes clear which of her major characters are Hutu and which are Tutsi, and she claims that she doesn't know herself. The ambiguity forces listeners to confront her characters as individuals while still not ignoring group tensions.

Sibazuri lives her philosophy. Her acting troupe is mixed, drawing from both groups, and although she and her husband are Hutus, people see her as having transcended ethnic identity. "No ethnic stereotype can fit her," says Adolphe Sururu, a Tutsi who has known her for many years. She's too open, too big."

She has paid a price for her openness, though. In 1995, she lived in a mixed neighborhood, when Burundi's Tutsi-run army retaliated against Hutus for attacks on Tutsis elsewhere. One morning, Hutu families were attacked. Her children's nanny was killed, and her husband was so seriously wounded by a gunshot that he had to spend four months in a hospital. Their house was set afire and looted. In the confusion, one of her children—her only daughter—disappeared and didn't turn up until weeks later. Sibazuri moved to another mixed neighborhood, where her family was attacked once again. This time, her husband sought asylum in Belgium, while she stayed on in Burundi for two more years.

The riots proved to be a decisive break in her life. She saw violence up close and lost something dear: sixty-seven plays she had written over twenty years. Most had been performed in Burundi but had not been published. In the second riot, an unfinished novel and a book of Burundian folk tales she had written were lost.

"I don't see the sense of it," she says. "I wonder if my writings served to wrap up peanuts."

But Sibazuri is reluctant to talk about her lost writings. She knows others have lost loved ones in Burundi's violence. Yet, as if making up for her losses, she writes furiously now, and with hope. She is such an intelligent optimist that a leading journalist in Burundi, Alexis Sinduhije, says that "the creator of this show should be the president of our country."

Sibazuri, who insists she'll return home to live someday, shakes her head in disbelief. "Do you see me in the president's skin?" she says lifting her eyes skyward. "I don't think so."

CHAPTER 2

ROOTS AND WINGS

People got to keep on movin'.

—JOHN STEINBECK

In 1996, more than half of the Dominicans and Mexicans who died in New York City were sent home for burial, as were a third of the Ecuadorians, a fifth of the Jamaicans and 16 percent of the Greeks, according to an analysis of city death records.

—*NEW YORK TIMES*[1]

In the 19th century and before, moving to a foreign country meant cutting close ties with the homeland for years if not forever. Modern conditions make it possible even for very humble immigrants to keep in touch with their place of origin. . . . Such links mean that immigrants find it far easier to maintain their cultural identity in a strange land. Psychologically they remain at home even when away from home; or more exactly, they are able to inhabit two very different worlds simultaneously.

—WILLIAM H. MCNEILL[2]

PEOPLE HAVE WINGS as well as roots. On a planet where distance is dying, the hybrid won't stay put. The breakdown of the unitary self, the rising appetite for diversity, the growing taste for gumbo, the proliferation of voluntary attachments to places, practices and communities—all those factors described in the first chapter—can occur within a single country, region, neighborhood or even family. There can be domestic mongrels and staying-put cosmopolitans. After all, nine of ten people on the planet live within 100 miles of their place of birth. But the hybrid on the move is an increasingly important pattern.[3]

In this chapter, I explain the rise of transnational identities: people with roots in more than one nation. These people are the fruits of new patterns in migration and mobility. They are the future.

Keep this rule in mind: People don't have to leave their original country permanently anymore. They can go home again. Roots are portable. Travel, once viewed as a wretched ordeal or as a way to break up a humdrum routine, is now an essential part of a good life. People discover their ordinary lives through traveling. They don't just travel for holidays, education, business, conferences. They make friends, learn languages, ignite passions while on the move. Travel is a way of life, not a vacation from a life.

Unlike hybrids who mostly stay put, transnationals are constantly in motion, crossing borders, changing forms. They are unmistakable. Soo Ing, one of my favorites, speaks three languages fluently and participates in four distinct cultures: south China, where her parents were born and raised; Canada, where she grew up; Germany, where she lives; and Mongolia, where she's worked professionally. Only thirty years old, she isn't finished moving. She may go to the United States next, or who knows where, only certain that she'll bring along her roots as well as wings.

"You reach a certain level of fluency [in a place] and there's no way back," she says. "I don't see any of these identities as a guise. I just see them as something I've always wanted to do. I have a great interest in peoples and cultures all over the world and I'm eager to learn." Whether it's coaxing an office meeting out of a diffident German professor, riding bareback on a Mongolian steppe or chattering in Cantonese with her sister, "I love diversity, whatever it brings. I'm not put off by what you're eating, what you wear, how you keep your hair, the language you speak, if you don't have electricity or running water. It doesn't matter. I really like different cultures, I like to learn."

Doubts about her own authenticity never occur to Ing, because—as if living Camus's philosophy—her existence precedes any debate over her essence. "There's never a debate inside me of what I am or who I am," she says. "I just am. I don't slip from one guise to another, it's all a part of me." Nor does she see herself as part of an elite, a self-styled "Davos man," in reference to the annual conference of global jet-setters held in the Swiss Alps. "I believe this capacity [for hybridity] is in everyone," she says. "We're all adaptable. We really do ourselves an injustice to say we can't adjust. We all can. We all have this latent potential to express the whole panoply of the human race."

Ing's hybridity is a call to arms, a declaration of freedom with responsibility. She gets diversity, and gets better at it as she goes on. The more she hybridizes, the easier it becomes. Still, her story is enriched by serendipity. Ing's affection for Germany was first sparked during a summer tour of Europe, when she met two German women near Avignon, France. The Germans invited her to a party in their country and later became Ing's pen pals. When she returned to visit them in Germany a second time, she became smitten with the language and the people.

Ing is a power-hybrid, or what sociologist Robin Cohen calls a "hyper mobile."[4] She's an extreme example, but not an uncommon one. The power-hybrid is everywhere:

He is an immigrant to the United States who visits his country of birth regularly, maybe holds dual citizenship, votes in both nations, owns property in his old home and a business in his new one.

He is the pensioner from New Jersey who retired to Costa Rica and gets a monthly check from the Social Security Administration.

He is the child of international parents who spends winters in one country and summers in another.

He is the international executive, working in Mexico City, who must stay close to Latin American markets but not lose touch with his company's headquarters in Los Angeles.

He is the political exile, the refugee, the spiritual chief of the Falun Gong sect who lives safely in New York while his faithful followers struggle to survive in China.

Transnationals aren't static. Soo Ing may move to Indonesia, where a close friend now works, or return to Mongolia, where she is an expert on fire and forestry in the Central Asian country. Or she may try a new country. Chiori Santiago has never lived abroad, but she could move to Puerto Rico, Mexico or even Japan in a heartbeat. Barry Cox, the English Canto-pop singer, moved from Liverpool to Hong Kong, chasing his dream of becoming a star in China.

Their fluidness makes hybrids more of a work in progress than other people. Sometimes their options are hard to keep straight. Anwar Elgonemy holds an Egyptian passport (from his father) and a British one (from his mother). He went to high school in Rome and university in Switzerland. He took his first job in Portugal. He's entitled to an Italian passport because he was born in Italy, but only if he lives there, which he doesn't want to do. Instead, he lives in the United States, which gives the only passport he wants but doesn't have.

"The world is a mish-mash," he says. "Citizenship is an artificial creation. It always was but now that's clearer to see since boundaries are falling." His attachments remain, though. He is a Muslim and visits Egypt at least every other year. "It's good to go back into a traditional mosque," he says. But long-term, he wants to stay in San Francisco. "It's the center of the new economy," he says. "Every other place is a step down." Still, he steps outside northern California often, since some of his most active clients are in Japan. Why not?

Such convoluted journeys are more common than many realize. Consider the resumé of Margaret Lee, a Manhattan attorney born in Korea. She came to New York with her parents as a child. They returned to Korea with her two sisters when she was in high school, but she stayed in the United States. She went to college and married an American artist. Her husband's parents live in Korea, though, where an art gallery represents his work. Her husband's links to Korea might make Lee's visits there more frequent except that her own parents recently moved back to the United States because, they say, the golf courses in New Jersey are cheaper than the ones they used in Korea. The precise term for the senior Lees' return to the United States, by the way, is "re-emigration."

The dual background of the younger Lees is being passed on to their only child, who has two names, Kevin and Keeho, suggesting his American and Korean options. Margaret Lee wants her son to get attached to her native country, not just appreciate Korean food and culture. "I hope for my son's relationship with Korea to be continuous, just as mine has been," she says.[5]

Connecting with the roots of one's parents isn't always straightforward. For mongrels, the biggest challenge is often, whose roots? Consider the choices presented to Juan Krijnen, a twenty-nine-year-old native of Amsterdam. Tall, handsome and well-spoken (in both Dutch and English), Juan manages apartment buildings in his hometown. A Dutch citizen, he keeps Holland's colonial history in his bones. His mother was born in Curaçao in Latin America of a Dutch father and local woman. Juan's father came from Indonesia, where a Dutch colonist married one of his ancestors. Juan's mother and father met in Amsterdam, a city teeming with foreigners, where racial and ethnic combinations are a source of fascination.

Juan is a product of Dutch tolerance and the peculiar legacy of the nation's imperial adventures. He solves the riddle of his identity with the simple declaration "I'm unique. I'm different from everybody." Who is he, really? He smiles: "I just follow my feelings and then I know."

Juan's answer sounds glib, but he walks the walk. He has many Dutch friends, speaks fluent Dutch and displays the Dutch zeal for American culture. His favorite sport is American football (he plays free safety for a local semipro team). He's never been to either Indonesia or Curaçao, but he's been to Chicago.

Still, Juan burned to build another self. He started with intimacy. He wanted a foreign lover in much the way that a wanderer might leave his home out of a belief that he was born in the wrong country. Juan knew many Dutch women, but they left him cold. He wanted a more mysterious passion. He dreamed of meeting a Latin woman, someone with the heat he felt that Dutch women lacked and that he associated with his parents' mixed marriage. One night in an Amsterdam club, he met a woman named Marita from Lima, Peru. Marita lived in Sydney, Australia, where she worked for a shipping company. She was on holiday in Amsterdam, visiting her sister, who then lived in Holland. The two women went to a club featuring Brazilian music, and Marita met Juan. They talked all evening. The next day, he called her at her hotel, and they spoke for two more hours. They were hooked. "It was like a dream," Juan says. Adds Marita, "It was love at first sight."

Marita, twenty-nine years old, was herself a mix. Her father's parents had emigrated to Peru from Italy, and she grew up eating fresh pasta, not beans, as the family staple. Visits to Italy were routine. She spoke Italian, Spanish and English.

After two weeks in Amsterdam, she returned to her job in Sydney. Juan kept courting her, sending love letters by electronic mail. He never enjoyed the computer so much as when reading her replies. "She's the same type as me," he says. "We have the same values."

Marita finally quit her job, joining Juan in Amsterdam. Three weeks later, they were married in a simple ceremony. At dinner afterward, they feasted on Thai food.

JUAN'S JOURNEY STANDS on its head the old cliché that an outsider marries into the dominant culture in order to win respectability. He has married out of the culture as a way of gaining a new dimension in his life. This is a singular achievement, a kind of mongrel's gold medal.

For another serial transformation, consider Sue Patterson. Born and raised in Ontario, Canada, she fell in love with a New Zealander named Mike who was attending graduate school in Canada. They married and moved to New Zealand, where Sue worked as a lab technician. After three years, they returned to Canada, living in Nova Scotia. Sue gave birth to a daughter and ran a family farm for several years. She returned to New Zealand with her husband, and after many years away from her family's Presbyterian church, she grew closer to religion. She attended a theological seminary and was ordained a Methodist minister in 1988. In 1995, her husband Mike decided to move to Scotland to strengthen his ties to the land of his grandparents. Sue joined him and got a job as a minister in a Presbyterian church in a town midway between Glasgow and Edinburgh. Now both consider themselves "new Scots," people who have chosen voluntarily to embrace Scottishness, not by virtue of blood tie but because they believe they can help build a "new" Scotland that builds upon but still transcends the traditional symbols and practices of Scottish life.

Sue cherishes her Canadian roots, loves Scotland but still worries that her transformations leave her wobbly. "Will we ever find peace?" she asks about hybrids, while celebrating her ability to acquire more depth and texture. She is fond of quoting a bit of folk wisdom from New Zealand's Maori tribe whose members say, "Don't tell me what you do, tell me where you're from."

Sue is proud that her daughter Alannah, nineteen years old, is smitten with Canada, a place she's never lived. Alannah holds a Canadian passport (by birth) and recently visited Canada with her Scottish boyfriend. The two talk often about moving to Canada and may do so if they marry (which would enable her boyfriend to gain Canadian residency).

Alannah's affection for Canada surprises Sue, who struggles for an explanation. She hits on an experience a few years ago when Alannah first visited Canada. It was winter and much colder than in Scotland, and her daughter did not bring a heavy coat. After the plane emptied, she shivered in the airport. Then one of Sue's cousins—there to greet them—pulled out a plush winter coat. She wrapped it around Alannah and whispered, "This is yours for as long as you're here."

She might as well have said "amen" to portable roots. They are there when you need them.

GLOBAL HYBRIDS

When hybridity goes global, the result is not a soulless transnational. Global hybrids are anything but. Yanni,[6] a seventeen-year-old girl, easily slides from her home in St. Paul, Minnesota, to her parents' birthplace in Tunisia. The shifts don't seem to faze her. "She's so good at this, no one can tell the difference," her mother says.

Is Sally Broughton, a North Carolina native, less substantial after spending two years in Macedonia, where she worked on educational programs promoting ethnic harmony and dated an Islamic man?

Who would question the heart of Patricia Hengelmon, a Scottish computer programmer who settled in Amsterdam twenty-five years ago, married and raised two children? She teaches programming to college-educated immigrants to Holland, helping them learn a new skill and teaching them about Dutch ways at the same time. She still retains a sense of being an outsider, yet this expands her value because she can relate both to natives and newcomers.

There's nothing flimsy either about Naysaa Gyedu-Adomako, the daughter of the Red Cross chief in Ghana who chose the University of Iceland for her undergraduate studies. Can anyone doubt that this twenty-five-year-old—having survived a few Icelandic winters, learned the country's distinctive language, graduated from college and gotten a job in Reykjavik—is not broader and stronger for her labors? And far from losing her Ghanaian identity, gaining an Icelandic one makes her ties to Ghana seem more real.

"Iceland has made me more aware of and attached to my Ghanaian heritage," she says. "I must admit I took a lot for granted before coming to Iceland. But living amongst Icelanders, who are so intensely proud of their heritage, made me more aware of how important my country and its customs and traditions are to me. It also made me understand why some Asians and Africans who live in other parts of the world insist on upholding some outdated customs, some of which are no longer practiced. Confronted with a new culture, there is always the fear of losing your own cultural identity: Some do, and others become more aware and attached to it."

"Before I came to Iceland, I looked in the mirror and saw a girl," she adds. "Now I look in the mirror and I see a black girl. My stay in Iceland has made me extremely race-conscious, and also conscious of the fact that some doors may be slammed in my face solely because of the color of my skin. It makes me sad and angry, but it prevents me from having any illusions about life. It would be nice to go on believing that we live in a world where color is irrelevant, where everyone has an equal chance to make it. But if that were true, we would rename the world Utopia, and that's a long way off. Maybe being aware of bias will not make my frustrations more tolerable, but I think it may help me find ways to deal with all this without losing confidence in myself and my abilities."

To be sure, Naysaa's ties to Ghana are now looser in the sense that she's more willing to live elsewhere and frankly admits to wanting to marry a non-Ghanaian man for the cultural variety (though she's not paired with anyone now). Still, she often hears echoes of Ghana, even in Iceland, where she rarely meets another African. "My connection with Ghana," she says, "is something that I carry inside me, and no matter where I am or how long I live abroad, those ties won't be severed. Thanks to modern information technology, I can communicate with my parents through e-mail every day. I read Ghanaian newspapers and listen to radio broadcasts on the Internet." If she ever has children, she adds, "I would make it a point to teach them Fanti, my mother tongue, and send them home to Mom as often as possible for deep Ghanaian socialization."

FOR CHILDREN of immigrants, the tension between the new and the old can be even more intense for first-generation wanderers such as Naysaa. Immigrant children, writes one observer, "inevitably find themselves pushed and pulled between the culture and values of their parents and those of the larger American society. Such ambiguities are perhaps never more acute then when a decision about marriage . . . is at hand."[7]

This tension is well illustrated by the example of Vinit Sethi, a native New Yorker and an investment banker, who agreed to allow his Indian-born mother to arrange a marriage for him with a woman from her country. To be sure, immigrants for centuries have sought wives in the old country, but today the ease of travel allows an immigrant to examine potential spouses himself and even have a wedding ceremony in his ancestral land, options unavailable to an immigrant to the United States a century ago. Just how Sethi selected a wife reveals much about transoceanic lives and the openness of the new cosmopolitanism. Mongrelization doesn't necessarily mean total acceptance of individualism or the denigration of tradition. It can also encourage provincialism, as Vinit's courtship showed.

His mother, Shahshi, felt her son was excellent husband material. At Stuyvesant High School in Manhattan, Vinit had excelled academically, but never dated. In college, he dated occasionally but never had a girlfriend. After graduating summa cum laude, he joined an investment bank and moved into an apartment across the hall from his parents. When he turned twenty-three, his mother told him to stop "goofing around" and marry. He could pick his own wife, she said, if he chose a vegetarian. But if he and his wife planned to live across the hall, she added, "I would have to get along with her and she would have to get along with me, emotionwise, foodwise and livingwise."

Vinit had no marriage plans but let his mother know that he preferred an Indian woman to an American. Shahshi saw this as a signal to search her homeland for a wife. She told friends and family in Bombay and Jaipur of her son's eligibility, but he refused to visit India to meet potential mates personally. Still, the word was out. Shahshi began receiving inquiries and even details about specific women. While on a visit to Bombay, one of the women, Anshu Jain, made a surprise appearance accompanied by her father and two uncles. As Celia Dugger recounted in the *New York Times:*

> The willowy, soft-spoken Miss Jain walked in [and] . . . quickly won over Vinit's grandmother, uncle, aunt, assorted cousins—and most important, his mother. "Anshu had a softness," Mrs. Sethi recalled. "She was very down to earth, very simple, very humble. It just clicked."
>
> When Mrs. Sethi returned to New York . . . she described the young women she had met, ranking the top four and their respective virtues. Always, Miss Jain headed the list. . . . Five months later, Vinit flew to Hyderabad to meet her. At a party before he left, one of his college friends brought out a cake topped with a plastic married couple and the words, Happy 17th Birthday, suggesting he was going to be married off to a teenager. "I was a little spooked by the whole situation," he acknowledged. But he told himself he could always refuse the match.
>
> The first day he and Anshu met, they spoke about hobbies, school, siblings. He was charmed, but he felt he needed to know her better. But Miss Jain's family customarily allowed its daughters only a brief pre-engagement glimpse of the men they were to wed . . . [yet] her father decided to allow another meeting. The next day, he sent [Anshu with] one of his veteran drivers to pick up Vinit. During hours of talk in the back of the car, she told him of her bare-bones needs: "A guy who's patient and who doesn't smoke or eat tobacco." He, in turn, told her about his more complex requirements: a woman with whom he connected emotionally and who shared his commitment to family.
>
> He knew there was no chance for a third meeting. He had to decide. He

flew to Bombay the next day and waited to see if the spell would lift. It didn't.

He said yes.[8]

The marriage of Vinit and Anshu took place in India. Vinit rode to the ceremony on horseback, dressed as a prince. After the wedding, Anshu flew to New York, moving into Vinit's apartment across the hall from Shahshi. The worlds collided. Vinit's mother wouldn't allow Anshu to leave her apartment alone and insisted she wear traditional Indian clothing, at least when receiving guests. Vinit acceded to his mother's dress code, but won Anshu the room to explore New York on her own and attend a university, where she studies business. The couple has even declared their intention to buy their own home, leaving their parents behind.

Shahshi is satisfied. "We are all trying to take the best of the two worlds," she said. "It's not a juggle or a struggle."

To be sure, the story of Vinit and Anshu raises more questions than it answers. Are they budding hybrids, or only transplanted natives? Will their attachment to Indian ways decay over time, so that their own children—which they hope to have someday—find the mind-set of Shahshi peculiar and alien? Is it possible to creatively juggle two styles as different as tradition-bound Indian and go-go New York? Will Vinit's world narrow over time, becoming more dominated by the values of his parents? Can Anshu find other roles besides that of dutiful wife? Does she have an "American" future, or will she be merely a spectator in the United States? If the couple has children, will this foster a decisive break with tradition, or can the "virtual India" created by Shahshi be sustained in New York?

I don't have the answers to these questions, but I favor a world in which they can arise. The hybrid spawns riddles, which expose the depth and nuance of life.

MOVIN'

Migration is the breath of life for hybrids. Like Vinit, they shuttle between multiple communities in order to flourish. In the future, many more will live this way. Levels of migration within the industrialized world are high, equaling or even exceeding in recent decades the great transatlantic migrations of 1880 to 1920. In this earlier period, 30 million people emigrated to the United States alone, pushing the percentage of foreign-born people in America to a record of 14.7 percent in 1910. One analyst estimates that the flow of people into rich countries from 1965 to 1995 more than tripled the transatlantic migration of a century ago. And because of slower population growth in Europe, "the European component of migration is probably as intense as the American experience at the turn of the [twentieth] century."[9] Another difference from the great migration of 100 years ago is that the migrants of the late twentieth century have come from a far greater number of countries. In this recent migration, the number of people "speaking a language other than English at home was not greater than 1910 or 1920, but the diversity of languages was much larger," notes Lawrence Fuchs, an expert on ethnic politics in the United States. In southern California, for instance, at least 1,000 students (not proficient in English) spoke one of fifteen foreign languages, including Urdu, Japanese, Russian and Armenian. Rather than two or three countries dominating the immigration flow, as they did in 1900, the top five countries in the 1980s and 1990s accounted for less than 40 percent of the annual flows. In the 1980s, immigrants to the United States hailed from an astonishing 174 nations and territories. Chinese, Tagalog, Korean and Vietnamese were each spoken by more than 500,000 newcomers. At least 200,000 spoke Arabic, Hindi, Thai and Persian. Oscar Handlin has called this array of newcomers "unprecedented in numbers and diversity."[10]

The effect of greater diversity is clear. "One consequence of these continuous movements is that, despite the supposed drive to protect the social, ethnic and cultural homogeneity of Europeans and Americans, the life of big cities continues to display increasing cosmopolitanism," one observer notes, concluding that "the growing diversity of sources is also remarkable, such that each major city appears increasingly like a microcosm of the world's peoples."[11]

"Even if migration were to stop tomorrow," say two leading migration experts, "this will affect [rich] societies for generations." But migration, they say, "shows few signs of ceasing and is indeed more likely to grow in volume as we move into the 21st century."[12]

Various factors should keep migration into wealthy countries high, if not push migration higher:

- There is rising inequality between rich and poor countries, which increases the incentives for skilled and ambitious people to move from poorer to richer countries (the World Bank estimates that the ratio of GNP per capita income in the top quintile of the world's population to the bottom quintile widened from 60 to 1 in 1993 to 74 to 1 in 1998).[13]
- Populations are aging and birthrates low in rich countries. This will likely cause periodic labor shortages in many of these countries.
- The legal means of importing people are expanding as citizenship

becomes more flexible (witness the exchangeable citizenship within European Union countries) and countries expand the varieties of "work visas" in response to economic and political pressures.

- Finally, the number of people who don't live in rich nations is staggering. Poor countries account for more than 5 billion of the world's 6 billion people. India and China alone make up more than 40 percent of the total. Some people in these countries will trade their homes for a rich home. And there is reason to believe that as the standard of living rises in poor countries, the beneficiaries of these gains will be more likely than before to move to a rich nation, at least temporarily. More aware than before about the benefits of wealth and more skilled, many people will find the best chance of realizing their rising expectations lies far from home. So much for the misguided notion, widely held by governments of some rich countries, that as poor countries develop, the flow of emigrants may decline. Indeed, development may bring about a rise in emigration precisely because larger numbers of people now possess the skills and mentality to thrive in a rich nation.

TWO DISTINCTIONS, one geographical and one social, are believed generally to describe migration through history. The distinctions, made by historian William McNeill, boil down to this: There were two types of migrants and they went different places. Elite migrants—aristocrats, missionaries, merchants and bureaucrats—moved from one power center to another. Mass migrants, on the other hand, were nomads or peasants who settled outlying lands.[14]

Today, such differences between elite and mass migrants are breaking down. A new picture of migration is emerging, in which elite and mass migrants travel the same routes to the same places and live parallel (though vastly different) lives. "The immigrant population is highly bifurcated," notes one observer. "There are many immigrants with few skills and many immigrants who are highly skilled," so that they "tend to be lumped at both ends" of the human scale.[15] Politically, this bifurcation can be interpreted two ways. Conservatives complain about immigration because they fear it "pollutes" their society with less-capable people. Liberals and progressives presume that admitting newcomers to their country helps truly needy people, not elite transnationals who arrive with college degrees and nannies in tow. These divergent views from the Right and Left share a common misperception about migration. Both accept the frayed distinction between elite and mass migrants. They fail to realize that the software engineer and the nurse take the same plane from Manila to Tokyo or London or San Francisco. The physician from Bombay travels the same path to Brooklyn as does the waiter from Bihar.

Because many of the low-skilled migrants provide personal services, the social circles of elite and mass migrants are intertwined too. The French business consultant in New York has a Guatemalan nanny; together they learn the transit system, where to find ethnic foods and what neighborhoods to avoid for safety reasons. They may practice their English on one another as well. These shared experiences knit them together in surprising ways.

Differences between elite and mass migration are eroding for other reasons. Mass migrants from developing countries are usually among the better educated in their society. They are, thus, not from the "masses" in the sense that many people in rich countries think of the term. They are not usually the people described by the inscription on the Statue of Liberty in Manhattan harbor; they are not the "wretched refuse" of the poor and the oppressed.[16] They are generally better off than most lower- and middle-class people in poor countries.

This is even true for those who lack the definable skills, such as university degrees, that give elite migrants from poor countries an edge. As Nigel Harris has noted, "Many rated as unskilled in developing countries may qualify as skilled in a developing country because they possess competencies taken for granted in one country but scarce in the other—the ability to read and write, to drive a vehicle, to undertake elementary calculations." These skills, so basic that they are rarely recognized as such in rich countries, often signal that a migrant is a relatively privileged member of his home country. Studies of domestic workers in Europe, for instance, found that they were generally "younger, fitter and better educated than any native equivalents." One study of Filipina maids working abroad found that more than half even had some university education. Another study, of Filipina domestics in Hong Kong, found that 55 percent were college graduates and another 21 percent had finished school; four in ten had worked in the Philippines as professionals, including many as teachers.[17]

Educated people are surprisingly well represented even among migrants from South America. In the second half of the 1990s, *The Wall Street Journal* found that "hordes" of midlevel professionals and recent university graduates took menial jobs in the United States following the contraction of Mexico's economy from the peso crisis. Engineers picked onions. Dentists carried bags to people's cars. Lawyers waited on tables. Even well-educated people who could land jobs in Mexico preferred menial jobs in the United States. One report described why Maria Castro, a qualified teacher, was picking vegetables in the United States. Her job in the field paid five times more per week than a Mexican schoolteacher earns. "I spent five years in college to pick broccoli," Castro said. Perhaps luckiest are people who live near the border between the United States and Mexico. Mexican professionals working in the Imperial Valley, a rich agricultural zone in California, can maintain their practices in Mexico. Mexican doctors in one city spent mornings in the United States picking vegetables only to return to Mexico in the afternoon to see patients.[18]

These situations make a mockery of simplistic notions about immigration, underscoring that migration is influenced by the sophistication, language ability and other know-how of the migrants themselves. This willingness of more advantaged people from poor nations to migrate to a rich nation isn't limited to times of economic crisis either. Some personal services in rich countries are lucrative enough to attract highly capable people from developing countries. On one taxi ride to Kennedy airport, my Egyptian driver turned out to be a Queens high school teacher who had been a math professor in his home country. The extra money he earned driving a cab he invested in Egypt, buying several Cairo businesses, which his brother managed. "This is my retirement," he said. "I couldn't do it without my brother. He knows the city. Ten years I'm gone from Cairo, and I don't know it anymore."

Nor are migrants who flee political persecution, or even take the drastic measure of paying a human trafficker for the service of getting them into a desired country, necessarily more representative of the "great unwashed" of a poor nation. This is one of the dirty little secrets of the refugee game. When I asked a senior official at the United Nations Commission on Human Rights about data on the socioeconomic background of refugees and asylum seekers in wealthy countries, he told me that the U.N. would rather not know the socioeconomic background of these people. What if it turned out that refugees who fled instability were disproportionately better educated and wealthier than the people who stayed home? Wouldn't this undercut the sympathy for refugees in the nations asked to absorb them?

The trouble with this thinking is that it ultimately weakens support in rich nations for immigration by depicting migrants as burdens, unprepared for competition. By hiding or ignoring the true character of migrants, do-gooders undermine public support in rich countries for the diversity brought by migration. By "dumbing down" migrants in the hopes of eliciting sympathy, do-gooders perversely create the combustible fuel to ignite a backlash. To be sure, some migrants are ill-prepared for the requirements of urban life and require charity, but then so do some natives.

McNeill's second distinction, between migration to periphery versus center, is also breaking down. Increasingly, migrants move to the same place: anywhere the economy is hot, money is flowing and they know (or are related to) someone. Indeed, familiar faces are crucial. Migration today is more akin to a chain letter than a random invasion.

One migration expert tells of this illustrative encounter with a Tamil, newly arrived in Europe from his native Sri Lanka:

"Why are you in Europe?" I asked [him].
"How many Tamils are there in Europe?" he replied.
"About 24,000," I answered.
"Then there are about 24,000 reasons why I am here."[19]

This is not an isolated example. At one point in the 1990s, half of the 8,000 Italian brickmakers in one British city came from only four villages in southern Italy. In a Canadian nursing home containing thirty-three elderly Filipinos, twenty-eight were from the same village. Of Bangladesh's twenty-one regions or districts, four supply the bulk of the immigrants. Five U.S. metropolitan areas attracted 40 percent of legal immigrants to the United States in the 1970s and 1980s. In the 1990s, six states accounted for seven in ten of all legal immigrants. The draw of an established haven for migrants can be irresistible. In the mid-1960s, New York's Chinatown contained 15,000 people in a six-block area. Two decades later it was home to 300,000 residents, 450 restaurants and 500 garment factories. In California's Silicon Valley, immigrants accounted for 32 percent of scientists and engineers in 1990. Of the 28,500 Indians employed in the valley, 98 percent were immigrants.[20]

McNeill's geographic distinction has less relevance today for another reason. The old definition of migration—a person moves from point A to point B—is also obsolete. This either-or definition is embedded in the popular understanding of migration. People moved and then stayed or returned home. Today people shuttle back and forth indefinitely. "This kind of circular migration is very common between Mexico and the U. S.," writes Peter Stalker, who observes that migrants "try to get the best of both worlds." International migration, he adds, "is this generating a new kind of social space, occupied by 'transnational communities.'

As Saskia Sassen of the University of Chicago has noted, Old concepts of belonging do not fit present realities." People now circulate rather than come and go, so that, Sassen writes, "the divide between origin and destination is no longer a divide of Otherness, a world in which borders no longer separate human realities."[21]

How and why this occurs explains much of the momentum behind mongrelization and the sustainability of new cosmopolitanism.

DIASPORA

The breakdown between elite and mass migrants has deep consequences for global hybridity. Migration is best understood as a mass activity that mimics elite patterns. To be sure, people will continue to migrate in traditional ways, but they increasingly will adopt one of two models of transnational life. The first is the diaspora model. The second is a model of "flexible" citizenship. These two models overlap, but merit separate explanations.

The idea of "diaspora" has a long history and varied meanings. In its loosest sense, it refers to any community whose members settle outside of their native land and maintain some connection with the "old country." But more commonly, the term applies to groups whose members are widely scattered around the world and face some special barriers to integration into their new homes. These barriers, mirrored around the world, create a sense of collective destiny for disparate peoples who share common values, or at least an outlook, even though they've never lived among one another.

The word "diaspora" comes from the Greek verb *speiro* (to sow) and the preposition *dia* (over). It is most commonly associated with the dispersal of Jews throughout the world. As Robin Cohen explains in his masterful introduction to the subject in *Global Diasporas:*

> The destruction of Jerusalem and razing of the walls of its Temple in 586 BC created the central folk memory of the negative, victim diaspora tradition— in particular the experience of enslavement, exile and displacement. The Jewish leader of the time, Zedikiah, had vacillated for a decade, then impulsively sanctioned a rebellion against the powerful Mesopotamian empire. No mercy for his impudence was shown by the Babylonian king, Nebuchadnezzar. His soldiers forced Zedikiah to witness the execution of his sons; the Jewish leader was then blinded and dragged in chains to Babylon. Peasants were left behind to till the soil, but the key military, civic and religious personnel accompanied Zedikiah to captivity in Babylon. Jews had been compelled to desert the land "promised" to them by God to Moses and thereafter, the tradition suggests, forever became dispersed.
>
> Babylon subsequently became a codeword among Jews (and ... Africans) for the afflictions, isolation and insecurity of living in a foreign place, set adrift, cut off from their roots and their sense of identity, oppressed by an alien ruling class. Since the Babylonian exile, "the homelessness of the Jews has been a leitmotiv in Jewish literature, art, culture, and of course, prayer." Jewish folklore and its strong oral tradition retold stories of the perceived, or actual, trauma of their historical experiences. The use of the word Babylon alone was enough to evoke a sense of captivity, exile, alienation and isolation.[22]

Scholars debate whether Jews are the "normative," or the classic, case of diaspora, but their global experience clearly influenced the perceptions of other great diasporas. The Irish Babylon was Ireland's great famine of the 1840s. The slave trade and slavery itself comprised the African Babylon. And the Armenian diaspora of the twentieth century was fired by the slaughter of an estimated one million people in 1915.

Whereas all four of these classic examples center on the brutality of the victimization of communities, newer diasporas hark back to the original Greek sense of the word, which referred to migration and colonization. Thus, a whole host of diasporas emerge in modern times, from Indian to Lebanese to Caribbean and Chinese. The victimization suffered by these "communities of dispersion" is more sporadic, and they are less committed to maintaining outcast status than the classic diaspora cases. Nevertheless, these overseas ethnic groups retain their differences as they participate in the mainstream of the societies they inhabit.[23] Their effort to do so isn't unprecedented but recalls W.E.B. Du Bois's concept of "double consciousness," which he saw as describing the special burden on African Americans that required them to juggle two lives and two self-conceptions. Today's diaspora communities view this condition of "double consciousness" in a benign way and see it as the basis for their own diasporic sense.

It is the durability of identity differences that has drawn attention to diasporas from opponents of homogenization—and hybrids seeking a model for what they view as the increasingly normal condition of staying and leaving. In this way of thinking, every hybrid is a Jew, and every aspiring hybrid wishes to participate in a diasporic consciousness defined by the Jewish experience of exile. In turn, this echoes Camus's concept of an "exile without remedy." For Camus, exile underscored the inevitability of fragmentation (of self, of culture). In his way of thinking, purity is not only a wrong turn but an impossibility.

The basic illogic of purity is a crucial point. Diaspora implies a commingling of races, an impurity, a radical mixing. Thus, even diasporic peoples may not be a single tribe as many assume. The Jewish exemplar bears this out. Cohen, reviewing the evidence, writes that "Jews are not a single people with a single origin and a single migration history." Indeed, in some ways the Zionist ideal, which flowers in the creation of the state of Israel, conflicts with the inherent variety of the diaspora that so appeals to multiculturalists who revel in the break between cultural communities and a specific territory.

Of course, to the extent that Jews flourish beyond the borders of Israel (which they indeed do), the relevance of this new diaspora model holds. And hold it does. The survival of diaspora communities—across great distances and over many centuries—is proof that "transnational bonds no longer have to be cemented by migration or by exclusive territorial claims. In the age of cyberspace, a diaspora can, to some degree, be held together or re-created through the mind, through cultural artifacts and through a shared imagination."[24] But this does not mean that every hybrid community is artificial any more than are the imagined bonds between a Jew in Morocco and a Jew in Maryland.

Loosely applied, the term "diaspora" helps to convey the idea of global hybridity to people stuck in "one-race, one-place thinking." As Cohen notes, diaspora is an "exciting way of understanding cultural difference and identity politics" that suggests a person can participate fully in a local society while maintaining a strong connection with a global one. This possibility shatters many old assumptions.

To those who dismiss humanity's capacity for protean attachments, hybridity only provides intellectual "cover" for smug posturing. Yet this is an uncharitable view. Hybridity seems to have as much legitimacy as the diasporic experience. As Khachig Tololyan has written, diasporas are "the exemplary communities of the transnational moment." They are, in short, metaphors for the human condition.[25]

It is absurd to say that everyone has a diasporic consciousness, but it is a noble aspiration nonetheless. To declare "We are all Jews now!" suggests both the predicament of identity in a globalizing world and a way out of the predicament. If loose language is the price of an intellectual umbrella for hybridity, then pay it. Sociologically, biologically, historically, we are all from somewhere else, outsiders to one degree or another. And so America remains the city on the Hill, the mythic Promised Land to the world's billions. "It's that same old, same old story," observes the American writer Fae Myenne Ng. "We all have an immigrant ancestor, one who believed in America; one who, daring or duped, took sail."[26]

Well, pull up anchor and take sail too, as did that forgotten ancestor. Diaspora, flaws and all, is the mother of cosmopolitanism. Now let's examine the father.

CITIZENSHIP

New forms of citizenship are emerging to accommodate hybrid identities. Growing numbers of countries permit their citizens to hold passports from other countries. No one knows how many U.S. citizens hold a second passport, but many millions are certainly eligible. Aihwa Ong, an anthropologist at the University of California at Berkeley, calls the new mind-set "flexible citizenship" to convey the open-ended quality of what was once viewed as a rigid relationship.[27]

Dual citizenship provides the legal underpinning for transnational hybridity in a world where nations still matter. For ties to deepen across borders, an individual must have the right to realize these ties. The ability to live in an adopted or native country, vote, own property and even participate in social and political organizations may depend on citizenship rights. For a variety of reasons, then, "flexible citizenship" provides public support for hybridity in much the same way as the concept of diasporic consciousness provides private support.

Dual citizenship is especially important because relatively few countries, notably the United States, Mexico and Canada, automatically grant citizenship to people born on their soil (of European countries, only France does so, but puts far more restrictions on it than the United States). In most countries, citizenship is not a birthright. It must be petitioned for and granted, creating uncertainty in the lives of many parents and children.[28] Generations of Koreans born in Japan, for instance, did not receive automatic citizenship. Until recently, neither did children born in Germany of Turkish immigrants or the children's children. In Macedonia, a former republic of Yugoslavia that has been spared civil war, the children of ethnic Albanians, the country's largest minority, routinely fail to receive citizenship papers and passports.

For most of the twentieth century, nations discouraged people from holding two passports and even revoked the citizenship of some who displayed too much loyalty toward another country. Some countries, including Germany and Sweden, still don't permit it. And the concept of dual citizenship remains controversial. Many claim it promotes divided loyalties that threaten the nation. In Turkey, for instance, a member of parliament was stripped of her seat because she failed to inform the government, as the law stipulates, that she had obtained a U.S. passport (while retaining her Turkish one). In Germany, a proposal to allow dual citizenship was stopped dead, despite the backing of the country's ruling coalition, by fears that the practice of allowing two passports would promote disloyalty among ethnic minorities in Germany.

At least in wealthy nations, the holdouts against dual citizenship are the exceptions. For example, in 1940, on the eve of World War II, a U.S. law codified the long-standing American practice of revoking the citizenship of anyone who participated in the political life of a foreign country. Merely voting in an overseas political election could lead to the loss of citizenship. A 1952 law tightened these restrictions. But in a series of Supreme Court rulings beginning in 1964, the limitations were effectively removed. Today dual citizenship is permitted in the United States. Although no law expressly approves of it, the concept is so entrenched in practice that when the Immigration and Naturalization Service grants citizenship to an immigrant, the agency doesn't even ask whether the person still holds another passport. Moreover, according to the U.S. State Department, no matter what an American does on behalf of another nation (so long as it doesn't violate U.S. laws), it "is no longer possible to terminate an American's citizenship without the citizen's cooperation."[29]

Millions of U.S. citizens are eligible to obtain another passport; these include not only naturalized Americans but also people whose parents, or even grandparents, were born in certain foreign countries. Ireland and Italy, for instance, have issued passports to the grandchildren of nationals living elsewhere. Using the birthrates of children born to foreign-born parents, one migration expert, T. Alexander Aleinikoff, estimates that the pool of Americans eligible for dual citizenship grows by at least 500,000 each year.

In the 1990s, many countries began to allow some forms of dual citizenship, including Mexico, Brazil and El Salvador. Such changes are generally welcomed by immigrants. Until Mexico changed its law in 1998 to permit its natives to hold a second passport, many Mexican emigrants to the United States were reluctant to obtain American citizenship. In Germany, residents of Turkish descent, even some born in the country, often won't seek German papers out of fear that they will jeopardize their right to live in Turkey.

The spread of dual citizenship has given rise to some curious forms of transnational politics. A retired U.S. bureaucrat was elected president of Lithuania. A U.S.-born son of immigrants from the Dominican Republic talks about winning the country's presidency, even though he lives in New York. The government of Colombia has debated whether to allow Colombians living in the United States to vote in elections at home. New York mayoral candidates routinely campaign for votes in Puerto Rico and the Dominican Republic because so many New York voters maintain ties with these places.

To be sure, politics is only one way that a hybrid can deepen ties across borders and not usually the most satisfying. In fact, dual citizenship is only the minimum requirement for hybridity. Legal rights usually don't address the social barriers to participation. In the European Union, for instance, anyone holding a passport for one of the fifteen member nations is free to live and work in any of the other countries. But only a minuscule number of people do this because most Europeans remain wedded to their localities, and a host of "soft" barriers, such as different languages and retirement plans, encourage people to stay put.

Despite limitations, "flexible citizenship" is a valuable concept. It promotes happiness and helps hybrids avoid falling into citizenship limbo. It also belies the outmoded image of the immigrant as someone who leaves one country and joins another without ever looking back. To accommodate the messier, more complex reality of hybridity, flexible forms of citizenship are a must. Combined with the concept of the diasporic consciousness, they give hybrids powerful tools to construct and reconstruct themselves and their communities.

Be clear, though, that flexibility is no backdoor into "world citizenship." The right to participate in a specific locale remains rooted in an authentic commitment: either through work, family or a shared passion for tradition or innovation. People want real transnational ties, not empty gestures, and hybrids are happier when they don't have to battle to achieve deep ties. The reason is existential: People want freedom. Why should they surrender their freedom to wear different guises when they need not? By creating plentiful options, both the practice of leaving-and-staying and the construction of hybrid identities promote happiness. Hybridity is the surest way to avoid the fate of the soulless business-class traveler, described by Pico Iyer, who "has all his needs taken care of, except the ones that really matter."[30]

MONGREL PAST

Global hybrids are new but not unprecedented. In premodern times, there were transnational people and civilizations. The Roman and the Ottoman empires absorbed a wide range of peoples into their international projects. The Catholic Church, another kind of empire, certainly traversed national lines and absorbed the talents of many societies. For the elites of these empires, nationality was no impediment to achieving power, money and status. As the review of diaspora communities revealed, transnational "tribes" have long existed as well. The Jewish diaspora from the Levant spread across Iberia, Italy, France, England and Germany from the fall of the Western Roman Empire until the tenth century, after which waves of expulsions from England (1209), France (1306), Spain (1492) and Portugal (1496) shifted the center of Jewish settlement to Poland, Lithuania and the Ukraine. Other "tribes," notably the overseas Chinese, also crisscrossed the globe, bringing a shared mentality to very different places.

Even in modern history, with its emphasis on national ties, it is striking how an awareness of national pride often flowers in a transnational setting. Sun Yat-sen, China's first modernizer, plotted his revolution of 1911 after an education in Hawaii and Hong Kong, where he trained and practiced as a physician. Gandhi, India's great liberator, drew some inspiration for his philosophy of nonviolence from the London socialists he knew while studying the law in England and began his life of activism in South Africa. Marcus Garvey, a native of Jamaica and the most important black nationalist between the two world wars, gained his zeal for what he called "universal Negro improvement" from a group of Pan-Africans in London, where he lived from 1912 to 1914. Eamon De Valera, the father of modern Ireland, was born in New York and returned to America at the height of the Irish independence struggle to rally foreigners to his cause. Even as president of the Irish republic, he relied on American money to fund the daily newspaper he controlled. The archetypal British bulldog, Winston Churchill, had an American mother. Ho Chi Minh, the Vietnamese nationalist, left his homeland in 1911 at the age of twenty-one, spending the next thirty years abroad. In seizing control of Vietnam from the Japanese in 1945, Ho realized an anticolonialist vision that he had worked out during significant stays in Paris, London, Moscow, New York and Hong Kong.[31]

Though hybrids have peopled world history, today's hybrids are different. There are four chief differences, which together suggest why a new cosmopolitanism will gain momentum.[32]

First, there's the matter of scale. The new cosmopolitanism is much wider and deeper than its premodern form. It doesn't involve only the wealthy or the favored few. "Massive numbers of people are moving across borders, making virtually every country more polyethnic in composition."[33] These wanderings show no sign of abating. If they do not, one respected survey predicted in 1999, "then the contemporary pattern of migration may supersede its predecessors in terms of intensity and extensity."[34]

Second, hybrids today are more defiant. Like Chiori Santiago, they are quicker to cry foul. Or like Barry Cox, they unabashedly declare new affiliations even when these may seem odd to many people. By contrast, in premodern societies, minorities generally accepted their subordinate status; they knew their place. If minorities somehow managed to assimilate into the dominant group, they usually aped the manners of their "betters."

Third, mongrelization occurs alongside the globalization of economic production and is encouraged by this globalization. Multinational corporations are committed to hybridity and spur mongrelization. In the past, even when multinational corporations had operations dispersed across many countries, they tended to draw upon national workforces and rarely mixed employees from many countries in a single location. Today, the best global companies—large and small—want hybrids in their organizations, from top to bottom, if possible.

Finally, the end of the Cold War marked a new phase in the history of nations. For nearly three centuries, large and small nations made concerted efforts to enforce a single culture and pacify, co-opt or obliterate minorities and nonconformists. In the twentieth century, such uniformity campaigns were shaped by wars, colonial exploitation and ideology. The retreat of this type of nationalism should not be confused with the decline of nations as such. Nations remain the most practical form of maximizing individual happiness and achieving cohesion within a diverse society. But the advent of a new style of nationalism, which allows space for both traditional minorities and newfangled hybrids to participate within and across national boundaries, creates unique conditions for the revival of cosmopolitanism and its expansion. The rise of a diasporic consciousness, the emergence of flexible citizenships and the demand for portable roots that reflect the practice of staying and leaving—all these forces set apart today's hybrids from yesterday's.

In this chapter, I've stressed the ability of hybrids to both incorporate and transcend the twin categories of ethnicity and nationality. But identity involves more than these two parameters. To start with, identity is highly personal. It arises out of intimate family and gender experiences as well as work, play and religious community. These experiences aren't national or ethnic in character. This is why I've punctuated my narrative with life stories. These vignettes aren't meant to be iconic. Each veers in unique directions and carries multiple, and at times conflicting, meanings. The stories aren't presented as parables but are meant to suggest the decline of familiar ways of labeling people. In this context, it is worth recalling Eric Hobsbawm's reminder about national identifications. "We cannot assume that for most people national identification—when it exists—excludes or is always ever superior to the remainder of the set of identifications which constitute the social being," he wrote in 1990. "In fact, it is always combined with identifications of another kind, even when it is felt to be superior to them."[35]

The question of just who values national identity above other affiliations remains open. Young people in rich nations seem less attached to the symbols of patriotism than do their forebears. That older people, in their anxiety, stoke nationalistic fires is understandable. But the nationalist explosions of the late twentieth century are likely a death rattle. Continued flows of people between nations, and radical mixing within them, will mean that those in wealthy nations who seek to lord national affiliation over other ties will pay an increasingly steep price for their vanity. Ethnic and national identities are neither as old nor as resistant to change as people assume. By demanding that newcomers "assimilate or else," nativists will grow isolated and ever weaker culturally, morally and economically.

BORDER JUMPERS

I can hear the objection now. Isn't the new cosmopolitanism really the same as the old? Isn't it practically impossible to carry roots about like luggage, checking in the bags when needed? Aren't youths like Barry Cox destined to revert to type as they age? Doesn't Michiko Nagasaka really face two stark choices, between surrendering her original identity or subordinating all her diverse experiences to it? Isn't Vinit Sethi just masquerading as a white financier when his heart actually aches for an unadulterated attachment to venerable India?

Such cynicism isn't new. In the nineteenth century, when nationalism flowered in Europe, the German philosopher Johann Herder asserted that there was no such thing as a man, only a German or an American or a Swede or a Jew. Without a national identity, a person was nothing.

Stated plainly, this narrow definition of identity—equating personal identity with nationality—sounds simpleminded, but it has surprising currency with many thinkers. Will Kymlicka, a Canadian philosopher and a leading authority on multiculturalism, asserts that the desire for an attachment to an *ethnos* or a people with a distinct culture springs from "deep in the human condition." He adds, "This bond does seem to be a fact . . . ." Kymlicka concedes that "some people seem most at home leading a truly cosmopolitan life, moving freely between different societal cultures." Yet these hybrids are a distinct minority and destined to remain so, he insists, declaring: "But most people, most of the time, have a deep bond to their own culture."[36]

Kymlicka, and those who agree with him, support governments that actively side with certain ethnic or national groups over others through intervention in schools, courts, media and the workplace. These interventions are easier if groups are viewed as fixed. But it's growing more difficult for a state to act in favor of specific groups, since the criteria for group membership is increasingly fluid. To create disincentives or deny people the right to choose new identities seems awfully unfair even if the benefit of doing so is to defend a besieged minority. This predicament highlights the challenge of basing public assistance on a single trait or affiliation, especially an inherited or involuntary one.

The freedom to choose one's identity is critical, since the sources of identity are shifting from "belonging" to "achievement." Speaking for many, Kymlicka says that "identification is more secure, less liable to be threatened, if it does not depend on accomplishment." But this is absurd. Achievement (playing the cello, passing the bar exam, publishing an article, winning a contract) increasingly is the basis for a satisfying life. To be sure, some people want unconditional acceptance by their "in" group. But more and more, people in rich countries achieve many of their identities. They choose their careers, friendships, allies, mixing and matching pieces and styles. Even their ethnic, racial and national affiliations are forged in various ways, despite the fact that a person's self-image depends partly on how he's viewed by others. Indeed, the ability to make one's own self is the essence of freedom. A good society recognizes and does not pit roots and wings against one another. If roots are the necessary condition for happiness, then wings are the sufficient condition. A good life is not possible without both.

Kymlicka, and other defenders of national identity, fear that wings become the enemy of roots. They fear that people abandon their ethnicity when they fly away. The characters in this book, I believe, show otherwise. The challenge of the new century is not that people will unthinkingly assimilate into an imperial norm. The bigger threat is that people will fail to realize their full humanity by ignoring their wings. The bigger threat is that they will stay so faithful to their roots that they will lack the flexibility and openness to forge new ties. Thus, wings and roots are inseparable. Roots provide a compass for those in flight. Wings endow greater meaning to roots.

Few people move between cultures, Kymlicka asserts; boundary crossing "is rarer, and more difficult," than most believe, and "there are limits on the 'cultural materials' which people find meaningful."[37] The evidence shows otherwise. Besides, who could possibly decide what the limits are and, for that matter, why there should be any limits at all? Are not people entirely free to remake themselves, drawing from whatever they have at hand? If Kymlicka wants to move to Hungary, is that a bad thing? Of course not, not for him or Hungary. It may even be necessary (say, if Kymlicka marries a Hungarian or chooses to study minority-rights issues there). In any case, such a move would hardly be surprising. In the new century, people, organizations and entire nations must begin thinking more like Barry Cox and Naysaa Gyedu-Ado-mako. If they don't, they'll find themselves falling behind while mongrels sprint ahead.

AN INDIAN ENGINEER
LIVES RIO TIME...
IN CALIFORNIA

CUPERTINO, CALIFORNIA—Radha Basu's job spans the world. Literally. She manages teams of software writers in California, Colorado, England, Germany, Switzerland, India, Japan and Australia. Born and educated in India, she earned a computer-science degree in the United States, is a naturalized American citizen and notched her first experience as an international manager in Germany.

"I feel like a global person," she says. "I feel I belong anywhere."

Her feeling fits, given the realities of business today. In many industries, gone are the days when a single location produced an entire project or product. The need to finish products and services quickly—and in varied enough forms to satisfy local differences—means that designers often must work around the clock. This approach of "following the sun" is more easily done when tasks are split up between continents. And as the search for talent gets more heated, global managers must be technically adept but culturally sensitive, familiar with corporate rules but flexible enough to bend when necessary. All in an effort to get their message across to people working across many time zones—fifteen, in Radha's case.

Large companies long have had foreign outposts. But thanks to advances in communications, computing and air travel, collaboration between far-flung coworkers has never been more intense, or intimate. Radha logs more than 100,000 air miles a year; even so, she often talks with groups of colleagues at Hewlett-Packard, the computer company, via video- or teleconferences. She exchanges scores of e-mails a day and sends simultaneous voice-mail messages to many of the 1,000 people in her division.

No matter how carefully she scripts her messages, impromptu conversations are the staple of her life. Shop talk can start early. One morning, she awoke to a phone call from her Swiss team, which was about to sign a deal to supply software to a major bank in Basel. It was 6:05 a.m. and Radha gulped. "Congratulations," she said, shaking off sleep. "Now what did you guys commit to?"

They quickly told her they planned to customize the bank's standard software, which would cut into the team's profit margins and time. A forty-minute conversation followed, during which Radha helped to refine her team's promises to the bank. While she talked, she also got dressed.

Like all of her international meetings, this one was held in English, which raises challenges of its own. English is the lingua franca for technical people worldwide, but it can also give rise to confusions by masking differences in style and practices between people of different countries. "We all use the same words, but we don't all mean the same things," says Christian Verstraete, a native French speaker who works in Brussels for Radha.

This became apparent once when Radha complained to Verstraete that some of her German engineers weren't doing what she'd asked. She had told the engineers they "should" do something. "To a German that means he still has the option of not doing it," Verstraete told her. He advised that she tell the engineers they "must" follow her directions, not only because she thinks it best for them to do so but because they have no choice.

Cultural differences can prove as formidable as linguistic subtleties. When her German code writers promise to deliver a program, they specify not only the day of its arrival but the time of day too. This punctuality has its benefits but means that the Germans expect her to deliver on her promises just as precisely.

RADHA HAILS from Madras, in southern India. She was born in 1953, just eight years after India's independence. Raised a Hindu, she was nonetheless educated by Irish nuns at the Good Shepherd Convent. Her father, an engineer on the Indian railways, thought the Catholics ran the best school in the area. "He taught me the value of being very solid in my basic foundation," she recalls. "He had real discipline." The youngest of three sisters, she attended Good Shepherd from kindergarten through high school. She got a strong injection of discipline at the school, but also lessons in Irish humor. Even now she will blurt out some humorous barb that will prompt a listener to ask how she gained her sharp wit.

Radha was a terrific math student, but when time came for her to apply to a university, her father forbade her to study engineering, her chosen course. "Engineering is too hard for girls," he told her. She applied anyway and took the entrance exam. Her father didn't know she'd done so until he read in the local newspaper that his daughter had notched the top score.

As an undergraduate, Radha lived at home. The engineering college had 2,700 men and 17 women. She graduated with honors and won admission to the University of Southern California, where she planned to study new areas in medical electronics not yet pursued by Indian universities. Her parents insisted she marry before leaving India. She refused.

A few years later, she did marry an Indian, a U.S. engineer who grew up not far from Madras. By then, she worked for Hewlett-Packard, where she rose rapidly. After two years in Germany, she was sent to India in 1985 to set up a software unit in the country. Hewlett-Packard was among the first multinationals to tap Indian software prowess by setting up local operations, and Radha was a formative figure in India's now-booming code sector. The assignment thrilled her; she had long wanted to give something back to her homeland. What's more, her six-year-old daughter came along, which gave her exposure to her mother's world.

Radha's four years in India were rocky. Her Anglo and European colleagues at Hewlett-Packard considered her ideal for the job, but local Indians resented her for leaving their country and returning as the standard-bearer of a U.S. company. "What I learned, and sometimes the hard way, was not to go into India and be the know-it-all," she recalls. Yet Radha's determination attracted the notice of the Indian government, which named her as an adviser on computer policy. By the time she left India in 1989, Hewlett-Packard's India offices employed 400 people and were one of the company's strongest offshore units. Her husband, meanwhile, launched one of India's first public computer networks.

Ten years later, Radha stays close to India. Besides helping to hire local software developers, she came up with a plan to help found local companies in Bangalore and Madras by having Hewlett-Packard contract with them for services. Some of the half dozen companies even set up shop in Hewlett-Packard's facilities in order to save money and obtain the proper support from the very start.

To be sure, Hewlett-Packard could hire these people directly, but Radha has long felt that "you don't have to own all of the organization in order to succeed." The idea of a big company serving as a seedbed for local entrepreneurs appealed to her, especially since in many places people with good ideas—but no track record—can't get funding. "This is a new way of empowering people," she says. "And not just in India. The idea applies just as well to China, Brazil, the Czech Republic and other developing countries with lots of technical talent."

PART OF RADHA'S FLAIR lies in her willingness to tackle national differences head-on, deflating them with her directness and sense of humor. Once, during a teleconference, she was settling the details of a joint venture with an Asian software partner. On the line were her own engineers from Singapore and Japan and a white male attorney from the United States. Also on the line were the partner's Asian attorney and president. The conversation was stiff, since it concerned contract language, but Radha felt that her lawyer's interruptions were making things worse. Noting that the Asian attorney was silent, she joked, "I think we need two Asian lawyers to finish this deal."

Humor cuts through tension, but misunderstandings are unavoidable. Besides, her teams aren't encounter groups; their goal isn't to promote multicultural harmony but to sell software. This focus on public results, as opposed to private attitudes, is a big help. It allows diverse contributors to adopt a common metric for success—and put a lid on differences when they don't advance team goals. It turns out, anyway, that diverse contributors yield better results. "We use this diversity to our great advantage," she says.

Radha means it. Look at her closest staff. One is a white American male who looks after two software groups in India. Another is a Taiwanese woman who lives in California and specializes in U.S. issues. Her software chief in England was born in Curaçao of Portuguese parents. Her top manager in Singapore hails from Norway. A key troubleshooter is an Indian native who works out of Bangalore, has a Canadian passport and does most of her work with customers in Latin America.

Radha tries to avoid a common trap of global managers who arrive in a city, rush to a plant, huddle with senior people, then give a canned speech to rank and filers before leaving. She prefers to spend a few days at each site, sometimes devoting most of her time to only a few teams or even a few people. "I need to dive into details," she says.

This personal approach takes time but gives Radha a better grip on her business and sets an example for subordinates who may have a different conception of management. Her top German manager, for instance, keeps a distance from his code writers and refrains from asking them about their work. But with Radha pestering him for details, he must change. He now tells his code writers: "Radha is doing this to me, so I'm going to do it to you." Still, the German manager is shamed by Radha's questions. "If I had done my job," he says, "she would not have to ask."

Other Germans feel the same way. When those on one small team learn of an impending visit from Radha, they try to anticipate her questions and meet to rehearse their answers. When Radha meets with the Germans, she grasps that the performance is scripted and tells them "to throw away your prepared questions. I want the natural ones." Her gambit prompts only a few fresh queries, disappointing her.

For Radha and her colleagues, it was another day of moving closer together, living a multicultural life that is becoming the norm "for us . . . and for the rest of industry."

CHAPTER 3

MONGRELIZE OR DIE!

The most important thing to learn is the value of impurity.

—SALMAN RUSHDIE[1]

The highly educated are sometimes trapped in habitual modes of thought which have proved successful in the past, but which militate against innovation. . . . The newcomer to a subject may see it from a point of view inaccessible to the professional, and thus produce something new.

—ANTHONY STORR[2]

If everybody in the room is the same, you'll have a lot fewer arguments and a lot worse answers.

—IVAN SEIDENBERG[3]

THE HISTORIAN David Landes offers an important warning in his wide-ranging book *The Wealth and Poverty of Nations*. "A common mistake of would-be scientific history," he writes, "is to assume that today's virtues must also be tomorrow's and that a given factor, if positive once, must always pay. History doesn't work that way." Instead, history teaches that success depends on "different strategies in different circumstances."[4]

This maxim is well worth remembering. My premise is that the circumstances that give rise to personal and communal vitality, well-being and prosperity have changed, and that people must pay more attention to an important variable they have largely ignored in the past. This variable is diversity, of the broadest type, which I call hybridity. The new importance of hybridity is a happy occurrence, since doing good and making good aren't always compatible. But this is one case where they are.

So far I have made the case that people can have both roots and wings and that, by having both, they help to preserve the inherited groups to which they belong while at the same time realizing their individual freedom and exposing their groups to nourishing outside influences. Hybrid lives, therefore, are good for individuals and good for the groups to which they belong. As such, hybridity is a quality many people will wish to possess. Hybridity will be seen as a sign of strength, not weak roots. People who adopt a hybrid style will contribute to social vitality and gain personal happiness by affirming their inherited identities and the additional ones they've chosen. Those who assume a hybrid stance will gain social, psychological and aesthetic rewards, but also economic benefits. In short, hybridity pays. And, in the present economic moment, hybridity pays well.

Be clear that I am not saying it will pay forever. I am not saying that mongrelization is the final stage of capitalism. It isn't. I am saying that capitalism and the conditions for creating wealth have changed in ways that play to the strengths of hybrid individuals, organizations and nations. And that those who wish to profit from changing economic conditions must view hybridity as their first and best option.

This bold claim warrants an explanation. The ability to apply knowledge to new situations is the most valued currency in today's economy. Creativity bestows more rewards than ever before, and hence curiosity about the source of creativity has never been higher. How creativity comes about is a great riddle, but a few things seem clear. Highly creative people don't necessarily excel in raw brainpower or test-taking. They are misfits on some level. They tend to question accepted views and consider contradictory ones. This appreciation for paradox, not coincidentally, defines the mongrel mentality—and gives rise to it. The mongrel is a bundle of contradictions, metaphorically, and exists at odds with others, actually. Discontent is the groundbeat of his life. His heightened sense of difference—of not fitting into molds—reminds him that every worthwhile creation is at once an act of love (of difference) and an act of rebellion (against formulas, pat answers, imagined harmony).

All these traits correlate with creativity. As the British psychiatrist Anthony Storr observes:

> Necessity may be the mother of invention, but dissatisfaction is its father. If we were perfectly content with the world as it is, we should not be moved to make scientific discoveries, invent imaginary heavens, write novels, paint pictures or compose music. Blissful happiness is not conducive to imaginative inventiveness. Therefore, it is surely to be expected that the most inventive and creative of mankind should also be those who are most at odds with the world and themselves.[5]

The American psychologist Howard Gardner also finds the source of creativity in what he calls "a lack of fit," or asynchrony. Highly creative people tend toward marginality, he finds, for a variety of reasons, including their nationality and ethnicity. These people learn to exploit their marginal position. What's more, marginality becomes a way of life. Since their success wins them acceptance, "whenever they risked joining the 'establishment,' they would shift course to at least intellectual marginality."[6]

The implications of this asynchrony seem clear: Divergent thinking is an essential ingredient of creativity. Diverse groups produce diverse thinking. Ergo, diversity promotes creativity.

This logic applies to those who cross academic or technical boundaries, hopping from one field of study to another, drawing fresh insights from inter-disciplinary investigations that consciously seek to break down intellectual walls. The same process animates the breaking down of walls in business. Cor-porate managers, planners, researchers, marketers and content creators ben-efit from diverse inputs. Those businesses that rely on diverse people, from top to bottom, are more likely to innovate than those that rely on similar people. This conclusion is backed by a body of scholarship that suggests that over the long term greater diversity in economic institutions will lead to more success-ful adaptations in a competitive environment. As the business historians Louis Galambos and Jeffrey L. Sturchio observe in their cogent study of the global pharmaceutical industry:

> Seen in this light, the corporations that are starting to shed their national identities are better able to take advantage of the creative tension between local opportunities and global resources; by drawing on the skills of a new cadre of "business cosmopolitans," they are better prepared to prosper in varied local economic and political environments.
>
> The new managers in these global corporations are attuned to a wide variety of customer relationships, cultural settings, government regulations, market conditions, patterns of industrial competition, and technological sys-tems. Their collective experience—shared with colleagues in different national contexts through the mobility of key players and institutionalized through focused learning networks within the firm—provides competitive advantage in an era of increased globalization. Firms that adapt to this new environment most adroitly are able to draw upon a larger, more diverse pool of candidates for their leadership positions and thus achieve [competitive] advantage.[7]

The same kind of benefits that corporations gain from diversity also accrue to cities, the most vibrant of which no longer draw on the energies of the nation in which they're located but on the energies of the entire world. Lon-don, San Francisco, Hong Kong, Miami, Paris, Tokyo, Bombay, to name only a few, have changed in function. In the last decades of the twentieth century, they ceased being national cities and became, as V.S. Naipaul has observed, "cities of the world, modern-day Romes, establishing the pattern of what great cities should be," great cauldrons of diversity, magnets for the talented and the misfits of the entire world.[8]

What is true for cities—that they must draw on far-flung talents to sustain and renew themselves—is fast becoming true for entire nations. Nations that welcome the contributions of outsiders and natives with different values are prospering; those who resist this are stagnating: To understand the economics behind this pattern, consider the concept of "social capital ," or "the ability of people to work together for common purposes in groups and organizations." Because social capital involves communal aims, numerous critics have presumed that homogeneous groups will score higher in this respect than diverse groups. In explaining the success of Asian economies in his book *Trust,* Francis Fukuyama concludes, "The most important variable is not industrial policy per se but culture."[9] Yet it never occurs to Fukuyama that it is not culture per se that shapes economic performance but a certain kind of cultural activity, the mixing of cultures. Thus, diverse America, with its tension between hybridity and harmony, has far more social capital than Japan. For Fukuyama, American success must be explained despite the country's diversity, not because of it, a view that flows directly from an unexamined belief in the superiority of the homogeneous.

Fukuyama isn't alone in making this mistake. Economists have the same blind spot. This is why the question of correlating hybridity with creativity, or perhaps innovation, never arises in their research. The conventional wisdom among economists is that diversity works against you. Jagdish Bhagwati, an international economist at Columbia University, nicely summarizes the prevailing view: "If everyone's alike, of course you're better off economically."

This belief flows from a mechanistic view of human behavior. If all people in a group understand the same language, or react the same way in the same situation, then of course it will be less costly (in time, energy, effort) to shift direction. When societies are modeled after machines, and individuals as cogs, the lockstep approach to organization makes sense. In periods of stability, or slow change, lockstep is wonderful. This perhaps explains why the role of diversity in the vitality of nations is curiously ignored by big thinkers through the ages. Adam Smith had nothing to say about it in *The Wealth of Nations.* Nor did Karl Marx discuss diversity in *Das Capital.* John Maynard Keynes ignored it too. Historians fare little better. Yale's Paul Kennedy, who wrote *The Rise and Fall of the Great Powers,* ignored both migration and diversity. Michael Porter, author of the influential business study *The Competitive Advantage of Nations,* never mentions either topic.

To be sure, a lack of diversity isn't always a signal disadvantage. Homogeneity can benefit a nation when it tries to catch up to economic leaders. When nations have a clear target—say, to imitate a leading competitor or to restore a well-understood but damaged industry—cultural sameness lowers the cost of mobilization. Germany and Japan posted dizzying growth rates after World War II partly because their homogeneous populations acted in concert, freeing attention to other areas. But once a country has caught up with political, economic or cultural leaders, then innovation carries a premium, and the need for diversity is more keenly felt. Thus, different stages, different needs.

OPENNESS

We are not in a lockstep era. The days of asking everyone to turn on a dime are over. Command economies collapsed. So did command leadership. Lockstep is the last thing companies or communities need. As Fukuyama notes, "The most useful kind of social capital is often not the ability to work under the authority of a traditional community or group, but the capacity to form new associations and to cooperate within the terms of reference they establish."[10] It turns out that at the start of the twenty-first century the best way to expand the capacity to form new associations is to rely on people who excel at doing just that.

Again, I can't give you a mathematical proof, but try the "quack" test. If something waddles like a duck, eats like a duck and quacks like a duck, then it's a duck. You don't need to submit the animal for DNA testing, or discuss classification schemes with a zoologist. A duck is a duck.

Look at professional sports. More than any other sport, soccer has been shaped by nationalism. Two countries even fought a war over a soccer match. Scores of nations have their own leagues, and each country periodically forms a "national" team out of its best players in order to compete in regional tournaments and the World Cup, which is essentially the Olympics of soccer. This dual nature of soccer contrasts sharply with Canadian and American pro sports, in which the top teams in baseball, basketball and U.S.-style football never seriously compete with teams outside of North America.

The stress on national achievement in soccer (or football as it is known everywhere in the world save the United States and Ireland) led inevitably to the rise of national identities in the sport. The English played long ball; the Brazilians showed flair and daring; Germans were disciplined and effective; Italians defended their goal at all costs; the French underachieved. Even as societies grew more porous to outsiders and more international in outlook, soccer retained its national traits, perhaps because shifts in the wider world made sports seem more precious to the patriotic.

Today soccer is a hybrid game. Nations still compete for regional and world championships, but the top domestic leagues are thoroughly cosmopolitan. Italy's Serie A league, probably the world's best, is loaded with talents from the world over. So too are the top leagues in Spain and England, two other rich soccer markets. The reason for blending players seems as straightforward as the decision in the late 1940s to allow the first blacks to play major-league baseball: Teams that do so win and the game itself improves. When the pool of potential participants is widened, competition increases, and athletes hone their skills too. Quality rises.

Even so, in Europe, where soccer is the most globalized, it required a ruling from the European Court of Justice in 1995 to end limits on the number of foreign players that a club could field. Those limits remain, but now apply only to players outside of the European Union. Most teams have added a few foreigners, and a growing number are bent on fielding what are essentially global all-star teams. Probably the most articulate advocate of radical mixing on the soccer field is Arsene Wenger, coach of Arsenal, a top London team in England's Premier League. Wenger is French and speaks of soccer as if it were a form of high culture (which it is). His team boasts a majority of non-English players and at one point had at least seven foreigners among the starting eleven.

When Wenger took over, fans were suspicious of him and his outsider ways. As one English observer recalled: "It would never work, [the fans] muttered knowingly into their pints. Not a chance. A foreigner teaching the English how to do something the English invented, and a Frenchman at that? A mixture of Dutch, English and French [players], thrown together in the fanciful hope of European harmony? Impossible. They would divide into national camps."

That was the sense in 1996. But within three years of Wenger's hire, Arsenal won the English league with flair, and their coach's philosophy looked visionary. Rather than try to alter the character of either his local or imported players, Wenger wanted each to bring a "new identity" to a collection of styles.

"Each person brings from his own culture the positive side, which all comes together in the service of efficiency," Wenger explained. "That is the beauty. It is almost magical." If not sheer poetry in motion, Arsenal football under Wenger was clearly more creative. "Arsenal was muscular and British, but stagnant [before]. 'Boring! Boring! Arsenal!' was a regular jibe from opposing hecklers. When the fans sing it now, it is with irony. The continentals, with less brawn, more flair, have brought new life."[11]

WHAT WORKS FOR teams also works for individuals. The sociologist Alvin Gouldner has argued that when a person draws on more than one "line of thought, and can thus escape the control of any one of them," and yet toggle between the two (or more) of them, then he or she is bound to forge new understandings. Psychological research bears this out. According to one respected survey, people from bicultural backgrounds (where they must hop between one cultural group and another) may be mentally more flexible and "find it easier to encode and access knowledge in diverse ways." They may have richer associations with a single concept than does a monocultural person. And they "may have a greater tolerance for ambiguity because they are comfortable with situations in which one basic idea may have different nuances" depending on the community they inhabit at the time. "Tolerance of ambiguity is considered a valuable trait for creativity because there is often a phase in which incompatible, ill-defined elements co-exist during problem solving." Biculturals often live in different places and participate in the rituals and activities of multiple ethnic or national communities. The experience may make them more aware of ambiguity and less frightened by it than those whose "activities [are] focused essentially on one cultural group." Biracial people may possess this same heightened awareness of ambiguity. By successfully participating in different racial groups, they bridge these differences and highlight what one scholar calls "the experience of both belonging nowhere and negotiating some belonging everywhere."[12]

I saw a bit of this myself growing up in a hybrid family. My father's parents were from southern Italy; my mother's parents from Russia. Both families yelled a lot, but for different reasons. My Italian relatives yelled over food, business and card games. My Russian-Jewish relatives yelled about feelings, either because their feelings were hurt or because they wanted to hurt someone else's feelings. What an outside observer might politely call ambiguity, I took as confusion. At an early age, I was forced to grasp the relativity of behavior. I learned that under the same circumstances, people could think and act in very different ways. Those on my father's side enjoyed themselves regardless of what other people thought, caused a ruckus and then laughed about it all. My mother's side worried about the price of not fitting in, didn't fit in and then felt guilty about not fitting in. Out of these contradictory styles came new perspectives, I felt, and an ability to react in very different ways depending on the needs of the moment.

I also came away from my childhood with a belief that intermarriages stimulate creativity among the spouses and their offspring. Children of intermarriages must contend with different perspectives. I know of no organized research into the creativity of children from intermarriages, but I am struck by how many highly creative people come from mixed backgrounds.

Consider Karim Rashid, a hot, up-and-coming designer of ordinary objects. Born in Cairo of an Egyptian father and English mother, Rashid has applied his taste to shopping bags, plastic chairs, even "very trippy" manhole covers. His Garbo wastebasket is considered a hit. More than one million of these curvy, translucent pails—in lilac, lime and ice blue—sold in North America in the late 1990s. The pail, priced at $10, caught the attention of art critics. A "Garbo" even ended up in the permanent collection of the San Francisco Museum of Modern Art.

Rashid was born in Cairo in 1960. His father painted sets for films and television shows. His mother taught school. Raised in England and the United States, Rashid studied industrial design in Italy and then worked in Canada. He speaks with a Canadian accent, is married to an American and won't call anywhere home. In 1993, he moved to New York, where he scored with innovative designs for ordinary objects such as a snow shovel and a plastic chair.

"I don't feel very culturally or racially attached to either England or Egypt," he says. "I jokingly say I'm nomadic. That's why I'm probably in America. You have an autonomy here that takes place nowhere else in the world. You don't have to have a [specific] heritage. This freedom allows me to be globally interactive. Because I don't feel I belong to a specific community, I feel I'm perpetually able to analyze it. So I'm always observing. That's the start of my work."

Outsider and yet insider, Rashid wants to turn design norms upside down. His fascination with plastic, a material that litters poor countries and represents tackiness in rich countries, reflects this. He favors what he calls "casual engineering" of ordinary stuff, so that "mass, everyday items gain the qualities of high design." This vision leads him to question many preconceived notions. "I try to let go of mental baggage," he says. "Who told us that this is the way we have to sit? Who told us I should be seventeen inches off the ground? We have shaped our own behavior; we have created everything we do. There's nothing 'natural' or 'intuitive' about it. So I ask myself, can I imagine a world that's completely different?"

Drawing on his own diversity, Rashid sees the world in unusual ways. One night at a restaurant, he sat in a flimsy and uncomfortable plastic chair. His back hurt so much he could hardly enjoy the meal. That night he had the counterintuitive idea "to elevate plastic to a new plateau of quality and good taste. It was time to drop the idea that plastic was a cheap material."

This insight led to his attempt to bring glamour to the lowly garbage pail. He named his pail Garbo in a frank attempt to associate trash with glamour (the name of the Hollywood star shares the same prefix as garbage). And the pail's striking shape flowed from Rashid's curious practice of studying waste containers in malls, grocery stores and offices. He even visited plastic-molding factories to learn the methods used to create his pail.

"We want rules and I'm trying to do the complete opposite," Rashid says. "To free myself from any preassociations. That's hard to do. A lot of times I get angry with myself that I'm not thinking out of the box enough."

His sense of life as a melding of the friend and stranger, the rooted and the winged, informs his designs with an unmistakably hybrid quality. They embody the sort of surprising juxtapositions that result from having crossed signals intelligently. In an arena where hype and high prices are the norm, Rashid's designs are appealing, original, practical and priced for the masses.

His aesthetic flows from his estrangement from cultures he knows well. Whereas others look for ways to make the expensive in a cheaper guise, he studies cheap things in order to find ways of endowing them with richness.[13]

SILICON VALLEY

The discovery of the connection between diversity and innovation is actually rediscovery. In the aftermath of World War II, homogeneity took the high ground. The postwar revival of Germany and Japan seemed predicated on their monolithic character. The Soviet Union, though comprising many diverse people, promoted one true way to its citizens. For a time, the simplicity and force of the Soviet message, and the huge economic and technological strides made by the country in the 1950s, won wide notice for its brand of monoculturalism. When in the late 1970s the shortcomings of the Soviet system became well understood, the communist regime was too unstable to attract from outside the fresh thinking it could not produce at home but desperately needed. Still, the Soviets survived. By the 1980s, monocultures thus seemed to be a fixed part of the geopolitical landscape. On the high end were Japan and Germany. On the low end were the Soviet Union and China. Notwithstanding the differing outcomes, closed systems were taken as normative. They cut across ideological lines, and few imagined a world without them.

The collapse of the Soviet Union in 1991 signaled the re-evaluation of heterogeneity, while the stagnation of Germany and Japan in the 1990s raised further doubts about the belief in the inefficiencies of mixing people. The U.S. economic boom of the 1990s finally brought to an end a half century of monocultural chauvinism. By the end of the twentieth century, U.S.-style diversity seemed an enviable approach to social, economic and political organization. In short, it produced more creativity. And the emblem of American creativity is Silicon Valley.

People can argue about what makes a fifty-mile stretch of northern California—loosely described as the land hugging both sides of the bay between San Francisco and San Jose—so successful. No one can argue, however, that the valley is a monoculture. It is a poster child for mongrelization, and the mixing of people is central to its success. "If you subtracted that," says Anna Eschoo, one of the members of Congress who represents the area, "the Valley would collapse."[14]

A pathbreaking study by AnnaLee Saxenian reinforces this view, outlining the profound influence of new Americans on northern California's high-tech mecca. At least one-third of Silicon Valley's scientists and engineers are immigrants. They come from everywhere: Europe, Latin America, the Middle East, but especially Asia. The vast majority of these immigrants are people of Chinese and Indian descent (51 percent and 23 percent respectively). Since 1980, the Chinese and Indian immigrants alone have founded 2,700 companies, which account for annual sales of $16.8 billion, or about 17 percent of all high-tech sales from the region. The companies employ 58,000 people, an untold number of whom are American-born.[15]

The role of mongrelization in maintaining Silicon Valley's creative edge has been apparent to me for some time. I saw the start of this relationship in 1988 while I was a reporter for the *San Jose Mercury News*. I wrote an article about why the valley really wasn't an American success story, arguing that the region's success depended upon a foreign import: people.

Silicon Valley's paper of record ran my story on the front page under the headline "Foreign Dependency." Like a lot of people back then who worried about American vulnerability, my editors (who wrote the headline) missed the big picture. The logic of purity doesn't apply to the world of hybridity. The rush of foreign talent into the valley made it more of a global place than a local place, more international than national, more postmodern than modern. Silicon Valley watchers missed this change in the rules. While the region's creative leaders were too busy to articulate the shift, they were happy to have the help. "This is good for the U.S. economy to have the best and the brightest from around the world assembled here," Robert Noyce, one of Intel's cofounders, told me.[16]

At the time, people actually thought this attitude was a shuck and jive. Oh sure, they'd say sarcastically, the valley's top dogs were junkies who needed another fix of foreigners. After all, the United States was heading down the tubes. Everybody knew that. American creativity was finished. We were a bastardized people. Too much mixing had overwhelmed the educational system, lowered standards, so diminished the national will that no one knew which way was up anymore. Lester Thurow, one of the most persuasive economists of his generation, even told Americans that the (pure) Japanese and Germans were about to bury them in "head-to-head" competition. I mean, look at how well their kids did on standardized tests. Or how many patents their corporations piled up. Comments like Noyce's seemed self-serving, the suspicion being that because Americans couldn't cut it on their own, they had to hire foreigners to handle the rough stuff. Meanwhile, the more independent Germans and Japanese, who had virtually no skilled immigrants in their workforce, could take care of their own business.

In the early 1990s, people really believed the dependency scenario. Think back. Few saw the big change. America wasn't "dependent" on foreigners; it was being liberated by them. And the foreigners (at least many in Silicon Valley) weren't hired hands. They were equal partners, owners of their own businesses. They hadn't elbowed aside Americans. Year after year, more Americans than ever worked in Silicon Valley. But so did more foreigners.

Even now, the place is still run mainly by native-born Americans. The magic is in the mixing. Successful immigrants long have said this themselves. For my "dependency" article, an Indian immigrant and leading venture capitalist told me, "Silicon Valley is very accepting of foreigners, more so than many other places in the [United States]. You don't feel out of place here." An Israeli engineer said, "It seems a safer place to come."

And why not? Everybody is from somewhere else. We are all mongrels here.

Even today, cynics sneer that this smacks of dirty pool. That it's so easy to rip off talent from the rest of the world by making them feel welcome when they arrive on American shores. Europeans are especially upset by this, seeing the tradition of Yankee mobility and openness as a cynical tool, another way for the United States to cheat its way to the top.

Get a grip. If it's so easy to cheat, why aren't other countries doing it? Why don't they use the same "subterfuge" to lure foreign talent onto their soil?

It isn't happening because it isn't easy to make foreigners feel welcome, especially talented ones. Try naming cities outside of North America where large numbers of foreigners are central to the innovation scene. It's a pretty short list. Maybe London. What about the superrich Stuttgart area in Germany's world-beating auto belt? Why doesn't it draw the best and brightest from abroad? Why aren't they flocking to Tokyo? Whatever happened to Moscow anyway? All these places have had, in economic and human terms, the right inputs: education, discipline, investment. But they missed an elusive factor: getting natives and strangers to form creative bonds.

To be sure, Silicon Valley is singular. Even native-born Americans must discover the place; they too are immigrants and the valley is their acquired home, their "invented tradition." And Silicon Valley natives must construct new identities because the region mutates with each passing technological generation (something like a period of five years now). Landmarks change. Success gets redefined. There's a new test for creativity.

Much the same dynamic can be seen throughout California, of course. As far back as the 1940s, Carey McWilliams referred to the state's capacity for innovation as "the edge of novelty," noting that "Californians have become so used to the idea of experimentation—they have had to experiment so often— that they are psychologically prepared to try anything." Almost no one is from California, after 150 years of ceaseless migration from elsewhere in the United States and abroad. Rates of intermarriage and percentage of foreign-born residents are the highest in the United States. One-third of America's foreign-born residents live in California. No Americans trade or travel abroad more. Californians are the ultimate mongrels. The state, Carlos Fuentes has written, "poses the universal question of the coming century: how do we deal with the Other?"[17]

CREATIVITY

Silicon Valley is not an aberration, nor is California merely an extreme example of the American norm. All across the United States, hybridity pays off—big-time—in higher-quality ideas, greater flexibility and tighter ties to places and people around the world. America offers the best example of what happens economically when an entire business class exploits hybridity. The new economic paradigm, though still poorly understood, matches the skills and mentalities of hybrids. It turns hybrids into a signal economic weapon. Because the United States has more hybrids than anywhere else, it gets the biggest bang from them.

There's no quantitative proof of this payoff, but there's plenty of other evidence to suggest that the open American culture largely explains the phenomenal U.S. economic boom of the 1990s. Defying naysayers, the United States posted higher rates of growth than any of its economic rivals, escaping a recession and growing in excess of 4 percent annually (or nearly triple the European rate) in the last years of the decade. The combination of rapid growth, ultralow unemployment and scant inflation reinforced the already huge lead America held in attracting talented foreigners to its shores.

No less an astute observer than Alan Greenspan, chairman of the U.S. central bank, invoked the term "new economy" to suggest that a different set of economic rules now holds sway compared with the period from the 1950s through the 1980s. Explanations of American economic resurgence are sought in the way information technologies are "transforming the way America does business," "revealing new opportunities for growth" and "helping companies to lower their costs." But this explanation fails to explain why the same technologies, also available to the European and Japanese economies, don't have the same tonic effect in these places. Preoccupied with technological determinism and bloodless quantitative models, economists and business gurus alike—pondering the mysteries of America's economic performance—ignore the most obvious difference between the United States and most other rich nations: the country's commitment to hybridity. In all the head-scratching over how the United States achieved such a virtuous economic cycle, leaving Europe and Japan in the dust, hybridity remains the missing link.[18]

This interconnection among hybridity, innovation and growth still eludes most Americans. In the "new economy," ideas and innovation—the chief currency of hybrids—are at the heart of commercial success. Whether a company makes a car or a razor or a software program, ideas are the defining element. The rewards for better-quality ideas are immense. Competitors are willing to bet more heavily than ever on their ideas, which accelerates the rate of technical change, rewarding those who apply more diverse minds to a problem. The costs of assembling the human minds required to develop a conceptual product is small compared with the potential rewards of setting a standard or creating a "killer application." So canny employers are actually willing to pay the finest foreign talent even more than they pay many locals, not underbidding for foreigners, as nativists fear, but often *overbidding*.

The economics of ideas means that even small differences in quality can yield huge differences in gain. This is because of the winner-take-all principle, whereby establishing the standard for a product ensures long-term profits. In the race to define the standard, whether of a computer printer, a tax program, an entertainment icon (the next *Star Wars*, perhaps) or even a wastebasket, the size of the talent pool drawn on by a company or country becomes critical. The bigger the pool, the better the odds of bringing together the right people at the right time.

The simple mathematics of creativity means that casting a wide net for key people is a necessity (just as it is in professional soccer). But the effect comes from more than just numbers. Strangers instinctively question things that natives take for granted. They stimulate new perspectives because, simply, many things strike them as odd or stupid. This is why it's great for any tribe to have a smart stranger injected into it. Under the right conditions, the newcomer aids the group. This aid is increased if the group is already mongrelized, because then resistance to the outsider is less.

Edgar van Ommen, managing director of Sony's unit in Berlin, calls this the "principle of the United Nations." His prime directive is to get the best people regardless of their nationalities. Sure, this makes life tougher for managers and poses challenges for companies with distinctive cultures and a suspicion of outsiders. But what is the alternative? To rely on a smaller pool of people— say, only Germans or Japanese? To the most idea-driven enterprises, nationality is too limiting. Ommen was raised in Austria, married a German, holds a Dutch passport and keeps a second home in Bangkok. Of his sixty-person team, two-thirds come from outside of Germany, representing more than a dozen nationalities. "The fact that all my colleagues come from different backgrounds and cultures is crucial in the realm of ideas," Ommen says. "The engineering of a concept is a lot easier because each person shows a different emotion as to what's being presented. This means the Germans may react one way, while the English or Irish say this is junk. Maybe the Turkish lady likes it, but the Sri Lankan doesn't." To think great thoughts, he says, employees must contribute their "whole being," not just their minds. Passion matters. Heated argument may spur fresh ideas.

Many business thinkers in Asia and Europe understand that good ideas often arise out of differences. But only American companies consistently exploit hybrid ideas because of the openness of U.S. society. American graduate schools attract the world's best students, in fields as diverse as finance and engineering, business strategy and physics. Foreigners run scores of top companies, and entrepreneurs often consider the United States the best place to launch an innovative company. Hybridity proves so powerful a magnet that even flourishing young businesses from Europe and Asia often decide to move to the United States in order to gain a better crack at talent and to absorb the intangibles in the world's largest market.

Egyptian-born Sam Gibari, chief executive officer of Goodyear, says the diverse backgrounds greatly benefit American companies and the U.S. economy. "It's a big strength that we have a cadre of multinational managers," he says. "We can better relate to other cultures."

Indeed, top U.S. companies have built entire strategies around the hybrid backgrounds of key people. When Motorola first tackled India's mobile telephone market, it assigned one of its executives of Indian descent to the critical task of dealing with government agencies. It wasn't until the man proved a star that Motorola realized he had never been to India. He was born and raised in Malaysia of Indian-born parents. Being an outsider to both India and the United States helped him succeed in his job, he says.

The diverse backgrounds of American factory workers help in similar ways. In Silicon Valley, makers of the most advanced high-tech products relied heavily on immigrants for routine test and assembly jobs. As their businesses grew and cost pressures increased, these companies seized on the possibility of moving factories to low-wage outposts in Southeast Asia. The shift proved formidable for many Japanese companies, which delayed moving production abroad for many years. But this seemed less daunting to American managers who were already used to training and hiring foreign labor right at home. This taste for diversity proved crucial in defending U.S. leads in a range of miniaturized technologies that seemed ready-made for Japanese dominance. Seagate, the world's largest maker of storage equipment for personal computers, was among the most successful at shifting production to Asia. The company chief, Alan Shugart, enjoyed visiting his burgeoning factories and took to wearing local attire on his visits. He also wore Yankee openness on his sleeve. In Penang, Malaysia, to launch a new factory, he ended a speech to employees and government officials by declaring, "I am a Malaysian!"

This openness, while cynically exploited at times, highlighted an astonishing lesson from the bruising competitive battles of the 1980s, when foreign products and companies made depressing inroads into American strongholds. The U.S. response depended on many factors, but a critical one was the ability to absorb talented foreigners who in turn led the charge against corporations from their "home" regions. By the 1990s, many American executives privately boasted that "our" foreigners were beating "their" foreigners in global competition. This insight became such a cliché that often the person saying it sometimes forgot he was a foreigner himself. I recall how one chief executive of a California chip maker proudly cited his company's ability to hire top engineers from Japan's own "backyard" in Asia. The executive so took for granted his American-acquired cleverness that he never thought of citing himself as a prime example of this openness. As his accent hinted, he was born and raised in Germany.

BRAIN EXCHANGE

The U.S. experience isn't some grand historical exception. Mongrels win. In the past, great leaps forward have been more often associated with hybridity than not. Nations long have relied on mixing local and imported talent to stimulate activity. They can do so again, en masse, if they dare. The means are clear: Movements of people are crucial to the diffusion of knowledge. People are the most effective culture-carriers, more effective than media or artifacts. The annals of espionage amply show this. Designs for weapons or factories or software programs or pharmaceuticals (or Picasso's paintings, for that matter) are often nothing without the people who made those designs and the engineers who can execute them. "Some know-how can be learned only by experience," David Landes writes.[19] In short, get the right people.

This truth is part of a larger truth. As Kevin Kelly quipped in his *New Rules for the New Economy,* "Follow the free." Open systems outmatch closed ones. As the record of innovation during World War II showed, Germany's initial technological lead was based on its openness prior to the war. During the war, it lost that lead because it was closed. The Germans drove away its premier Jewish scientists, including one (Albert Einstein) who wrote a letter to the president of the United States convincing him to launch a program to study the building of an atomic bomb. During the war, the United States and Britain overwhelmed the Axis powers with innovations, drawing winning vitality from cross-cultural teamwork wholly absent in Germany, where even Hitler sympathizers like the seminal physicist Werner Heisenberg stifled their creative impulses out of fear of what fellow Nazis would do to them if they failed. By contrast, Britain shared its technologies with the United States, laying the basis for a stunning burst of creativity. Innovations arose from English, Scots, exiled Germans and Americans, working side by side in laboratories. Though these teams were nowhere near as diverse as today's best teams—there were virtually no blacks, Asians or women in the World War II combos—they still put to shame the uniformity of Axis research. Against Germany's mastery of rocketry, the Allies countered with radar, the proximity fuze and then of course atomic weapons. These are the only the best-known innovations. A more detailed scorecard shows a one-side Allied victory. After the war, research leaders in the United States knew well it was the country's freedom and openness that enabled them to out-innovate Germany and Japan.[20]

It seems each generation needs to learn the lesson of openness, the link between mixing of people and creativity. The historical precedents certainly predate World War II. A complete catalog of creative mingling might comprise the story of human civilization itself, so critical are alien encounters to sparking fresh thinking and acting. As Thomas Sowell concludes in his history of global migration, "What migrations have meant has not been merely a relocation of bodies but, more fundamentally, a redistribution of skills, experience and other 'human capital' across the planet. It is this process of cultural change which has transformed nations and continents."[21]

MIGRATION IS OFTEN seen as a push by poorer people to improve their material lives, epitomized in the image of the United States as "a land of opportunity." But migrants are just as often pulled by a city or state trying to keep pace with rivals or to plug an obvious gap. Frederick William, in the second half of the 1600s, selectively invited outsiders to move to his Prussian kingdom, "consciously choosing settlers who would bring money, expertise and skills." By 1725, one-fifth of the residents of his kingdom's Brandenburg province were born abroad. Prussia saw this surge of incomers not as a sign of weakness but as a badge of merit. Berlin, its capital city, "was transformed by the energy and skills of the immigrants," who came in large numbers from Denmark, Sweden, France and Bohemia. Throughout Germany, migrants played important roles; one study estimates that they comprised half of the traders in Germany's commercial hubs.[22]

The industrial revolution offers another example of how newcomers can stimulate a society. In the 1700s, Britain took the lead in building a production system in which machines did the work of people and vastly more powerful engines powered those machines. In response, France, in the words of David Landes, "launched a systematic pursuit of British technicians: clock- and watchmakers, woolen workers, metallurgists, glassmakers, shipbuilders—some two or three hundred people." Britain replied by banning the emigration of certain skilled craftsmen. This did not halt the inevitable—hundreds, even thousands, left Britain. By the early 1800s, "skilled craftsmen, like savants and artists, took all of Europe as their home. . . . Some of this emigration was solicited: foreign governments paid people to come and helped them set up in business."[23]

Indeed, the winners and losers among nations can be charted by tracking where the talent goes. Think of Paris in the 1920s. "In Paris to be smart was smart," wrote Clive James. "Paris was an all-star spectacular of brilliant foreigners who were there for the exchange rate, the tolerance, the intelligence, the style."[24]

But importers of talent must realize that migrants can be only a supplement; they can't be a substitute for a fertile local environment. Migrants can always return home, or move elsewhere for higher returns. In the mid-1800s, Britain raced to the forefront of the new industry of chemical dyes. But German chemists in London had played a decisive role in the launch of this industry. When they returned to Germany, the technology moved with them. By 1900, Germany produced 80 percent of chemical dyes.

In theory, today's major importers of talent are vulnerable in the same way. In the 1980s, people worried that the United States might sputter if large numbers of highly skilled migrant groups, such as Taiwanese or Koreans, suddenly packed up and went home. But this fear faded for two reasons, one obvious and the other not.

The obvious reason was that the sources of skilled immigrants to the United States are so diverse that no one country supplies too big a share of them. The not so obvious reason was that there's also been a shift in the boundary between "us" and "them." Many talented migrants no longer see themselves wholly in or wholly out of either the country they work in or their country of origin. They have, as the prior chapter showed, roots and wings. Thus, hybridity shifts the terms of the global talent chase. To the receiving nation, the question of national loyalty is irrelevant.

To the country exporting talent, the question is different, or at least seems to be. Leaders of developing countries long have complained about "brain drain." To be sure, many talented people leave poorer countries. One study found that India, China, the Philippines and Korea lost 145,000 scientifically trained people to the United States from 1972 to 1985. Of the 2.7 million scientists and engineers working in U.S. industry as of 1993, 13.2 percent were foreign born.

This migration is usually considered a complete loss to the exporting country. But patterns are shifting. "Brain drain" is giving way to "brain circulation," a process in which well-educated people move through a cycle of study and work abroad followed by a return to the home country and then further travel. Such cycles involve everyone from Africans, Latin Americans and Indians to Europeans (indeed, the term "brain drain" was first used to describe the flow of British engineers and scientists to the United States in the 1960s). From 1986 to 1996, 40 percent of the Germans who pursued graduate studies in the United States planned to remain for some time after gaining their degree; 52 percent from Britain planned to do so. Fewer of these students stay for good, but U.S. experience gives them a lifetime network of helpful associations.

On their return home, brainy migrants often bring with them skills and capital that they could not have gained at home. For some, staying home would have meant squandering their educational endowment anyway. Having grown through exposure to the latest techniques in advanced countries, they may even steer promising opportunities to their home turf. "Even when these skilled immigrants choose not to return home," according to one study, "they still play a critical role as middlemen" between their adopted and ancestral homes.

The evidence of brain circulation is intriguing, if not definitive. From his survey of the data, Allan Findlay, a Scottish expert on migration, concludes that "brain exchanges" are "critical to the global economy." Another researcher found "extensive" efforts by Asian-born engineers and scientists in the United States to help their home countries develop technology industries. Taiwan provides perhaps the best-documented example of this. A growing number of Taiwanese technologists split their time between Silicon Valley and Taiwan's Hsinchu region. These commuters "have the professional skills to function fluently in both the Silicon Valley and Taiwanese business cultures and to draw on the complementary strengths of the two regional economies," Saxenian finds. In 1996, eighty-two companies in the Hsinchu Science Park (or 40 percent of the total) were formed by returnees to Taiwan; about 2,500 returnees worked in this one park alone.[25]

Highly skilled people from many countries, even rich ones, are relying on both roots and wings to further their careers. The very process of circulation breeds more circulation. This in turn, notes Nigel Harris, "speeds up the process of social fission and fusion, of innovation, which are the essence of dynamic cultures."[26]

PURITY

The movement of creative types preceded modern times; indeed, movement may have been greater in a premodern era when national boundaries were less important. "Only in remote and barbarous lands did ethnic homogeneity prevail," writes William McNeill. In ancient times, labor requirements resulted in "ethnic mixture and pluralism on a grand scale in major centers of imperial government." Another factor that assured ethnic mingling was trade. A third was conquest and enslavement. The different ethnic groups, McNeill writes, "entered into conventional and relatively well-defined relations with one another." McNeill calls this condition, commonly found in the world well into the seventeenth century, "an ordered ethnic diversity" in which, interestingly, "no one supposed that uniformity was desirable or that assimilation to a common style of life or pattern of culture was either normal or possible."[27]

Not only were strangers tolerated in premodern times; they were often cheered. "What makes [these] migrations alien events to us today is that they were welcomed, on the whole, by the receiving community," writes Saskia Sassen. Governments wooed migrants without fear of political backlash, as the history of Amsterdam illustrates. From 1600 to 1650, Amsterdam's population nearly tripled, rising from 60,000 to 175,000. Some migrants had fled persecution elsewhere, but jobs were the chief draw. More than half of Amsterdam's sailors were foreign, mainly from Germany and Norway. Amsterdam's capital also came from far and wide. "Frenchmen, Venetians, Florentines and Genoese, as well as Germans, Poles, Hungarians, Spaniards, Russians, Turks, Armenians and Hindus traded not only in stocks but also in sophisticated derivatives. Much of the capital active in Amsterdam was owned by foreigners or immigrants."[28]

Amsterdam's rise to global financial prominence in the seventeenth century is often noted but rarely for the right reasons. "Max Weber [the great German sociologist] never bothered to look at migratory patterns when he came up with his speculation that Amsterdam owed its success to the Protestant ethic," observes Robert Brenner, an economics writer. "Although Weber's idea has been quoted frequently enough to pass for fact, it wasn't true in Amsterdam or in any other prosperous trading cities or states. Educated and ambitious trading immigrants, tied in to ethnic networks around the world—brains and trust, that is—turned 17th-century Amsterdam into a miracle."[29]

Mixing also increased vitality in the Middle Ages. In Eastern Europe, cities were home mainly to foreigners rather than the indigenous people of the countryside. Craft workers routinely traveled widely as they gained competency in their field. When the Ottoman Empire offered greater tolerance to Jews after their eviction from Spain in 1492, they flocked there. By the early 1500s, the medical staff to the Ottoman sultans consisted of forty-one Jews and twenty-one Muslims. Japanese emigrated to Korea and the Philippines in the fifteenth century; 3,000 of them lived in Manila in 1606.[30]

In modern times especially, cities have been magnets for talent, havens for hybrids. The eminent urban historian Peter Hall says in his exhaustive survey, Cities in Civilization, that "creative cities were nearly all cosmopolitan; they drew talent from the four corners of their worlds, and from the very start those worlds were often surprisingly far-flung. Probably, no city has ever been creative without continued renewal of the creative bloodstream." Hall explains the reasons why, highlighting the importance of tension between native and newcomer, a tension that is best managed but not resolved. "Creative cities," he says, are "not comfortable places at all." Crucial to their vitality "is that this clash [between new and old] is experienced and expressed by a group of creative people who feel themselves to be in some important sense outsiders: they both belong and do not belong." A creative city, Hall notes, "will therefore be a place where outsiders can enter and feel that state of ambiguity: they must neither be excluded from opportunity, nor must they be so warmly embraced that the creative drive is lost." In short, they must keep both their roots and their wings.[31]

Hall's analysis supports McNeill's view that the ideal of national unity, based on ethnic homogeneity and assimilation of outsiders into a fixed norm, is an aberration. This state of affairs held only in Europe from 1750 to 1920 and then only partially. Mixing is the norm, the human condition.[32]

When people go against this norm, they hurt creativity and vitality. There are enough historical cases of migrants being expelled from a society to support this conclusion. After Spain evicted its Jews, who played a distinctive role as middlemen, its economy and culture faltered; the country never regained its previous heights. Germany's extermination of its Jewish community destroyed the country's creativity in many fields. Immigrants of Indian descent were so entrenched in Uganda that they accounted for a third of the country's output in 1972, more than a decade after African nationalists unleashed successive waves of harassment against them. When that year Idi Amin expelled 50,000 Indians, virtually the entire remaining number, Uganda's economy fell apart. Twenty years later, in 1992, new Ugandan leaders sought to persuade Indians to return, even offering to restore property to these exiled businessmen. Few took up the offer.[33]

Sometimes, the scorned do return, but not to rebuild. Consider the area once known as the Pale of Settlement, today part of Moldova, a former Soviet republic. The Pale was the area to which Russia's czar consigned the Jews. By 1897, 5.2 million Jews lived in Russia, most in the Pale. The heart of the Pale was the city of Chisinau, where the play *Fiddler on the Roof* was set. Jews were the commercial leaders of Chisinau in the nineteenth century, but a series of violent pogroms, starting in 1881, traumatized the community. The czar's draft also was a fearsome prospect, since he could demand twenty-five years of military service. In the early decades of the twentieth century, millions of Jews left Russia. Those who remained were spared the Holocaust, but Stalin erased any semblance of traditional Jewish life. Since the fall of the Soviet Union, some people of Jewish ancestry in its territory are finding their roots, but the limited revival is bringing no Jews back to Chisinau. Quite the opposite is occurring, as I learned one day when visiting the Prietenia Hotel in Bendery, a deteriorating town across the Dniestr River from Chisinau.[34]

At the front desk, a woman sat at attention. After twenty-two years on the job, she was devoted to this hotel, even though its elevator was disabled, its lobby looted and a bug had fallen from the ceiling onto her forehead.

Once newlyweds from around the Soviet Union flocked here to enjoy the mild climate and the fine local foods and wine. The staff greeted visitors in traditional costumes, carrying bread and salt for luck as they ushered them into honeymoon suites overlooking the river. "Now very few people stay here," she told me, sending the bug flying with the flick of her finger.

The woman had a gift for understatement: Only one of the hotel's 300 rooms was occupied.

To be polite, I asked her the room rate. Only sixteen dollars for a two-room suite. I was about to reply when a crowd of people entered the lobby. They were so energetic that the smell of decay suddenly vanished. I asked the woman about them. "The Yiddishers," she said. "Here for their regular meeting."

Hmmm. I make a note to ask her about this later. For the moment, she agreed to show me one of the hotel's honeymoon suites. We walked up four flights of stairs. Painted on the door of room 408 was a small white dove. Inside, the view of the tree-lined river was still romantic. But the room wasn't. It had no phone or TV. Only one light worked. The paint was peeling and the bathroom stank. We left quickly. I felt bad and now wished to give her a little money. When the state stopped owning the hotel—and gave it to employees like her—her salary also stopped. I asked about the hotel's restaurant, thinking I would buy something there. She took me to a dining room.

There I saw the Yiddishers. Three women and two men ate at a long table. While I bought several bottles of local champagne from the bar, I told my translator to please introduce me to the Yiddishers if they looked my way.

My instructions were unnecessary. One of the women greeted me in English. "We are Israelis," she said. Her group was charged with offering college scholarships, and the right to reside in Israel, to local high school graduates who could show some Jewish ancestry. I asked how closely they examined the backgrounds of people for proof of their Judaism. Not very, she said, explaining that they were after talent, as much as Jews, for Israel's own knowledge economy.

"We only take the smart ones," she said. "We need them." Before she could say more, one of her colleagues shushed her. She had said enough.

WIRED

The persistent link between migration and creativity makes it reasonable to wonder whether the two qualities—the desire to move about and the capacity to create fresh ideas—spring from the same seed. The notion that people are "hardwired" to benefit from encounters with people very different from them resonates with experience. Who hasn't seen evidence of the old saw "Opposites attract"? When one person confronts a profoundly different person, might this trigger a kind of psychobiological reaction that spurs creativity? This possibility flies in the face of the conventional wisdom—peddled relentlessly by such alarmists as Robert Kaplan and Samuel Huntington—that people are biologically programmed to stick with their own kind and that mixing is incendiary because it somehow goes against the grain of humanity.

Biological metaphors are the rage in both popular and intellectual circles, and their appeal is not without hazards. Biological concepts, from DNA to genetic inheritance, are constructs that seek to describe reality; they don't exist in the same way that my proverbial duck quacks. Tribalists misunderstand this. The case for a biological basis for mongrelization is more compelling, and inspiring, than the racialist presumption of the superiority of sticking with one's own kind.

Mixing and mongrelization make evolutionary sense. As biologists have shown, interbreeding broadens the genetic variability of a population, and as variation increases, the odds also increase that the population—or at least part of it—will develop specific characteristics that aid in survival. A good example of this can be found in fish hatcheries. The idea for hatcheries is pretty simple: In order to maintain stocks of fish at acceptable levels, scientists supervise the breeding of fish before releasing the spawn back into the wild. But hatchery operators faced limits. They were breeding all of this stock from a limited number of adult fish. They also knew there were inherent limitations on mating combinations because most fish lay a lot of eggs, so few parents could produce a large brood. As a result, genetic variation was generally narrow.

Consider this comparison. Imagine the same two humans having child after child. The children would look different, and their personalities might diverge as they aged. But genetically, their differences could be only so great because they shared the same parents. This limitation explains why many attempts by hatcheries to replenish fish stocks have failed.

One of Darwin's great insights was that minute genetic variations, produced by interbreeding and mutation and then amplified by further breeding, can make a particular animal—human or otherwise—better suited for its environment. The more genetically diverse a species, the more likely it is to possess an adaptation that helps it survive in a specific environment. This is one way of understanding the phrase "survival of the fittest." Thus, when scientists tried to restore salmon to rivers in which they had once thrived, they were bitterly (and yet predictably) disappointed. Hatchery-raised salmon showed little genetic diversity; they failed to adapt to changing river conditions. In the Pacific Northwest, where wild salmon are approaching extinction, huge numbers of hatchery salmon were released into the rivers only to encounter a new ecosystem. Logging had left the banks bare of trees. With no trees to shade the river, water temperatures rose slightly. Warmer water meant an increase in certain diseases that were uncommon in chillier days. The result: The fish were devastated by disease. Had the salmon population been the product of sustained interbreeding—mixing and mutation involving a large, diverse adult population—then perhaps some salmon would have survived by being able to better fight diseases and other new threats. But highly similar to one another, "hatchery fish lack stream smarts and are easily scarfed by predators," writes Carl Safina, an expert in marine life.

The failure of hatchery salmon was worse than this, however. Not only did these fish die in droves, but their introduction into rivers robbed resources from the few remaining wild salmon, thus reducing essential diversity. Perversely, "hatchery fish out-compete local fish and then themselves die," Safina adds.[35]

This fate, then, suggests the danger of ignoring the logic of diversity. In human society, opponents of mixing would prefer a fish-hatchery model of existence. They'd favor a fish tank in which Chinese breed only with Chinese, Germans with Germans and Serbs with Serbs. But just as this model fails to create a thriving salmon population in rivers of the Pacific Northwest, so too it would fail to create thriving human communities around the world. The stubborn reality is that dynamic environments—for salmon or humans—result from mixing and diversifying. The Darwinian message: Mongrelize, or what happened to hatchery salmon will happen to your people.

SOME OF THE ISSUES that bedevil fish hatcheries can be grouped together under the rubric of combinatorial science. As people become specialized in their skills and interests—as their hybridity becomes more distinctive—there is an explosion in diversity because of the exponential growth in what can mix and match. Whereas this process only slowly unfolds in nature, it can be seen more rapidly in computers, which are a powerful tool for the study of nature. The reason has to do with being digital. Software is all about ones and zeros (called bits). Evolution is all about ones and zeros (called genes).

A friend of mine, the journalist and author Tom Petzinger, has teased out some of the implications of this process. A few years ago, Petzinger visited a company in Atlanta named ASSI, owned by a Joyce and Vic Roberts. He observed:

> Vic was an architect, Joyce a construction manager. They were early and eager adopters. They knew CAD [computer-aided design] like Ford knew cars. Their clients were the big-name architects who created front elevations

and plastic scale models for new buildings—then hired their company to grind out the thousands of drawings necessary to actually build them.

Joyce and Vic were so committed to quality they resolved to employ nothing but top graduates of the best architecture schools. Work poured into ASSI from an up-and-coming retailer called Home Depot. Before long, Joyce, Vic and their dozen young employees appeared on the cover of *Fortune* as a company of tomorrow. The cover kids of ASSI.

Deep down, though, Joyce and Vic sensed problems. When the company moved to bigger offices, everyone wanted a cubicle with a view. Joyce and Vic accommodated the staff to the point of seating everyone next to a window—no small feat in a modern office building—only to hear the staff complain about glare. When Joyce or Vic tried to have a private lunch with a staffer, the entire staff assumed that something was amiss. "We couldn't do anything right," Joyce told me. "It was like a spontaneous unionization drive."

Then, within barely a year, the cover-kids staff walked out. En masse.

Only in retrospect did Joyce and Vic realize their error. Their rigorous hiring profile—only the best grads from the best schools—effectively guaranteed a monocultural workforce, one that was young, single, childless, white, from well-to-do families and from the Northeast. That's a lot for any dozen workers to have in common. They thought like a bloc. Acted like a bloc. Walked out like a bloc.

The exodus left Joyce and Vic with bills piling up and clients awaiting drawings. ASSI needed staff instantly, but this time such selectivity was no option. If you qualified for the work, it was yours. That architect from Vietnam? Hired. A woman re-entering the workforce? Hired. People who had attended lesser schools in the South. People who didn't grow up as rich kids. People with spouses (and not). People with children (and not). People with mortgages (and not). Part-timers as well as full-timers. Ultimately temps, contractors, even employees shared with other firms.

This crazy-quilt crew was never going to win ASSI a return trip to the cover of *Fortune*, but it was a crew that worked together brilliantly. When problems came up—business problems, personality problems, whatever—the diversity of views tended to dampen them. Beyond that, the greater number of sensibilities created a greater number of potential solutions to any problem. However unplanned, diversity had rescued the company.

A coda on Petzinger's reflections: While thinking about the experience of Joyce and Vic, he happened to pick up Jane Jacobs's *The Death and Life of Great American Cities*. Diverse street lengths, building sizes, building ages and business types, she shows, made cities not only more beautiful and energetic but more efficient and wealthier too. About then Petzinger also turned to Stuart

Kauffman's *At Home in the Universe*, in which the theorist of complexity concludes, "Diversity probably begets diversity; hence diversity may help beget growth."[36]

Petzinger was puzzling over this when he learned about a vile computer virus that devoured the contents of files with extensions named .doc, .xls, .exe and .ppt. The virus was designed to attack Microsoft software programs while leaving unharmed Unix, Mac and other diverse platforms.

ExploreZip was still spreading when Petzinger heard from a software writer with a degree in evolutionary biology who worried that too little diversity among the world's computers left them vulnerable to a crippling epidemic. His warning had a familiar ring: "With 90%+ computers being PC with Windows, most of the world's computers aren't like clones, they are clones," he wrote. "They share all of the core internal components, with only superficial diversity, like facial features (monitor size and resolution). Any group of highly similar individuals are highly susceptible to disease, such as the virus that devastated captive cheetah populations in the U.S. a few years ago. Captive cheetahs are more similar than siblings and almost as similar as identical twins due to in-breeding. . . . [They are] like a giant mono-culture of trees planted after cutting down a forest. Mono-culture tree farms are profitable only as long as the trees are not attacked by the same devastating disease."

So radical mixing was the friend's remedy for computer viruses. "The answer is not to be found in the anti-virus companies," he wrote. "They're simply locked in an arms race, one that they cannot win. . . . The only true security is to be found in widely divergent—and incompatible—computer products. Macs and PC's, Linux, desktops and hand-helds. This proliferation will mean that the industry as a whole will grow more slowly, and be more complex and riskier for new companies unable to strike deals and leverage millions of customers at a stroke. But the complexity will improve our security as viruses and hackers can only attack small and medium sized ecosystem-markets."

Pondering his friend's words, Petzinger queried a professor at the University of Pittsburgh named Bill Frederick. "Not only computer viruses, but computers themselves, are literally just another form of nature," Frederick explained. "They are not mere analogies or metaphors of natural processes. Computers, viruses, and worms live within ecosystems composed of neurological fragments generated in the human brain, and like all living things they are vulnerable to attacks on their ecological niche by competitors or predators. Their quasi-mechanical or computational form should not mislead one to believe that computers and their viruses are therefore not a direct manifestation of nature."

Though Frederick's answer sounded like a monologue from Fox Mulder of *The X-Files*, it pulled things together for Petzinger. He suddenly realized that mongrelization tied into the rhythms of the universe. And without warning he sent me an ode to the mongrel in us:

> So diversity, too, is a universal strength in living systems, whether those systems are jungles, computing environments or architectural services concerns; whether we're talking about the corporate or the corporeal, organizations or organisms, economies or ecologies. Diversity fosters creativity. Diversity creates defense. Diversity defends itself.

Indiana Jones Discovers Thomas Jefferson... on a Soviet Farm

NISPORIN, MOLDOVA—In a cool gray room, a dozen men watch their hostess, Elena Rabu, enter with a plate of steaming mamaliga, a local cornmeal staple that resembles polenta. Setting the plate next to a roasted leg of lamb, she eyes the American at her table and whispers to her son, "Is he the one who got us our land?"

The son nods. Elena smiles, baring three silver false teeth. At the far end of the table, Vince Morabito raises a glass of homemade red wine in toast. There's reason to celebrate. A few months before, Vince broke up his first collective farm in this former Soviet republic, securing for the Rabus—and two thousand others—ownership of a few acres of land each.

Vince cries out the traditional salute, "Narok!" and, following local custom, drains his glass in one gulp. Impressed, one of the men shouts, "Morabito, you are practically a Moldovan."

Actually, Vince hails from San Pedro, California. The grandson of European immigrants to the West Coast, he is a wiry fifty-five-year-old, with short black hair, thick wire-rim glasses and the map of Italy on his face. Call him the Indiana Jones of rural development. He's been kidnapped in Guatemala, shaken down by Russia mobsters and caught in the cross fire between peasant rebels in Southeast Asia. Early in his career he helped to assemble farm cooperatives; now he is ripping them apart.

"I'm a Republican now," he says, "but I didn't start out that way." In the mid-1960s, he joined the Peace Corps. He was essentially a socialist, a believer in communal ownership. Because he spoke Spanish, he was sent to Honduras. The experience only hardened his views. "I saw landless peasants gunned down in the streets," he recalls. "I saw a priest not giving a confession unless he was paid. The world wasn't supposed to be this way."

A born hustler with the heart of a poet, he's still trying to make the world, or at least his little piece of it, the way it is supposed to be. He brings a romantic, even dashing, enthusiasm to this task. He's a hybrid with a cause. In the process, he's become adept at moving around his roots. "I don't have a home anymore," he says. He lives in Chisinau, the capital of Moldova, gets medical treatment (for a troublesome prostate) in Vienna and relaxes in Budapest, the capital of Hungary, where he owns a gorgeous flat near the Danube.

After three decades working with peasants, Vince is realistic about how hard it is for them to get power and keep it. He's too tough to qualify as a bleeding-heart liberal, and too radical to be trusted by conservatives. Pragmatic and flexible, he long ago set aside ideology. He's an old-fashioned populist who tries to help farmers in far-flung places improve their living standards and get more justice. And this can't be done without land ownership. "Empower people through the land," he says. "Give them the opportunity to make change and a little advice—and then get out of their way."

These aren't the words of a tweedy academic or a policy wonk who spends years prowling the halls of the World Bank in Washington, D.C. Vince has lived in the field with peasants from Central America to Southeast Asia to Africa. He even ran a big farm himself in Nebraska for ten years, trading bulls and growing so much popcorn he got himself elected president of the national popcorn growers association. After splitting up with his wife in the early 1980s, he went to Egypt with his two teenage daughters and then to the Dominican Republic, where he helped boost exports of fresh fruit and vegetables.

In the Caribbean, Vince rekindled his passion for the underdog. "He knows in any country there are haves and have-nots and that you've got to understand both," says a friend in the aid game. Vince helped a large U.S. fruit grower, backed by wealthy locals, to export cantaloupes from the Dominican Republic. The operation employed hundreds of illiterate peasants, which was the attraction for Vince. The grower did well for a few seasons, but then overexpanded, lost money and suddenly closed, owing the laborers two weeks' pay. In the Dominican Republic, workers had to stand in line with other creditors, waiting for payment that might never come. Vince refused to accept this. He had sold the laborers on field jobs in the first place as a path to a better life. Now they were bereft again.

"You can screw suppliers but you can't screw the little guys," Vince told the grower. Under his prodding, the grower agreed to meet payroll, but the question was how? The laborers couldn't be paid out in the open, else other creditors might cry foul. So Vince concocted a plan to avoid their scrutiny. The grower handed him $50,000 and

Vince, following the payroll ledger, stuffed the right amounts into hundreds of envelopes and then personally delivered them to the laborers. This was his last attempt to make good to them on his promises of "development."

Soured on Latin America, Vince went to Eastern Europe in 1991, when the Soviet Union fell apart. He broke up some of the first farm collectives in Russia before moving to Hungary, where he also privatized state enterprises.

Moldova is his latest stop. George Soros, the billionaire financier, hired him through one of his foundations to run a land reform program here. Vince is one of a small number of consultants charged with teaching the basics of capitalism to the 4.3 million people in this landlocked nation sandwiched between Romania and Ukraine. As usual, the medium for Vince's message is land. A thousand large farm collectives dominate agricultural output, and half the population still lives off the land. Stalin ended private ownership of farmland in the late 1940s, collectivizing production and sending to Siberia those families who resisted. Many peasants still grow white-hot with fear and anger just at the mention of Stalin's name.

When Vince arrived in Moldova in 1995, not a single collective farm had been broken up. The government feared losing control over the peasants. Four years after the collapse of communism, not a single peasant owned any land. The government actually opposed private ownership, insisting that this could result in peasants getting swindled out of their land by unscrupulous operators. Instead, officials proposed that the collectives restructure—that is, adopt better financial and farming techniques so that they would be in better shape when they finally privatized.

The policy made no sense to Vince, who decided to buck it. When a government minister asked him to advise one of the largest collectives, the one in Nisporin, on financial matters, he decided to use the occasion to pitch his privatization ideas. Shortly before Christmas, he made a tortuous ninety-minute drive to the collective, which grows fruits and grains and operates a winery. It snowed the entire trip. In the winery's small office, lubricated by big mugs of the house red, he gave his spiel. Break up the collective, give land to each of the members, and they could decide to farm on their own or band together—perhaps by leasing their land—to form a larger operation. Either way, the peasants would benefit from ownership. And in the same stroke, they would realize the ideals expressed by Thomas Jefferson, the third U.S. president, who passionately believed in the power of private property to transform a republic. Envisioning America as a nation of small, independent landowners, Vince saw a link between commerce and citizenship. An owner would have a stake in the justice system, because rule of law would protect his property rights; he would have a stake in the function of markets, because it would afford him a better chance to receive a fair price for his crops; he would have a stake in infrastructure, because through this he might improve the value of his holdings.

To empower people, "I don't know a better way than ownership," he said. Give farmers land, from which they learn about markets and credits, freedom and responsibility. "I've seen what happens when peasants get land," he added. "They suddenly stiffen up. They suddenly are less submissive and more demanding. They can turn themselves into something."

Vince went on and on about the Jeffersonian ideal. As he spoke, the snow kept falling and the room got colder and the snow piled higher until it pressed up against the windows. In Moldova, the cold is menacing because the heat is poor. The government lacks money for energy, so entire neighborhoods—hooked into a communal grid—go cold when the supplier isn't paid. Vince often wears a hat and coat in his office. He has slept wearing earmuffs and mittens—and that's when he's inside a down sleeping bag.

But this night the wine flows, and Vince stays warm. A hardy drinker, he seems impervious to its effects. Raising another glass to toast his new friends, these long-suffering survivors of communism, Vince exclaimed, "In America people financed their social mobility through land ownership. It can happen here too. Of course, you can't keep all these people on the farm, but the medium of exchange will be the land. That's the only social safety net." The government hasn't the resources or the expertise to protect people. "I can sit here and give you human tragedies," Vince said. "The point is Moldovans can't look to their government for solutions. People will have to go with what they've got. Privatizing land, empowering peasants, that's the only possibility." He wished the situation were different. He took off his glasses, squinted, chugged more wine. "The fact is no one has enough money to fix the problem. We can't just quit. We have to start. We can't wait for the perfect scenario. We know some of these farms will fail, but we have to try."

By midnight, Vince's relentless advocacy began to take effect. The collective's chief, Vasilie Carajia, agreed to support privatization: a complete breakup. "All of us will have to do this sooner or later," he said.

Vince and his team from the Soros group plunged into the task of preparing for the breakup. Dividing the land was tricky because no one wanted poor land and some of the best land had already been grabbed, informally, by about a quarter of the collective's 2,136 members.

Because many members were too old or disinterested to run a farm, Vince advised them to lease their land to trusted neighbors. About half a dozen men wound up with large blocks of land. The biggest went to Carajia, who convinced about 360 people to lease their land to him. This result, which seemed to create a minicollective out of the corpse of the old one, upset the World Bank, which advised the government on farm policy. Bank officials accused Vince of allowing a few farmers to win big at the expense of others.

Vince, cornered, hit back. He chided his critics for their paternalism, saying the peasants were not stupid; they could lease their land to someone else if they felt they got a raw deal. "Protecting the little guy from the little guy, that won't work," he said. "Leaders emerge. You can't hold these people back. Call them whatever you want—entrepreneurs, elites, dealers, robber barons. They emerge. Even under communism, they did."

The debate dredged up memories of wrong turns he'd made in the past: how in the 1970s, he had failed to appreciate the importance of personal initiative and accountability. One of his most beloved projects, a fruit cooperative consisting of 600 Honduran farmers, failed for precisely this reason. Vince had felt burned; he had promised the farmers the coop would prosper. Yet nearly all failed. "It was what we thought was right and just at the time," he recalled. "You treated everyone the same. It was a way to define social justice. But you didn't get justice. Things got complicated very fast."

Given his passionate defense of privatization, Vince wondered whether Nisporin was the last collective he would break up in Moldova. Then in spring 1996, Moldova's deputy president summoned him to talk about the peasantry. Vince was so skittish he brought along the U.S. ambassador and proposed breaking up only five more collectives. "Why not seventy?" the Moldovan asked. Vince agreed.

ON ONE OF HIS trips to the countryside, Vince visited a collective in Ungheni, near the Romanian border. It was among the seventy collectives chosen for breakup, and one of the farmers invited him to lunch. The group quickly grew to include the mayor and his family and the farmer's family and his neighbors. The whole group sat around a long table and listened as the men gave toasts. The wine flowed and the words and then came the steaming mamaliga and the beef and the vegetables. The farmer thanked Vince for his helping to get people their land and the mayor did. Then an old man said this was the second time he'd met an American; the first time was fifty years ago when he was in the Red Army and his unit entered Berlin to liberate it. He met American soldiers then and now Vince.

Maybe this time was better than the first, the old farmer said. Stalin took away their land, made them into slaves, now they were free again. Now this American had set them free.

Up went the glasses again. "Narok!" said the Red Army veteran.

"Narok!" replied his listeners. And the wine flowed, the wine from the vineyards out there, from the casks they'd made with their own hands.

It was hard for these people not to see Vince as their liberator, as the man on the white horse riding into town to save them. In his rough-and-readiness, Vince resembled that man: the Clint Eastwood character who deflects all challenges and wins a measure of justice for those around him. But Vince talked a lot more than any Clint Eastwood character ever did, and that was only the start of it. As an American he was expected to have all the answers, to know it all. Even those who resented Americans for this very reason were disappointed when an American did not display willingness to tackle anything. After all, everyone wanted the chance to play in a cowboy movie. To stand tall and win big. Vince understood that. He understood that the fantasy of American omnipotence was so real to most foreigners that if you denied them that fantasy they would not thank you, they would hate you. So he acted as if anything was possible: no mountain too high, no river too wide, that sort of thing. Wherever he went, people loved that. They needed it. Because their experience was with limits and losses, getting knocked down and not getting up. People might rail against American illusions, about misplaced confidence, about arrogance—and it was all too true—but deny them the can-do dream, the dream that anything is possible if only the Americans say it, and these people never forgive you.

Vince knew this in his bones, so he wore the metaphorical six-shooter and the Stetson hat, even though he saw the irony of it all: Vince a guy who rarely strayed west of Budapest actually having to work at pretending to be an American because he painted dreams for poor people but never made any promises. He'd learned not to do that too. It was a thin line to walk, this thing of giving complete strangers their dignity, their dreams, but still not leaving them up the creek without a paddle. After all, he wasn't about to rescue anybody. That's what made Vince a big improvement over the old Ugly American. Not only wasn't he going to save anybody, because he couldn't, but he wasn't going to put anybody in a position to be saved. After all, he often wondered who was saving whom? Was he saving them, or were they saving him? After years sitting down with peasants, close to the earth, near to the heart, he no longer could tell. Or probably he could tell: They were saving him.

At least at this moment, as his turn came to give his toast, he was sure they were saving him. After twenty years outside of the United States, two-thirds of his adult life, and in places that weren't Paris, he felt he'd lost his identity. That's the price you pay for wandering, he told himself. Maybe three years ago, he still had some traces of an imagined identity, but not now.

Someone filled his glass again and it was his turn to give a toast. He first toasted the woman of the house, then said nothing for a while and finally took another draw on his glass. "I'm grateful for your hospitality," he said. "I only wish that someday I can have you in my home and we can sit around a table like this and enjoy wonderful food and each other. I am only sad because I know this will never happen."

Vince's translator stopped for a moment, but Vince looked at him hard as if to say go ahead, and the translator did.

No one seemed to mind. "Narok!" the mayor said. Then he toasted Vince, the American who would ride off into the sunset, just the way he should.

ONE NIGHT I tell Vince that maybe he's more Moldovan than he thinks. Maybe he belongs there. Maybe the peasants are right. He drinks like a Moldovan, toasts like one, even thinks like one. Maybe he is one. I tell him my duck theory. If it quacks like a duck, it's a duck. "You quack," I say. "You're a duck."

He shakes his head. We are sitting in his Budapest apartment. Vince likes to visit on weekends. Budapest is a short flight from Chisinau, and Vince has many women friends here. A sworn bachelor, he finds hybridity good for his romantic life. His strongest attachment is with a young artist in Bucharest, Romania, but he seems to play the field. He's been so many places, and has so many stories, that he's certainly entertaining. And even in romance, he sometimes can't resist mounting his white horse and coming to a woman's rescue.

Budapest is a racy city but is as European and cultivated, in its history, as Paris. Vince lives on the fourth floor of a vintage nineteenth-century building with a beautiful inner courtyard. He has tastefully restored the apartment. On the walls of his living room are impressionistic paintings, made by artists of the former Soviet Union. Vince is a collector. He plans to open a gallery here to display and sell the paintings of these artists. That alone will bring him back to Moldova, but perhaps only that, after he's done with land reform there. He privatized Nisporin, then seventy more collectives. With the government's blessing, he's now breaking up 600 more. After that, the rest of the collectives can break apart on their own, if they wish. Vince thinks that the peasants are happier as landowners and that their farms are more productive. But ownership hasn't unleashed the democratic forces that he still pines for. People don't show the backbone that he thinks they should.

"It upsets me," he says. "I get angry." He pauses, then says, "You know the problem with the lack of heat," talking about how cold Moldova's buildings are in winter. The country is saddled with a wasteful Soviet-style heating system and dependent wholly on imported gas and yet lacks the money to pay its heating bills. When the unpaid bills get too big, the heat is shut off. That includes hospitals, even maternity wards. Which is what happened one December day to a friend of one of his Moldovan staff. Vince had been in Chisinau maybe six months at that point; it was his first winter and he was shocked by the cold. This woman had her baby and the hospital was freezing and the nurse took the baby away from the mother to give her some rest. The nurse put the child in another room—an unheated room—and the child died.

Vince can't get the story out of his mind (later he checked it out and yes, it happened). "I could never make this my adopted country," he says.

He reminds me of the time he helped a young Moldovan open a movie theater. Her idea was to show English-language movies, which had never been done in the country before. She was so inexperienced she didn't even know to name her theater. In communist times, stores had numbers. She thought her theater would have a number too.

Vince told her to give it a name. She called it "Movie House."

She rented a vacant auditorium and even before she set an opening date, the local mafia demanded one-third of her ticket revenues as protection money. Vince got angry when she told him. At least wait until she has customers before you shake her down, he thought.

He told her to make the mafia sign a contract for security services and to let them have a percentage only of concession sales rather than ticket sales. She got them to agree.

This is a big victory in Moldova.

CHAPTER 4

NATIONALISM, DIVERSITY AND ETHNIC STRIFE

It is good for everyone to know how to forget.
—ERNEST RENAN[1]

All origins become mysterious if we seek far enough into the past. And almost all peoples, when we look at their earliest origins, turn out to have come from somewhere else.
—NOEL MALCOLM[2]

Successful modern states make a virtue, not a blood feud, out of ethnic and religious diversity.
—BILL CLINTON[3]

It makes no sense to hate. Whoever you hate will end up in your family.
—CHRIS ROCK[4]

ETHNIC DISPUTES RAGE all over the world. Fueled by rival readings of race and identity, these disputes shadow and shape civic life in the Balkans, the Middle East, Northern Ireland, India, Indonesia and many parts of Africa.

These disputes rarely grow violent in rich countries, but cracks show. A significant minority of people in Scotland wish to secede from Britain. Canada must accommodate demands by the French-speaking province of Quebec and its Native American population. Belgium is held together by an awkward sharing of power between French and Flemish speakers. The United States faces separatist movements in the state of Hawaii, Puerto Rico and island territories in the Pacific. On the mainland, various ethnic groups demand language rights and preferential treatment in gaining public jobs. Even France, which proudly upholds the ideal of a unified culture, faces demands by speakers of sixty-eight regional and minority languages who want representation in schools, workplaces and the media. The island of Corsica, a French territory in the Mediterranean, harbors an independence movement.

Many rich countries, meanwhile, suffer from isolated outbreaks of hate crimes. In 1999, a lone bomber in London targeted blacks, Asians and gay people. A racist gunman in Illinois methodically killed a black and a Korean. In Los Angeles, an anti-Semite attacked a Jewish community center, wounding children. In Germany, attacks on foreigners are common, and the elected head of the country's Jewish community, before his death from illness in 1999, said he wished to be buried in Israel because he feared that his grave in Germany would be desecrated.[5]

Isolated attacks on minorities don't tar a whole society. But they suggest that accommodating diversity isn't easy. It is a central challenge for rich nations, for two main reasons.

Self-styled "purists" want to limit mingling in order to preserve "blood-lines." Proponents of such views, though marginalized politically and socially, are nonetheless a force to be reckoned with. On the other end of the spectrum are defenders of minority groups who think too much mingling threatens their existence. Viewed as liberals, these minority advocates often defend the status quo and deride new cosmopolitans. In the United States, they insist on retaining outmoded racial classifications out of fear of diluting their group power. They oppose, for instance, giving people the choice to refuse to give a standard racial description in college admissions or job applications.

Opposition from both racial purists and defenders of rigid ethnic categories raise doubts about whether mongrelization can survive. Is it possible that as mingling deepens, and it becomes more difficult to sustain conventional distinctions between people, hybridity will consume itself? Explaining why this won't happen is the purpose of this chapter.

At first blush, the very existence of communal violence and individual hate crimes would seem to contradict my central thesis. I argue that under the right conditions hybridity promotes harmony and thus becomes a powerful catalyst for happiness and wealth. The very absence of support for hybridity is a leading source of ethnic strife. Under the right conditions, communal violence is least likely to occur in mongrel societies. Ethnic conflict, far from repudiating the benefits of mongrelization, actually confirms them.

In this chapter, I will explain why this occurs. First, I will distinguish between societies that tolerate diversity and those that support and welcome the supercharged form of diversity that I call hybridity, mongrelization or the new cosmopolitanism. All three terms suggest the emptiness of the words "diversity" and "multiculturalism." They can mean almost anything, from accepting outsiders but keeping them in their place, to tolerating their differences but freezing ethnic and racial categories through law and custom. Neither approach unleashes the benefits of hybridity. The failure to define "What kind of diversity?" sends a society into a vicious cycle. Even when the dominant group responds with recognition of minority claims, its members are rewarded with more strident minority demands. That minorities often don't specify their diversity requirements only compounds the misunderstandings.

Next, I describe various ways nations use history to influence their capacity to accommodate differences among members of their societies and thus either expand or limit their growth as hybrid nation-states. To grow a hybrid nation, certain ways of using history are essential. National myths must be restructured in order to reflect the shifts in identity and diversity that promote mongrelization. These myths must be linked to power-sharing arrangements that shape daily life. Finally, I explain why hybridity is sustainable. The mechanics of power sharing are less important than the consistency with which power is shared. But any legitimate power-sharing arrangement must not rely on the false and misleading dichotomy between integration ("the center holds") and disintegration ("things fall apart"). Proponents of integration unwittingly accept the basic premise of disintegrationists and thus give the latter significant momentum. Pro-integrationists often favor the sorts of radical mixing that I describe, but may endorse policies and practices that heighten communal tensions and reduce the space for hybrid identities. These outcomes are regrettable, since many integrationists are people of good will. But they undermine themselves by framing the debate as either-or.

What follows isn't a philosophical defense of the sustainability of hybridity. I am not giving a moral "proof," but describing various ways of reacting to social change. Mongrelization proceeds, even where conditions aren't optimal. Purposely refusing to create optimal conditions won't prevent mongrelization but will make the transition from a monochrome world to a mongrel world more painful. There is no keeping the mono world of yesterday, not unless a rich nation wishes to become a poor one. The only way to stay "pure" is for a society to wreck its standard of living. The alternative to hybridity is poverty, something no democratic nation would choose. Diversity must be accommodated, and not with hollow nostrums. There is no escape.

MACEDONIA

In every rich country the line between diversity and hybridity is blurry. All rich countries have some means of taking in outsiders and, at least formally, propose to treat minorities equally. But in practice they make a variety of discriminations and distinctions between natives and newcomers. In some cases, rich nations may hold up a single model, or a common destination, for group identity, which implies denial of difference. Other rich countries support hybridity by affirming the desire of groups and individuals to pursue diverse and multiple identities. Yet even in these countries, pressures to assimilate and conform to a single standard remain a still-visible ideal.

To better grasp the distinction between toleration for difference and active encouragement of it, consider an extreme case. Extreme cases help highlight distinctions and reveal the range of issues displayed in milder cases. My extreme case is Macedonia, the only former Yugoslav republic with a significant minority that has avoided communal violence. In the late 1990s, Serbs and ethnic Albanians killed each other in the Serbian province of Kosovo. In

Macedonia, the dominant Slavs and minority Albanians lived in peace. They not only tolerated one another but struggled to share power in ways that validated the hybrid selves of Macedonia's Albanians.

This was no storybook accommodation, however. During a visit I made to the country, one Albanian asked bitterly, "What do we have to look forward to? We are second-class citizens here, and even worse off than Kosovo. How do we build a future?"

Muhamed's plight is common. He was born in Macedonia about thirty years ago, at a time when Skopje, Macedonia's capital, and Pristina, the capital of Kosovo, were part of the same country. The two cities are about a two-hour drive apart. Because there is no accredited university in Macedonia that teaches classes in the Albanian language, ethnic Albanians attended school in Pristina, at least before the Serbs shut down the university. When Serbia rescinded Kosovo's autonomy in 1989, many of Kosovo's elite helped to form an unofficial university in the Macedonian city of Tetevo, where most of the country's Albanians live.

The mingling between Albanians in Serbia and Macedonia makes a mockery of the borders that run through this lush, mountainous region. Muhamed's wife, an ethnic Albanian who was born in Macedonia, can't get citizenship papers or a Macedonian passport because her mother was born in Kosovo. But she isn't entitled to a Serbian or an Albanian passport either. As a result, Muhamed's two children are stateless, even though they too were born in Macedonia.

Albanians comprise at least a quarter, and perhaps as much as a third, of Macedonia's population of two million. But the denigration of Albanians in Macedonia doesn't stop with the denial of basic documents. They are subjected to relentless political surveillance by the Slavic majority. They are more often searched and arrested than Slavs. In one major outburst in July 1997, police beat hundreds of people who were protesting a government ban on flying the Albanian flag.

Petty harassment is common. Six policemen once visited the home of Hazbi Duraku, a shopkeeper in Tetevo, and searched his house for weapons. Durako said he had no weapons. The officers trained their guns on his children and kept searching until they found a set of German-made kitchen knives. "You can pick these up at the station," they told him. Duraku, angry and humiliated, never did.

Influential Albanians aren't exempt from police harassment. Tetevo's mayor, an Albanian named Nurtezan Ismaili, refuses to fix the broken door leading into his private office. Police broke it open when they arrested his predecessor for complaining about the government's suppression of Albanian cultural life. The former mayor was banned from politics as a condition of his release. Ismaili, his replacement, is convinced he is under surveillance. "They are probably listening to us now as we talk," he told me, pointing to the ceiling.

Macedonia is often viewed as the one part of the former Yugoslavia where different ethnic groups coexist. Yet relations between Slavs and Albanians are poor. In daily life, Albanians and Macedonians almost never mix. Children attend separate schools. Intermarriages between Christian Slavs and Muslim Albanians are rare. The two groups tend to live and work separately. Albanians fear Slavs are plotting against them, and Slavs generally see Albanians as dishonest, shiftless and conspiring to secede from the country.

The leading Albanian politican in Macedonia, Arben Xhaferi, wants to transcend the stereotypes. He believes people of different religious and ethnic backgrounds can live peacefully together. He doesn't want the largely Albanian western part of Macedonia to secede and unite with Albania or Kosovo. But for Albanians to remain within Macedonia, he argues, they must have more power; otherwise they will be eradicated by the Slavic majority. For Albanians to survive, Slavs cannot simply tolerate them, though that would be a good start; they must also recognize their differences. To Xhaferi, who was a Belgrade philosophy professor in the old Yugoslavia, the solution to the Albanian problem isn't to redraw the map but to guarantee minority representation in the country's institutions. In early 1999, he wagered his reputation on a plan—forged jointly with the ruling Slavic party in Macedonia—to bring more Albanians into authority positions in the police, hospitals and cultural organizations.

This frank attempt at what philosopher Charles Taylor calls the "politics of recognition" carries risks, because if Slavs interpret it as a form of surrender, they may strike back at Albanians. Xhaferi feels the risk is worth taking. "In Macedonia, we have the marginalization of the Albanian," he says. "Here we are alone." Albanians need more than protection against persecution. They need real power over their lives, and the only way to get it is to prove to the dominant Slavs that they can wield power responsibly and for the common good. He vows that Albanians are committed to this and challenges Slavs to reciprocate. "If citizens show more loyalty to the state than their ethnic group, the state will be more stable. But for that to happen here, the state must buy the loyalty of the Albanians."

TO UNDERSTAND HOW Macedonians might win the loyalty of Albanians, meet a tough cop named Ismail Bexheti.

An ethnic Albanian and a Muslim, Bexheti is chief of police in Tetevo. His district is composed almost entirely of Slavic Christians. He is the first Albanian ever to be police chief in Tetevo, despite Albanians comprising 90 percent of his jurisdiction. This may not sound like much but is the rough equivalent, in American terms, of Chicago naming a Black Panther as its top cop in 1968. "This is a big step for Albanians in Macedonia," says Gilles de Rapper, a French anthropologist who has studied the region. "Even if it turns out to be only symbolic, it can give Albanians a sense of belonging."

The drive to belong, however, may consume Bexheti. His new job, which forces him to sleep some nights on a moldy couch in his office and take calls at home in the middle of the night, "has destroyed my peace," he says.

From the start, Bexheti, who is forty years old, faced a rebellion of senior Slavic officers who were mortified by the prospect of working for an Albanian. The squabble wounded Bexheti. "I don't trust most of my people," he says.

They don't trust him. Sixty days into his tenure, four Macedonian cops beat up an old Albanian, claiming that the man attacked them with a knife and then tried to escape. They threw the man in jail and left. When Bexheti learned of the incident, he decided the police story "defied logic." He opened a personal investigation and quickly found that the officers carried Kalishnikov rifles and were younger and more fit than the Albanian. And the knife couldn't be found. So Bexheti freed the old man and tried to discipline the officers. But his actions so incensed the Slavic officers that he couldn't punish the offenders; the most he could do was warn them not to beat anyone again.

Bexheti considers such compromises unavoidable. "I am not God," he says. "I can't see everything." He realizes that the gulf between Macedonians and Albanians is large, and not just on the police force. This makes the country's effort to diversify its police crucial to building ethnic harmony. "The only way a police force can be acceptable to a society is if it is a reflection of that society," says Anita Hazenberg, a senior Dutch police officer who has advised the Macedonian government on behalf of the Council of Europe. "You have to represent society or you can't serve it."

Ethnic Albanians now comprise only 3 percent of the department's 9,000 employees nationwide and 10 percent in Bexheti's region. The idea of putting an Albanian in charge, and gradually adding more Albanian officers, is based on the assumption that treatment of Albanians will improve. Although proud of Bexheti's appointment, many Albanians in Tetevo think he can't change the police. "From one flower, spring will not come—even if the flower is the chief," says Abdul Xhelil, who runs a sandwich shop near the main station.

Others insist that Bexheti is a tool of his Macedonian bosses in the capital city of Skopje, a forty-five-minute drive away. They cite his inability to hire people—this is done centrally—and his lack of control over his own budget. He can't, for instance, order spending on overtime without Skopje's approval. Critics worry that Bexheti's presence is designed to silence them. "Now it makes it harder for us to criticize the police because they can say the chief is Albanian," says Abdul Alieu, an Albanian who serves in Macedonia's parliament.

Bexheti's experience suggests the complexity of the situation. Soft-spoken and stylish, he is the youngest son of a successful local family. One brother is mayor of a nearby city; another is a leading physician; and a third works as a government labor inspector. "I was the stupid one who joined the police," he says. Having been weaned on Hollywood cop movies, "I thought I'd have a glamorous job."

In 1983, at the age of twenty, he attended a police academy in Skopje, then part of Yugoslavia. He joined the force in Tetovo as an ordinary officer. Work was tedious. His Albanian ethnicity limited his advancement and earned him the mistrust of the Macedonian officers. Among the few Albanian officers, he became known for his ability to endure Slavic insults without exploding.

After the breakup of Yugoslavia, and the independence of Macedonia in 1991, Bexheti gained his own command, of a small village outside Tetovo. One day he received an order from Skopje to begin ripping down the distinctive black-eagle flag of Albania, which many locals display as a way of asserting their cultural difference. Bexheti refused the order. He was stripped of his command, but not fired, so as to avoid making him into a martyr.

Back as a beat cop, Bexheti thought of quitting. "My friends encouraged me to stay," he says. Because he was one of only a few Albanian officers, "they said I could do a lot of good for my people," he recalls. "But the job didn't do much good for me."

Languishing in the department, Bexheti was a pariah. The department's chief, a Macedonian Slav, not only refused to discuss problems with ordinary Albanians but wouldn't even see Bexheti. Still, Bexheti kept a reputation for honesty, effectiveness and even occasional heroics.

In 1998, when the nine-year-old son of a prominent family was kidnapped, Bexheti learned where the child was held from one of his informants. He led a dramatic rescue, surrounding the kidnappers' hideout and forcing them to give up the boy. He even personally arrested one of the kidnappers, knocking him to the ground. He broke his left leg in the arrest.

When the government launched its power-sharing plan in 1999, Bexheti was considered the natural choice as chief. "He's clean, and he's not one of those Albanians who treats his own people worse just to show the Macedonians he's fair," says Xhaferi, his political patron.

For a novice chief, Bexheti is a canny operator. Ordinary people can see him in his office, or on the streets, at the Bolero café where he often sits outside drinking a cappuccino, or while driving his department-issue Volkswagen Golf. One afternoon, he wheels the car through the center of Tetovo, playing the celebrity. He slows to allow an old woman to cross the street and she stops to chat with him, asking about his family. Two men jump out into the street and say hello. A well-dressed woman hails him. She is a local Albanian folksinger, and Bexheti asks where she will perform next.

Everywhere he goes, people know him. "They know me, but I don't always know them," he quips. If they need him, he tells them to visit his office. If they say that Slavic officers refuse to let them enter the station—as some say happens—he growls in his characteristically faint voice, "Tell them the chief sent you."

Inside the main station, a ramshackle four-story building left over from the communist era, Bexheti is decidedly less partisan. "I will not act only for Albanians," he told his Macedonian officers when he took office. Rather than issue orders, he tries to coax them into trying new methods. He's won fans for supporting a pay hike for his men. And he keeps his cool. "He never raises his voice," says Sonia, his secretary, who worked for two prior chiefs.

He does argue, though. Chain-smoking Marlboro Lights in his unadorned office, he spends hours on the telephone with higher-ups in Skopje lobbying for more Albanian officers. They have promised him thirty more, but won't say when. One recent morning, he pulls out a blueprint for his most ambitious plan, a redesigned police station. Residents would obtain basic services through clear-glass windows, which would have the added benefit that supervisors can see if the officers are indeed working. Today, cops work behind closed doors and often are mysteriously busy for long stretches. There are no benches or waiting rooms, and visitors must either stand outside or sit on the bare ground.

"My dream is to hire pretty policewomen who will smile a lot," Bexheti says. "No longer will the officers be unfriendly."

His plan makes sense, but his bosses rejected it, saying they couldn't afford it. Such setbacks make Bexheti reach for one of four bottles of whiskey he keeps on the floor under his desk. Sipping a Johnny Walker one recent afternoon, he says, "I have a lot of plans but low means."

With a salary of only $250 a month, he isn't getting rich either. While he admits that low pay encourages corruption, he says he doesn't take bribes. He lives in a four-room apartment, with his wife and three children, on the tenth floor in a building with a balky elevator. Without the earnings of his wife, a schoolteacher, he could barely pay his bills.

As chief, he logs long hours; he hardly sees his kids or his parents, whom in more relaxed times he visited twice a week in his childhood village. Yet his presence as chief has lifted the morale of the Albanian officers, who are playing important roles in monitoring refugee movements and camps. Besides domestic murders and theft, Tetovo has its drug smugglers and extortion gangs. During the Kosovo war, in the spring of 1999, Bexheti's biggest headache was policing the two refugee camps in his district. Elsewhere in Macedonia, where Albanians had virtually no role on the force, refugees repeatedly complained of police brutality and even staged protests calling for NATO forces to replace Macedonian police at the camps.

Under Bexheti's watch, complaints were far fewer, chiefly because he has stationed ethnic Albanians in key spots. At a refugee camp two miles from the center of Tetovo, I watched three of Bexheti's cops listen to an old man explain why a family of eight people should leave the camp with him. He wanted to give them dinner in his home. Two cops drift off, the Macedonian ones, leaving the third man, an Albanian, to sort out the situation. There are 7,000 refugees in the camp, too many to allow them free roam. But the Albanian cop sympathizes with this uprooted family. After fifteen minutes of talk, he lets them go on the promise they will do the paperwork later.

As the group walks through the camp gate, the officer smiles. "I have been a policeman for thirteen years," he says. "I am also an Albanian, and these are my people."

GROUP RIGHTS

Macedonia's police reforms resemble the type of affirmative action practiced in the United States for the past thirty years. Xhaferi calls the approach "American-style power sharing," and he is right to do so. The United States isn't the only government that practices power sharing, but it is the most significant.

The United States certainly has a history of denying power to substantial groups. It perpetuated the enslavement of African Americans. It exterminated Indians—stole their land and destroyed their traditions. Even today, the United States remains divided over communal rights. The nation's legal system is predicated on the ideal of affording rights to individuals, not to groups. In many ways, this is an admirable tradition. Groups—from unions to religions—have tended to limit the freedom of their members. Some of what accounts for loyalty to ethnic, racial, religious or union affiliations arises out of fear, anxiety, explicit coercion or subtle peer pressure. Yet groups matter, and group feeling is genuine (though probably less heartfelt than many think). Thus, groups deserve, if not irreducible rights, then at least practical considerations. It is in this spirit that preferential hiring and promotion procedures, commonly known as affirmative action, are supported.

Language rights are similarly defended whenever ballot measures are presented in other than English; court interpreters are supplied; or bilingual instruction is provided. "Hate" speech is curtailed in workplaces and universities, so that one worker or student can't harass another with denigrating comments about his or her race, religion or sexuality, even though such speech is permitted in public space.[6] Courts have sharply limited the use of communal privileges too. The space afforded affirmative action, for instance, has steadily narrowed. But to say, as some do, that the United States shuns communal rights, though perhaps formally correct, ignores the countless practical accommodations between and within groups that honeycomb American polity.

The United States achieves these accommodations by constructing its history in order to promote consensus, optimism and the value of moving ahead. Through management of national symbols, or myths, the United States repudiates the tired "melting pot" metaphor for assimilation and creates fertile ground for transnational communities, where new cosmopolitans can keep one foot on American soil and another, if they wish, in midair.

To begin to explain the informal way in which the United States has essentially squared the circle of communal strife, I want first to describe the way

Americans approach their own history. In an age when ethnic strife is fueled by rival readings of history, the penchant of Americans for distorting their history in ways that reduce group tensions holds interesting lessons for the world. The U.S. approach is selective forgetting, amnesia put in the service of social cohesion. This practice disturbs some because it smacks of escapism, but Patricia Nelson Limerick, a historian of the American West, admits it isn't so bad when the world is choking on bad memories. "Most of the time, I would be inclined to see the loss of memory as a shame," she observes. "But given what's going on elsewhere in the world, forgetting may be something of a virtue."

To be sure, Americans distort historical images, but rarely in order to ignite communal strife. For the most part, Americans set aside disturbing memories, or touch them up for the purposes of nostalgia. The so-called winning of the West, in which white settlers routed Indian tribes, was so brutal that some historians view it as a forerunner of the "ethnic cleansing" campaigns in the Balkans and Africa in the 1990s. "For most white Americans, memory of the gritty horrible elements of the Indian wars are either lost to amnesia, or distanced into a colorful, even chipper memory of Wild West days," says Limerick (though this is hardly so for Native Americans who find this kind of "forgetting" deeply offensive).

Recent traumas, which might be expected to spark a desire for revenge—such as the Oklahoma City bombing or the 1983 massacre of 241 U.S. soldiers in Beirut—rapidly fade. And the willingness of victims of injustice in the United States to seek redress through the courts runs deeps. Or consider the 1967 assassination of Martin Luther King. His death resulted not in revenge killings common in some other nations, but in efforts—admittedly not always successful—at racial reconciliation. Yes, there were riots over the next few years that were linked to King's death and the unresolved challenges of civil rights. But today King's national holiday isn't an occasion for blacks to recall centuries of white violence against them, but instead is a time for all Americans to celebrate the ideal of brotherhood. Not only have whites collectively sought redemption through marking King's death; even King's widow and son Dexter embraced the convicted assassin, James Earl Ray, before Ray died of natural causes in prison. "For all our country's failings, there is an impulse to rectify injustice here," says Paul Boyer, a cultural historian at the University of Wisconsin.

The Civil War is perhaps the best example of how many Americans mold history to suit their constructive purposes. Many Americans view this bloody conflict, which 135 years ago left more than 600,000 dead, as a redemptive drama in which the United States expunged the evil of slavery and set the stage for its emergence as a world power in the twentieth century. Both the war, which began in 1861, and the South's defeat, in 1865, have come to be seen as inevitable—and morally correct—because of the North's superior industrial strength and its opposition to slavery. Once the war was over, the nation faced two main challenges: to heal the regional division and to give the former slaves a fair shake at decent lives.

Difficult as it was, healing proved the easier of the two, probably because whites in both North and South shared a language, a history, even a sense of America's destiny in the world. But the drive for black equality expired. "The great tragedy in Civil War memory in this country is that [America] eventually had a great deal of healing without justice," says David Blight, a historian at Amherst College.

By the 1880s, soldiers from the North and the South were holding reunions together, brought together by a common memory of the horrors of war, not the differences that had started it. With the abandonment of Reconstruction, Southerners were free to paint the effort as an invasion by greedy Northern "carpetbaggers" who really weren't interested in former slaves. One magazine, aimed at former Confederate soldiers, routinely carried articles about how happy and contented slaves were. Even Northerners, meanwhile, began to prefer an idyllic picture of the antebellum South, devouring tales of plantation life that culminated in the 1930s book *Gone with the Wind*.

But for blacks, the promise of the war proved hollow. The commitment to black equality, which partly motivated Northern resistance to Southern secession, expired after the war, and by the 1880s blacks fell prey to a resurgent Southern racism that culminated in the rigid system of segregation and exploitation that went by the name "Jim Crow." By the early 1900s, from Virginia to Florida, most blacks were left impoverished, second-class citizens subject to the whims of white supremacists. Says historian Edward Ayres, of the University of Virginia, "The congratulatory story we tell ourselves masks generations of injustice."

Blacks weren't the only ones to pay a price. Native Americans did too. After the Civil War, thousands of soldiers, who might otherwise have struggled to find a peaceful role for themselves in the United States, headed west to fight Indians. "Some of the biggest Indian fighters—Sheridan, Sherman, Custer— were important Civil War generals, so that the winning of the West becomes a unifier for both North and South" says British historian Susan-Mary Grant.

The view of the Civil War as a "salvation drama" is epitomized by the final scene in Ken Burns's 1990 documentary on the subject. Set in 1913, on the fiftieth anniversary of the Gettysburg battle, one of the war's bloodiest, the scene captures old Blue and Gray soldiers on grainy film footage charging across the battlefield once again, only this time to hug one another. Such images are attractive today when most Americans, rather than examine their failures or setbacks too closely, prefer to move on.

The September 11, 2001 attacks on the U.S. will sorely test the ability of Americans to move on—to selectively forget the past in order to forgive, reconcile and get on with life. In the months following 9-11, revenge was the rage in America and the so-called war on terrorism, whatever its merits, carries risk of dragging the U.S. into an unending cycle of violence, where terrorists reply to each American response, prompting more severe forms of retaliation.

Perhaps an awareness of these risks—and the limits of military power—will help Americans to realize that forgiveness, not revenge, is a main theme in the American experience. The tale of the Hatfields and McCoys, the legendary feuding neighbors, stands as a caution against the damage done to the quality of life when the desire for revenge goes unchecked. To be sure, forgiveness and a selective amnesia are no panaceas. The U.S. faces significant threats from around the world and these cannot be wished away. The U.S. must secure its borders against terrorists and it must disrupt, or eradicate, terrorist organizations around the world who wish to commit crimes on American soil. But as a highly diverse nation, the U.S. needs to accommodate differences in order to remain dynamic. And that means the U.S must remain open to foreign influence—and the people who carry them. America is not invincible. It never was. And the open society, to paraphrase the philosopher Karl Popper, has always had its enemies. There are no more enemies today, and probably a good deal fewer, than in the 1930s when Hitler and Stalin held sway over much of Europe. Yes, the U.S. must punish terrorists who commit crimes in our country. But in so doing, we must remember that punishment ought to satisfy the needs of the living and not only honor the dead.

If the U.S. does become consumed with revenge, it will be doing what many other countries do—promote conflict in a bid to "get even." The chief means of settling scores is to invoke historical events—real or imagined—that justify violent actions of the moment. "Each side tries to legitimize their aims by appealing to history," says Norman Davies, a historian at Oxford University.

Rival interpretations of history inspire rival conceptions of justice. Serbia's attacks on Kosovo, which culminated in its mass evictions of ethnic Albanians in 1999, were justified in part as payback for a series of betrayals—and outbreaks of violence in the twentieth century—that link back to a primary betrayal that allegedly occurred in 1389. Serbs say they lost their medieval kingdom because Albanians aided Turkish invaders. This casting of history helps explain an apparent puzzle: How is it that the ethnic group in power keeps justifying its actions by invoking its own victim status?

Serbia's defeat in 1389, on the Field of the Blackbirds, inaugurated 500 years of Turkish domination. The date of the battle, June 28, so underpins the Serb sense of victimization that not only is it a religious holiday but on that very day, in 1914, a Serb nationalist assassinated Austrian Archduke Franz Ferdinand, triggering World War I. Yet the battle itself is shrouded in myths. No contemporary report of it exists. The Serb kingdom, though diminished, still survived for another seventy years. Much evidence suggests that Albanians even may have fought alongside Serbs, making them allies and not enemies. Some historians think Serbia actually won the battle; others think the Serbs perhaps fought to a draw.[7]

About the only thing everyone agrees on is that the Serb leader, Prince Lazar, was killed in the battle. This fact is critical, since Serb nationalists through the centuries have sought to associate themselves with the myth of their valiant prince. Lazar is recalled as a martyr who embodies Serb greatness. When in 1989 Slobodan Milosevic rescinded the autonomy status of Yugoslavia's Kosovo province, he draped himself in Lazar imagery. After one million Serbs gathered nearby at a monastery for the first public viewing of what were said to be Prince Lazar's bones, Milosevic arrived by helicopter at the Field of Blackbirds. Addressing a throng, he reached back to 1389, declaring, "The Kosovo heroism does not allow us to forget that at one time we were brave and dignified and one of the few who went into battle undefeated. . . . Six centuries later, again we are in battles and quarrels."

The Kosovo performance marked a turning point in Serbian nationalism. By identifying himself with Lazar, and thus with the central myths of Serb history, Milosevic succeeded in prompting his fellow Serbs to enter what Michael Sells, a professor of religion at Haverford College, calls "collapsed time," psychologically returning to the Middle Ages. "When Serbs talk about 1389, they are living in 1389," says Sells. "They are so transformed by the ritual that they no longer think of themselves as an audience looking at a past event." In the minds of many Serbs, Milosevic becomes Lazar.

That Serbia's readings of history promote conflict and justify cycles of revenge is sadly all too common. Memory lies at the heart of many ethnic contests. It validates resistance to diversity; it normalizes the status of monocultures, transforming them from aberrations to a mythical state of grace. Large-scale mixing of people throughout history is the norm. Virtually every contemporary state has a messy, mixed-up social substratum (perhaps only Japan and Iceland can honestly cite an absence of mixing, and this is due to their extraordinary isolation prior to the nineteenth century). Even lands traversed by a multitude of people through the ages inspire claims of purity and uniqueness that defy the literal record. Consider the situation facing Israel and Palestine. This may be the world's most difficult historical dispute because the history seems, well, so ancient. In reality, it isn't. The core disagreements all date within the past 100 years—a long time, to be sure, but not on a biblical scale.

"There is a tendency to see things as going back to time immemorial," says Rashid Khalidi, a Palestinian American who teaches history at the University of Chicago. "Arabs and Jews haven't been killing each other for thousands of years, not even hundreds of years. In fact, theirs is a very recent conflict. It is 50 to 100 years, not millennia."

Before this century, a small number of Jews lived alongside more numerous Arabs within the Holy Land. Palestinians arguably didn't exist as a distinct group before the twentieth century. Historians generally date the first flowering of Palestinian identity to the 1920s. Similarly, Israeli identity arose only in the twentieth century, as embattled European Jews sought a home in the Middle East. To be sure, many Jews long saw Palestine as a historical homeland, but curiously some Sephardic Jews—descendants of people expelled from Spain in 1492—longed to return to a "home" in Spain. Zionist Theodor Herzl even seriously considered a British plan to create a Jewish homeland in Africa.[8]

Disagreements abound over interpretations of more recent events. For example, the first great wave of Arab protests over Jewish settlements came in 1936, when Britain controlled Palestine. Palestinians remember the protests as an "uprising" of huge importance, whereas Israelis dismiss them as a mere "disturbance," despite their lasting three years. Or consider the bitter argument over why Palestinians fled their homes in 1948 on the creation of Israel. For decades, Israeli leaders have insisted that Palestinians left voluntarily or as part of an Arab conspiracy to embarrass the new Jewish state. Palestinians counter that Israel forced them out, destroying hundreds of their villages and even marching them at gunpoint into neighboring countries. Respected historians give succor to both sides. In northern Palestine, many Arabs left of their own accord. But in the center of the country, Israelis destroyed hundreds of Palestinian villages and forced thousands of people out.[9]

The contest over historical "facts" highlights the importance of the past in maintaining contemporary differences. The veneer of historical legitimacy allows both sides to continue fighting over who "deserves" control of the land because of that side's purportedly unique association with it. In this case, national myths are managed in order to heighten conflict and promote a winner-take-all view of society. These myths are about origins: where people are from and where they are going. But myths, as made, can be remade in response to new conditions. In Israel's case, the Middle East peace accords, which called on both Israelis and Palestinians to promote the concept of coexistence among their populations, is driving a change in history books.

In the fall of 1999, Israeli schools introduced new textbooks that, one observer noted, "make plain that many of the most common Israeli beliefs are as much myth as fact." The effect of the new history curriculum is to accent a more conciliatory attitude toward Palestinians. A textbook in 1984, for instance, wrote that Jews were "horrifyingly" outnumbered in the war to create Israel and that "the chances for success were doubtful," conveying a sense that Israelis overcame great odds. The new textbook stresses that Jews were better prepared militarily than the Arabs, so that their victory was less surprising than once thought. "On nearly every front and in nearly every battle," it reads, "the Jewish side had the advantage over the Arabs in terms of planning, organization, operation of equipment and also in the number of trained fighters who participated in the battle." The restructured myths of Israel's origins balance the picture in the spirit of U.S. power-sharing approaches, which I describe next.[10]

POWER SHARING

Power can be shared in many ways. It can be doled out in degrees, by the tea-spoon or the barrel. To manage national myths so that they promote hybrid-ity requires compromise, rule of law and a concern for both individuals and group needs. The idea that all people get their day in court—before a judge, administrator or legislative body—has much to do with why Americans view history so differently from people in other countries. Belief in fair play is strong. Every American expects some redress for past wrongs; indeed, the surest sign that an immigrant has acquired American attitudes is when he starts thinking his complaints will draw positive responses.

Even the most mistreated of all Americans think this way. Despite a history of broken promises, "many Native Americans believe the American system is going to solve the problem of inequalities and injustice," says Marcus Lopez, a director of American Indian Airways, an independent radio network.

An illustration: Members of the Lakota want the International Court of Justice, in the Netherlands, to weigh the tribe's territorial claim (dismissed by U.S. courts) on a swath of the American Midwest where the buffalo once roamed. The United States seized the land after routing the Lakota. Courts are slow and often unyielding, but the Lakota view them as their best hope. "We don't feel any animosity toward whites," says Germaine Tremmel, a tribal lawyer. "That isn't our way."

With few exceptions, revenge isn't anybody's way in the United States. Indeed, it requires a huge leap to imagine Serbia-like conditions in America. "Consider how different the U.S. might be had the Congress agreed, in 1818, to set aside a chunk of Ohio for Irish immigrants, or in the late 1840s, a chunk of Texas for German immigrants," says David Hollinger of the University of California at Berkeley. "It's inconceivable."

Nothing close to that happened. Yes, blacks ended up as half the population of Mississippi, Mormons predominated in Utah and the Navajos ultimately controlled a wide area of the Southwest. But individuals always had the chance to step outside the informal boundaries, and the state endorsed eth-nic-only territories only in the case of Native Americans. African Americans generally fought not for autonomy but for inclusion. Rather than try to "take over" a Southern state, blacks streamed North, depleting their ranks (and potential influence) in the deep South. Outsiders gradually moved to Utah, lessening Mormon power. And the enormous Navajo "reservation" never received statehood because the United States, notes one scholar, "made a deliberate decision . . . not to accept any territory as a state unless national groups were outnumbered." The American system fostered individual iden-tity, not ethnic-group identity.[11]

It also promoted reconciliation. Consider one of the more peculiar disputes in American history: over land in what today is northern New Mexico. The land was awarded by Spanish and Mexicañ governors of this territory, prior to U.S. conquest in the war of 1846. Under a treaty ending the war, the United States pledged to honor these grants, but over the years the grantees—Hispanic and Indian families, descendants of some of the oldest settlers in North America—gradually saw their holdings whittled away. Dishonest government surveyors, unscrupulous developers and uncharitable judges combined to reduce these pre-1846 grants, with white developers or the federal government benefiting.

For decades, resentment simmered in New Mexico. Anger finally boiled over in the 1960s. The land-grant families seized a courthouse, destroyed property and threatened rebellion. But the attacks failed. "From then on, a lot of people saw that violence was not going to work," recalls Roberto Mondragon, a land-grant heir who lives in La Loma, New Mexico. "Eventually we sought a peaceful solution."

The protesters turned to politics. They ran for local offices. Some won, including one man involved in the courthouse seizure. By the 1990s, people of Spanish and Mexican descent controlled almost all the local governments in the land-grant areas. Heirs of the land grantees then convinced their congressman, Rep. Tom Udall, to back legislation authorizing a presidential commission to study ways to return land to families deprived of it. "That alone would give recognition of the injustice," says Udall. Such a bill seems likely to pass sooner or later, even though Udall says his fellow members of Congress have little patience for talk about a 150-year-old land dispute. "This country has a tradition that when major injustices are done that we sort it out," Udall says.

The land-grant heirs certainly expect movement. "We all have a glimmer of hope that some leader will come through and present a mechanism whereby people can present their case and get their day in court," Mondragon says. "Hope may not get us fat, but it keeps us going."

By defusing disputes with the prospect of a compromise in which each side gets something, the United States avoids communal violence. How else to explain the New Mexico situation, where an aggrieved minority, dispossessed of its land by invaders, then becomes subjugated by them? Sounds like the Balkans, right? Only without a crucial ingredient: Serbia won't share power with ethnic Albanians. In New Mexico, power is spread around, and hope abounds. "America is very co-optive," says Peter Skerry, a professor at Claremont College who has written widely on Hispanics. "It responds in ways that drains the energies out of violent and radical changes."

Co-optation is widespread in the United States, rendering formal policies less important than they appear from a distance. This pragmatism undermines the practice of majority rule and boosts so-called consociational tendencies. Rule by majority presumes a roughly homogeneous body politic; winners and losers both accept the same rules. Consociationalism looks to forge a modus vivendi, or a treaty among contending groups. This approach addresses, as

Michael Lind observes, "the possibility that a given political community may be made up of two or more enduring, distinct communities defined by extra-political characteristics, such as regional, racial or religious identities." It views democracy as a means of achieving consensus among rival groups, not simply expressing the will of the majority. In the United States, consociationalists see the separation of powers—the principle by which courts can act as a check on a majority-controlled legislature, for instance—as crucial to "reducing dangerous strife, by giving as many groups as possible a stake in the system, and minimizing the possibility that one region, or one race, or one religious denomination, can use the power of the state to exploit others."

Lind highlights the American flair for holding together a polyethnic society in the face of the divisive forces that so worried the Frenchman Alexis de Tocqueville, who in the nineteenth century wrote of the United States: "Picture to yourself ... a society which comprises all the nations of the world— English, French, German: people differing from one another in language, in beliefs, in opinions; in a word a society possessing no roots, no memories, no prejudices, no routine, no common ideas, no national character, yet with a happiness a hundred times greater than our own. . . . What is the connecting link between these so diverse elements? How are they wedded into one people?" A sort of answer lies in the American concern for stakeholders, not just for the majority bloc. "Every numerical minority in a society cannot be placated," Lind writes. "But no effort should be spared to co-opt substantial minorities, if social peace hangs on the result."[12]

Indeed, Americans usually spare no effort to balance the tradition of majority rule with the demands of an increasingly hybridized nation. The town of El Cenizo, in southern Texas, provides a good example of how rival tendencies complement each other in the United States. Disenchanted with the task of translating into Spanish its local government meetings, voters passed an ordinance allowing public business to be conducted in Spanish. Another ordinance ordered the city's employees, all six of them, not to aid the Immigration and Naturalization Service in catching illegal aliens. Nearly every resident in El Cenizo, population 7,500, is an immigrant, married to an immigrant or the child of immigrants. Paranoia about the INS is so high that town workers are routinely accused of assisting in the capture of illegals. The town's mayor hopes the new laws will dispel such charges, prompting one observer to write, "The laws reflect not so much a rejection of American culture but acknowledgment of a border culture dominated by Spanish and haunted by Border Patrol search vehicles."

Cultural purists cringe over examples such as this. But no one seems harmed—certainly not the INS, which has ample legal powers to track down illegal aliens, nor advocates of English, who have only the world's most popular language to promote. So why stop a small community from exercising its preferences? El Cenizo's language law draws attention, but the law is apparently legal. As one advocate for Mexican Americans says, people should do what works. "It appears these folks clearly understand these communities do not speak English and this is a way of providing a service."[13]

THE IMPORTANCE OF NATIONS

A recognition of both individual and communal needs is the legal and political foundation for hybridity. Only nations can supply this foundation. International organizations are too weak to do so. Generally, the United Nations and various regional organizations don't have the authority to intervene in the internal affairs of a sovereign nation in order to protect the rights of an aggrieved minority or to help forge a more just relationship between contending groups. In those rare cases when they have authority to protect a minority group (as in East Timor, after Indonesia agreed in 1999 to allow a vote of its people on independence, or in U.N.-controlled Kosovo), international organizations fail to deliver on their promises. Tribal or ethnic organizations, meanwhile, fail to guarantee the freedom of their members to exit their group or to seek a just settlement of disputes that stem from a complaint against group rules. Religious courts, for instance, consistently fail to uphold individual freedoms against the needs of the group. To be sure, the purpose of these ethnic organizations is to preserve the group, but the group is generally defined in static, unchanging terms. Hybrids seek to transplant their roots into new soil, or cross traits with other groups (as in an intermarriage). Ethnic authorities rarely endorse such activities.

Only national governments can secure the conditions out of which hybridity springs. Flawed though they are, nations are the best arbiters of fairness on matters of communal and individual import. Only nations can manage the complex cross-currents between individualism and communalism. Despite all the loose talk of the decline of sovereignty and the irrelevance of borders, strong national government remains the best remedy for most of the challenges posed by diversity. This doesn't mean that international organizations or tribal groups are unimportant; they have their place. But nations matter most. As local ties and affiliations grow in importance to people and as they desire to forge intimate relationships (whether in political, business or personal life) across the globe, only nations can serve as the neutral arbiter required to ensure that the multiplicity of individual ties do not collapse in conflict. This belief in the primacy of the nation is, of course, unfashionable at a time when people the world over bemoan the "loss" of national sovereignty to international outfits such as the World Trade Organization and to all manner of multinational corporations. Of course, nations are constrained by global economic forces, technological change and a patchwork of multilateral and bilateral agreements. But nations have always been so constrained; sovereignty never has been unconditional, not even for historical superpowers. Moreover, for all the hand-wringing about the flaws of nation-states, no compelling alternative to them has emerged. Not even far-fetched replacements for the nation have won much of an audience. As the scholar Jeffrey Herbst has noted, "there has been startlingly little creativity in devising alternatives to the nation-state."[14]

Thus, it seems fair to say that fears over the supposed decline of the nation are overblown. This hysteria is unfortunate, because in the panic over the rise of global forces beyond local political control, too many people have ignored the possibilities for expanding democracy and resolving social conflicts at the national level. Even with the emerging constraints on nations from global forces, the potential for nations to promote happiness and prosperity along hybrid lines remains largely untapped. This means that people who wish to realize their capacity for roots and wings must care deeply about the health and wealth of the nation. There is much they can do locally to improve their situation.

How nations cope with the competing needs and demands of their diverse citizenry is thus the central political and moral question of the time. This question is all the more difficult to answer because no nation can simply carve in stone the very rules that balance individual and communal claims. They cannot merely issue a set of rules that enable citizens to mix and match cultural elements across ideological, religious, ethical, racial and ethnic lines. Any such rules would surely face endless challenges, so the nation must actively and constantly exist in relation to its hybridizing society. This is because individuals vary and change over time. A Baptist converts to Catholicism. A tuba player switches to the French horn.

Groups also vary and change over time. No government should freeze the terms of membership even if asked to do so by a group. Consider the case of people of Chinese descent living in Europe and the United States. A nation might consider certain safeguards for the society and culture of the Chinese, so as to aid in the effort to maintain Chinese roots. But just what are those roots? What is Chineseness? This isn't obvious, neither to politicians nor people of Chinese descent. Perhaps some Chinese people in America and Europe will someday insist on identifying themselves more with their regions of origin than they do now. Instead of identifying themselves as representatives of a nation (China), they may become, through an act of reinvention, Hokkiens, Yunnanese or Guandongese (or other regional identities). As Thomas Sowell notes, "like other minorities, Chinese may 'all look alike' to outsiders, but their internal differences are sharp and enduring, both in China and overseas. Chinese from different parts of China not only speak in ways that are mutually unintelligible, but also operate overseas in different social networks that are often mutually exclusive in both personal and business matters."[15] In short, Chinese diversity can be viewed as composed of different groups, not merely a variation on a single theme.

The Chinese case suggests the dangers posed by shrill advocates of freezing (or "defending," as some would say) group identities. By taking this stance, well-intended cultural guardians may frustrate the very people they seek to protect. There is an absurdity in defending and preserving a group label—and its coincident characteristics—that was invented in response to circumstances that no longer apply. In the case of the label "Chinese," it was the relative ignorance of Westerners and the historical existence of a Chinese empire that spawned the practice of calling these migrants "Chinese" when even they usually called themselves something else. The reasons for calling these people "Chinese" may no longer apply; hence there may be no further need to defend and preserve "Chinese" culture within a multiethnic state. Indeed, there may not be a "Chinese" culture to protect.

Similarly, the concept of "Hispanic" may have outlived its usefulness. Some Hispanics say they are white; some say they are black. Some are from Europe; some are from Latin America. Some have no history of speaking Spanish (Brazilians, for example). Indeed, the differences between Cubans and Colombians, people from Spain and Guatemala, are vast. The same point can be made about the category "Asian American." Once a valuable tool for raising awareness about historical discrimination in America against Chinese and Japanese immigrants, the label now obscures more than it reveals and probably makes it more difficult for white Americans to understand the vast differences among "Asians" themselves, who hail from such diverse places as India, Japan, Vietnam and Indonesia and who intermarry (between their respective groups and with whites) at an astonishing rate. As Eric Liu observes in his meditation on ethnicity, *The Accidental Asian:* "The Asian American identity as we know it may not last another generation. Which makes doubters like me grow more doubtful—and hopeful. . . . From the perspective of my children and their children . . . it may seem that 'Asian American' was but a cocoon: something useful, something to outgrow."[16]

The willingness to constantly refresh the boundaries and language of group identity should not be so hard to accept, but identity lobbies and interest groups have a stake in the status quo. The challenge for governments is to protect recognized minority groups, but not in ways that make it impossible for group identities to shift ground in order to better reflect group members. Communal identities are no less flexible than individual ones.

LOSING OUT

Hybridity is sustainable. Through power sharing and the adroit use of myths and history, the United States manages most of the tensions spawned by a hybrid society. But some fester. They don't spoil the mongrel dream, but they are troubling.

These tensions fall into two categories. The first type flows from inequalities in wealth. These inequalities cut across traditional lines of race, class, gender, religion and ethnicity. The United States, notwithstanding its flair for power sharing and hybridization, supports an economic model that results in increasing disparities of wealth and income. Other rich countries, though also showing widening disparities, have stronger social safety nets in order to better protect those on the bottom.

The second type of tension arises over race. Mexican Americans, other Hispanics and Asians face discrimination from some parts of the United States. But the success of these groups belies the suspicion that they are subject to widespread, persistent and systematic bias. The case of American blacks is different. Antiblack attitudes are widely held by white Americans. They are even voiced by many immigrants to the United States, indeed many of the very immigrants who claim themselves to be victims of discrimination. For example, many of them arrive with antiblack attitudes, and their experience, contending with blacks for space and opportunity, only deepens these attitudes. Citing the widespread reluctance of immigrant entrepreneurs to hire American blacks, one report concluded that "while they are minorities themselves, many immigrant bosses are refusing to employ the nation's largest minority [blacks], sometimes invoking troubling stereotypes to explain themselves."[17]

This pattern can be seen in many American cities, where immigrants have brought energy, vitality and investment to depressed urban neighborhoods. Although many blacks benefit from these changes, some are left behind. From Brooklyn, New York, to Houston, Texas, to Oakland, California, newcomers have succeeded in rebuilding urban areas where government programs had failed. Even smaller cities in outlying areas see gains from immigrants—and tensions, as white employers prefer them to blacks. As the case of Utica, New York, shows, the resulting tensions aren't easily resolved.

Since 1960, Utica has been slowly dying. A decaying industrial town along the Mohawk River, Utica's population fell from 101,000 in 1960 to 58,590 in 1968. Large knitting mills, which once buoyed the economy, moved to the South in the late 1950s. By 1991, five factories once operated here by General Electric were closed. An Air Force base, which employed 5,000 military and civilian workers, closed in 1996.

Decades of decline left Utica with plenty of room for immigrants. Starting in 1993, Bosnians arrived. Fleeing persecution in the former Yugoslavia, about 3,000 arrived in a six-year period, giving Utica the fourth-largest Bosnian population in the United States. The Bosnians, generally Muslim, joined about 2,500 Russians who began arriving a few years earlier.

The influx of newcomers boosted Utica's economy, especially because many of them received state and federal subsidies. They bought unwanted homes (at 1960s prices), filled low-wage jobs that might otherwise go begging and moved into dilapidated city-owned apartment buildings that were once nearly empty. The ease of their entry, however, angered poor blacks in Utica, who say the popularity of the immigrants stems from their skin color, not their character. They say that immigrants are grabbing aid that should go to them and that local businesses bypass blacks to hire Bosnians or Russians. "There's an acceptance for the refugees that isn't there for people of African-American descent," says a reverend at a black church. The head of the local Head Start program, also black, claims Utica employers told only the immigrant community about job openings.

Utica's white establishment denies these charges, but fans suspicions by saying that immigrants are better prepared and harder working than some local blacks. "I don't want to say other ethnic groups are not of good quality," one city official says. "But they are a better quality of people than the others." The city's schools chief, in response to complaints that blame immigrants for overcrowded classrooms and deteriorating school quality, believes, "These people will be part of our rebirth, not our demise."

Still, blacks and other minorities in Utica reportedly have shown restraint. Puerto Rican and Bosnian teenagers once clashed with rocks and bottles, fairly tame combat for the United States. More curiously, Bosnians and Russians have taken offense to some American traditions, forcing the cancellation of an annual Halloween parade at a diverse elementary school. The newcomers felt that by wearing costumes, their children were partaking in some kind of "satanic observance." American parents then cried foul, saying their kids were being denied a good time because of spurious concerns. In a characteristic example of American co-optation, the school chose to hold dual Halloween events: the traditional parade for those who wanted one and a movie screening for those who didn't approve.

In the same spirit, teachers in Utica—ignoring the raging philosophical controversy over the merits of bilingual education—try various ways to ease the transition from a foreign language to English. Immigrant kids were initially placed in regular classroom and given scant extra help—the sink-or-swim treatment, which immigrants received a hundred years before—but results were too poor. Schools now assign each student an English-speaking buddy and provide heavy support from special staff. While policymakers and demagogues often want a single answer in this contentious area of linguistic and educational integration, Utica's educators stay flexible. With kids, one size does not fit all. They learn at different speeds. At the 800-student Columbus Magnet School, one of Utica's ten elementary schools, two dozen different languages are spoken, and a quarter of the students speak little English. "Some immediately reach an advanced level," says the principal, "while others take much longer."[18]

UTICA'S EXPERIENCE reinforces the view that diversity brings vitality to flexible communities and suggests that hybridity satisfies not only the elite but nearly everyone. This is an important point, because cosmopolitans are often accused of elitism. The accusation is unfair, though why it is takes a bit of explaining. If identity arises more from achievement than from belonging (as explained earlier), then it follows that people less able to achieve may resent this new order. Yet this logical conclusion is based on misunderstanding the nature of achievement as it applies to identity formation. In this context, "achievement" does not mean worldly success, wealth, acclaim. "Achievement" is a part of being human. To paraphrase Jesse Jackson, anyone can be somebody. This sense of "achievement" derives from passion, the effort a person puts into an activity. To think of himself as a trumpet player, a young man need not play like Miles Davis. A person can proudly cook in the Provençal style without serving as a chef in a Marseilles restaurant. A cabinetmaker who outfits a kitchen need not think less of his work because it isn't displayed in an art museum.

I have often recalled a speech Martin Luther King Jr. delivered from the pulpit of the Ebenezer Baptist Church in Atlanta, two months before his death. The speech gained fame because excerpts of it were played at King's nationally televised funeral, and people mostly recall his stylized humility in calling himself "a drum major for justice" who saw his worldly achievements—such as winning the Nobel Peace Prize—as "shallow things." Yet his sermon's larger message was that accomplishment wasn't about acclaim, but inner pride and generosity. This was "your new definition of greatness," he said, and "by giving that definition of greatness, it means that everybody can be great." Even a street sweeper can be great, if he sweeps the streets with "grace"—if in his heart, honestly, he's giving his all. Of greatness, King said, "You must earn it. True greatness comes not by favoritism, but by fitness."

King's existential sense of achievement—his suggestion that belonging is earned through right livelihood—recalls the notion of persistence considered by Camus as the core of hope. It is this sense of achievement—a fitness that flows out of persistence—that is the ground out of which identities spring. This is why I spend so much time describing the inner lives of people. Hybrid identities arise out of an inner sense of accomplishment, and that accomplishment can only be illustrated by an actual life. Of course, not every source of identity arises from accomplishment. A sense of belonging is basic to the well-being of every person. The love of parents, the acceptance by an extended family, the surrender to an ethnic or religious community—these are all basic human experiences. But they are not the boundaries of human experience. Achievement, in King's sense, complements the unconditional acceptance that underpins traditional identities.[19]

This understanding of achievement, I must admit, is not widely shared (nor was it in 1968 when King delivered his sermon as an attack on the pernicious logic of "trying to outdo the Joneses"). Americans are a success-oriented society, where merit poses as master, and sports as a metaphor for life. Achievement means winning. It shouldn't. Games produce winners and losers, not life. In life, people just get to play the game. And even when life delivers a rare, clear-cut result, people often learn more from losing than winning anyway. So what's the point of "winning" when "losing" promotes learning? Few see the scoreboard so metaphorically. In the crass, corrosive calculus of popular achievement, people with low salaries, mean bosses, lousy houses, junky cars and little chance of upward movement are viewed as unlikely candidates for appreciating the virtues of cosmopolitanism, where accomplishment—not inheritance—drives status.

It seems no coincidence, therefore, that in addition to poor blacks, those most threatened by a cosmopolitan America are whites in socioeconomic retreat. They may face stagnating wages, outmoded skills, failed marriages, insecure futures. They are young or middle-aged men, frustrated by some setback, who start shooting people and, often, themselves. Less successful people are nostalgic for identities based on belonging; they wish to define their lives by blood and surrender. Some say this is a human trait—an intrinsic part of the human condition. But why should this be so when, for these people, feelings of belonging seem heightened by feelings of hatred and even paranoia toward another group? This suggests the possibility of a perverse kind of accomplishment: an excellence in showing disregard for others and for proving "I am not one of them."

Those bewildered by hybridity and frightened of falling behind should consider the possibility that the logic of impurity applies even to their circumstances. Hybridity sustains itself when power is shared. National myths must promote the recognition of difference and the potential for diverse people to work together, even if working together only results in their working separately when they wish. This is not a riddle. It is an aspiration. The great task for new cosmopolitans is to build societies where those who wish to withdraw into uniform subcultures are free to do so. I'm not talking about a retreat into walled-off zones, but porous enclaves. People come and go, move from zone to zone, affiliation to affiliation, community to community, maybe so fast and frequently that the walls can be seen only after the fact.

Tolerance can have no free riders. It rewards everyone, but it exacts a price too.

A BLACK HUSTLER BAKES
BREAD...IN MAGDEBURG

MAGDEBURG, GERMANY—One hundred billion dollars a year, and everybody wants a piece. It's a big number that gets the attention of people. Even a guy from Togo, West Africa.

Madison Ouro, the guy, doesn't know that $100 billion is what the government of Germany spends to raise the living standard of its former communist East Germany, absorbed into the West a decade ago. He doesn't know that West Germans are so committed to equality that they flood the East with money in order to lift the wages of Easterners. All Madison knows is that Easterners have plenty of money and so avoid gritty, tedious work, like standing in the market square of this drab city, peddling cheap clothes.

Madison is needed here, to handle the dirty work, and he stays even though Magdeburg is a hothouse for racists and political extremists called "skinheads." Blacks are routinely harassed here. Madison's skin is coal-black and, as if to declare his roots, he wears around his neck, dangling on a leather cord, a polished animal tooth. He doesn't say how he arrived in Germany, only that he fled government repression in Togo, home to Africa's longest-running dictator. Madison won't speak of the circumstances of his departure from Togo, but the very fact that we are conversing in English (and Togo is a French-speaking country) suggests that he is from a privileged background. His elite background may explain how he discovered that East Germany was a land of opportunity. You don't come to Magdeburg on a guess. The city has no night life and even if it had a night life an African couldn't enjoy it because, well, blacks don't walk the streets here after dark. The skinheads don't like that.

I ask Madison about the skinheads and suddenly he grows friendlier. "The Germans don't want us here," he whispers and asks me to return to his shop after closing so that we can speak more freely.

I NEVER MADE IT back to the market. I figured I knew this guy's story anyway. In any big city, in any rich country, you meet guys like Madison. Young sharp hustlers, who somehow managed to reach the Promised Land and now want to stay. They want their piece. And why not? Can any city in a wealthy country prosper without guys like Madison anymore? I don't think so. I know I can't survive without them. I think of my own experience. I renovated a hundred-year-old house in Berkeley, all to building code, all with permits, a complete makeover, from the foundation to the roof. At one time, I had a Mexican drywaller, a German carpenter, a Guatemalan electrician and an English painter, all in the place at the same time. All had originally arrived without work in the country; all stayed because they were needed and they were good. All spoke English (sort of). All made a good living and were either permanent residents or citizens now.

So I know the story. Immigrants staff hospitals, schools, factories. They teach my children; they collect my garbage. I compete with them for jobs, and I sell them my services. And it's the same all over the world. So I know the story.

Only I didn't know Madison's story.

I AM STANDING outside what Germans call an "asylum house." It's where refugees live for their own protection. The one in Magdeburg is hard to find. The first evidence is the barbed wire. I'm walking alongside a tall stone wall, nearly seven feet high, and I see the wire. I grab the top of the wall and lift myself up, so I can see over it. This is the place. There are a half dozen buildings and lots of people milling about.

At the end of the road, there is a parking lot and then an entrance to the compound. Two security officers check all the people coming and going. Around Germany, asylum houses have been set on fire and attacked in other ways, so the government makes a big show of protecting them. They won't allow me in. "You need the government's permission," one says. I won't live long enough to get that, so I walk off, glum. It is about 6 p.m., and people are streaming into the compound, probably coming home for dinner, so I think rather than argue with the police I'll stick around the parking lot and see what happens.

For a while nothing does happen, and then a van pulls into the lot driven by the guy with the animal tooth hanging from his neck. Madison. Our eyes meet. I go over to his car and he rolls down the window. "You had dinner?" I ask. "I'm hungry."

He points to the African guy in the front seat with him. He is also from Togo and has lived in the asylum house for four years. "I need to get something from him," he says. "Wait here, and I'll be back."

Madison returns fifteen minutes later. His friend is afraid to work in Magdeburg or walk outside at night. "I'm scared too," he says, "but I force myself to travel around. I won't stay inside in fear."

We are in his van now, which is owned by his boss, an African (not from Togo) for whom he sells clothes at various markets around Germany. Madison must give the day's sales to his boss and return the van. He's late and afraid of upsetting his boss.

He heads toward the city center and, still near the asylum house, sees two black men walking toward him. They are from Togo and greet him in his local language. Until six months ago, Madison lived in the asylum house himself, so he knows many people there. "I got crazy inside," he says. One day he packed up and left. Nobody stopped him; nobody has tried to bring him back. Still, he feels like a fugitive now. By leaving the house, he has set himself apart from the Togoans, yet he feels no kinship with the Germans. At a traffic light, he pulls alongside a car full of young Easterners. "It isn't funny here," he says. "People are looking sad. Everywhere is sadness."

The conversation stops, and I can hear the engine whirring. Madison makes a sharp turn, and I compliment him on his driving. He says he learned to drive in Togo and recalls the streets and then his mother, whom he misses and calls regularly on the telephone. Then he stops, perhaps thinking he has given away too much. How many people, after all, have phones in Togo?

I ask him about his necklace. "It's for my father's ghost." He tugs at the string and the tooth jumps. The sunlight reflects off its shiny surface. I wait for Madison to tell me how his father died, but he does not.

HE PULLS THE VAN into a parking lot behind a petrol station. This is where he leaves it every night. He locks the doors and goes into the station's convenience store. He hands the keys to a man behind the counter, buys a soda, then uses the phone. I watch him through a glass window. It is past 7 p.m. now and the summer heat is starting to cool. I put on my leather jacket, and I decide that Madison won't have dinner with me. I am sad.

"My boss wants his money," he tells me. "I must go."

"How can I get to the train station?" I ask.

"We can both take this streetcar," he says. The stop is directly across from the station.

We cross the street and wait. A German woman looks at us. She averts her eyes when I look at her. "If I walk ten meters—no, even two meters—they look at me because I am black," he says. "It will take time before this will change. I hope it will."

The tram squeals to a halt before us. We enter from the rear and then stand close to each other. Madison is shorter than me, but thicker and stronger. The hair on his chest is soft and matted, and his face looks worn and grooved. His eyes shine brightly. He seems ageless to me, not twenty years younger than I am.

He notices me staring at him. For a moment, I am conscious of how I am studying him and feel guilty about the gulf between us. It is not just racial. I get to leave Magdeburg at the end of the day. He stays.

"I don't pretend," I say, "to look at you the same way as I look at the Germans, the whites."

My confession relaxes him. Perhaps he senses that I am speaking my mind and that my admission somehow separates me from the quiet people, those who cannot say he makes them uncomfortable.

"I cannot be honest with anyone," he tells me, getting close to my ear because the tram is noisy. "I can't say what's inside of me."

He taps his chest with one hand. He must even keep up this facade with his girlfriend, a pretty German schoolteacher who works nearby. He enjoys her company but holds out little hope that she can understand him. "She tries. I give her that," he says.

I suddenly feel his loneliness, realizing it has been there all along. His easy smile and banter now seem less a sign of assurance than a screen against unwarranted intrusions and a practiced means of satisfying strangers. "People are closed here," he says. "I don't know what happened to them." Communism is only a word to him. He was fourteen when the Berlin Wall fell. He says that his French-educated father was a government official and for a time a minister in Togo's cabinet. By his own standards, he is worldly, but he can't begin to grasp the divisions between Germans.

The tram screeches to a halt. This is my stop. He climbs down from the tram with me. There is a café just ahead and I suggest we have a drink. He agrees, saying he can keep his boss waiting a little longer. We find a table on the sidewalk and order Pilsners. Without prompting, he pulls out his wallet and shows me an identity card. "My given name is Ouro-Babang," he says. "I left Togo after my father was murdered." He doesn't say how and won't when I ask.

Sipping the beer, he says he wants to stay in Germany but worries that he will be forced to leave. He may run out of money or be run out of the country. When I say he can marry a German woman, he looks embarrassed, though he knows this is a way to remain. I look past him for a long time, letting my suggestion die. Finally, I ask him what he would do in Germany if he could do anything. He smiles, big and wide. "I would be a baker," he says. "Bake breads, cakes, pastries."

I am astonished by his dream. The simplicity of his request—set against the obstacles he faces—makes me angry. I ask again about his father. "I will tell you the next time I see you," he says. But not tomorrow, because he must work the market in Chemnitz, another city in the old East. He gives me the phone number and address of his girlfriend, then offers to pay for the beers. I stop him. I fear I will never see him again, and I am angry about that too.

OUTSIDE OF THE city's train station, I see a gang of skinheads. Two of them are fighting near the front entrance. They are adorned with tattoos, clad in leather, looking slightly pathetic and fearsome at the same time. Cheered on by pals, they are hitting each other. One of the fighters takes a punch to the nose and blood runs down his face. This seems to arouse him. I consider speaking to the skinheads, telling them about my encounter with Madison and his dream of baking bread. Would they listen to me explain why his simple ambition is no threat to them and that immigrants to their country give as well as take?

As I watch the two men batter each other, I decide I shall not speak to them today. Instead, I make a wish. I wish that Madison is already a baker and that I can bring these skinheads some steaming bread from his oven. I watch the Germans eat and tell them that the bread comes from the hands of a black man.

Would this enrage or delight them? Would it educate or aggravate them? Suddenly, my optimism deserts me, and I consider my dream a cheap trick. It is not only these men who must eat Madison's bread but many others. What of the two sick Texans who tied a black man to the back of their truck and dragged him to his death? Or of the Hutu priest who encouraged the massacre of his Tutsi neighbors? Or of the depraved teens who tortured and murdered a gay college student in Wyoming? Is there enough bread in the world to sway these frightened and frightening opponents of diversity?

CHAPTER 5

EUROPE AS A MONGREL SPACE

You learn nothing about people as a child in Germany.

—ROLAND BERGER

We are not a country of immigration.

—HELMUT KOHL

Integration shouldn't mean assimilation.

—MEHMET ERBAKAN

*The biggest problem in Germany is not to attract people. The problem is
to get them in. Because the German government doesn't like excellent
people to stay.*

—ERIK MASING

*Germans have bungled everything possible in dealing with migration.
We ended up with no economic benefits, no public support and a drain on
society.*

—BARBARA JOHN

OLEG KOVRIGIN SAW the future. It was 1990. He headed the artificial intelligence division at the Russian Academy of Sciences. Just before the Soviet Union collapsed, he spent three months in Berlin, visiting with computer scientists, engineers and software writers. A German was impressed with his ability to create complex programs. He offered to start a company with him.

Kovrigin wears a bemused look on his face. He can make light of his frustrations. He speaks English with a Russian accent. He prefers short, clipped comments to lengthy declarations. When the German made his offer, Kovrigin had a salary of less than $100 a month. His entire net worth was $300. So in response to the offer, he replied, "My brain, your money."

The German accepted. He then sought a work permit for Kovrigin. German officials, who review permit applications, repeatedly turned him down.

Finally a German scientist vouched for Kovrigin, calling him Russia's best researcher on computer intelligence. Germany issued a permit.

Kovrigin moved to Berlin with his wife and only child. The business went poorly. Kovrigin had never written a commercial program and didn't target potential customers. His German backer had little sales ability and, anyway, had another company that took up his time. Cash dwindled. At one point the venture stopped paying Kovrigin's salary. For eighteen months, he took a construction job, wielding a jackhammer. Since the job was "black," or off the books, he needed no permit.

One day, Kovrigin met another German in a Berlin café. The two got to talking about mathematics and complex systems. On the construction site, Kovrigin didn't have much chance to talk science, so he grew excited. The German, younger than Kovrigin, had a good business idea, a logical way to speed the process of updating old "legacy" programs so that they worked on newer computers. This is probably the biggest technical hurdle facing large corporations around the world. Telephone companies, insurers, banks, brokerage houses, big retailers—all have lots of important data and business systems trapped on perfectly good programs that run on outmoded computers. Sometimes they have to build their own spare parts to keep these old dogs humming. These companies will pay a lot of money to convert programs to faster machines, since the conversions can take years.

The German in the café, a young Berliner named Erik Masing, had a theoretical approach to speeding up conversions. Kovrigin immediately understood it, since the core idea came out of his specialty area. He told Masing, "You have an approach, but can you implement?" Masing said no. Kovrigin said, "I can."

The partnership began, sort of. This was Masing's first business. He had been a consultant in Germany, worked in Eastern Europe and studied in Paris, and he spoke French and English fluently. His father is an ethnic German from Estonia, who came to Germany in 1949. His mother is Austrian. Masing was born in Germany, south of Frankfurt, but feels ethnically mixed. He liked the idea of working with a Russian. He took most of his savings, about $30,000, and formed a company.

Then something upset his plans. Kovrigin's work permit specified that he could work only for his original company. It didn't matter that the company paid him only sporadically and might go out of business at any time. If he switched to another company, even one that he helped to found, the government would force him, his wife and his son to leave Germany within twenty-four hours. Not only that, he would lose three years' credit toward gaining a permanent visa. This was a big loss, because if he worked five years without interruption in Germany, he would gain the right to work there forever.

Masing wanted Kovrigin for his venture and saw a solution, albeit a nutty one. "To get this one man, I will buy his company," he said. The decision was risky, since the moribund company might have hidden liabilities. "It could have a dead body on its balance sheet," Masing said.

It took the better part of a year for Masing to complete the transaction. And even then labor officials in Berlin complained to Masing about his attachment to Kovrigin. It didn't seem to matter that the Russian was a shareholder in the company. One bureaucrat was convinced that somewhere there was an unemployed German programmer who was as good as Kovrigin. Or at least someone, somewhere, in the fourteen other European Union nations whose citizens have rights to work in Germany.

Masing protested. "Let's analyze what you've said," he told the bureaucrat. "There are unemployed software engineers. I cannot believe it. Perhaps they can write software, but better than Oleg, no."

"My problem is that I want him," Masing went on. "I want to buy a product, and you tell me I want a German. I don't want to buy a German. I want the Moscow product. Do I have the right of choosing or not?" He did, but the Arbeitsant, the labor office, told him he should first advertise within Germany for Kovrigin's job. Maybe he could find a better German.

So Masing advertised and interviewed sixty applicants. He rejected them all and kept Kovrigin.

Once the German and the Russian got together full-time, they jelled. Their company, founded in 1994, employs twenty-five people in Berlin, half of them programmers from outside of Germany (mainly Russia). Importing talent is essential but difficult. Masing estimates that at least one-sixth of his software development costs goes toward gathering evidence "to convince people in the Arbeitsant to let these people come here."

Masing's most recent hire is an Indian who earned a master's degree in engineering at a German university, working for the giant German company Siemens as an intern while he studied. Foreign students can work legally but are expected to return home upon graduation. This Indian wanted to stay, and Masing found him through an executive recruiter. The Indian understood German and English and wrote excellent code. The headhunter advised hiring him on a freelance contract, so Masing could skirt the law requiring the Indian to get a work permit. Masing refused. He wanted to treat the Indian as a permanent employee, the equal of a German. He asked the government for a work permit, saying he would employ the Indian while awaiting a ruling.

Months went by. No ruling. The Indian programmer settled into Masing's company. Then one day the government ruled that the Indian had to leave Germany: If only Masing looked harder for a German, he would find one to replace the Indian.

The rejection bothered Masing, but the seeming inconsistency of the ruling bothered him more. "What surprises me is that in a country which applies rules so thoroughly, there aren't any rules in this area," he said. Local labor officials have much discretion over which workers they allow in. The latitude is convenient, since the issue of jobs for immigrants—when official German unemployment exceeds 4 million, or about one in ten of the labor force—is too controversial for the federal government to set a countrywide policy.

Kovrigin wishes the system were different. As the software chief, he must consider how best to pursue customers in the United States and Asia. He needs more programmers, and this is what the government bureaucrats don't grasp. Does he bring Asian and American programmers to Germany, or does he manage them remotely, locating them abroad? Either way, a German doesn't get the job. He gets it only if he's good.

This rankles some Germans, Kovrigin says. Why else do they hold onto their crazy system? he wonders. Although he is thankful to work in Germany, he remains angry that his wife, who speaks six languages, could not legally hold a job in Germany for a long time. The government banned her from Germany until Kovrigin had spent nearly six years on a German payroll. "Perhaps the German government thought it enough that my 'foreign' family had one salary," he sniffs.

The indignities, meanwhile, haven't ceased. When in 1999 his son turned eighteen, Kovrigin received a letter from the German government informing him that the boy would be deported after graduating from high school. The boy could stay in Germany only if he enrolled in a university.

COLD SHOULDER

Kovrigin's tale says much about modern Germany. The country is open to newcomers. It has the highest percentage of foreign-born people of any of the large European countries. Yet for all its immigrants, Germany lacks the hybridity factor, because unlike the United States, which relentlessly woos talented foreigners, Germany does not. "This is a big mistake," Masing says. "These [skilled] people will never sell drugs in the street. They will never go and shoot someone. They are security number one. These people want to think and earn money, and that's what we need."

Masing's views are heretical in Germany, though sensible, as I hope this chapter will convey. Germany is critical for my hybridity thesis. If a country so monocultural has the potential to go hybrid, then all of continental Europe can do so too. To a greater or lesser degree, Germany's neighbors face the same situation in terms of failing to benefit from diversity. To be sure, Holland is better than Germany at integrating poor and low-skilled workers. And Britain is better at attracting and retaining skilled foreigners.

But no country in continental Europe sees diversity as central to national vitality and economic competitiveness. A detailed look at Germany reveals the reasons for this—and the reasons why it is futile for Europe to oppose hybridity.

If one listens only to Germany's elite—from government to unions, charities to social welfare agencies—it seems the issue of diversity has nothing to do with the country's rejuvenation. Germany's chattering classes are obsessed with retooling the welfare state: fiddling with tax rates and benefits, jawboning Germans to become slightly more entrepreneurial, making the system more flexible at the margins. When the topic of immigration comes up, debate centers on how much to help the needy. Germans are experts at doling out their compassion by degrees. To borrow a phrase from the sociologist Birgit Brandt, Germans are caught between "pity and contempt" for immigrants.[2] At best, absorbing newcomers is seen as an act of charity, not an opportunity to reinvent the country.

To outsiders, this attitude seems odd. In the 1990s, the country admitted more refugees, asylum seekers and indigents than the rest of Western Europe combined. In the same period, it also admitted 2.3 million ethnic Germans from the former Soviet bloc, many of whom had only a tenuous connection with German culture and came "home" with few skills or savings. The country also absorbed the 17 million people of the former East Germany. This latest wave of immigration followed an earlier period, from 1955 to 1973, when labor shortages prompted Germany to open its doors to hundreds of thousands of guest workers. These *Gastarbeiter* were supposed to return home, but many didn't. Berlin ended up with a larger population of ethnic Turks than all but four cities in Turkey. Besides Turks, 12 million ethnic Germans—living outside of Germany's borders—returned to the fatherland in the years immediately following World War II. In the second half of the twentieth century, Germany absorbed more newcomers, as a percentage of its population, than any other large country in the world. Twenty million people moved into the space that today contains about 80 million Germans. About one in eleven Germans is now foreign-born, only a slightly lower percentage than in the United States.[3] This is why some Germans laughed whenever Helmut Kohl, best known for reunifying Germany as chancellor, described Germany as "not a country of immigration."

In fact, without immigrants, Germany's population falls precipitously because of the country's ultralow birthrate. Without immigrants, Germany's economy contracts. In the coming decades, the country will face worsening labor shortages. Without immigrants, fewer people will speak German, raising the costs of sustaining the language against the global spread of English. Without immigrants, Germany's generous retirement system buckle because the country won't have enough young workers to pay the freight. Without immigrants, Germany's global influence declines.

So why don't Germans love immigration?

They should. Immigration ought to be what computer people call a "no-brainer." Yet it's such a simple fix, with so many good ripple effects, that it seems like cheating to many Germans. Like the Japanese, whose history resembles theirs, Germans are divided by the idea of newcomers. "For someone to be a German and a non-German seems to offend the German sense of tidiness," notes one writer.[4] Adds Ilka Schroder, at twenty-two the youngest German ever elected to the European Parliament, "If people understood that diversity is good for society, on whatever terms, that would be a paradigm shift. But right now Germany sees diversity as a burden." Sadly, even young people feel this way, Shroder says.

A chilling example of Germany's divided attitude toward newcomers was seen when the new Social Democratic government failed in 1999 to achieve a complete reform of Germany's archaic citizenship laws, which were based on alleged blood ties. Under the system, children of immigrants had no automatic right to citizenship, and naturalization, whereby an immigrant becomes a citizen, was extremely difficult. Reformers wanted to normalize immigration policy, allowing citizens to hold multiple passports and removing other barriers to nonethnic Germans. A huge outpouring of opposition scuttled the landmark program. Instead, citizenship laws were only modestly streamlined.

There are other problems. German industry fails to attract talented people, sending highly educated Germans abroad in far higher numbers than educated foreigners come in. Of the big rich nations, only Japan attracts less foreign investment; Germany receives even less foreign investment than Ireland, a market twenty times smaller.[5] The picture of top German companies seems even bleaker: After decades of investing heavily at home, they now routinely make more than half of their investments abroad. Since people follow money, this further spurs the outflow of talent.

German universities do the same. "So few foreigners come to German universities; that's a tremendous handicap for the country," says Andrei Marko-vitz, a professor of politics at the University of Michigan and an expert on Germany. German universities were the envy of the academic world as late as the 1920s, but they no longer rank among the world's top educational institutions. Outside of Europe, few of the brightest students attend German universities. The country lacks a first-rank business school and lacks a tradition of private education. None of its professional schools draw overseas students at anything like the rate of a Harvard, a Stanford or a London School of Economics. Some of this failure stems from the requirement for study in German, but an ossified academic culture, suffocating on status and cut off from the stimulation of lived experience, consigns universities to mediocrity. Given their problems, German university administrators could be shamelessly wooing foreign students with promises to accept degrees from and courses taken in other countries. Incredibly, they refuse to give credit for any but the most advanced, specialized academic work abroad. They won't offer equivalent degrees either, so a graduate from, say, Yale University can't get his degree accepted from even a second-tier German graduate school. This practice guarantees that all but the most intrepid students will bypass German universities. "I don't see when this will change," Markovitz says. "It's a very entrenched system."

It gets worse. German academic and professional elites don't promote the ideal of diversity and, unlike their counterparts in Britain, the United States and Canada, simply won't lobby for a widening of the talent pool beyond member nations of the European Union. In short, they fear competition from talented foreigners, especially those from the United States and Asia. "The German elite is afraid the Americans will Americanize them if they let them in," says Ghia Nodia, a professor of politics in the country of Georgia who has taught in Germany. This attitude is shared by Germans themselves. "The country doesn't want talented immigrants," says Rainier Munz, the foremost living scholar on migration in Germany. "Immigration is seen as a burden. If we take people, it's for humanitarian reasons, not because we want them." German residency is "an offer to the lower classes," Munz adds, because Germany's highly educated people "want to avoid competition." They like their cozy world the way it is, he says. And by pointedly pushing for lower-class migrants, they keep the moral high ground.

The upper ranks of Germany's corporate society also enjoy their comfortable vanity. Executives at the country's best corporations similarly grow visibly pale at the possibility that they must import foreign talent in order to stay competitive. When asked where their Asians are (on the premise that without the best and brightest Asians, no corporation can succeed internationally), German executives proudly declare, "In Asia." The same attitude extends to workers closer to home. The chief economist at Siemens once told me that the reason for investing so heavily in Eastern Europe was to keep Poles, Ukrainians and Slavs from storming Germany. When asked what he meant, he waited for me to smile knowingly, and when I didn't, he said, "You know, the Poles, the Ukrainians, the Slavs—they will stay put if we provide them with jobs." Few German companies have upper-level foreigners at home. And if they do, they darn well keep it a secret because many Germans have a "zero-sum" view of labor markets. A job taken by a foreigner is one stolen from a German.

Thus, reformers are hampered by three factors. First, as Munz suggests, many Germans see immigration as an act of charity, a freebie for poor people from Eastern Europe, Africa and Asia. Under this tortured reasoning, they prefer disadvantaged people from poor countries, rather than educated ones, because the latter—it's assumed—can cope back home. And they recoil at the "immorality" of creaming the best researchers, engineers and executives from a poor country, unaware that "brain circulation" has replaced "brain drain" as the model of skilled migration and that, rather than stagnate at home, many of these folks will join and strengthen competing economies. Unlike Canada, which sets immigration targets based largely on potential economic benefit, Germany does the opposite, maximizing its economic burden by chiefly accepting those less prepared to live there.

The failure of German intellectuals presents a second problem. No leading social thinker in Germany grasps the implications of fluid identities for German social cohesion. No one seems to realize that there can be varieties, or types, of assimilation. The shared assumption is that either immigrants "integrate" (the preferred term in Germany for assimilation) or remain locked in a diasporic state, awaiting return to their homeland. If immigrants can't integrate, it is because of "racism," or their unwillingness to Germanize sufficiently. It is taken for granted that people must integrate or pose a threat to Germany's survival. The poverty of social thought in Germany limits policy options and even distorts the reactions of ordinary people. Most Germans can't conceive of the kind of dual consciousness possessed by hybrids. Having created a false dichotomy between integration and balkanization, social thinkers fear immigration even as, in some cases, they promote it.

The third problem (following logically from the second) is the failure to redefine Germanness. If immigrants can't act like real Germans, yet they are essential, then by implication Germans must reconstruct their identities. This is a pressing matter; the need for change should not be an affront to German sensibilities. Former citizens of East Germany rightly seek a new definition of "Germanness" so that they are not simply colonized culturally by West Germans. Easterners represent a significant reason for Germans to give a new answer to the question of what it is to be German. Even with the new watered-down citizenship law, German identity is no longer explicitly a matter of blood lineage. Yet what is it? The positive answer is relevant not only to Easterners but to the whole world as well. Few Germans link the difficulty in absorbing the East with the inability to woo talent from the rest of the world. To see this link means to admit that Germanness is, if not a fiction, an identity in need of retooling. Germanness is cultural clay, not stone. But German habits of mind are fixed. Germans heap scorn on their rigid (Nazi?) side and romanticize their sensitive (Goethe?) side, while smugly congratulating themselves for their competency and discipline. This swing between the yin and yang of Germanness blocks any review of how Germany's national myths and founding narratives can be revised. And not just revised in order to nurture a multicultural Germany but a mongrel Germany. Such a revision would stand German history on its head, and to good effect.

Amid the wreckage of missed opportunities and absurdities in Germany's diversity policies and practices, one person stands out like a beacon of good sense. Barbara John is Berlin's *Auslanderbeautagte*, or chief advocate for foreigners in a city with more of them than any other place in Germany. She is a stately, gracious survivor of German politics. A centrist, she was appointed to her post in the early 1980s and is admired by both the Left and the Right for her principled and effective promotion of tolerance, multiculturalism and social harmony. Through her office's educational and media campaigns, she nudges the debate over foreigners toward a realization that immigration benefits both immigrant and native German. One stunning poster from her office, entitled "We are Berlin," shows the faces of twenty-five Berliners surrounding the phrase "We are light and dark." The array of faces is staggering, including various mixed-race children and adults, Eastern Europeans, Asians and a dark-skinned man with dreadlocks. Only one person's hair is blond, and that hair seems to have been dyed. Another arresting poster, "Was ist deutsch?" lists scores of contrasting aspects of German life, presented as brief questions. Conveying the paradoxes of a diverse Germany that remains in denial, the answer "Lothar Matthaus?" (Germany's most famous footballer) is followed by "Anthony Yeboah? Roy Black? Roberto Blanco?"—three Berliners with decidedly non-German names.

John, a fiftyish woman with deep-set, penetrating eyes, wears a grave expression. She carries the weariness of a committed public servant. Even after nearly two decades of multicultural campaigning, she questions the readiness of her country to move from showing grudging tolerance of foreigners to viewing them as a cornerstone of a German revival. But if such a shift ever occurs, she believes Berlin will be at the center of it. "Berlin is an anomaly, a workplace for multiculturalism and integration," she says. "Germany is composed of smaller cities, and Berlin is the only really large one. Even though the same conditions don't apply everywhere, Berlin can act as a model for Germany. The city has always had a big influx from the outside. It is used to absorbing people. To host foreigners first and then make them feel at home."

Creating this capacity for welcoming others is the challenge for the whole of Germany. "We are not an immigration country," John says, sarcastically. "That is still in German minds and laws. We never intended to become more diverse. We didn't want to create diversity, and in the face of the fact of diversity there is a sense that it shouldn't have happened."

Her face crumples for a moment as if this is the saddest thing she can say about her people. "What we most need is the positive attitude to the diversity we already have," she says, then adds quickly: "And then to enjoy it." Those who want to know who is to blame for the presence of so many foreigners "are looking for the negative," she says. "People must push themselves to see the positive."

I ask John if German leaders, especially from business and labor, realize the damage done to the country's economic competitiveness by Germany's failure to attract and retain talented foreigners. Do they understand the logic of drawing on talent from the whole world, in an era when quality of ideas trumps quantity of production? Immigration provides the United States an inexpensive, relatively controlled means of increasing the skills and the youth of its labor force. Lucky for America, I say, that Germany and Japan, its foremost economic competitors, remain trapped in traditions hostile to immigration.

John shakes her head. No large company in Germany imports talent, she says. Upstarts like Masing, maybe, but not the country's industrial titans. "Germany wouldn't allow a big company to bring in a smart guy from Korea. It's not possible. You can't do it." She's bewildered by this. "We don't have a program for this. Our laws inhibit it. Yet America, even Ireland, is far ahead because they just do it. We don't even talk about it. I don't understand it. It's a damage to the economy, and it's a damage to the migrants we already have."

For John, the reluctance to tap talented immigrants exposes Germany's pathologies and the still onerous burden of its history. "We are so unselfish," she says, sneering now. "Altruistic! We only want the very poor. Fine. Very good. Take them. But you must balance them. You must bring in talented, skilled people, people who can help others."

By admitting only the poor and less skilled, Germany actually undercuts support for the very people its political establishment claims to want to help. Migrants get stigmatized. If their ranks were leavened by college graduates from around the world, the instinct to label them as the dregs of society would be checked. "It makes diversity look like a cost you must bear for years and years," she says. "You should see the diversity at the top too. You should see immigration on the winning side."

Perversely, Germany routinely pays for the education of some bright foreign students, then relentlessly sends them home when they graduate. If Germans realized the potential economic gains of immigration, they might also understand that newcomers to the country must have the freedom to retain their own ways of doing things. Openness without diversity is no help. "Nobody has a duty to integrate," John says. "Once you are here, integration can't be enforced."

Many Germans, of course, want to enforce it, tolerating immigrants only so long as they act, speak and think like the ideal German. Foreigners can have pride in their own culture, learn their own traditions, but in the public sphere they must display their German side, which notably includes speaking German well. If immigrants behave in this manner, and Germany somehow halts further immigration, then perhaps the monoculture can be saved. John thinks it is too late for that. "Diversity is a self-perpetuating system," she says. "Even if you don't like it or didn't intend it, diversity still goes on. People are no longer just immigrants. They are no longer leaving everything behind as they have in the past. They keep in touch. Because it gives them more options. They will be the first generation who can move in more than one country quite easily."

These new cosmopolitans are increasingly visible in Germany but represent "only one track," John explains. They are opposed by a powerful "second track, the national political track, which says everyone must integrate." She adds, defiantly: "The politicians say that transnationality is a threat to Germany. They are wrong."

There are signs, however, that Germany's rigid politicians are starting to see the light. After taking a beating from the media and high-tech entrepreneurs over Germany's failure to attract foreign talent, Chancellor Gerhard Schroeder pledged to waive restrictions on importing software programmers and electrical engineers in the hopes of bringing into Germany some tens of thousands of computer professionals, mainly from China and India. While a pale imitation of programs run by the United States and Canada, Germany's response seemed surprisingly daring to its own citizens. Conservatives blasted the plan, labeling it as unfair to German workers but also to those developing countries whose talent was being filched. But nativist anxieties were clear. One opposition politician even provocatively called for *Kinder statt Inder*: more (German) children instead of Indians. This reference to Germany's ultralow birthrate, which is viewed as the reason why foreign talent is needed, profoundly misses the point that Germany would benefit from ethnoracial mixing even if German couples were having larger families. Reform-minded Germans grasp this instinctively, however. Citing reports that German industry may lack some 300,000 specialists over the coming decade, reformers complained that the proposed opening up of Germany to skilled foreigners was still a matter of too little, too late, and that it would take more forceful measures to redress many years of ignoring Germany's failure to attract highly educated people from other countries. There was even a concern that many reformers who favored importing more talent still held out the hope that somehow these foreigners could be sent back home once the labor crisis passed. Notwithstanding the claim by the German government that it doesn't wish to invite outsiders on a temporary basis—like the *Gastarbeiter* (guest workers) of the 1960s—many Germans will be tempted to think of these foreigners as just that: a stopgap until German universities produce enough experts in high-demand fields. Yet attitudes are changing: The very act of trying harder to attract the world's best professionals to Germany will carry many lessons. Perhaps the most important will be that Germans will begin to see more clearly than ever how far their business and social practices must be altered before superstars from Asia and North America flock to Germany.

NEW GERMANS

In spite of Germany's polices, hybrids are on the march. It is as John says. Diversity sustains itself. Rolls on like a river. Germans are riding this river. They are giving lie to the country's reputation for inflexibility. Secure in their native identities, they are hybridizing in various ways. One in four Berliners, for instance, is marrying outside of his or her ethnic group. Besides intermarriage, many Germans are working abroad, returning home with new attachments and perspectives. It is harder, of course, for auslanders to brave Germany. Some newcomers—white Americans and northern Europeans—slip easily into the society, even gaining recognition for their differences. But talented people of color—blacks and Asians notably but also Turks and Arabs—face greater barriers. They need an indomitable will to make it in Germany. But some are making it, and changing German attitudes as they do.

MEET CORBETT SANTANA, owner of the Black Bar in Kreuzberg, the funkiest, most ethnically mixed part of the old West Berlin. Born in Brooklyn, he came to Germany a decade ago from Manhattan to work as a video editor and stayed. He's forty-four years old and speaks enough German to get by. He's tall, thin and when he talks, he moves around a lot. Three years ago, he opened his bar. In Berlin, bars can stay open all night, which is fine with Santana, who's a night person.

"The Wall coming down, that attracted me," he says. He never expected to stay in Germany. Most American blacks in Germany served in the U.S. military, which still has a large presence in the country. For a black with a college degree like Santana, who was working in Manhattan in 1991, moving to Germany seemed strange given its history. London, Paris, maybe. But Berlin, Hitler's headquarters and nerve center of the infamous Third Reich?

Santana liked the city immediately and decided to settle there. He admits that part of the appeal came from what he calls "the exotic factor." Berliners have "a fascination with newcomers," he says. "Like, wow, there's a black guy, or an Arab." Corbett liked being seen as a novelty, even though he realized that some of this flowed from the stain on Germany's soul. In the 1960s, German youth rebelled against their parents and Germany's postwar dependence on the United States. They rejected, one scholar notes, "any notion of national identity, incorporated into a nation-state they saw as inheriting the guilt and responsibility of the Third Reich." They sought what they considered "authentic cultures," viewing American blacks, indigenous people and other "primitives" as desirably different. By exalting the foreign as exotic, "as that which can only be experienced elsewhere," German youth celebrated Otherness, as if finding in the non-German a freedom from moral impurity "worthy of admiration."

Germans still exoticize the Other, but they've grown more adept at doing so. Blacks aren't lumped together but rather distinguished by their place of origin: the United States, Africa, the Caribbean. The same goes for Asians. Germans don't expect a Korean who came here as a guest worker in the 1970s to share much with a Vietnamese communist who came via East Germany. That he isn't pigeonholed gives Santana more freedom to define himself, which is useful because he embodies impurity: His mother, a nurse born in Pennsylvania, has both black and Hispanic ancestors, and her Spanish side comes by way of Puerto Rico, itself a mélange. His father is also a racial mix.

"Look at me," Santana says. He is dressed in all black: turtleneck, pants and shoes—and the dark color of his clothes stands in contrast to his tawny skin. "Obviously, I'm not black. My clothes are black, but my skin is brown if you want to be exact. So I'm brown, but in America I'm black."

Growing up in New York, Santana was drawn toward both Latino and African-American styles, but felt forced choose one over the other. He faced the added pressure of having a mother who wanted him to sound white. "I'd imitate white people on television," he says, recalling a special attraction he had for the news anchor David Brinkley, a 1960s media icon. "Speak like a white man," his mother told him. And he did, but with people of color he rapped, rolling easily into what he calls "ghetto talk." After years in Europe, though, he has added a new dimension to his chameleon quality. After some years in Berlin, he visited New York and one day at Coney Island, as he was standing in a line at Nathan's, near the beach, and placing an order for fried clams, a black guy listened to him and exclaimed, "You're not from around here, are you?" That's when Santana realized he had become a Berliner, sort of.

In Berlin, he faces no pressure to pick sides. He's a one-off character, a relaxed impresario running a kind of Rick's Café for jazz, latin and blues musicians and their fans. Santana plays the Bogart part, welcoming the strange brew that assembles here nightly. Though he cultivates other acts, he sometimes takes the mike himself, backed by a pianist. Santana is a spoken-word artist in the style of Gil Scott-Heron, the jazz singer and godfather of rap. He can sing straight blues or jazz, but prefers songs that suit the cadences of his poems. While his subject matter is freewheeling, he writes most movingly about the plight of Turks, Germany's largest minority:

The Underdog, The Worker
Good Cheap Labor
I Don't Want To Do A Job Like That, The Germans Say
You Know, They Built This City Up Again
To Its Former Splendor And Glory
And What Do They Get In Return?
A Second-Class Citizenship Is Their Glory
The Problem Is The Same
In All Of Our Souls
So Turn To One Another And Say
Turks Look Like Puerto Ricans, Anyway

Santana's sympathy for Turks seems genuine. He feels as if he's walked in their shoes. There are relatively few American blacks in Germany, so unlike in the United States, he's not part of the main minority, the chief threat to a white society's alleged purity. The Turks play that role. About 2.5 million people of Turkish descent live in Germany, with Berlin having the largest share of them. "The Turks are in limbo land, culturewise," Santana says. More so than he, the Turks experience "the streak of racism that runs through this whole society. You know how in the U.S. when something goes wrong, it's 'blame it on the black people.' Well, here the Turks get blamed."

One night the club has no scheduled act, but about midnight some of Santana's friends drift by and the music starts. A black Army veteran, who stayed on after discharge and now works construction, sings gospel-drenched blues. After a half dozen songs, the place is packed: a rapt crowd of Germans, blacks and amazed visitors. On his break, downing a beer, the Army vet says in a southern drawl, "I'm no German, no Berliner," as if anyone wondered. A new singer now has the microphone, and he's doing smoother pop tunes, his dreadlocks swaying as he dances. He's a tailor and costume designer from Los Angeles who came to Berlin six months ago on a hunch. No job, no contacts, he just had a feeling. This sounds like a recipe for disaster, but then a smile appears through the forest of his dreadlocks. "I've gotten more love here than anywhere else in the world," he declares. And he doesn't mean only the romantic kind. He works for a German company, designing clothes for a boutique. "Ideas are hot here," he says. "I get shit done."

He sings on the side, though with more feeling than flair. When he takes a breather, a new singer comes on. He's Irish, plays the piano and does the kind of barroom ballads sung by Tom Waits. It's 2 a.m. and Santana's favorite pianist shows up, a white German who can apparently command the keys. Santana is now ready to run through a few of his own protest songs, backed by the German, but the Irishman won't quit. It's as if he doesn't know this is the Black Bar. After four songs, some of Santana's pals nudge him, but he barks, "Let the white guy sing." It's still early, and his turn will come. After all, he owns the place.

IF SANTANA IS hypersocial, surrounded by musicians and drinkers and lovers of the exotic, Sook-hee Kwak is isolated, unable to connect with Germans. Kwak is from Korea and is a thirty-six-year-old sociology doctoral student at a university in southwest Germany. She is serious, forceful, polite and an excellent student. In Korea, she learned German, gained a passion for the country's literature and, after some years working as a teacher, won a scholarship to study for her doctorate in Germany. She speaks German fluently and loves the language.

Kwak is single and the first person in her family to live outside of Korea. She knew no Germans on arrival. Her graduate adviser was open and supportive, but German professors have a deserved reputation for detachment, and even the friendliest won't easily pal around with even a graduate student. Gradually, she got to know other students, but only casually. This did not bother her, though, because the intensity of Korean social life—the stress on family obligations and proscribed roles—had worn thin. "I was exhausted in Korea from always having something to do with other people," she says. So at first, distance from people appealed to her.

Her single-mindedness paid off in her studies. She mastered the rigorous German examinations and held fast to a well-ordered curriculum that overwhelmed some foreign graduate students. But she realized, "I have just studied without life. I have to live."

She tried. Few Asians lived in her small university town, and almost no other Koreans. She was certainly exotic. If not glamorous, she was attractive and spoke bluntly, a quality many Germans admire. As she spent more time with Germans, though, she found them cold. She would spend time with a person, man or woman, and then "hit a wall. This wall was always there, and I couldn't get over it."

At the university, she began noticing that people said good morning to her, but nothing more. She went to the office for foreign students, but the staff helps only with university procedures and housing, not social and psychological issues. She did, of course, have Asian friends, the few at the university, and she saw them often. But she had come to Germany to meet Germans, and it bothered her that if she needed something, only Asians would help her. Never a German.

To be sure, some of Kwak's disappointments centered on her unmet romantic aspirations. She wanted a lasting relationship with a German man.

She'd had brushes with success: dated two for a few months each, only to have the affair run down. Although she never put romance before her studies, part of her reason for coming to Germany was to form an intimate relationship. She found Korean men boring. "Perhaps a relationship with a German will be more interesting because of the diversity," she thought.

She also expected German men to take her more seriously as a person and thinker. She resented that Korean men pigeonholed her. Why should an educated woman accept that? She expected German men to admire her mind and her fortitude, not see her only as a woman. At least so far, she found German men no better than her homeboys. "German men think that Asian women are very obedient and very domestic," she says. "To a certain extent that's true— and maybe in comparison to some German women. However, the Japanese and Korean women who come here are actually the most independent women in their countries. That's why the German man's expectations of me aren't met. I start from a different place than they want, and they start from someplace different than I expect."

Kwak's admission is difficult for her. She doesn't wish to seem obsessed with romance, when she's actually obsessed with finishing her dissertation on feminism in Asia. Writing (in the German language) consumes her days. When she finishes her book-length study, she will celebrate by leaving Germany. She's not sure where she will go, perhaps to the United States. "Even if given the chance to stay in Germany, I would not stay," she says. "Germans are honest, so I can work with them, but that is not enough. Personal relations are why I can't stay here."

One night, Kwak shares Chinese food with one of her Asian friends, a younger female graduate student who has a German boyfriend and a feistier attitude toward taming the German academy. Talk turns to life after Germany. The friend, the child of Chinese immigrants to Canada, tries to predict where Kwak will end up. The United States? Canada? Back to Korea? She teases that Kwak might like Canadian men, even the Chinese ones. They sip tea and eat eggrolls. Kwak's mood lightens and she spoons some kung pao chicken onto her rice. Her friend tells her not to look at her experience in Germany as a failure, reminding her that she isn't alone. "After eighteen months here, I start to get ill myself, psychologically, mentally," the friend says. "I get exhausted. I feel like if I don't recharge, I'll never be healthy again."

"And you're so damn positive," Kwak says, smiling.

"What else can you do?" her friend protests. "But the Germanness still gets you down." She sighs and lifts some food with her chopsticks. "Its like a heavy blanket hanging over you. Maybe it's protecting you, but it's hard to shake off. The only way to get the strength to carry the blanket is to leave."

Kwak agrees, and for an instant the women look at each other and shiver. Is it possible that they'll carry this blanket for the rest of lives?

KWAK'S TALE highlights a challenge for Barbara John and other advocates of hybridity. Germans can open their doors to talented foreigners, but people must step through them and then stay the course. This requires immense determination. Ibrahim Aslan is one of the diehards.

Aslan came to Germany in 1975, at the age of twenty-one. Born in Turkey, he came as a student and stayed. In 1982, he formed a company that is today Berlin's biggest Turkish-owned printer. The business grew by meeting German prejudices head-on. Aslan set out to specialize in printing the German language, with all its odd accents and squiggles. His ambition must be set against the reality that most Turkish businesses serve Turkish clients. Today, nine of ten of Aslan's clients are German. His German speech is indistinguishable from that of a native.

Aslan is a slim, small, proud man. He wears a suit and keeps a trim mustache. He speaks quietly, so that even with no presses running (it is after hours) my translator must urge him to talk louder. His plant employs twenty-five people and has the latest in computerized typesetting equipment. He mainly prints books and commercial papers. He clearly wants acceptance from Germans, though he realizes this comes only slowly. When he first started the business, German competitors laughed at him, then thought they could pry loose his customers. They couldn't. Aslan based his business on quality, tolerating zero defects in his print runs. He initially combined his perfectionism with prices that were slightly below those of his German rivals. As years went by he charged higher prices than some German printers because customers rewarded him for his habit of meeting deadlines, quality and knack for solving problems. He even landed Berlin's Technical University as a client, a boon because of its massive print needs.

Aslan took pains not to run a Turkish shop: All but one of his printers were German because he felt the Germans were more qualified than Turks. This was partly because Turks were underrepresented among printing apprentices and the craft generally, but mainly because few knew the German language well enough to meet his exacting standards. "They must know German perfectly," he says. Only third-generation Turks usually know German well enough to suit Aslan. Though he expects the ranks of these Turks to grow, he insists he has no special obligation to hire them. "I take the best people," he said. "My clients know that."

In another place, Aslan might be lulled into thinking Germans were accepting him as one of them. In another place, he might be called an "Uncle Tom"—Turkish on the outside, German on the inside. But Germans remind him all too often of who he is and is not. For five years, he had a running battle with a few of his printers who, he's convinced, resented having a Turk for a boss. He is a quiet man, and the irony of his worker rebellion is still lost on him. In the fifth and final year of the fight, the renegades openly campaigned against him. "It came to the point that we were nearly enemies," he says. Nearly?

Aslan's experience again made me wonder whether Aslan felt inferior to Germans and so cannot bring himself to challenge them. He answered by saying that he finally forced the ringleader off his payroll. Relations with his printers have improved. Now they at least show respect to his face, though he still presumes that privately "they do not respect me."

This bothers Aslan, though not as much as it would some others. He seeks hybridity, not assimilation, so that a part of him is German now and there's a part of him that the Germans can't touch. "We should keep our culture," he says of the Turks. "But we shouldn't be a ghetto. We are obliged to learn the ways of the country in which we live. It would be stupid not to. But Berlin is a *multikulti* city and we must keep it that way."

Perhaps because of his success, he shows more generosity toward Germans than, say, an educated immigrant to the United States would show to American citizens. In time, Aslan will learn whether his respect (bordering on meekness) is met by an open hand or a closed fist. For now he says "it may take generations for Germans to accept someone like me as an equal."

When I say that "generations" sounds like a long time, he looks right through me as if the people in whatever land I come from must be morons. "After ten years," he tells me, his voice now rising for the first time, "the East Germans still have problems. Of course foreigners will have them too."

LESS IS MORE

Aslan gets me thinking because, it is true, an ordinary East German is, in many ways, more of an alien than an educated, cultivated Turk like himself—and this is precisely the most troubling paradox of contemporary Germany. Some of those whose Germanness is unquestioned act less German than those labeled aliens. With the notable exception of Barbara John, the West German elite doesn't think about diversity in sensible ways, and so accommodating the diversity of East Germany is more difficult than it should be. Ten years after unification, the East remains a region upon which West German culture and expertise must be imposed. "Easterners . . . still resent the way that the West has simply taken over the East as a kind of colony, imposing its own systems and standards, without much regard for local feelings," notes one observer. Money does not seem to paper over these differences. Despite the transfer of nearly one trillion dollars to the East (or about $53,000 per citizen), the gulf between the two regions is large. One survey found that only 38 percent of the Easterners like living in a democracy, and one in seven prefer a return to a separate communist state.[6]

In the celebratory atmosphere after Kohl pulled off his lightning reunification in 1990, few anticipated the economic, social and cultural problems
that lay ahead. By the mid-1990s, the dream of a monolithic Germany had
given way to the grudging acceptance that a mental "wall" now divided the
country. Official unemployment in the East is about double the West's rate,
and one respected estimate pegs the actual number of jobless Easterners at 30
percent, if those in training classes and heavily subsidized private jobs are
combined with the jobless. The situation inspires growing cynicism and the
realization that Germany may have wandered into a situation somewhat like
what the United States faced after the Civil War: The North tried to reinte-
grate the South into the union but essentially gave up within a decade, leaving the South to follow a separate and quite different path of development.
From the 1880s to the 1950s, the South was an island of backwardness
within a surging United States, made all the more isolated by the local practice of racial segregation.[7]

The parallel is increasingly realistic. Demands by Easterners for recognition of their distinct culture grow more shrill: Old products from the German
Democratic Republic (GDR) days, left for dead in the flush of unification,
have returned. Economic vitality is far greater than in communist times but
still lags. Industrial productivity (output per person-hour) is only about two-
thirds that of the West. The gap is closing so slowly that Robert Barros, a distinguished economist, estimated that the East won't reach the West's
standard for perhaps fifty years. The Organization for Economic Cooperation
and Development, the club of rich nations, made the same point more
politely, concluding, "The catch-up process in eastern Germany is proving
painful and slow." Even West Germans are coming to accept that an economic divide has replaced a political one. One poll of 800 business executives, by Germany's leading financial newspaper, found that two-thirds
expect it will take more than ten years for the East to gain economic parity
with the West.[8]

Even this dour forecast seems optimistic. The old GDR was a Soviet puppet
whose planned economy badly trailed the West and imploded as soon as the
Soviets loosened their grip. But many Easterners still believe in the ideal of
socialism and insist that the GDR failed only because it was a bad version of
socialism. This outlook explains the striking electoral success of the former
communist party in the East. Many of the party's supporters seethe with rage
that Eastern distinctiveness isn't recognized in a unified Germany. The bad
joke is that the West, after studying all of the East's practices, adopted only its
rule of turning right on a red light. In short, Easterners feel shut out even as
they've been let in. They feel erased, denied their minority culture. This is sad-
dening. Ursula Gerlach, a Russian translator in the old GDR, says of herself and
old comrades: "We are deeply hurt over being excluded from [the new Ger-

many]. Despite our views, we were all ready to give our best. They didn't—and don't—let us."

Gerlach is a passionate, articulate woman whose feelings are so strong that she cannot speak very long about the past without breaking into tears. She now works as a secretary at a leading German research institute in Berlin; her husband, a former member of the Communist Party, doesn't work at all. A smart and blunt woman, she realizes that the difficulty with incorporating Easterners into a unified Germany is only one aspect of the larger problem: Germans have difficulty recognizing that immigrants wish to retain distinctive attitudes and habits—not as a rebuke to Germans or as a signal that they wish to retreat into ghettos, but in order to more freely acquire German traits. The premise of German immigration policy is that an ethnic German born outside of Germany—a blood-tie German—shares something basic with the old West Germans. Gerlach believes this isn't the case and that it will be as hard for many Easterners to forge a dual, or hyphenated, identity in Germany as it would be for Madison Ouro or Ibrahim Aslan.

Her idea is intriguing, but the logic of it isn't immediately obvious. Gerlach begins with the premise that unification was neither necessary nor desirable. "We could have had two states in parallel for a time," she says. "We could have had it." And while the notion of two Germanies after the fall of the Wall struck many as absurd, people have now accepted that there exist two Germanies of the mind—so divergent are the paths of East and West. This was not planned, just as Germany was not supposed to become an immigration country. But it happened. No one can deny that. The further irony, of course, is that the greatest hostility in Germany to foreigners, especially nonwhites, appears in the East: Easterners show spite (and, at times, act violently) toward the very people with whom they share the most in today's Germany. This situation is more than sad, and is perhaps the latest (if not the last) of the curses visited upon the German nation for its aggression during World War II. That the unification of Germany becomes another cross for Germans to bear is predictable. The best chance for a resolution is less so. The surest escape from the double alienation that many Germans feel toward the strangers around them is to redefine what it means to be German.

BUT HOW? Wolfgang Meckel has one answer. He and his wife Sigrun Marcks, schoolteachers in Berlin, had one child and decided that was enough. But when their daughter Natasha was five, they adopted a boy from Peru. Then they adopted a child from Brazil, then another and finally two more. The last two were orphaned sisters living on the streets of São Paulo—rescued by a Brazilian social worker. For nearly a year, a local judge delayed and delayed completing the adoption. Then one day the social worker called to tell Meckel that one of the girls had fallen ill and might die. He flew to Brazil and won permission, finally, from the court to take the sisters. He arrived in Germany with a very sick child and her frightened sister. Both survived.

Meckel and Marcks are part of a generation born in the years of deprivation after the end of World War II. Coming of age in the 1960s, Meckel and Marcks held out one goal for themselves: "to be better." They became schoolteachers and created a remarkable family. Their diversity is captured in family photos: two brown-skinned children, three darker-skinned children and blond nineteen-year-old Natasha, the light-skinned child who plays big sister to this brood. One evening, mother and father relax in their spacious living room, the top-floor apartment of a building once used to house officers in Kaiser Wilhelm's army. Casually dressed and wearing Birkenstocks, Marcks serves chamomile tea. She and her husband talk openly of their adopted children. The three oldest sit nearby, listening intently. Benjamin, eighteen, is about to finish secondary school and spend a year in national service, a requirement for all German youth. Joshua, fifteen, is tall, talkative and a big basketball fan: His bedroom is filled with posters of professional players, all American. Rebekka, fourteen, has large brown eyes, an Afro hairdo and a passion for gospel singing. (The two youngest girls are asleep, and Natasha is in Brazil, working in a poverty program before attending the university.)

The children are strikingly different, though share a devotion to their family and a sense of gratitude for being welcomed into their corner of Germany. Benjamin feels the most German. He resists discussing his feelings, talking uneasily about his skin color and the still-thorny reality of racial prejudice in Germany. "Skin color doesn't matter," he says bravely. "People accept me as I am."

Benjamin sees no special need to befriend non-Germans. Joshua, on the other hand, says it is important for him to hang out with a diverse crowd of nonwhites and immigrants. "When I see other colored people on the street, we greet each other warmly," he says. "They make a good impression on me." His best friend is from Rwanda. He attributes his greater race-consciousness to the fact that he came to Berlin as a boy (not as a newborn, like Benjamin). "I had no friends, and I had to learn the language," he says. Rebekka, meanwhile, has something of her father's flair for philosophical pronouncements. She has an infectious smile and a warmth that immediately puts visitors at ease. Many Germans are frightened by her multicultural family, she admits. "They long for the kind of family we've achieved, this kind of brother- and sisterhood," she says. "But they wouldn't dare try this themselves. They don't have enough trust in themselves."

Meckel and Marcks are proud of their children. "They are German, but of course they have their roots," Marcks says. "It's a big richness. They are Germans but more than Germans. They have their heritage and they bring it to German society." How to strike a balance between their children's need to adapt to Germany and their desire to affirm their differences is a constant challenge. For the two girls from the São Paulo streets, this tension remains a pressing issue even after three years in Germany. Although the other kids are more settled, none have completed their basic schooling, so questions remain about their experience in Germany. Building a mixed-race family puts strains on the parents too. Meckel and Marcks are asked again and again by critical Germans, "How can you do this to nonwhite children, bring them into our monoculture?"

They are firm in their answer. "If we did not adopt them, then the segregationists would have won," Meckel says. He expects his children—all of them—to be accepted in Germany. "I demand it. They are Germans, fully German," he says but concedes, "Without our principles, our passion, we could not do this." Indeed, both he and Marcks advise parents considering international adoptions. They tell them about the disappointments and frustrations as well as the joys. For many couples, adopting nonwhite children is too much to tackle, they admit.

But for Meckel and Marcks, this is their mission. They envision a mongrel Germany, a Germany as mixed as the whole world. "We're a small laboratory," Meckel says. In this Germany, the native lies down with the alien, the self and the Other commune. Their cosmopolitan vision might seem like empty cocktail-party chatter were they not so obviously doing what parents always do, which is to give, give, give to their children.

"We're all one big family, that's my credo," Meckel says. He means this to serve as Germany's credo too. Halfway measures have no place in his thinking. There is no such thing as a "little" diverse. In his mind, diversity is all or nothing. To those who say radical mixing can work in the United States but not in Germany, Meckel replies, "The segregationists will not win. They will never win."

When the conversation fades, Rebekka and her mother show me their collection of gospel recordings. They put on a tape, and we listen for a bit. It is late, though, and Rebekka must attend school the next day, so it is time for goodnight. Marcks embraces her daughter, holding her close. With the sounds of a joyous choir in the air, Rebekka smiles, her eyes bright and face radiant.

MANY PEOPLE COULD not muster the passion and intensity of Wolfgang Meckel and Sigrun Marcks. But there are cooler, more pragmatic routes to a mongrel Germany. Lothar Lange travels one. He manages clinical trials for the pharmaceutical company Schering, a venerable German firm. Tests of new drugs are handled in labs in Germany, Japan and the United States. For decades, the staffs of these labs largely kept to themselves, or shuttled back and forth to the German office. But as competitors pushed the pace of their innovation, Schering fell behind. When Lange got his job four years ago, he decided to gradually bring more foreigners to Germany, where by tradition the major decisions were made on which drugs to develop fastest and how.

Of ten managers, six are German and four are not. Of the latter, two are American, one is Canadian and the other is British of South Asian descent. Lange thinks the diversity brings better, quicker decisions and more perspective over the long run. But most of his German project managers still aren't happy with his decision to diversify. They find the outsiders too pushy, too eager to promote themselves and their projects. Part of the frustration is understandable. Lange requires all documents and presentations to be made in English. This obviously gives native English speakers an advantage, and rankles German colleagues. As one pointedly told me, "We can't make ourselves understood in your language."

Lange's rejoinder is to present well in English himself. He says it's possible for other Germans to do so, if they apply themselves. Besides, choice of a working language isn't a matter of taste. Pharmaceutical research now is conducted in English the world over.

There are differences of style, however. In presentations, "Germans don't perform as well," Lange says, noting that the Americans and British "put more salesmanship into their pitches." To Germans, this seems like faking, and Lange finds his German managers grumbling about how superficial their foreign colleagues are.

Lange does not indulge these complaints. "What I always tell them is use the example, do it yourself," he says. This is how he wants his German managers to behave, with more flair, gusto and the relentless optimism that Americans bring to their jobs and that seems, well, so un-German. "But this is something that's difficult for them and they don't want it," Lange says. "And it creates a lot of problems."

Day by day, so gradually that few notice, the style shifts. Lange tries to avoid pushing too hard, but his intentions are clear. He wants the Germans to expand their portfolio of traits. They also must squarely accept diversity, not just tolerate others, but accept them—weave these differences into the fabric of their own lives. Someday soon, Lange predicts, diversity will be "present every day, and if you don't take care and appreciate the differences, then you can't work."

There's no clear recipe for hybridity. "It happens somehow," says Lange, who thinks it has happened to him. "Somehow you become international. You remain a German but you somehow become less a German when you work in such an environment."

IS BECOMING "less of a German" really a break with Germany's past, or is it an unexpected resumption of tradition? Isn't German nationalism, and the cult of homogeneity, from Bismarck to Kohl, the aberration?

Although in this chapter I have concentrated on how the collision between Germans and immigrants in Germany alters both, hybridization emerges in another way—when Germans leave their country. As a people, Germans have a history of making their way in the world, a great wanderlust. In the early 1700s, rulers of various German principalities (there was no unified state until 1871) tried to slow or ban emigration with little effect. Emigration increased in size and diversity for 150 years. In 1709, 11,000 Germans moved to Britain. Nearly 4,000 moved to Ireland. Three thousand moved to New York. Later in the 1700s, Pennsylvania became the main American destination because of its toleration of religious diversity. In the 1760s, 30,000 Germans moved to Russia. Nearly 20,000 went to Hungary. As late as 1834, nearly all German emigrants came from the German southwest, but within a decade five-sixths were from other regions. From 1816 to 1830, half of the emigrants went to South America, but for the remainder of the century, 90 percent went to the United States.

As Thomas Sowell observes, "German emigrants did not simply leave Germany. They took part of Germany with them, preserving its culture not only for themselves but also making it part of the larger culture of societies in which they settled." They spread technical skills, arts and crafts, science and engineering. They placed a high value on education: The kindergarten and the research university, both German innovations, were widely imitated elsewhere. And men of German ancestry held high posts in czarist Russia, in South America and in the United States from the Revolutionary War through World War II.[9]

This tradition of German wandering is reviving, as the stigma of the Nazi era fades and poor job prospects at home spur more people to seek their fortune abroad. Franc, from Berlin, travels the world building pipe organs by hand. On a trip to Japan, he met a Japanese woman at the Goethe Institute, the center for German culture abroad. Harry, a carpenter and gifted furniture maker from Aachen, took his fascination with Native American beads, leather and archery to the United States, traveling the Southwest, camping out and visiting tribes. He works in California now, applying his exacting standards and sensitive taste to the task of remodeling homes. Rainier, a software programmer, writes code in the United States, though he could surely find the same job closer to home.

At the start of a new century, Germans living outside of Germany probably see their country more clearly than those who have stayed behind. The German penchant for complaining at home has a cascading effect, which distorts diagnoses of the country's problems and robs people of their capacity for inspiring dreams. People under age forty already live the insecure, contingent Americanized life that people over forty swear they will prevent from coming to Germany. All ages share a sense of diminishing possibilities, a belief that the future will be a long goodbye to the welfare state and that little good can come from retrenchment.

German self-pity seems tiresome and somewhat embarrassing even to Germans who live abroad. I was reminded of this one afternoon when lunching with Bernd Kupper, a German schoolteacher from Munich who had moved to Poland three years before. He teaches German to Polish university students, courtesy of the German government. The experience of living in a country on its way up has unshackled him. "I realize now how spoiled and fragile people in Germany are," he says. "I can't believe my ears when I listen to the moaning and groaning over the threat of getting too small of a raise or giving up a piece of benefit." By contrast, Poles seem bursting with energy and optimism, even though materially they may not reach German living standards for a long time, if ever.

Bernd thinks Germans should spend more time outside of their country in order to shed their negativity. Not by going on holiday but by living normal lives elsewhere. He thinks only by removing themselves from Germany can they discover what is best about their national traits.

His idea makes me think that the German diaspora, as old and as watered down as it is, may play a critical role in the remaking of Germany. Living abroad makes Germans less German in the intangible way perceived by Lange. When these people return to Germany, they will do so as strangers in their own land, budding hybrids who embrace Germany's aliens while Germanizing them at the same time.

A NIGERIAN PRIEST
GAINS A PARISH...
IN DUBLIN

DUBLIN, IRELAND—The priest, draped in purple robes, holds high a Bible from his perch at the altar and launches into his sonorous reading from the Scripture. It is a March Sunday in Dublin, Ireland, and at this very moment, hundreds of Masses are being said all over this heavily Catholic nation. But none are like this Mass.

The priest is black. His name is , Father Livinus Onyebuchi. He isn't Irish, although sometimes he feels a little Irish. The first white man he ever saw was an Irish priest. Some of his schoolteachers in southern Nigeria, where he grew up, were Irish. When he entered a seminary, his mentors were Irish. Father Onyebuchi, at the age of thirty-six, has so many Irish friends from Nigeria—many now back on the Emerald Isle—that when he arrived here in 1997, he recalls, "I felt like I was coming home."

Fifty years ago, young Irish men facing few prospects in their own desperately poor homeland flocked to the priesthood, far exceeding Ireland's needs. These men moved on to parochial schools and parishes in Chicago, Boston, New York—and all over Africa, especially in Nigeria, where entire regions were taught Christianity by Irish priests.

Today Ireland is short of priests. Not only has the country stopped exporting them, it can't fill vacancies at home created by retiring clergy. So Nigerians are coming to help.

This is not just the Christian thing to do; it's also an aspect of globalization. Nigeria, an English-speaking country in West Africa and a former British colony (as was Ireland), has what economists call a "comparative advantage" when it comes to the production of priests. It costs as little as $500 a year to educate, feed and house a priest in Nigeria, a tiny fraction of what it costs to produce a priest in Ireland or in the United States.

Nigeria is home to one of the world's largest seminaries, with an enrollment of about 800. There's also the factor of religious hunger. In Ireland, young men see their destinies elsewhere—in the fashionable high-tech or finance sectors, for instance. Not so in Nigeria, where an economy devastated by corruption and civil disorder means that the priesthood remains a prime career path—and an exit strategy.

Father Onyebuchi's religious order in Nigeria, the Missionary Order of Saint Paul, has twenty-five openings a year and receives twenty to forty times that number of applicants—and this for a chance to endure a seven-year course of study that, on completion, qualifies the graduate for a life of celibacy. While India and a few other nations produce more priests, Nigeria probably exports more than any other country. The Vatican doesn't compile statistics on priest exports by country, but the U.S. Conference of Bishops estimates that Nigerian priests are the most mobile.

Hundreds of Nigerian priests work in Catholic dioceses in the United States, filling a growing number of vacancies. Nigerians are also prominent in Britain and Germany, where the number of vacancies has risen. In the Vatican, a native Nigerian, Cardinal Francis Arinze, is a contender to succeed Pope John Paul II.

For a century, the Irish played the role of Catholicism's reserve army. Now it is the Nigerians' turn. "They are picking up the historic role that the Irish played," says Tony Byrne, a Dublin priest who spent ten years in Nigeria. "Increasingly they are the public face of Catholicism."

In Ireland, this takes getting used to. Until the late 1990s, there were almost no black people in Ireland—priests or otherwise. Even now, more than 99 percent of Ireland's population of four million is classified as white. Father Onyebuchi is the first black man many of his parishioners have ever seen in person.

After Father Onyebuchi's Mass at Church of the Holy Name, a neighborhood church that was used in the film *Angela's Ashes,* two elderly women stroll out of the church and into a cool Dublin afternoon. "He's a colored priest, a nice priest," one woman says. The other replies, "Oh yes, but he's very hard to understand at times."

Father Onyebuchi speaks standard English but not with an Irish accent. Diction isn't his only challenge. In Nigeria, he gave sermons lasting half an hour or longer, speaking without notes, "as the spirit moved me," he says. Now he types his words in advance in order to keep within the five to seven minutes allotted for a sermon here. In Nigeria, the tall and broad-shouldered Father Onyebuchi kept a Mass going for several hours—and belted out hymns from the pulpit. In Ireland, such singing is considered undignified, and the Mass is tightly scripted, lasting less than an hour.

Morgan Costelloe, the senior priest at the Church of the Holy Name, likes it that way. Father Costelloe, sixty-seven years old, once had three assistant priests but was down to one before he hired Father Onyebuchi in September 1998. The move made Father Costelloe something of a pioneer. A spokesman for Ireland's Catholic Church says that the Church hasn't encouraged its parishes to fill priest vacancies with Nigerians or other immigrants, and that foreign priests attached to parishes remain rare in Ireland.

Nonetheless, a handful of Nigerian priests work in Ireland, and Father Costelloe, who has lived his entire life in the country, expects the number of African priests here to grow. He describes Father Onyebuchi's presence in his parish as "a sign for the future." Trying to be positive, he tells the Nigerian priest that "people don't even realize you come from Africa. You are one of us."

The color-blind view propounded by Father Costelloe is laudatory, but it is inaccurate. Black people are routinely discriminated against in Ireland, harassed in public places and menaced in the night. Nigerians as a group get a bad rap too. "Two Nigerians a Day Arrested for Credit Card Scams," screamed one headline in the *Irish Independent,* the country's best-selling daily newspaper. Over the past two years, about 4,500 Nigerians have entered Ireland illegally and applied for refugee status, which would make them eligible for welfare payments. The rise in welfare seekers has led to a round of Nigerian bashing that worries some Irish people, who fear that the criticism exposes racist attitudes in their society.

"We've discovered that racism is latent in a lot of us," says Donal Dorr, a Dublin priest who taught Father Onyebuchi when they both lived in Nigeria.

Father Onyebuchi says that he hasn't felt the sting of bias personally and that he takes comfort in some of the small changes he sees. When he first arrived in Ireland, he says, "I could walk the length of Dublin without seeing a black person," he recalls. "Now, nearly on every street, I'll see one."

Sometimes he'll see black faces in church too. In February, after he finished a Mass, an older black woman greeted him warmly, then pulled him along to a house up the street from the church. The woman burst inside, shouting at her daughter, "I found a black priest!"

The older woman, a Haitian immigrant to the United States visiting her daughter, who had recently moved to Ireland, asked Father Onyebuchi to bless her daughter's newborn baby. The woman's discovery of the priest helped ease her concern that her daughter, a Haitian-American stewardess who had attended Catholic schools in New York, might be too isolated in Dublin, where she had moved with her husband, a white American who works for a U.S. high-tech company.

Other moments can be more awkward for Father Onyebuchi. After the first time Moraid O'Brien watched him celebrate Mass this year, she wondered whether to describe the priest as black or colored. "Which do you think he'd prefer?" she asked.

Father Onyebuchi's earnest, energetic demeanor and his disciplined personal life—he doesn't drink alcohol or smoke—wins him respect. One afternoon, he sits in Elizabeth Sitton's kitchen as she heaps a pile of potatoes onto his plate. "I'm sorry they're not yams," she says politely, referring to the favorite food of his region of Nigeria. Father Onyebuchi laughs and says dryly, "It's a long time since I've had potatoes."

After lunch, the two move to the parlor and discuss the shortage of priests in Ireland. Sitton is a retired government employee who is active in a group working to persuade Irish men to become priests. She has been a member of the Holy Name parish for her entire life—and was stunned to learn recently that the entire Dublin diocese had ordained only one priest in the prior year.

Thinking of how the Irish once took care of the spiritual needs of the Nigerians and how the roles are starting to reverse, Sitton says, "When I was a child, I used to ask my mother for a penny for the black babies in Africa."

The money, collected by the parish, paid for Irish missionaries to educate men such as Father Onyebuchi. At the time, and for many years afterward, she never thought she'd meet a Nigerian. Now, looking across the room, she declares proudly, "Here's my black baby, back!"

She means no offense by this comment, and Father Onyebuchi takes none. But the racial talk reminds him that some Irish are uncomfortable with new—and nonwhite—faces. He can live with those people, however, because he sees a new Ireland rising. "Many others make it clear that Irish people have been economic migrants down through the centuries," he says, "so they must be able to receive others in their own land."

CHAPTER 6

DIVERSITY BY DESIGN

*Look closely and you will see what an enormous variety of human types
are represented in the huge crowd.*

—SHIMEI FUTABATEI[1]

*you start to walk. she comes closer and rubs her nose in your jeans. you
keep walking. she meows and meows and you still keep walking, a little
faster. she stops. the fun is almost over. there is kinship in the game just
played. she stops and knows she cannot follow you forever. you know you
cannot follow her forever. as you walk away, you think about this beautiful catwalk, this rhythm of exchange, this bond of being.*

—KIRPAL SINGH[2]

If you bring forth what is within you,
What is within you will save you.
If you do not bring forth what is within you,
What is within you will destroy you.

—JESUS IN THE GNOSTIC GOSPELS[3]

NATIONS[4] MATTER in a mongrel world. Their governments, their laws and
policies, their civic life—all matter, perhaps more than ever. In the
bygone era of monocultures, the task of civic life in prosperous nations was to
create a common ground, drawn from essentially the same human material.
Fairness meant applying one set of rules, uniformly. Equality meant everyone
had a fair shot to climb a single social ladder.

After more than two centuries, a range of forces ended the age of monocultures. An identity revolution, described in the first two chapters, gave birth
to hybrid societies that now spawn creativity while sustaining and defending
themselves. This pervasive process of mongrelization, described in Chapters 3
and 4, occurs in cities, regions and entire countries. It is not limited to wealthy
parts of the world, but is most evident there. Hybridity is most pronounced in
the United States. By virtue of scale and scope, not flawless performance in
achieving social harmony, America is the world's leading mongrel nation. It is

the master example, the exemplar, of hybridity and an incubator for new cosmopolitans.

In Chapter 5, I described Germany's handling of diversity and the ways in which the country has wasted the economic and political benefits of opening up to large numbers of outsiders. Just as the United States is a master example of mongrelization, Germany is the exemplar of the monoculture in retreat, the homogeneous society under siege. Germany is one of the most diverse nations in the wealthy world, yet no nation has done less with its diversity. But as I have argued, Germany can turn a negative into a positive. It has the pieces in place to turn on a dime. Germany only must show the will, and it can reap the boon of hybridity.

Germany's potential for mongrelization is significant and not only for the obvious historical irony that the land that spawned the most vile ideology of purity now possesses the ingredients for the sort of radical mixing that was anathema to Hitler. Indeed, Germany's future will be defined by the success of its auslanders. If Germany can go hybrid, then surely all other rich nations can too.

To be sure, no country is a mere proxy for others in the world, but the tensions within Germany over diversity are mirrored elsewhere. Studies of France, Switzerland, Sweden, Australia and the Netherlands reveal basically the same story. These countries are diverse, and home to foreigners who have notched impressive achievements. But diversity is not central to these nations, and aliens remain stigmatized. Moreover, these countries do not woo talented foreigners in a frank effort to make their societies younger and more vital, improve the competitiveness of key industries or aid in the reinvention of national myths and symbols. In short, the German experience says much about the way many rich nations cope with diversity.

The United States and Germany are thus convenient bookends, marking the boundaries of the mongrel world. Within these borders exists a great deal of what's right and wrong with diversity in advanced countries. But these two main cases are limited. In this chapter, I will examine two exceptions to the America-Germany polarity.

First, I will look at how small nations can organically redefine their identities. Because of their size (and sometimes their relative isolation), small nations can leverage diversity more quickly and forthrightly than larger countries can. Ireland's recent experience illustrates this. Despite its image as a monolithic place, the country is breaking free of its tradition of ethnoreligious purity.

In the second half of this chapter, I look at Japan, the only great nation with scant diversity and no evident willingness to redesign itself along hybrid lines. Japan illustrates the limits of plasticity and presents a useful test case. If a nation can avoid mongrelization, Japan will find a way.

VANISHING IRELAND

I am in Kilkenny, a charming medieval city about two hours south of Dublin that has winding alleyways, a restored castle and a river running through its ancient walls. I have just walked the castle grounds, returning along the river and then emerging across the street from a sandwich shop. I'm hungry and go in and place an order. John, the manager of the place, serves me. He's an American, and when he tells me what he's doing there, I am reminded that Ireland is no longer for the Irish. It's for everybody now.

John graduated from Yale University two months before. For those who don't memorize university rankings, Yale is among the most prestigious schools in the United States, and is about as hard to get into as Harvard. John wasn't a dance major either. He studied business and economics. After weighing a half dozen job offers in the spring of 1999, he decided on Ireland. "My best opportunities are here," he says.

When I stop laughing, I tell him I didn't know that Yale grads had to fly to Ireland just to get a fast-food job. I thought there were plenty of those jobs in New Haven, Yale's home. I ask him to tell me why he's really here. His parents are Irish? He's Irish? His girlfriend is Irish? His girlfriend's parents are Irish?

No on all counts, he says. I tell him he must be joking, and he answers impatiently, "Look, I could end up part owner of a bunch of these places before I'm twenty-five." He then explains that he's opening shops around Ireland for investors and gets a piece of the ownership each time he does. Over the next year, he might open ten shops in Ireland.

If I needed further evidence of a sea change in the world, John provides it. Ever since the potato famine in 1848, people have left Ireland in droves in hope of a better life. Or they left Ireland because of its overwhelming monoculture (as James Joyce did in 1904, returning to visit only twice thereafter). People continued leaving in the decades after World War II. They left in the 1970s and the 1980s. Only yesterday, it seems, they were still leaving.

Now, in one of the wackiest reversals in history, Ireland is a magnet for the young and enterprising. People move to Ireland looking for a better life. Not only are Irish people coming from abroad, but so too are other Europeans and Americans. In John's case, he even brought along his girlfriend, another Yale graduate. When I met him, she was vying for a job with the local milk coop. What's the world coming to when Kilkenny dairy farmers are getting applications from Yale graduates?

This situation is so improbable that the mind rebels. Yet it isn't as strange as it seems. By joining the European Union in 1972, Ireland began moving out of Britain's shadow. "I have come to the paradoxical conclusion," Garret FitzGerald, a former Irish prime minister, once said, "that it is in the process of merging its sovereignty with other member states of the European Union that Ireland has found the clearest ex post facto justification for its long struggle to achieve sovereign independence from the United Kingdom."[5]

EU membership boosted Irish confidence and the country's economy. Before 1973, 61 percent of Irish exports went to Britain and only 9 percent to other EU countries; by 1996, exports to these EU countries accounted for half of all exports and double those to Britain.[6]

Ireland's European awakening wasn't only economic. The Irish began seeing international organizations as a means of achieving their ambitions. As a small neutral country, Ireland offended no one (save perhaps Britain, over the status of Northern Ireland), so its people were welcomed by international agencies, especially those of the United Nations. Mary Robinson, U.N. commissioner for human rights, was the best-known Irish internationalist, but scores of lesser-known people—and many women among them—held important posts in the U.N. system. The effect was to give the best and brightest of Ireland a sophistication and global reach that they previously lacked.

To people such as Deirdre Clancy, a human-rights specialist who has worked in France and New York, Ireland is already cosmopolitan. A twenty-something graduate of the law school at Dublin's Trinity College, Clancy finds that Irish sentimentality obscures the new realities of her country. "Rather than pretend that we are isolated on the edge of Europe and more at home with members of their own tribe, the Irish should admit what's been true for a long time: that we are a cosmopolitan people," she says.

Much of Ireland's new worldliness stems from its economic boom. Standards of living rocketed in the second half of the 1990s. Ireland was no longer among the poorest European nations but heading toward the wealthiest group. The change was so rapid—and came at a time when so many other European countries were stagnating economically—that many Irish worried the boom was an illusion. When will the bubble burst? they asked one another.

An Irish crash isn't likely. As part of the European Monetary Union, Ireland shares a common currency with slower-growing France and Germany, and because of low European interest rates, money remained cheap in Ireland even as its boom persisted. Jobs went begging and the call for more immigrants grew louder. In August 1999, just two weeks after I met the Yale grad, I read a screaming headline in the *Irish Independent,* the biggest daily: 15,000 FOREIGN WORKERS ON WAY TO JOBS HERE.

The accompanying article explained that for the first time the Irish government had issued a realistic projection of the number of workers it would import over the next eighteen months. These newcomers would come on top of 5,700 foreign workers—from 112 countries—already admitted to Ireland that year. A Dublin economist explained in the newspaper that the immigrants weren't hurting any Irish residents, at least not financially. Although Ireland's official unemployment rate sat at 6.6 percent, or about 200,000 people, the economist said this reflected only the generosity of Irish welfare benefits and the ease with which benefits could be fraudulently obtained by those working off-the-books. "There is an unquestionable excess of job offers over possible job seekers," the economist wrote.[7]

Word gets around. In 1999, a thousand people entered Ireland each week to live or work, and many were neither Irish nor residents of EU countries. "In Dublin's pubs and restaurants these days you are more likely to be served by a Spaniard or Italian or Australian than by anybody Irish," *The Economist* wrote. Irish farmers, short of field hands, searched in Poland, Latvia and the Czech Republic for help. One meat packer hired thirty Polish butchers, while another imported fifty Brazilians. Even highly skilled, educated foreigners arrived, chiefly to join the growing ranks of Irish software developers or to staff the scores of multinationals with operations in the country.[8]

By the spring of 2000, the flow of foreigners into Ireland had increased, fueled by government reports of "an unprecedented" 70,000 unfilled jobs. The number of vacancies had jumped 30 percent in twelve months to a record high. The need for foreign workers was most severe in the Dublin area and among global high-tech companies that view Ireland as the best place to service their customers throughout Europe. One major U.S. computer company, which already employed more than a thousand people in Ireland, was so bent on expanding that it was trying to convince the Irish government to help it bring as many as 4,000 service workers from China. But smaller companies were frantically seeking staff abroad too. Pub owners were collectively importing thirty bar staff each month from Italy, Portugal and Spain. Even historically depressed Irish regions, such as Connemara, were hiring manual workers from Finland, the Czech Republic and Estonia.[9]

The torrent of immigrants reflects Ireland's position as Europe's fastest-growing economy. In the late 1990s, Ireland posted a torrid 8 percent growth rate four years running. From 1994 to 1998, employment in the country grew by an astonishing 27.5 percent, or nearly twice the rate of growth in the labor force. The robust economy acted as a magnet for foreigners, almost overnight turning Ireland from a sender of people to a receiver of them. In 1998, 17,500 non-Irish people moved to Ireland—the third year in a row of positive migration. In a country of four million people, the number is significant, and not only because Ireland is thought of as an exporter of people. Non-Irish mothers delivered one-third of the Irish newborns in 1998. Not since the English subdued Ireland in the 1700s had so many foreigners chosen to call the island home. Enthused by the prospect of talented immigrants, some experts urged the government to go all out to attract highly skilled and university-educated foreigners, and not only those with an Irish lineage.

"Ireland now faces . . . a skills shortage," notes James Wickham, a professor of labor at Trinity College in Dublin. "There is a crisis in the software industry. And it is clear that the problem is not going to be solved by the skilled [Irish] emigrants of the 1980s returning. Firms and recruitment consultants are now negotiating for labor permits for non-EU citizens and demanding that the government speed up processing such requests." Wickham thinks Ireland has a chance to reinvent itself as a multicultural nation, with immigrants adding diversity and lifting the Irish economy to new heights. "An immigrant population," he thinks, "can now make an important contribution to creating a more dynamic Ireland."

Ireland is well suited to cultivate diversity for three reasons. First, Ireland can use people. It remains thinly populated, except in Dublin. (This is a country that had a larger population in 1881 than in 1981. It had more people in 1841 than it does today, even if the people in Northern Ireland are included in the total.) Then there is the basic Irish sympathy for the underdog. For two centuries Irish people left their homes to find opportunities elsewhere in the world; they understand the mentality of the economic migrant. Finally, there is the matter of size. When it comes to diversity, small nations have inherent advantages over large ones. A behemoth like Germany can stigmatize newcomers, forcing them onto the margins, but Ireland is simply too small to do so. Relatively few newcomers can alter its character, while at the same time natives aren't numerous enough to keep immigrants permanently in a lower class.

But why can't Ireland assimilate immigrants (make them Irish, so to speak) rather than allow them to retain ethnic ties and thus broaden the meaning of Irishness? The logic of size again suggests an answer. Ireland is too small to pursue the sort of cultural-preservation strategies common in France and Britain, two postimperial powers that still insist, in legal and informal ways, that newcomers mimic natives. In absorbing people from their far-flung colonies, both France and Britain have demanded a public conformity, or assimilation, to the mainstream. Hyphenated identities (black-British or French-Algerian, say) continue to arouse great anxieties within many large countries, and few policymakers appreciate the value of compound identities (black *and* British, French *and* Algerian). Multiple loyalties seem alien to Ireland too. Yet paradoxically, Ireland's history of emigration—and the existence of an Irish diaspora spanning the globe—obviate the need for a domestic strategy of cultural preservation. Irish culture is preserved (albeit beyond Ireland's borders) by the diaspora. No one can argue that immigrants threaten the survival of "Irishness" because Irishness thrives outside of Ireland (in Australia, Britain and the United States especially). And no matter the changes in Ireland, Irishness will endure.

Irishness as an identity has thrived for so long outside of its territorial home that a hybrid Ireland seems both just and inevitable. This may come as a surprise to older residents of Ireland and members of its overseas diaspora, but younger Irish people actively discuss new ways of being Irish. "Everyone writing [today] in Ireland reinvents the place," quips the Wexford novelist Colm Toibin, who observes that the Irish have traded Catholic nationalism for an urbane Europeanism. Eager to cast off sentimental images of themselves, Irish youth reject the equation of Irishness with Catholicism, conformity and a misty-eyed attachment to the "old sod." But this rebellion against a frozen-in-time Irish identity is still largely underground. Donal Scannell, a Dublin music producer and book editor, declares, "The old guard still rule our roost economically, politically and culturally. Whilst we have hordes of frequently praised and displayed 'cultural ambassadors,' those outside Ireland get a particularly distorted view of what's really making this new Ireland tick."[10]

The "new" Ireland represents money, diversity and a fresh disregard for limits that, taken together, mark a departure with the country's monoculture. "Financially, we're more successful than ever," says Shane, a university grad in his midtwenties who works at a Dublin software company. "Before, the country's focus was on pain and victimization. Now the focus is on freedom. We used to be sheep; now we're shepherds. It allows you to take any direction you want. We're no longer a backwater. We're independent. We go where we want to and when."

BOOMING IRELAND is no fluke. Now is a good time to be small and hybridizing. Small countries have no choice but to open themselves to diversity—and benefit disproportionately from multinational ties. The dominant economic strategy of the 1980s and 1990s—export-led growth—was tailor-made to lift incomes in small nations, which had small domestic markets anyway. Indeed, studies show no statistical relationship between country size and economic growth rates. Even people who argue that the size of a home market is important concede that because of the effect of other economic factors, high internal demand doesn't guarantee that a big country will outperform a small one. Moreover, there is reason to believe that some big countries—particularly those well endowed with oil, minerals and other resources—actually underperform smaller countries because of what political economist Terry Lynn Karl calls "the paradox of plenty." The experience of Nigeria, Iran and Indonesia— all big resource-rich countries—suggests that the "instant bonanza" brought about by commodity exports can reduce a country's competitiveness. By contrast, adversity has a healthy effect on many small nations, forcing them to work harder and smarter to gain economic advantage.[11]

Economics is only part of the surging outlook for small nations. At a time when economic victory often goes to the player who arrives first to a destination, small nations are inherently faster than big ones at making decisions and shifting gears. Just as small companies can hybridize more quickly than big ones, small nations can more quickly than big nations seize the benefits of hybridity. Mongrelization, in short, favors the small over the big.[12]

This is a historical reversal of grand proportions.

Small nations (those with small populations of, say, less than five million, or small land areas of, say, roughly the size of a small American state) once were viewed as mere fodder for big nations because they were thought to lack the internal resources to achieve wealth.[13] Economists thought that nations prospered by first exploiting domestic demand, then moving into international trade, so that the bigger a nation was, the better. For the past two centuries, small countries were seen as "material" out of which to build big ones. In 1843, one respected political observer said it was "ridiculous" that Belgium or Portugal should be independent. Giuseppe Mazzini, the nineteenth-century unifier of Italy, said the ideal number of European nations would be twelve (as opposed to fifty today).

The twentieth century proved no kinder to small countries. Consider the Netherlands, which built a sprawling colonial empire in the Pacific. The Soviet Union, China and India absorbed smaller neighbors unapologetically. Germany took the first step toward World War II when in 1938 it seized what was then Czechoslovakia. One rationale for these power grabs was that none of the absorbed countries—not Tibet or Kashmir or the Baltic state of Estonia—could survive on its own.

Not so. Economists now say almost no nation is too small to prosper. Many small countries outperform economically much larger nations, and for sound reasons. "Since the economy is so global now, the costs of being small have gone down," says Alberto Alesina, an economist at Harvard University who studies small nations. "You can afford to be small." So it seemed to the late Ernest Gellner, a political theorist, who wrote in 1997: "What makes you big, important, rich and strong in the modern world is not acreage but rates of growth."[14] This helps to explain why there are more small nations in the world than ever, more than 190 in all, up from 74 in 1946. Of these, 87 countries had populations below 5 million, 58 less than 2.5 million and 35 less than 500,000. "If the critical ingredient has shifted from natural resources to knowledge," says futurist Paul Saffo, "then the successful country is the one not with the most brains, but the most brains that can act in concert."

Even though countries with small populations would seem to be more threatened by immigrants than big ones—after all, there are fewer of "us" in small nations compared with arriving "them"—the relative ease of reaching consensus in a small nation can result in faster responses to shifts in population. In Ireland's case, a lack of official government policies and rules for guaranteeing ethnic rights and promoting diversity has allowed both Irish natives and immigrants more freedom to experiment with new identities. This was certainly not the intent of government inaction but was the effect nonetheless.

The lack of a political response to diversity is only another example of how politicians are the last to begin to adapt to Ireland's rising flow of incomers. People outside of government see more clearly Ireland's drift toward hybridity. Garret FitzGerald illustrates this. He served as the country's Taoiseach, or prime minister, for six years during the 1980s. Retired from politics, he remains a pungent observer of his country and one of the deepest thinkers on the new Irish diversity. "We were a very closed society, a censorious society, a rigid society until thirty years ago," he told me when I visited his home in Dublin. "The fact that the Church had held up change for so long, there was bound to be rapid change once the dam broke [in the 1970s], and that's what happened."

FitzGerald listed the profound shifts: a steep decline in Ireland's birthrate; delayed child-bearing; a sharp rise in sex outside of marriage and births out of wedlock; a slow but steady growth in failed marriages; and even a rise in abortion (by Irish women flying to England).

By the 1990s, Ireland "became an extremely tolerant" society, but too flush with prosperity, FitzGerald believes, to examine patiently the new face of Irish identity. The country, after all, had been defined by its Catholicism and an attachment to an imagined Gaelic past. Both sets of ties were challenged by a better-educated and more widely traveled younger generation and the rising numbers of Irish returnees and immigrants. This traditional concept of Irishness was also challenged by the need to resolve the dispute over Northern Ireland, where a Protestant majority claims that their group interests can never be satisfied in a united Ireland.

Protestant concerns about Irish tolerance aren't hollow. While Catholics complained about the history of discrimination against them in the North, Catholic discomfort with Protestants in the Republic of Ireland was no less real (if more understandable given the centuries of English repression against the Irish Catholics). The Protestant decline in the Irish republic (from its formation in 1922 until 1946, the Protestant population fell by 24 percent) stood as a warning to Protestants in the North that they might fare poorly in a united Ireland.[15] Nor did the experience of Ireland's small Jewish community, which steadily shrank after World War II, inspire visions of a multicultural Ireland.[16]

Nevertheless, Irish Catholics are increasingly solicitous of the needs of those different from them. As a sign of this new broad-mindedness, FitzGerald cites the legalization of divorce and the 1998 change in the Irish constitution that ended Ireland's territorial claim on the six counties in the North. Both moves helped to reduce Protestant fears that Ireland would impose a Catholic moral code on Protestants (and other non-Catholics). These steps also suggested that it was no longer obvious what it meant to be Irish.

Although the new meaning of Irishness isn't clear to FitzGerald, "someone can't say now that he will impose 'our' culture on people who are also Irish, but just not 'our' kind of Irish."

This shift at the end of the 1990s was a watershed in Irish history. From the time of the Easter Rising against British rule in 1916, Irishness was equated with the Church, the Gaelic language and Republicanism, or the insistence on a united Ireland under Catholic-Gaelic rule. "Irishness" is now being reinvented at least by those in Ireland (as opposed to those in Boston or Sydney or elsewhere in the Irish diaspora, who may hold onto their nostalgic image of the country). In a typical expression of soul-searching, the Irish journalist Fintan O'Toole writes of "the disappearance of a fixed Irish identity," asserting that "the central fact of [Irish] culture is that it knows no borders."[17] This is a provocative insight. FitzGerald won't go that far, but he concedes that "the Irish are fundamentally rethinking their identity."

THIS RETHINKING is painful, especially for minorities. Blacks face the greatest barriers to inclusion in an expanded Irish identity. Blacks who live permanently in Ireland number in the hundreds, but in recent years an estimated 4,500 Africans have entered the country, seeking legal residence under the European Union's asylum rules. These newcomers report bias, harassment and even beatings. The worst of these incidents occur in Dublin, and often in the poor sections of the city, where migrants compete for space with the least educated Irish natives. In March 1999, a Nigerian was dragged from a Dublin restaurant and beaten by a gang of youths who hurled obscenities at him. The year before, in broad daylight, a pregnant woman from Angola was assaulted. A migrant from the Congo was attacked with dogs. One African woman claims that people refuse to serve her in shops and won't sit next to her on the bus. A retail clerk from Malawi was told by his Irish coworkers that he could not enter the employee break room. Many Irish are still so unfamiliar with Africans or African Americans that they muse aloud about whether to call them "colored" or black people. An Irish priest, who worked for a decade in Nigeria before returning home in the mid-1990s, expresses the general view of Ireland's struggle over racial mixing when he says, "The Irish are finding that racism is latent in us all."

Some critics blame Ireland's new wealth for its failure to squarely confront societal racism. "Ireland is riding so high the Irish no longer feel the need to accommodate anyone else," says Mary Valarason-Toomey, a native of Sri Lanka who has lived in Ireland since 1967.[18] The task of integrating blacks is made no easier when at the same time the country must adjust to what appears like a flood of foreigners. Not all the newcomers are highly talented or arrive with jobs in hand. By early 2000, some 7,000 refugees lived in Ireland, all entitled to basic welfare support until their claims of political asylum could be either sustained or dismissed. Banned by the government from holding jobs, these refugees seemed parasitic, surviving on welfare benefits. Many Irish believed these newcomers were bent on taking advantage of them. The Irish media did their part to promote this view, reporting such dismal stories as "Two Nigerians a Day Arrested for Credit Card Scams." Such reports placed a cloud over all people of color in Ireland, since many Irish could not easily distinguish between legitimate and illegitimate immigrants. That such a distinction was ironic—given the history of Irish emigration to so many places in the world—made it no less powerful to people who felt threatened by outsiders.[19]

The backlash against nonwhites in Ireland seems likely to continue, as does the battle for Ireland's soul. "The Irish are on a precipice now, they can go one way or the other," says Sarah Nelson, a black American who lives in Dublin with her white husband, an executive with a U.S. computer company. "A lot of Irish people tell me this," she says. "'We're in a test mode,' they say. 'We can see ourselves becoming negative'" if things go awry. The child of Haitian immigrants to the United States, Nelson is Catholic and attends her local parish church. She mingles freely with the Irish and has grown accustomed to stares and surprised looks. "The Irish are just now getting used to black people," she says. But her husband adds: "When they meet you, you get a smile. But when you walk away, you get whispers." Nelson is optimistic. Ultimately Ireland will see its race "problem" as an opportunity, she thinks.

But big tests lie ahead, and those who wish to preserve Ireland as a white bastion have yet to show the depth of their resistance. Still, just as attacks on blacks in the United States don't empower white supremacists, neither will they do so in Ireland. This is partly because none of the country's three major political parties show much sympathy toward immigrant-bashing. Indeed, even as politicians complain about the cost of caring for refugees, they positively exult over Ireland's new status among global professionals and skilled workers. The rush of immigrants underscores the new Irish confidence, coming after decades of self-denial and doubt. Besides, there is little Ireland can do to erect walls even if it wants to. As a member of the European Union, Ireland is legally bound to accept anyone from the fourteen other member countries (just as the Irish can live and work in these countries). Ultimately it may be other white Europeans who move to Ireland in the greatest numbers, and their potential to change the country's character is surely vast. Italian investment bankers now stroll Dublin streets, and American high-tech executives are snapping up high-priced homes. The west of Ireland, meanwhile, is now home to hundreds, perhaps thousands, of wealthy Germans, attracted by the scenic beauty and the relatively low cost of living. The German influx has boosted home prices and injected needed enterprise and cash into depressed rural areas, but has spawned resentment too. When the first anti-immigrant group surfaced in Ireland in the late 1990s, it targeted not Africans or Asians but Germans as the main enemy. The absurdity of their position quickly made the group into a butt of jokes.

The presence of white Europeans doesn't usually raise objections from native Irish, but they still challenge the idea that Ireland exists only for its own. Consider Annabelle Konig. Born in the Netherlands, she spent eight years as a child in Ireland. At the age of twenty-five, she returned to Ireland, where she has now lived for ten years. She speaks English with an Irish accent, knows her Irish folklore and even has an Irish mate. Konig is a teacher, painter and artist by profession. She designs gallery installations and film sets. Fiercely passionate about Ireland's virtues, she nonetheless sees herself as an incendiary outsider who can shake things up. She finds Ireland quite conservative (by Dutch standards) and does her bit to change this. Her mate, Liam, is the father of her one child, but she won't marry him, preferring to live together outside of marriage. Such an arrangement is common in Holland but unusual in Ireland, where marital breakups and living out of wedlock still carry a stigma. She finds it absurd, for instance, that Liam, with whom she has lived for a decade, must adopt their son in order to gain some legal sway over the child.

"We don't get married as a kind of protest," Annabelle says. Still, when she visits hospitals and schools with her son, she often wears a wedding ring. "When I don't I've been treated badly," she says.

Annabelle's Dutch precision and punctuality will prevent her from ever "becoming Irish," she says, but she's attached to the people and the landscape. The Irish have an open friendliness and an enviable spontaneity that many northern Europeans lack. While enriching her life, Annabelle's dual consciousness at times upsets her. She has the Dutch passion for cycling, but Dublin lacks the neat, ubiquitous bike lanes of Amsterdam, where riders are so pampered they can even freely borrow bikes conveniently stashed around the city. Dublin's cascading traffic jams pose a problem for her. She has been knocked down twice by cars in recent years. Still, she won't blame the Irish. The auto mess is "bad planning, not any Celtic defect," she says, showing pride worthy of a native.

Of course, the odd artist and writer always moved to Ireland, but what's different now is the potential scale of mixing. With Ireland's economy booming, any number of the 4 million unemployed Germans might decide to try their luck in Ireland. Even the return of Irish migrants adds diversity. Since 1993, 115,000 Irish emigrants have returned to Ireland, with many bringing new attitudes and expectations.

"You learn that returning to Ireland is not going to be like coming home," says one returnee. "It's going to be like re-emigrating all over again. You have to go through the pain of rejection, the feeling that 'Ireland, my own country

doesn't want me' and I don't belong." Added another returnee, "People accli-
matise to where they have emigrated to and they are not the same people
coming back."[20]

As Irish, Germans, Dutch and other white Europeans bring diversity to Ireland, the pressure to accommodate outsiders is becoming overwhelming.
Thus opponents of diversity target people of color, so-called visible minorities
whose members are easiest to stigmatize. Until recently, almost no nonwhites
lived in Ireland. But this has changed. Ireland complies with Europe's vague
and generous provisions for those seeking asylum from repression at home.
The number of people seeking asylum in Ireland rose dramatically in the second half of the 1990s, bringing a burst of nonwhite people to the country for
the first time. It didn't help that asylum seekers weren't allowed by the Irish
government to work (a decision rescinded only in 1999). Thus they became
easy targets for accusations that they lived off government welfare or crime.

Until the mid-1990s, many Irish believed they harbored no racial prejudices. This myth has been put to rest, and many Irish activists now combat
racial intolerance. Suzanne Smith, one antidiscrimination campaigner, is an
Irish native married to a man from Detroit. They were married in a Catholic
church in Ireland and decided to live near Dublin. Her husband is a popular
chiropractor in a country that has only several dozen of them. Her marriage
to him would be banal were he not a black American.

Smith's parents accepted her husband, yet her intermarriage alerted her to
the sensitivities of racial mixing in Ireland. Some friends advised her against
marrying a black man, and strangers still stare at her and her husband on the
street. Smith condemns discrimination but understands the Irish predicament. "After all, we're just starting to accept Protestants in our society—and
they're all white and have lived here for centuries," she says.

With other Irish natives, Smith encourages schools, government and the
media to adopt more positive images of nonwhite immigrants and other cultures. She helped to found the first support group in Ireland for mixed families. "We want to show that diversity is actually positive, that it provides
opportunities of all kinds for our society," she says.

Irish leaders are starting to agree. In 1999, the country's deputy prime minister, Mary Harney, pointedly praised the "positive benefits" of foreigners. And
Bertie Ahern, the current prime minister, favors the celebration of diversity
and opposes any backlash against immigrants.

Official Ireland can go much further in departing from traditional norms.
The government gives scant support to ethnic communities. School curricu-
lums don't reflect Ireland's new diversity. And no group exists that specifically
advances immigrant rights. "The next real push for the republic will be to
embrace multiculturalism," says one diversity proponent.

This push should be interesting, since the government no longer imposes a single standard of Irishness. For newcomers, all that is expected is that they speak English and do an honest day's work. They aren't expected to master Irish humor or the proper way to pour a pint of Guinness. And the Catholic Church isn't about to stand in the way of diversity either. A series of scandals has weakened the Church's credibility, driven down mass attendance and created an unprecedented opening for secularism. In another weird switch, foreign religions, from Mormonism to born-again Christianity, are proselytizing more aggressively in Ireland than is Catholicism. Just as newcomers don't expect to become fully Irish, many Irish want the enrichment that comes from learning the ways of strangers. From such cultural collisions, Irish cosmopolitanism will flower.

In Cork, at the National University of Ireland, Piaras MacÉinrí speculates about just how this may unfold. MacÉinrí is a former Irish diplomat who now directs the Irish Centre for Immigration Studies. He combines a flair for practical accomplishments with intellectual daring. As a diplomat, he cut his teeth on the civil war that destroyed Beirut in the 1980s, acting as a mediator between warring factions. As a scholar, he's once more trying to build bridges, only this time between Ireland's past and its future.

MacÉinrí speaks quietly, has a gentle manner and is exceedingly polite. These traits, I suppose, are the residue of his career in diplomacy. But his ideas are anything but diplomatic. He calls for nothing short of a revolution in the Irish mentality, the replacement of simplistic notions about diversity with an image of a multilayered Ireland powered by a dynamic economy. Foreigners will increasingly hold down significant jobs in Ireland, with the country's non-Irish character steadily growing. Despite the often shrill warnings of activists and the ill-conceived, fitful opposition of nativists, a hybrid Ireland is here.

"Ireland itself has become a new, more pluralistic place," MacÉinrí writes. "It has also become a place in which migrants are visible for the first time, sometimes awkwardly so. Their views and decisions will increasingly count."[21] Moreover, hybridity will cement Irish prosperity. "For the first time [in Ireland's history] we have the opportunity to redefine ourselves, even to re-invent ourselves." This is not a zero-sum game, in which adding other cultures means subtracting Irishness. MacÉinrí observes:

> There is a crying need in Ireland to subvert the assumptions underlying our monolithic public culture. Mainstream culture has nothing to fear. Irish Catholic mass attendance has not dropped because of the Bosnians. The extraordinary vitality of Irish traditional music is not affected by the presence of foreigners—except in the sense that exciting new hybridities have been incorporated into the music, here and elsewhere. We now need new and more complex definitions of Irishness to take account, not simply of the stranger who is here, but of the "stranger within."[22]

JAPAN ALONE

To imagine Japan's capacity to hybridize, consider Richard Curtis, an American who lives and works in Kanazawa, a city on the Sea of Japan about five hours north of Tokyo.

Curtis is from Napa, California. But he has given himself to Kanazawa, best known for its old samurai quarter. He came to Japan twelve years ago, at the age of twenty-three. He is married to a Japanese woman. His four-year-old daughter is Japanese. He speaks Japanese. He works for a Japanese company. He can't imagine living anywhere else. He loves Japan and its people.

So why can't he fight fires?

I forgot to say that Curtis has a hobby. He belongs to a local volunteer fire-fighting company. The experience is intense. The volunteers practice marching in formation. They perform the traditional Kaga Tobi, in which they do acrobatics on top of ladders. They conduct a winter ritual, in which they strip off their uniforms, plunge into the Sai River and shoot water hoses across the icy rapids.

Curtis joined the Bababundan fire company seven years ago. With the passing of time, the group came to trust him more. He helps hold the ladders during the acrobatic feats. He maintains fire hydrants. He helps to teach classes on fire prevention. He does everything every member of Bababundan does. Everything, that is, but fight fires.

Curtis wants to fight fires. He's trained to fight fires. But he can't. Japanese law bans foreigners from municipal activities that "exercise administrative authority" or provide a means "to influence public opinion." The wording seems vague enough to permit Richard to fight fires, but the government insists it must ban foreigners from fire fighting. What would happen, for instance, if in the middle of a conflagration Curtis's Yankee patriotism kicked in and he decided to let a building burn simply to get even with Japan for World War II?

It's an absurd possibility, but local fire companies say they must go along with the national law. Curtis's Bababundan colleagues are torn. They inducted him six years ago without thinking anything was wrong in accepting a foreigner as long as he was willing to put up with the traditional Japanese way of fire fighting. The restriction shocked the two dozen members of Bababundan. Richard wasn't asking for any special accommodations. He was acting like them even if he didn't look like them. "In our hearts [we feel] he's one of us," says one. Still, the meaning of the law is clear: no gaijin battling blazes.

"Bababundan has accepted me like no other organization I've been a part of in Japan," Richard says. "And at the same time, joining has led to my worst experiences of prejudice here."

What's amazing, though, is that Curtis has gone as far as he has. He is believed to be the only foreigner ever to join a volunteer fire department in Japan.[23]

Curtis could become a full-fledged firefighter if he became a Japanese citizen, for which he is eligible because of his marriage to a Japanese national. Japanese citizenship wouldn't even jeopardize his U.S. status. But he refuses to play his marriage card, saying it's ridiculous that someone should have to be a citizen in order to volunteer to fight fires. He also cites another concern. "I won't humor the Japanese government and change my nationality for philosophical reasons," he says. "I think it should be a moot point anyway. I'd prefer to see the world going without borders. Changing your nationality verifies this notion of a world broken up by walls."

But the walls are there, and Curtis must either scale them or tear them down. Neither is likely. His Bababundan members have given up trying to make him an official member so that he remains, perpetually, a "candidate." Still, he stays with them. He has cried, at times, watching the company perform without him. The situation angers him, yet he's pleased by the moral support he's received from his community. "Most people exhort me to never give up," he says. Even the Bababundan's outgoing chief, a few years back, told him that, despite the opposition to Curtis's participation from other fire companies, he shouldn't give up. "Don't ever let them make you quit," the chief said.

Curtis has been heartened by the local support, which he says "has shown me that a lot of the problems with racism in this country are not shared by its citizens and not as deeply ingrained in the national collective psyche as Japan's officialdom would sometimes have us believe."

So he tilts against windmills. It helps that he's encouraged by his company, a supplier of textile-making equipment. As manager of the company's overseas section, he deals chiefly with foreign customers, acting as a bridge between them and the Japanese. "That's why I'm considered valuable by my employer, because I have this dual consciousness," he says.

RICHARD CURTIS'S situation is absurd. As a symbol, it presents a bizarre image of a country so intent on maintaining purity that it can't easily accept help from outsiders even in emergencies. When I first learned of Curtis's plight, I wondered why a far-thinking bureaucrat didn't quietly make an exception and allow him to fight fires just to spare his country the embarrassment. But just the opposite occurred. When newspapers reported on his situation in 1998, officials privately vowed they would not bend the rules for Curtis. To be sure, there is talk of changing the law that justifies Curtis' exclusion. Talk, but no action.

On the subject of immigrants and diversity, Japan appears paralyzed. Of all its differences with the world's other rich nations, this is the most profound and potentially damaging. Commentators can chatter away about the lack of transparency in Japan's financial system; its low birthrate and aging society; the half-hearted commitment to democracy and the unchallenged power of unelected bureaucrats; the resistance of corporations to downsizing; the immense pork-barrel projects that spell enormous waste; the veiled protectionism that costs Japanese consumers plenty; the daily crowding that undermines the spirit of innovation. To be sure, these factors burden Japan, but to one degree or another they burden all advanced nations. Only Japan ignores its diversity and the prospects for more. Only Japan still relentlessly maintains that, whatever the cost, its social monolith must stand.

Only about 1.5 percent of Japan's 125 million people are foreigners. The percentage is tiny; foreigners make up a larger share of Iceland's population. But the actual percentage in Japan is even lower, since many people born in the country are classed as foreign. Still, their small numbers don't translate in the Japanese mind into a small threat. Look at how one observer describes Japan's treatment of people of Korean descent, who at about 650,000 are the country's biggest minority:

> There is a long list of things the Koreans cannot do in Japan. They cannot expect to attend a major university or work at a leading corporation. They pay taxes as if they were citizens, but they cannot partake of many of the social benefits their taxes help finance—public housing, for instance, and government health-care programs. They cannot vote, stand for public office, or support a political party. Nor can a Korean, even a third- or fourth-generation Korean who has never been to Korea, carry a Japanese passport. They travel on Korean documents and cannot leave Japan without a reentry visa. In effect, Koreans must have an official permit to make a journey outside of Japan.

The treatment of Koreans is unfortunate, but it is consistent with Japanese attitudes toward foreigners generally and even those toward a stigmatized group of natives, known as the *burakumin*, who are genetically identical to other Japanese yet comprise a historical untouchable caste. Patrick Smith, a fine observer of Japan, concludes that the Japanese "have been relentlessly prejudicial toward others for as long as they have recorded their own history." And once a foreigner, always a foreigner in Japan. Naturalization, a fairly routine process of gaining full citizenship rights in the United States, "is so difficult" in Japan, notes one observer, "that it takes a missionary's persistence to accomplish."[24]

Complicated, mysterious and ultimately contradictory, Japan's discriminatory attitudes toward newcomers prevent the country's leaders from dealing with their crisis in the most direct way possible: by importing people. Demographers say that if current birthrate and immigration trends hold, Japan's population will shrink by nearly half over the next century. The country's current population of 120 million will fall to 100 million by 2050 and just 67 million by 2100. Under this scenario, the country's working-age population is expected to drop by 650,000 people annually. This in turn would cause Japan's economy to shrink by 5 percent over the next fifty years, leaving the country with only one-third of the global output it now holds.

Yet despite such a scenario, the Japanese government remains hostile to foreigners, making it exceptionally hard for them to obtain Japanese citizenship or the right to work in the country. Japanese companies, meanwhile, rarely employ foreigners in Japan in professional or skilled jobs.[25] This policy of exclusion "frees" Japanese natives of the burden of having to get along in close quarters with outsiders. They are spared the trouble of having to treat aliens as equals and to adapt to the ways of outsiders.

Japan's leaders are well aware that the surest, fastest way to defuse their demographic time-bomb is to let in outsiders. An official commission on the country's future has called for a gradual change in immigration policy, declaring, "We should set up an explicit immigration and permanent-residence system to encourage foreigners who can be expected to contribute to the development of Japanese society." This was followed by a decision to loosen regulations on what types of jobs foreigners can hold in Japan and then an announcement by the country's Justice Ministry urging the Japanese to "aggressively carry out smooth acceptance" of foreigners.

This is easier said than done, however. That Japan could admit immigrants selectively, giving preference to the skilled and educated in a manner clearly motivated by self-interest, still seems objectionable to many in this insider nation. One national poll found that eight out of ten respondents opposed allowing any more immigrants into the country. The entire topic, meanwhile, is virtually taboo. Toyoo Gyohten, an economist who advises senior members of the Japanese government, finds "a total aversion" to immigration among the country's elite. Masakazu Yamazaki, a playwright from Osaka University who also advises the government, says of the Japanese, "We face tremendous handicaps to internationalize our country."[26]

No doubt millions of poor people would move to Japan if given the chance, and some can even boast of having Japanese blood. Brazil and Peru took in relatively large numbers of Japanese migrants before World War II. Peru was the first Latin American country to have diplomatic relations with Japan, and Japanese farm workers began coming around the turn of the century. In 1970, Peru had 50,000 people of Japanese descent. Even more Japanese went to Brazil, starting in 1908, when 800 arrived to work on coffee plantations. By the mid-1990s, Brazil was home to roughly 1 million people of Japanese descent. From 1985 to 1996, the Brazilian community mushroomed from a mere 2,000 to 200,000 people. The number in Peru rose from 500 to 37,000.[27]

In 1991, Japan gave these Latin Americans of Japanese descent the right to return, live and work in Japan. Large numbers of these people—called *dekasegis* in Japan—immigrated, attracted by Japan's booming economy and the difficulties of life in South America. Japanese employers welcomed the newcomers because they took unpopular jobs, which nevertheless paid higher wages than those in Brazil and Peru. When a Brazilian dentist of Japanese descent joined the exodus in 1999, he gave a simple reason for his decision to take a job at a Japanese auto plant. "A lot of yen," he said, noting that the monthly pay in the auto plant was double what he earned as a dentist in São Paulo.

The lure of jobs and better wages, however, can't mask the difficulties faced by these newcomers, despite their Japanese looks. Many don't sink roots in Japan, sending money back to Brazil and Peru, either to support families or launch a business. The remittances totaled an estimated $2 billion in 1999 alone. That the *dekasegis* prefer to invest in South America illustrates their uneasy entry into Japan despite their having maintained Japanese traditions in Brazil and Peru. "Although our appearances are so similar, there is little contact between the groups," says Lili Kawamura, a Brazilian sociologist of Japanese descent who has written a book about the *dekasegis*. "Brazilians end up creating their own peripheral economy within Japan," acting as if they are sojourners rather than melting into the Japanese mass.[28]

The uneven experience of these reverse migrants highlights the challenges facing all outsiders. "Japan is the insiders' paradise, the stakeholders' dictatorship," writes one American observer. "God help the newcomer, for the Japanese won't."[29]

In other rich countries, the best corporations often favor more relaxed immigration policies in order to combat labor shortages. Historically, Japanese corporations have preferred exporting capital (to set up plants in other countries) to importing unskilled labor, as Germany, the United States and many other nations have done during periods of rapid growth. Although they hire large numbers of foreigners outside of Japan, Japanese corporations are nearly blind to the need for a diverse workforce at home. Only Sony, the least typical of Japan's global pacesetters, shows a flair for diversity of talent that's increasingly the standard of international business. Typical small or medium-size companies in Japan have no foreigners on their payrolls, and even giant companies have only a few. Toyota, one of Japan's most admired companies and one of the world's largest automakers, employed just 24 foreigners in Japan as of December 1998. Another 105 foreigners worked in Japan, but they were short-term transfers from Toyota's overseas operations.

Japanese multinationals once boasted they didn't need foreigners at home, but such claims are rare now. And when global mergers began to dominate the business headlines in the late 1990s, Japanese companies stood on the sidelines, seemingly paralyzed, unable to broker the sort of cross-border business deals that were an increasing sign of international competitiveness. "The inability of these managers to work comfortably with people outside of Japan is one big reason for the cautious approach to global mergers," says one leading Japanese economist. A senior executive at Toyota added, in a private conversation, that the company's dearth of diversity made virtually impossible any large acquisition of a foreign automaker.

One way to avoid the need for outsiders is for Japan to rely more heavily on its women, who now contribute little to Japan's economic strength. Yet Japan also discriminates thoroughly against women; the government, for example, permitted birth-control pills to be sold only in 1999 after decades of debating whether allowing women to use them was safe and proper. Even then the government limited the variety of contraceptive pills and refused to let the state insurance fund reimburse women for their costs. "I don't expect the pill to be used widely among Japanese women because the concept of taking full control of your own body has yet to mature in Japan," says Ruriko Tsushima, a female gynecologist and sexual-health advocate.[30]

How the country expects to compete globally with such biases against women remains a mystery. Not only does sexism offend talented foreigners; it forces Japanese women to the periphery of the labor force. The government's latest research finds that women account for only about 1 percent of senior management, 2.4 percent of middle management and about 8 percent of lowest management. In the United States, women make up about 45 percent of all managers, though they are less well represented at higher levels.

Japanese companies aren't very clever at rationalizing away their sexism. According to one survey, managers claim that women lack skills, experience and decisionmaking ability. Such attitudes rile women, which may explain why they aren't likely to respond to calls for them to have more babies either (another improbable escape route from Japan's demographic demolition).

"Unless we do away with the basic thinking that women should stay at home and shouldn't be working, things aren't going to change," says Kazumi Suzuki, a twenty-six-year-old employee at an American bank who quit a Japanese firm after three frustrating years. "I've had it with Japanese companies."[31]

Indeed, Japanese sexism is the last straw for firefighter Curtis, who worries about his biracial daughter. "This is not an easy place to raise a child of mixed ancestry, no less a girl," he says. "As much as I love Japan, I have to be realistic. I'd hate my daughter to be a second-class person in her own home."

SOME JAPANESE reject mainstream prejudices and even excel at acquiring multiple affiliations and a passion for diversity. A person born in a monocultural nation can still go hybrid. A thirty-two-year-old Japanese man, whom I must call J. S. at his insistence, is living proof. J. S. was born in Tokyo, reared partly in Germany and educated at universities in the United States. He is remarkably at home in three cultures, fluent in the language of each and quite adept at calling forth literary and historical allusions from the respective traditions to bolster his own observations.

One summer day, I lunched with J. S. after visiting the offices of a leading Japanese multinational, for which he works. When I met J. S., I was struck by his rare intimacy with the world's three richest countries. He possesses a triple consciousness and slips gracefully between perspectives. A global hybrid, he refuses to pit one location against another. "I've decided to say, for simplicity's sake, that where I live and work, at any point in time, is who I am," he says.

His father, a trader, brought him as a child to Düsseldorf in the early 1970s. On weekends, he often would go for walks in the woods with a German boy and his family. "We would spend days strolling," he recalls. After several years back in Tokyo, the time came for him to attend a high school. His father encouraged him to choose one in the United States. He then stayed in America for a university degree. In one of the many oddities that mark his life, J. S. served as the president of his high school's German club in Charlotte, North Carolina. After graduation, he got a job with one of Japan's biggest companies. Work has brought him back to the United States and Germany.

J. S.'s character has been shaped by his diverse experience. He has expertise in finance and information technology, but he's essentially a cultural broker, mediating among the Germans, Americans and Japanese at his company, which has major units in the three countries. His perspective on diversity is worth reciting.

"What is America?" he asks. "It's not a melting pot. It's more of a salad or a pizza. But even that confuses people. America isn't even a place anymore. It's an understanding about life that unites Americans, not a location." Successful diversity, he adds, requires that "people become more insensitive to cultural differences. Whereas if you're in Germany, you'd better speak German. And in Japan, you'd better be Japanese. Not only that, your grandfather better be Japanese too."

J. S. realizes that the Japanese way falls short. "You win with diversity now. It's so basic it's almost a technology. Mixing is a kind of engineering. The Japanese are good engineers, yet human engineering . . . . "

His voice trails off and he looks away, momentarily embarrassed. I think of Japan's history. The Japanese people established themselves on their islands in prehistoric times, avoiding invasions and erasing any ethnic diversity save for the distinction between the Japanese and the Ainu, who were gradually pushed to the northern reaches of the archipelago. In the sixteenth century, European missionaries and traders were welcomed, and some Japanese even converted to Christianity. But when Western ideas began to compete for Japanese loyalties, the government repressed Christianity and expelled the Europeans. Two hundred and fifty years of isolation followed during which the shoguns forebade emigration from Japan on pain of death. The sudden opening to the West came with the arrival in 1853 of Commodore Matthew C. Perry of the U.S. Navy. Perry was not the first to knock on Japan's door, but he was the first to gain entrance. After concluding a trade treaty with the United States, Japan rapidly did the same with other nations. Soon, the country raced to modernize.[32]

Japan succeeded brilliantly. By the 1930s it rivaled the biggest European nations in power. But under the sway of militarists, it cruelly invaded China, longed to conquer Southeast Asia and launched an ill-conceived attack on Pearl Harbor, triggering a war with the United States. Defeated in 1945, Japan resumed its historical arc with the postwar American occupation. Over the next two decades, it became an export juggernaut, equaling or surpassing Europe and the United States in electronics, steel, car manufacture and other key industries. Large numbers of Japanese traveled the world: to follow their investments, study, trade or simply relax. Fewer foreigners came to Japan, and those who did almost never gained entry. The same situation continues to this day. Historian W. Scott Morton calls Japan's unease about foreigners its most intractable problem. The need "to open up Japan" has such profound psychological implications that perhaps "the Japanese are not aware of" the extent of their isolation.[33]

Presented with this thumbnail history, J. S. reminds me that Japan's separateness is considered the basis for its virtues. "The reason Toyota was so successful was that it wasn't diverse. The Japanese notion of unity, single-mindedness—diversity would have upset this." The intense focus on internal resources contrasts sharply with Germany's outward bent. "If you read Goethe," Germany's most beloved writer, "he really becomes a European on his trip to Italy," J. S. says. "The whole notion of a voyage of discovery is so un-Japanese. This urge to overcome your parochialism is one of the most attractive of German attitudes."

The point makes J. S. recall his father's advice to him about identity: "'Son,' he told me, 'you should be proud of your Japanese heritage, but you should also overcome it. You can learn to accept other cultures and even strive to find a common element between them.'" J. S. took his father's advice and never regretted it. "For me an international community is a training ground," he says, then turns to his lunchmates, neither of whom is Japanese. When talking to them, he says, "I realize that my Japaneseness may prevent me from saying something I really should say."

This makes him sad, but also helps him grow more aware of the limitations of the Japanese and German sides of his character. "It's a two-way thing," he says. "As a tribe the Germans and the Japanese really haven't discovered the world yet. I know this sounds wild, but Germany and Japan were hampered in discovering the world. Everyone thinks about the end of the Cold War, and the fall of the Berlin Wall and the unification of Germany, but really the ghosts of World War II still haunt Germany and Japan. A half century has passed and diversity still hasn't internalized for us yet. We're more comfortable with other members of our tribe." And uncomfortable talking about diversity. "The topic is taboo in Japan," he says. "Partly this is self-denial. People don't want to think about Japan's aims [in the 1920s and 1930s] to colonize Asia. People don't want to think about our tradition of mistreating the Koreans. Even those born in Japan carry an ID card, are discriminated against. And yet when I look at a third-generation Korean I can't tell they aren't Japanese."

J. S. now sits upright in his chair, breathless, not eating. He's wanted to say this for a while. I tell him that perhaps it will take the Japanese a century to adapt to this new mongrel world. After all, how can the Japanese be expected to accept outsiders when they can't even face up to the little diversity long present in their society?

"The Japanese mind wants to keep the illusion of oneness," J. S. says. "Oh, sure, Japan is a homogeneous nation," he says in a mocking tone. "What about Hokkaido and Okinawa [the islands to the far north and south of Japan]? They are very different. An Okinawa guy is physically different. What about the untouchables? The Koreans? This is a sensitive issue, better forgotten." On delivering those words, J. S. laughs bitterly. Official Japan's obsession with purity angers him.

Another day, I meet him for dinner at a restaurant near his office. We eat a meal of miso soup, sashimi and teriyaki, then stroll down a darkened street toward his train stop. Before we part he wonders, "What will happen to my country?"

IN THE SECOND HALF of the 1990s, the status of non-Japanese people rose, underscoring the possibility that Japan might begin slouching toward hybridity. Foreigners have become a more common sight in Japan's big cities. The media portray non-natives more positively than in the past. The problem of discrimination has at least become a topic of discussion. Languages other than Japanese are afforded more space. Tokyo and two other cities even have multilingual radio stations. Ohata Kohei, managing director of the Tokyo station, echoes the shift in attitudes when he says that immigrants "have a right to be informed even if they don't speak Japanese."

Non-Japanese remain stigmatized, if not demonized, at the national level of Japanese government and society. Japan's elites have had "no serious discussion of what it might mean if Japan were to become a multi-cultural society."[34] But at a local level, non-Japanese are gaining a higher profile, if not exactly gaining more power and acceptance. In 1997, Kawasaki became the first major city to allow non-Japanese to sit for exams for all regular government jobs. The same year it also established an assembly of foreign residents that gives suggestions to the mayor. Tokyo and Kanagawa now do the same. Some local governments, meanwhile, are asking that non-Japanese be allowed to vote in local elections. One even has asked the central government to allow foreigners to run for and hold local offices.

The tension between national disregard for the special needs of non-Japanese residents and the more solicitous attitudes of local governments makes for a confusing situation. One study found that Tokyo had "no general guidelines for dealing with foreign residents," but that city boroughs with a high concentration of foreigners had informal programs, helping them in various ways, from printing informational leaflets in other languages to hiring multilingual staff to providing full-time interpreters. Florian Coulmas, the study's author and an expert on Japanese attitudes toward diversity, thinks that local governments are more interested in solving practical problems than debating principles and so are more willing to help non-Japanese in specific ways. He thinks that Japan is starting to accept diversity at the grassroots level. Basic values are changing, and natives are growing more tolerant of difference. "Minorities have come out of the shadow of the ideology of social uniformity," he believes. "The push for a pluralistic Japan is welcomed and supported by many Japanese." Thomas Berger, a Japan watcher at Johns Hopkins University, echoes this view: Japan's "usually fractious intelligentsia seem to be groping toward a pragmatic acceptance that a certain level of immigration is both inevitable and in Japan's national interest."[35]

Tolerance of outsiders is one thing. Resistance to supplanting a monolithic Japanese identity with a multicultural one is quite another—and an enormous challenge. Even small changes in Japan's approach to non-Japanese within its borders raise the specter of a nationalist backlash. Xenophobia stands at the core of Japan's popular mentality. Indeed, ordinary citizens are quick to turn on foreigners and blame them for Japan's problems. The sport of baseball offers a continuing reminder of this mentality. The Japanese are avid fans of the country's professional league, and they usually welcome (at least initially) the dozens of foreign players who add skills and luster to Japan's largely homegrown teams. Each team can field no more than three foreign players at once. Many of the imports are American; some are black. Well paid and lavishly feted, these players are intensely scrutinized and often found wanting. This cycle of acceptance and rejection occurs regularly in Japan, exposing the country's underlying ambivalence over relying on outsiders to enhance its most popular professional sport.

Foreign players usually resign themselves to disappointing the Japanese, and staying quiet about it. Occasionally, the lid flies off. In one such case in 1999, an American pitcher on the Hanshin Tigers wrote an open letter in which he accused his manager of not wanting foreign players to be part of the team. The American, Darrel May, was suspended for the rest of the season for his outburst. The incident reinforced the widespread view that outsiders disrupt the team. As one Japanese baseball official l~ter said, foreign players "don't contribute to harmony."[36]

STRANGER WITHIN

In Ireland and Japan, the mystery of the stranger lies close to the surface, concealed but present. In Ireland, tribalism begins to give way to an ironic, postmodern sense of the nation as a human construct, capacious enough to include anyone who shows up. As James Joyce wrote in *Ulysses*, "A nation is the same people living in the same place." Having been down so long, the Irish still can't quite believe they're up. And if the price of winning is mongrelizing Irish society, why not? It beats being poor again. In Japan, no sense of irony exists about the nation. Japan has never been successfully invaded by outsiders in war, and peaceful "invaders" may find the country's social defenses no easier to thwart. Too, the Japanese recall their powerhouse years of the 1980s and yearn for an explosive resurrection. The idea of Japanese greatness, born of purity, is hardly a distant thunder.

Ireland and Japan struggle with the emergence of radical mixing as a central force that is reordering the world. Each nation cobbles together a set of defenses and strategies to cope with hybridization. Governments talk of policies and programs, laws and mechanisms, but deep changes comes from individuals. In his astute account of the Japanese, Patrick Smith takes note of "their separateness from themselves and the rest of us." He then cites a remarkable passage from Julia Kristeva, a French psychoanalyst who was raised in Bulgaria. She observes that we learn to accept others by realizing

> our own disturbing otherness, for that indeed is what bursts in to confront that "demon," that threat, that apprehension generated by the projected apparition of the other at the heart of what we persist in maintaining as a proper, solid "us." By recognizing our uncanny strangeness we shall neither suffer from it nor enjoy it from the outside. The foreigner is within me, hence we are all foreigners. If I am a foreigner, there are no foreigners.[37]

A DAYAK LOGGER DOES HIGH-TECH...IN SILICON VALLEY

SANTA CLARA, CALIFORNIA—The shiny steel machine bellows like a whale. Donald Jagau, his long hair wrapped in a net, leans over the belly of the machine and shifts the position of a small circuit board inching along a conveyor belt. Holding a gas torch in his gloved hand, he burns some excess solder off the machine's scrubber. Sweat runs down his forehead, gathering in a pool above his plastic goggles.

It is ninety degrees in the sealed, brightly lit "hot-air" room. But Donald steps lightly. He's used to the heat. He grew up in the jungles of Borneo, where the heat is worse. His small kampong, or village, is on Malaysia's side of this storied island in Southeast Asia. Reteh, as his kampong is called, has no plumbing or electricity. A dozen families share a gorgeous bluff above the winding Kayan River. The river is the center of life for his Bidayuh people, one of Borneo's largest indigenous Dayak tribes. The people of Reteh bathe in the river, wash their clothes in the river, play in the river and use the river as a highway. The river is the main link to schools, friends and Kruzen, another village that unlike Reteh is connected by road to Kuching, the largest city in the Malaysian province of Sarawak.

One day in the summer of 1995, while cutting down a tree in the thick forest surrounding his village, Donald heard an announcement on his portable radio. An American company was looking for workers to hire and train for skilled jobs in one of Kuching's first high-tech factories. The only requirement was a knowledge of basic English and a high school degree. Donald had both. He also had a desire to earn more than he could cutting down odd trees and growing rice in nearby paddy fields. He asked his father's advice about getting a job in the city and then decided to apply.

The American company, Hadco, made a printed circuit board, a piece of electronics that went into cordless phones, computers and other gadgets. The PCB was a precision device, assembled out of individual chips, and then blended together with a standard of cleanliness and accuracy that no auto plant or even hospital could match. A worker might handle a machine worth $500,000. Learning the intricacies of this machine was the core of his or her job. Hadco had only one factory in Silicon Valley but it needed a foreign location to cut costs. It chose Kuching, an hour's flight from Penang, Malaysia's established high-tech center; the move meant lower costs but also recruiting an entire workforce from scratch. To guarantee that new employees understood how to run an advanced electronics plant, the company planned to send about 100 of them to the United States for an eleven-month apprenticeship.

It took Donald three hours, traveling by riverboat, van and then bus, to reach Kuching. He first took a written test, in English, in a towering Hilton hotel in the center of the city. He usually spoke his native Bidayuh language, but he spoke Malay, the country's official language, fluently, of course. He almost never spoke English, but when he saw the exam questions the words made sense to him. The were mainly about understanding procedures and solving math problems. The test lasted an hour and Donald went home. Two weeks later, a friend of his father's visited Donald's village, carrying a letter from Hadco. Donald had passed his test, and the company wanted him to come for an interview.

Donald returned to the Kuching Hilton at the specified date and time. There he met Bob Snyder, an American whose job was to launch the factory in Kuching. Snyder was a tall, casual, friendly Midwesterner who was on his first foreign assignment. About fifty, he was an experienced high-tech production manager. Open and unpretentious, Snyder knew almost nothing about Borneo's complex tribal structure and the often contentious relations between dominant Malays and the Chinese ethnics who essentially ran business in Kuching. Snyder greeted Donald and asked him to sit down. Glancing up from Donald's file, Snyder looked over the Bidayuh villager. Donald, then twenty-seven years old, was about five feet, eight inches tall, tawny in color, squat and powerfully built. He had a broad nose, narrow eyes and wore his black hair long and loose. His smile revealed two gaps in his top front teeth.

Donald intrigued Snyder. All the other candidates came from either Kuching or cities in far more industrialized East Malaysia, separated from Borneo by the South China Sea. Only Donald came from a jungle village. Only Donald, of all the Dayaks from the hinterland to apply for factory jobs, made the first cut. Snyder was glad Donald did, too, because he worried that Kuching, with about 300,000 people, wasn't large enough to supply all the workers he might need. If many high-tech factories opened here, the city's laborers would be snapped up, and companies, if they wanted to avoid raising wages, would have to begin hiring from the jungle villages. "Maybe Donald Jagau is our experiment," Snyder thought. If he could take a man out of the jungle and turn him into a reliable worker, then he had nothing to worry about.

Snyder asked Donald some polite questions about his life. He was surprised to learn that Donald had worked on construction sites in Singapore for about a year and then sold books and encyclopedias, of all things, around Sarawak. But two years ago, he had returned to his village and now eked out a living cutting down trees with his brother, who owned a chain saw, and farming with his father. He'd never used a personal computer or seen a printed circuit board, but he'd taken apart an outboard motor.

It all sounded fine to Snyder. He asked Donald if he would come to California for nearly a year as a trainee in Hadco's factory near San Francisco. He would not be able to visit Borneo during the training, and when he returned he would have to work for Hadco for at least three more years. He then told Donald the starting salary: about $275 a month, higher with overtime. And while Donald was in the United States, the company would pay for his housing, food, clothes, transportation, even his entertainment.

Donald took the job.

IN CALIFORNIA, Donald thrived. His easy manner and infectious laugh won over Americans and put at ease, too, the many Mexican immigrants who worked in Hadco's factory. He had a knack for understanding the way machines worked. In training classes he said little, but understood a lot. After work, in a bungalow he shared with five other Malaysians, he made detailed drawings of the arcane machines used by the factory. He pored over manuals, written in dry English, memorizing the daily routines. At the start of each day, for instance, he had to complete seventy-five distinct actions—such as cleaning manifolds and solder rollers to remove excess oil—designed to keep his machine on course. The prep process alone took an hour, but it usually guaranteed that his machine was then in good working order for sixteen hours. Small glitches could send it off course, however. Printed circuit boards are so temperamental that any imperfection can spoil them. Donald quickly learned that "troubleshooting is my number one priority. There's no other thing. If you know troubleshooting, no problem."

I met Donald in May 1996, near the end of his eleven-month stay in California. He had been to Disneyland, attended a Giants baseball game, watched enough professional wrestling on television to recognize Hulk Hogan and learned how to find pancake mix at the local Safeway, the largest supermarket Donald had ever seen. During the entire time, he hadn't spoken to his wife, parents or three children. Not even exchanged a letter. It didn't seem to bother him. His family had no phone and no official mail delivery. Bidayuh men often went on long journeys, and this was no different. He was building a better life for his family, he told himself. And why think about them? He would only miss them. He remembered in Singapore, at the construction site, how a man talked so much about his wife and children that he finally quit and went home. So no one at the company even knew he had a wife and children. Everyone thought he was single. Everyone except one friend, Frankie, a Dayak trainee who had a degree in engineering from a U.S. university. Though Frankie was higher in the organization, the two were like brothers. They talked constantly about work. Frankie even shared with Donald engineering documents, which they discussed, because it made Donald a better troubleshooter.

On a visit to Hadco's plant—arranged because I'd learned the company had a large group of Malaysian trainees who were about six weeks away from returning to Kuching—Snyder introduced me to Donald, whom he considered a prized recruit. We first looked at him through a glass window that opened onto the hot-air room. By this point, Donald worked regular shifts without supervision, and he was nearing the end of one. I peered through the window and watched him, all dressed up, working the machine like a champ. He moved around his machine gracefully, his fingers running over pieces of it, doing tasks that bewildered me. When his shift ended, he joined me outside in the corridor, with Snyder and two other managers sticking close.

I was immediately taken by Donald's enthusiasm and sincerity. As I kidded him about the heat inside his sealed room, he joked back, and the two of us started teasing one another. We were so giddy that Snyder grew nervous and his two colleagues tried to shoo me away. I stood my ground and told Donald that I planned to visit Kuching in two weeks. "Can I visit your village?" I asked him.

He looked gleeful. No one from the company had visited his village, or even bothered to find out how his parents were doing. "Yes, you can," he shouted. "And my father knows English, so he will have no problem understanding you."

"That's terrific," I said. "Give me his phone number."

Donald fell over laughing. "Funny," he said when he caught his breath. "In my village, no phone." He started laughing again, and then, realizing how little I knew about his world, repeated three or four times, "No phone!"

I got the picture. "Maybe I can just show up," I said. By now one of Snyder's people had a hand on my arm. "I can have somebody drive me there. That's great, right?"

"Yes. You are lucky because there is a great road to my village."

Beautiful, I'm thinking. "Give me the directions."

"Take the road to Serian," Donald said carefully, spelling out the name. "Then head west to Mongkoss." He spelled the name again. "Then you stop at a village, Kruzen, along the river, and you get a boat."

Ah, not so simple after all. I told Donald I would try nonetheless, and he thanked me. "My father will be glad. He likes meeting Americans."

The casual way Donald said this made me ask, "He's met some before?"

"Yes, yes, many times," Donald said, explaining that the Seventh-Day Adventists had converted his father years before and that he knew the local pastor well.

I FOUND Donald's father through that pastor, a kind, nearly deaf man named Dindall Rahoon. He arranged for Donald's father to meet me at the pickup point in the river. Thanks to him, I saw Donald's family and returned to California with news that they were well. I brought back pictures and a tape recording of his mother and father asking him questions. They worried about Donald and wondered not only when he would return, but why he never sent any money home.

I asked Donald where his salary went. He explained that the company deposited it in a bank in Kuching. He would like his wife to get some of the money, but she could not read or write and no one in his family ever had a bank account. All along, he planned to give his father a lot of money when he arrived at home. That's good, I told him, because his father complained that his portable generator won't work so that now he has no electricity, even for a few minutes, to watch the tiny television he owns. He can't afford an outboard either, and everyone else in the village has one now. So instead of smoothly gliding along the river, pushed by a 2.5-horsepower engine, he had to push against the riverbed with a long bamboo stick. This doubled what was a twenty-five-minute journey from his village to Kruzen.

His brother was broke too, I told him. He couldn't even afford to fix his chain saw that needed repairs, so he sold it. Loss of the chain saw was a setback. In the jungle, a chain saw meant a livelihood. With the saw, his brother had felled trees and carved them into wood planks that he sold to the people in nearby villages. The saw cost more than a thousand Malaysian ringgit, or about what Donald earned in a month.

The news stunned Donald. He groped for words, then asked me again and again whether the chain saw was really gone.

It was.

Returning home meant facing all this, but there was more, much more. Donald was about to begin living in two worlds, simultaneously, for the first time. In California, he could pretend that he wasn't a Bidayuh plucked out of the jungle by some mysterious American corporation and transported to Disneyland. He could imagine himself as any other of the dozen nationalities in the factory. Like he belonged there, as much as the Mexicans or the Vietnamese. His English was even better than what most of these other immigrants spoke. But back in Kuching, he could not escape his past, his ties to the Bidayuh and to his parents and, most of all, to his wife Lucy.

He worried about Lucy, a pretty, shy woman from the nearest village across the Kayan River. She was a good Bidayuh wife and she liked his mother, which was good. But he wondered how he would feel about her now. She had never attended school and spoke only Bidayuh and a little Malay. Donald feared he would find Lucy unattractive now. "I am modern; she is not," he told me as we made the short walk from the factory to his bungalow. He had an e-mail account, and the person he cared most about had never heard a dial tone.

I tried to grasp his situation. Dual identities stretch people, I realized, but could someone stretch this far? Could Donald appreciate his old way of life, or had his life in the factory—and in the fast lane to Disneyland—spoiled it for him? Could he be both high-tech man and Bidayuh, human asset for an American corporation in Asia and a Malaysian struggling to make his way into his country's middle class? And even if he showed the maturity and wisdom required to straddle two worlds, would rising expectations eat away at his justifiable pride in his accomplishments? Could he somehow strike a balance between his traditional village, and his new world, where he now raced constantly to gain better skills, higher pay and a brighter future? Or would he ditch one world in favor of the other, because—as some skeptics insist—it's just too hard for a person to live in midair.

I wanted Donald to pull it off, and so did Snyder, his mentor. But in early June, as Donald prepared to return to Borneo, Snyder wondered about his future. "I worry that when he gets home, he may just go back to his village, take his vacation time and disappear," Snyder said. "I just hope I'm wrong."

WHEN DONALD ARRIVED at his village, his mother Daot saw him from her doorway, climbing to the top of the stairs from the river. She waited for him to reach the door, watching him walk along the path as if he'd left this morning for Kuching.

"How is California?" she asked.

"Normal," Donald said.

They did not hug or kiss. But Donald took a photo album from his bag and showed his mother pictures of himself at Disneyland.

Before long the whole village gathered around him. His daughter, Phillipa, a few months old when he left for California, didn't recognize him and clung to Lucy.

A neighbor, Mambang, wasn't impressed with Donald's pictures but liked his looks. "You've grown fat at least," he said.

Although Donald was trim by American standards, he'd lost the emaciated look of his father, who typically went around shirtless, showing his ribs. His father didn't greet his son, only said simply, "I need money."

Donald quickly promised to give his father a monthly allowance and buy him an outboard motor. His pledge ignited a family celebration.

While he sipped rice wine, surrounded by his family, Donald did figures in his head. His salary, without overtime, was 1,100 ringgit. After giving his parents 200 ringgit a month, he would be left with 900, or about $225 a month. Out of this, he must pay for a house within commuting distance of Hadco's factory in Kuching. He couldn't live in his village, which was too far away. The city was expensive, however, and houses were in short supply. It would be hard to find a place he could afford. Even Snyder, the factory manager, worried that Donald would lack the money for a decent place. Yet Donald wasn't even thinking about decent. Can he afford a shack? he wondered.

Before looking, Donald visited a Chinese moneylender in Kuching who lent money to Bidayuh in need. Bidayuh rarely borrowed money from banks because they lacked collateral and a knowledge of finance. Informal loans were common, despite high interest rates.

Donald had no plans to borrow money. He owed too much already. Three years before, he had borrowed 3,000 ringgit at a yearly interest rate of 120 percent, or 10 percent per month of the total debt. This meant he must pay 300 ringgit a month merely to stay current. The moneylender allowed Donald to suspend payment while he worked in the United States, so now he had to pay a year's worth of back interest, more than the original amount he borrowed. This was a big chunk of the money he'd saved. He could stiff the Chinese man but he feared retaliation. The Chinese is a nice guy as long as you don't make trouble for him, Donald thought. He handed him a stack of bills and left.

After paying his debt, buying his father a motor, giving his parents their first allowance and buying presents for his sister, brother and wife, Donald had little money left, only enough to rent a small windowless shack off the main road to Serian, the nearest big town to his village. The shack was about nine miles from Hadco's factory. It had no toilet and only a shower stall with a hose connected to a spigot, not a fixture. There was no kitchen. Lucy had to cook on a kerosene stove. The floor was bare concrete with a few patches of vinyl covering. Flimsy foam pads, two of them, served as beds. He had a nine-inch television in one corner of the room. No other furniture.

The shack, one of two dozen separated by a dirt lane, had no address, got no mail. If Donald needed to make a call, there was a pay phone about fifty yards from his door, along the busy Serian road.

AFTER TWO WEEKS, Donald resumed work at Hadco, whose factory was ready to launch. On day shifts, he rose at 5:30 a.m. to an alarm clock. He washed by tossing cups of water on himself in a shower stall, then dressed without waking his wife and waited on the main road for a company van to pick him up. He did not wish his coworkers in the van to see his home. "I am ashamed of this place," he told one. At the factory, he ate breakfast—often pancakes, which he grew to like in the United States.

After breakfast, he put on his work clothes and the fun started. He was good at his job, completely serious. His machine enveloped his mind; it was no surprise that he often dreamed about it. Having never owned a car, a bicycle or even a lawn mower, Donald had a sort of first love affair with a thing. After six months, Hadco asked him to begin training others. The company even began hiring people on his say-so—people from his village and neighboring ones.

Donald's expanded role lifted his sights. "If I had money, I'd go back to school and become an engineer," he thought.

The responsibility of a family made this impossible. The nearest he could get to engineering was to hang out with Frankie, his pal from California. Donald idolized Frankie, who was everything he wasn't. Frankie was an expert who earned many times more than Donald did. Frankie had a proper house and a car. And he had no wife or kids to slow him down.

Frankie talked engineering with Donald and drove him places in his car. They teased each other a lot, something they couldn't do at work, where Frankie had to be super-serious. One night, they went to a posh party at the Hilton hotel. Another guest asked Frankie for his business card and when Frankie gave it to him, the guest asked Donald for his card. Embarrassed at not having one, Donald shook his head, speechless. Later he and Frankie laughed themselves silly over this. Once Frankie teased Donald about not having a business card and explained the joke to me, while Donald laughed uncontrollably. "You are the 'other engineer,'" Frankie told his friend.

But in the factory, Donald was a hot-air man who occasionally gave talks to coworkers on improving their maintenance techniques. He was a factory worker, too low to show up on an "org" chart. The highlight of his week often was a visit to a spacious badminton court that Hadco rented out for its employees (Malaysians take to the sport as Americans do to basketball). Newly resurfaced and flanked by nine rows of spectator seats, the badminton court gave Donald a feeling of prosperity. Wearing Adidas sneakers, shorts and a white shirt, he played doubles, covering the court quickly and wielding a killer forehand at the net. His racket, his one real luxury, cost him the equivalent of one month's rent.

On the court, Donald was the equal of his superiors at the factory, and his natural personality came through. With little urging, he broke into gags. After scoring a point one night, he danced in a small circle, waving his arms. During the game, he forgot his money troubles—and almost imagined himself in Silicon Valley again.

But off the court his bubble burst. He was often too tired to play with his two youngest children, a consequence of switching back and forth between day and night shifts. He described those days as "work and sleep, that's it."

Lucy, meanwhile, was glad Donald had a steady job and paycheck, but she missed her village. In Reteh she had spent her days helping in the fields, picking wild fruits and vegetables in the jungle and making rugs and baskets. In idle moments, she turned discarded aluminum soda cans into bright flowers, by carving the cans into strips and then assembling them into a metal mosaic that she hung on the walls of the Jagau house. Her parents and siblings lived nearby, so she was never lonely. In Kuching, she endured a numbing routine. Her one diversion was food shopping. Each day a traveling grocer visited the dirt lane, and Lucy picked out what she needed.

Donald let his wife keep all his cash. He didn't trust himself with it. Besides, the moneylender kept his bankbook as security. In a humiliating ritual, Donald had to visit his office and get the book in order to withdraw funds from his account.

One night Donald awoke from a fitful sleep and cursed his creaky shanty. "Why am I so stupid as to pay him 300 ringgit a month?" he wondered. "This is killing me."

Without the debt, Donald thought, "I can make a good life." But out of a sense of pride, he wouldn't ask Hadco for a loan. Some U.S. companies in Malaysia have set up credit unions for their local employees, but not Hadco. The company won't even offer financial counseling to its employees. That's probably needed, since some aren't used to receiving a regular paycheck. Donald knew of coworkers who owed money to local sharks, as he did. It was so normal that he never thought to complain about it.

The debt drove him to improbable fantasies. One night, about a year after returning from California, he told Frankie that he imagined being hired by another U.S. company and sent to America for more training. Frankie said this wasn't realistic, but Donald didn't believe him. Later, after Frankie left, he sat on the floor of his shack, wearing a "Great America" tank top, and said glumly, "I am very sad. More than a year since California, and I am still sad."

Donald wanted to shake his sadness. In the last few days of 1997, he decided not to pay the January rent on his shanty, hoping the landlord would let him catch up later. Then he took his meager savings and a small gift from a relative and paid off the moneylender. He got his bankbook back and his self-respect, but worried that his family would run short of food.

"I am bankrupt now and still living in this rotten house," he wrote one night on his computer at work.

His predicament made the memory of California grow brighter. "I want to go back," he said. "I will go back. In my dreams I am thinking this."

DONALD DREAMS of California less now. Since his return to Borneo in the summer of 1996, I have stayed in touch with him, visiting him several times and exchanging many e-mails. I admire Donald, and when I see him, we have fun together. I usually rent a car, and now, even without Donald's help, I can find the spot on the river where a boat will ferry us to his village. I am no longer astonished at the sight of naked women bathing in the river, or rice farmers steering traditional flatboats with Johnson outboard motors. A third of the way to Reteh, a rope bridge spans the river about twenty feet aboveground, which always reminds me that I must ask Donald to cross it with me some day.

I am past the point of thinking I will find the answers to the questions posed by his life. These are not Donald's questions, they are mine, and he is no hurry to answer them. I am sure I still hardly know him at all, and he is bewildered by me at times. He and other Bidayuh quite freely litter, discarding empty cans and packages in the forest near their kampong and even along the river. One time I told him sternly that I thought littering unwise. He was unconvinced, although out of respect for me he stopped littering at least while I was in view. He can't understand why I'm always taking notes, and hurrying to get somewhere, or who would pay me to do what I do or read what I write.

For all our differences, we share an irreverence toward social conventions and a curiosity about how other people live. In short, we are drawn toward strangers and so to each other. Of my oddities, Donald is quick to cry foul. Once I drove him, Lucy and his kids to the beach on the South China Sea in a rental car, and Donald teased me the entire trip about my zany turns and willful ignorance of traffic rules. "Cowboy driver!" he kept shouting. "Cowboy driver!" Another time, Donald came up to my room in the Holiday Inn and watched me open my computer database and then rattle off a half dozen phone calls to Bangkok, New York, London and, for all he knew, Timbuktu. "You know everybody in the whole world," he exclaimed, knowing I didn't.

Donald is a kind of rebel. As a Bidayuh, he must survive in a country that relentlessly elevates Islam and the Malay people, who colonized Borneo centuries before the British. His father's conversion to Christianity was part of a defense against the encroachments of Islam in a country where all nonbelievers who marry a Muslim must themselves convert. Donald's whole life, in some sense, is a continual rebellion against Malay dominance. His insurgence doesn't stop there. One night he, Frankie and I were in a restaurant about to order dinner. It was a traditional Malay seafood place, where diners made their own dishes by choosing from a wide array of fresh fish and jungle vegetables. I stood up to view the day's offerings, and while my back was turned, Bob Snyder, Hadco's chief in Kuching, walked up to Donald's table. It was an indelicate moment because, after initially introducing me to Donald and arranging interviews with his coworkers, Hadco had decided not to help me any further. The company feared I would somehow fail to celebrate sufficiently its beneficence toward Donald and other Malaysians and that Americans might get the impression that a company who had almost no African-American employees in California was somehow willing to lavish training on foreigners when it wouldn't do that for an American without skills.

Snyder was stunned to see Donald and Frankie sitting with me at his favorite restaurant. "What are you telling him?" Snyder asked Donald.

"Only about me personally," Donald replied. "Not the company."

Snyder reminded him he had been asked not to speak with me, but Frankie defended him. "You can order him at work, but this is his own time," Frankie said. "You are not paying us while we eat dinner." Donald smiled, giving his approval, but said nothing more. Snyder retreated.

When I returned to the table, Donald said let's go, and Frankie explained what happened. I apologized but Donald said I didn't need to. We moved to another restaurant. Snyder watched us go.

IT IS EASY to paint Donald as a creature of an American multinational. Cynics paint these corporate behemoths as bloodsuckers, but I have seen countless examples of how they can transform the material and psychological lives of employees. And not just in developing countries either. The best multinationals are dynamic agents of change that create insurgents within the societies they invade or, at the very least, foster centers of excellence. These insurgents then fan out through a society, carrying a greater sense of professionalism and more powerful technical skills than possessed by those in the strictly local economy. This sense of fair play, expressed through professionalism, can be strikingly at odds with local practice. In many countries, work is still shot through with nepotism and the "old-boy" network. Having the wrong last name, coming from the wrong class, getting the wrong grades on standardized tests—all these can still doom a person to obscurity in many countries regardless of a person's drive and competence. The best multinationals set a higher standard for excellence in countries where jobs are considered handouts and not won through merit and hard work.

This sense of fairness turns work into a haven from inequities found elsewhere in a society. Donald is my favorite example of this, if only because he has traveled further—from his childhood until now—than anyone I know. He is a multinational corporate asset. And as that asset, he has seen California and traveled to London and Edinburgh for two weeks of training on new machinery. He has a pile of training certificates and in fifteen minutes can explain enough about making printed circuit boards that scores of factories around the world would hire him in a minute. Yet when I walk into a store with Donald, the shopkeeper sees him as a Bidayuh, maybe a stupid and timid one too (since Bidayuh are famously quiet and calm; in bygone days they were not fierce headhunters, but a pastoral people). From this world of belonging—no one joins his Bidayuh tribe but is born into it—Donald has moved into the world of achievement, where his sense of self derives increasingly from what he has accomplished. Whatever he thinks about Hadco, he can thank them for that, for without Hadco, Donald surely would be cutting down trees at a timber camp (as his brother did for many years), roaming Southeast Asia looking for temporary work or growing rice and pepper in his home village.

Donald's pride over his accomplishments surfaces now and again and sometimes even gets the better of him. In early 1998, Donald moved out of his shanty into a newly constructed modern house on the edge of Kuching. The house had three bedrooms, a kitchen, a living room and a bathroom with all the expected plumbing. The house made Donald happy. The owner was a Bidayuh who gave Donald a good deal because he grew up near Donald's village and knew his father.

A few months after he moved in, I showed up for a visit and was delighted to see Donald's new home. His children were healthy and Lucy seemed much happier. Donald wasn't. He was frustrated with Hadco despite a stream of praise and small gains in pay and status. He spent more time training others now, even writing short manuals for coworkers on how to carry out certain tasks. Still, he barely earned $300 a month, and (with the downturn in Asian economies in 1998) his overtime hours had fallen. He complained (rightly) that he deserved more money and a better schedule, maybe all days and no nights ever. With more money, he could buy a motorcycle and get to work on his own, no more rising early to catch a lift with the company van. He wondered whether he should quit Hadco. Maybe another

American company would pay him more. Or maybe he'd be better off living in Reteh. "I could earn almost as much money working in the jungle," he said. Still, the idea of living off the land again seemed a distant possibility. Better to find another high-tech job. He pulled out a letter he'd written to another company that people believed would soon open an electronics factory in Kuching. "I know I can do better elsewhere," he said, then asked if I could help him with a résumé.

Listening to Donald, I thought about the perverse ironies of his life. In bringing him into their tribe, American executives believed they would create the stereotypical Asian worker: grateful, docile and loyal to his own detriment. Instead, Donald seemed eerily American, consumed with thinking about bettering his lot and seemingly dismissive of the company's claim on him.

His individualism actually worried me. On this visit, I gave him about $250 in Malaysian ringgit, which I considered a token of appreciation. I'd never promised him any money, but I was so pleased he had gotten out of debt and into a new house that I thought he deserved a housewarming gift. As we sat in my favorite restaurant (the one Bob Snyder liked too), I discussed with him his options. The $250 was enough to buy a decent refrigerator, which I thought Lucy would appreciate since her house had no appliances. But Donald wanted the motorcycle, and my money would cover the down payment on a purchase of one. I worried that the motorcycle dealers, all Chinese merchants in Kuching, would charge Donald a fortune in interest and then never give him proper title to the bike down the line. We even visited a few bike shops, and every dealer refused to give any proof of ownership, only writing in a small book what Donald would owe and how much he should pay monthly.

I also thought that buying a motorcycle seemed a selfish purchase and that he owed Lucy some kind of gift. He countered that Lucy would benefit from a bike; he could shop for groceries. I told him I feared the motorcycle would become his means of disappearing, so that Lucy would be alone with the kids even more than she was now. He shook his head, but I was serious. Having a refrigerator would empower Lucy, I thought, making her seem more modern to Donald and thus more appealing.

For two hours, we debated the purchase: fridge or bike. Finally he agreed to let me buy the fridge, though he seemed unhappy about it. I arranged with the shopkeeper to send the fridge to Donald's house and advised Donald to check the model when it arrived to see that it matched what we had bought. I had to leave for the airport that afternoon, so I hurriedly said good-bye but left Donald the telephone number of my hotel in case something went wrong with the delivery.

I flew to Kuala Lumpur and the next morning, in my hotel, I was awakened by the telephone. I said an unsteady hello into the receiver and heard Donald's voice. "Lucy is so happy," he said. "I start filling the refrigerator today."

I did not ask Donald with what. Shopping he knows. Indeed, some months later he bought a motorcycle on store credit and by my next visit was a seasoned rider. For the fun of it, I had him drive me around the block on his bike. Now I call him "cowboy driver."

THE TRAPPINGS of modern life do not diminish Donald. His experiences in America, his mastery over an aspect of the bewildering technological jungle, his rising material life in Kuching, his growing sense of self-worth—all these factors make Donald more, not less. To him, affiliations can be piled up like chips on a card table. They are not opponents of his inherited identity. Even as his horizons broaden, he retains his passion for his village, his parents and his Bidayuh past. Roots are not a zero-sum game. One attachment does not lessen another.

The last time I saw Donald, he told me something that made me think again of roots and wings. He no longer talks of quitting Hadco. The company has him on days-only now, and his salary is slightly higher than before. He realizes that hot-air machines, and the precision world of electronics, are a part of him now that he doesn't wish to give up. If he did not work for Hadco, he would work for someone else. The fantasies of returning to the jungle are gone. But they are not forgotten.

Donald's dream now is the dream of hybridity. He wants to live a double life, with one foot in his village and the other in "the modern world." As we walk in the jungle one day, past one of his father's abandoned rice paddies, Donald tells me of his goal to organize a large pepper garden, building on the expertise of his father and the villagers. Pepper prices are rising, and Sarawak pepper (white and black) is of good quality. Even with his small savings from work, he can provide the money for his father and neighbors to expand their output. The land around his village is communally owned, meaning only the villagers can use it, so the basic element—land—is free. And aside from fertilizer and seeds, pepper gardens require no cash. The clearing of the land, the tilling of the soil, the nursing of the trees—all is done by hand. The result is beautiful to behold. Many of the gardens slope down the side of hills, so that they seem like picturesque vineyards.

Donald's timing is good. Reteh has no phone or electric service, but finally the government is building a road that will cross the river and come near Donald's village. The road will bring electricity and phone lines in its wake. The improvements should turn what is now a three- to four-hour journey to Kuching into perhaps a sixty-minute trip. Suddenly, the distance between city and village will diminish, and Donald's ability to straddle the two will expand. Soon, he may easily bike to Reteh and the peace and pride from the jungle he knows so well. Soon, he may even be able to telephone his father, who has never received a phone call in his life. The elder Jagau already has selected the spot where he wants the communal phone installed (he doesn't want a phone in his house).

For me, Donald's straddle—helping promote pepper farming while working in high-tech—embodies the spirit of hybridity. He is a Bidayuh, or "normal," as he would say, and can return home from his life in another world. This first caused me wonder, but no longer. I used to consider his living in two worlds as the great riddle I had to crack, but no longer. Whatever the secret of Donald's roots—and perhaps the secret of roots as such—it is too elusive for me to plainly state. Donald's Bidayuh roots have endowed him with an enviable inner calm and confidence. The notion that Donald might lose his roots—and become a deracinated cosmopolitan—makes no sense to him. I can recall the first time I visited Reteh, when Donald was still in California, and his father and mother were so worried about him. I asked his father how eleven months in California had changed Donald. For a journalist, this was one of those zinger questions designed to force a brilliant insight to the surface—the sort of insight that can elevate my craft to the reaches of literature. I expected some meditative answer from old Jagau about the perils of losing one's culture amid the lure of the big city. About how he might not recognize his son. About the war in the Bidayuh soul between tradition and modernity.

I was disappointed. Jagau, who is shorter than Donald and has sharper facial features, raised both his eyebrows and looked at me as if I were mad. He tugged on his face. "Has Donald's skin changed?" he asked.

I said no.

He pointed to his eyes. "Have his eyes changed?" he asked. No, I said.

Then he moved on to other parts of his face. "Has his mouth changed? His lips? His ears? His hair?"

No on all counts, I told him.

He smiled and began to laugh, relieved and yet still puzzled. I think he wondered why I would ask a question when I already knew the answer. Or perhaps, for a moment, I had him thinking Donald would return looking like a blond surfer in a beach movie. To him, Donald is still Donald as long as he can recognize him.

The years go by, and I see no reason to disagree with him.

CHAPTER 7

THE MULTINATIONAL
CORPORATION

We are in a war for talent. And the only way you can meet your business imperatives is to have all people as part of your talent pool—here in the United States and around the world.

—RICH MCGINN[1]

Diversity is not an optional byproduct of high culture; it is at the very heart of a world that has abandoned the need for closed encompassing systems.

—RALF DAHRENDORF[2]

If we don't welcome talent, we can't grow.

—PHILIP YEO[3]

HYBRIDS ARE everywhere, but multinational corporations are hybrid hothouses.

The best corporations set the pace in diversity. Their mission is to match people and needs regardless of nationality, race or ethnicity. Managers want employees to retain their differences in order to make the most of their uniqueness and the creative tension spawned by a collision of these differences. Employers don't want hollow harmony. They want a cosmopolitan corporation.

Hybrid teams are the new corporate ideal. Listen to Goran Lindahl, chief executive of Zurich-based Asea Brown Boveri, one of the world's premier project managers. "It's better to have natural cultural diversity in your management team," he insists.[4] A decade ago, Lindahl, who then oversaw electric-power transmission business, began the practice of requiring that at least three different nationalities be represented on any management team. Besides gaining creative energy from the mix, "I avoided a lot of conflicts in the organization," he has said, "because you create a sort of general spirit that we are together in a global context and we solve global problems."

To be sure, global companies are freer to diversify their workforces than are other institutions. Laws may limit the ability of government agencies to hire foreigners. Smaller companies may lack the resources to hire workers in one part of the world and move them to another. Sending an employee abroad can cost two to three times the person's salary. And multicultural teams must spend substantial time together, which means travel to and from an organizational hub as well as phone, e-mail and other electronic connections.

Global government bodies also rely on diverse people, but are also constrained by political mandates. The European Union, for instance, takes elaborate steps to guarantee that each member nation gets a proper voice in EU affairs—a mandate that flows all the way down to where employees come from and who gets what jobs. But as in most international agencies, when people represent nations—when leadership posts are parceled out along national lines—hybrids don't thrive. Rather than providing a platform for mixing, national affiliations set boundaries. Defending one's national or ethnic style against rival encroachments is considered the goal of many pluralistic international organizations. Finding a synthesis of differing styles—of selectively applying various distinct styles—often lies outside the vision of a global agency.

In contrast, private corporations have the most freedom of all cross-border players. Merit is their master. Performance is king. To be sure, an "old-boy" network exists, but it has been radically altered. That "old" network depended on social status, nationality and ethnicity. The "new" network increasingly depends on qualifications, university connections, job experiences and passionate interests (which may include race, ethnicity and nationality). If they see the need, private employers can select those who show the most aptitude for dealing with diversity and weed out those who do not. A whole country doesn't have such an option.

Careers are now made or broken over diversity. "Every company wants to know what type of person will succeed as an international manager," notes one corporate psychologist.[5] Increasingly, the ability to work well abroad indicates how successful a person will be at home, since—with high levels of mobility—the domestic workforce is starting to resemble the international one.

The triumph of English as the language of international business makes it easier for corporations to hire the best and brightest around the world and then mix them. A growing number of European companies based in non-English-speaking countries—from Daimler Chrysler and Deutsche Bank (Germany) to Philips (the Netherlands) to Nokia (Finland) to LaFarge (France)—conduct much of their business in English. A common language makes trade in managers easier. Employers insist on English competency, even for some secretarial and factory jobs. No longer must Americans on overseas assignment speak the language of their new residence. They are asked to speak English.

International mergers also spur the trade in managers, which in turn promotes mixing. Marriages between Daimler (Germany) and Chrysler (United

States), Citigroup (United States) and Nikko (Japan) and BP (Britain) and Amoco (United States) force managers to confront diversity and communicate their ideas and goals more skillfully. When a German firm and a U.S. company merge, for instance, the two nationalities mix, but the enlarged company also finds managers from other countries more attractive. These "neutral" nationals—whether Swedes, Indians or Mexicans—seem more valuable because they don't instinctively side with either dominant group.

The mongrelization of management goes all the way to the top. An unprecedented number of foreign-born CEOs run major companies in the United States, Britain and several other countries, according to a study by Denis Lyons, an executive recruiter in New York. "The dawn of the millennium is ushering in a true global marketplace for CEOs," he writes. "An increasingly borderless global marketplace is absorbing top-level executive talent with diminishing regard to national origin."[6]

The list of border jumpers is impressive. Jacques Nasser, born in Lebanon and raised in Australia, runs Ford in the United States. Danny Rosenkrantz, born in Kenya of Polish parents, heads Britain's BOC Group. Fernandez Pujals, born in Cuba and a U.S. citizen, leads Telepizza in Spain. Deutsche Telekom's CEO is from Israel. Andy Grove, a Hungarian immigrant, chairs the board of Intel. Charles Wang, of Taiwan, runs Computer Associates. Philip Morris has an Australian CEO. A native of Morocco, who holds a Brazilian passport, runs Alcoa. Becton Dickinson's CEO, Clateo Castellini, was born in Italy, speaks English, Italian, French, Spanish and Portuguese and has worked in Italy, Brazil and the United States. A Frenchman runs Britain's Body Shop. An American is CEO of Britain's Pearson publishing empire. The Anglo-Dutch consumer giant Unilever is chaired by Niall Fitzgerald, an Irish native. A Dane runs the Anglo-American drug-maker SmithKline Beecham. An Australian is the chief of Coca-Cola.

As chief executives circulate, they become a global fraternity, not unlike the aristocracy of the middle ages whose members followed booty and glory irrespective of national borders. To be sure, CEOs are a special case, but they are also the model for the business hybrid. Where CEOs go today, white-collar professionals will go tomorrow. People working in law, health care and a host of other fields, where standards are set by government or quasi-governmental bodies, are among the most defensive about transnationality because their training is country-based and national differences in education, regulation and custom often prevent them from simply hopping from one country to the next for work. But as international standards proliferate, this defensiveness will turn to acceptance—as it has in finance, marketing, technical writing and other "soft" fields, where barriers are easing and the trade in these fields grows steadily.

In "harder" technical fields, borders mean less and less. In engineering, physics, code writing and all types of design, people carry their roots with them like the sixteenth-century explorers who sailed ships for wealthy patrons. U.S. corporations get their pick. The Indian or Chinese engineer in America is a cliché, but less is known about American architects, salespeople and shopping-mall developers who serve foreign corporations. Some live abroad; others shuttle back and forth. A "day at the office," for these folks, can be a trip to another continent.

An example is Tom Eddy of Napa, California. He is part of a small, obscure cadre of flying winemakers. To scour the Venezuelan Andes looking for good places to grow grapes, he flew to Caracas, then took a puddle-jumper 300 miles into the mountains searching for what he calls a "Shangri-la zone." At elevations of about 2,000 feet, he tried growing grapes at various sites, experimenting with microclimates, gauging the effects on established grapes. His aim, of course, is to jump-start wine production in a country with no wine-making tradition, but he also gains a lesson in hybridity. The diversity of the world's wine varietals is enhanced by his experiment, which could excite the palates of wine enthusiasts everywhere.

McKINSEY MAN

Corporations did not always seek diversity or exploit its advantages so relentlessly. Hybridity is new. From the first international corporations in the late 1800s through the 1970s, the leading corporations in every rich nation essentially reflected the character of their home nation. Foreign staffers, other than those in lower-paid manual work, were exceptional. Even in highly diverse countries such as the United States, upper management of corporations remained American, white and male. In the 1980s, the first cracks appeared in the corporate commitment to national identity. In the 1990s, more companies globalized their workforces. Among the best companies, building diverse teams became a routine part of business and a central piece of their strategy.

McKinsey, the Chicago-based consultancy, illustrates this trend. In the 1970s, most of its consultants were American, and its foreign contingent came from about twenty countries. By the mid-1980s, Americans still counted for more than half of the consultants, though the company drew from a wider group of non-Americans, perhaps from thirty countries. In the 1990s, the trend accelerated. By 1999, McKinsey's chief was a foreign national (from India), and only 40 percent of the company's 4,800 consultants were American. Foreigners came from more than forty countries. The largest groups by country were from Germany (700) and Britain (250). But India supplied more consultants than Italy, France and Canada, and the Taiwanese contingent was larger than the Dutch, Swedish or Norwegian groups.

The diversity at McKinsey means there's no dominant group—or identity mold. And the company's "United Nations" profile isn't a reflection of customer locations either. The idea isn't to assign Indians to Indian customers, say, or French to French customers. That's old thinking. New thinking presents hybrid teams as a positive agent. Many of McKinsey's forty-odd nationalities aren't where they "should" be. "If you let a meritocracy prevail you're bound to get a lot of diversity," says McKinsey's chief partner, Indian-born Rajat Gupta. He adds: "When you lack diversity you can see the difference in terms of a poorer grasp of context, perspective and the ability to think out of the box in a situation. There's no question about that."

McKinsey encourages an appreciation for difference by having each of its offices evaluated annually by a consultant from somewhere else in the world. The head of the San Francisco office may review Düsseldorf. Paris may do Mexico City. The process contains checks and balances between the partners by preventing too much coziness forming between partners in a country or region. But a side benefit of these evaluations is to raise cultural sensitivity and to promote the intermingling of traits. "There's an obligation to see things from other points of view," says one McKinsey partner. "That's hard-wired into this place."

As markets become more international, many companies say they get better results with diverse teams. "When you bring different people together, the boost to creativity is big," says Radha Basu, the Indian software manager. "The advantage is you get the whole world. From the Singaporeans you get process knowledge and discipline. From Indians you get outside thinking. From Germans you get reliability and accuracy. From the Brazilians you get snazziness. From the Japanese you get correctness; every 'i' is dotted."

Ethnic and national traits can blur as teams mature. People may start swapping characteristics, trying out different mixes. A German software programmer tries looking past his immediate task to longer-term conceptual issues, imitating the Russian at the next desk. After winning a big deal, a Japanese investment banker sambas in the office with a Brazilian colleague. An in-your-face New Yorker borrows the studied detachment of an English marketing manager.

Cosmopolitan corporations don't localize overseas operations, but seek a dynamic blend between colliding strangers. This is quite different from what passes for diversity in some U.S. companies that practice "ethnic" marketing, such as hiring a black to manage accounts in Harlem, or a Hispanic to handle the south Texas region. Ethnic marketing is blithely presented as multiculturalism, but it smacks of tokenism and is based on a dubious business model. To be sure, certain sales activities may go more smoothly when the race or ethnicity of the seller matches that of the buyer. But just how far this goes isn't clear. Would a Mexican American rather buy life insurance, or a car, from another Mexican American? Do blacks prefer eating in a McDonald's franchise owned by another black rather than by a Korean? Does a Taiwanese American prefer to get medical exams from an ethnically Chinese physician?

Such questions, though inspired by obvious business opportunities, don't reflect clear thinking about multiculturalism. Some ethnic groups are ignored because mainstream businesses can't or won't pursue them. Language is sometimes the issue. Obviously, reaching California's Spanish speakers requires Spanish-language advertising. But there is more to it than that. Businesses that pursue specific ethnic groups are likely to learn much about their particular needs. Ethnic banks, for instance, have mushroomed in the United States, partly because bank consolidation has left fewer banks to tend to small businesses but also because Asian, Indian and Hispanic small proprietors sometimes don't speak English (or not very well) and operate cash businesses. For instance, Houston, whose Asian population soared from 2,500 in 1965 to an estimated 100,000 today, has six Asian banks. Why not? Houston's ethnic bankers have more sympathy for their customers and, probably, more ability to help them than do the national chains.

But ethnic marketing isn't cosmopolitan enterprise. Companies aren't pro-diversity when their aim is merely to segment the market along identity lines. The approach may meet a real commercial need and is certainly morally better than purposely ignoring a class of customers (as many companies have done). To be sure, people should have the opportunity to buy preferred foods, hair products, religious articles and other distinguishing gear. But the limits of ethnic marketing underscore the confusion over multiculturalism. People belong to many overlapping groups—with shifting levels of intensity—so that any "scientific" attempt to pin them down seems doomed to fail. One market research firm, Ethnic Technologies, boasts that it has a software program and computer database that can classify people by 173 ethnic groups, 9 major religions and even by language preference. This feat is accomplished through study of first and last names. Even misspellings purportedly don't matter.[7] With better software programs and further intermingling of people, market researchers could offer a bead on hundreds of hyphenated ethnic groups and many new ones discovered by peeling the social onion. Yet as the Dutch political theorist Bart Tromp observes, "Every minority has its own minority." So the task of parsing group identity becomes endless in an age of radical mixing.

Rather than try to pigeonhole its customers, the hybrid enterprise acts as if they are all mongrels. Hybrid marketers don't seek one-dimensional terms to describe them. Their approach contradicts the premise of ethnic marketing: to put people in boxes. Ethnic marketing may work for a time, but it won't endure. It will end up chasing the shifting borders of identity and alienating potential customers. Market researchers will end up talking about the specific buying habits of, say, "second-generation Bolivian-Japanese males married to fourth-generation Russian-Arab women with a university degree and less than two children."

Surely, ethnic marketing is only a stopgap measure. It seems reasonable for employers in search of diversity to hire from different groups in order to put a black or brown face in front of black or brown customers. It may be easier to reach certain customers this way. But the tactic has risks too. Companies must be alert to changes in identity and the perils of tokenism. They must not merely replicate an ethnoracial grid that is losing relevance. If a customer thinks of himself as a Korean American, isn't it bad marketing to pigeonhole him as an Asian American? Marketers need a dose of what David Hollinger calls "postethnic" thinking. This applies both to domestic and international ventures. Many international companies still operate along ethnic lines. When they open an overseas unit, they usually assign foreigners to run it at first. Over time, locals are given leadership posts, but the most senior managers often remain foreign. Management scholars Robert T. Moran and Philip R. Harris call these "ethnocentric corporations." "All the key management positions," they write, "are centered at the domestic headquarters. Home-country nationals are recruited and trained for all international positions. . . . International strategic alternatives are limited to entry modes such as exporting, licensing and turnkey operations because [of the attitude] 'it works at home, it must work overseas.'"

Many U.S. companies do things differently. They seek to localize their foreign operations, using only a few Americans (or hyphenated ones) at the top. The Americans act as go-betweens, sending a representative group of middle- and lower-level workers to the United States for training. Bob Snyder of Hadco typifies the go-between, and Donald Jagau shows the breadth of the training experience. Moran and Harris call this approach "polycentric":

> The polycentric firm establishes multinational operations on condition that host-country managers "do it their way." The polycentric message is: "Local people know what is best for them. Let's give them the responsibility and leave them alone as long as they can make us a profit.". . . Host-country nationals have high or absolute sovereignty over the subsidiary's operations. There is no direction from headquarters and the only controls are financially oriented. No foreign national can seriously aspire to a senior position at headquarters. . . . Strategically, the multinational corporation competes on a market-by-market basis because it believes that "local people know what is best for them."[8]

Both ethnocentric and polycentric corporations have strengths. The former quickly achieve quality and consistency. The latter promote self-reliance among workers and managers in the field. Both styles also fall short. Ethnocentric corporations can seem imperialistic and create a permanent dependency relationship with locals. They also don't create a pool of senior locals who can move to the head office, bringing a new perspective. But at polycentric companies, locals can be cut off from the expertise, ideas and financial controls of the mother ship. In pursuit of corporate goals, they may use tactics that violate the parent company's ethics. Polycentric approaches seem progressive but aren't. The parent company doesn't wish to confront cultural difference, so it rules by neglect. In the worst cases, disasters strike, such as when IBM's Argentina unit became linked to a bribery scandal and Citigroup's bank operation in India was found to have hired a goon who hounded delinquent borrowers with threats that they could sell their body parts in order to raise the funds needed to repay loans.[9]

A hybrid approach, melding the best of both approaches, is emerging. The result is a cosmopolitan corporation that gets results. Look at the record of U.S. investment banks. In the 1980s, they realized that their old method of sending Americans over to European branches would not work. But they were leery of localizing, of just hiring Europeans and letting them loose. The companies' systems and skills were so specific that they worried their European offices would become too alien. Instead, the American bankers sought to create a hybrid: a controlled collision between European values, style and competency and an American commitment to skills, techniques and flexible, fair procedures. U.S. investment banks recruited promising young Europeans, trained them in their New York operations and then sent the best of the lot back to Europe. The shift was striking. In 1993, Goldman Sachs had nineteen American managing directors in Europe and eight Europeans; by 1999, it had thirty-seven European directors and twelve Americans. Americans held 66 percent of Morgan Stanley's European posts in 1979 and only 8 percent in 1999. The story is similar at other U.S. banks. In investment banking, creativity is measured by deals. Powered by a hybrid ethos, U.S. bankers are notching more European deals than ever.[10]

BODY AND SOUL

At the lower corporate levels, hybridization occurs too, as the experience of Donald Jagau suggests. Many of Donald's trainers in California hardly qualified as "white-collar." The need to train low-skilled people, even those who will ultimately work in developing countries, means that all sorts of workers in the home country will inevitably have much contact with foreigners. Lower-skilled workers can be as resistant as elite professionals to foreign competition, but they still can show compassion to the stranger. In Donald Jagau's Santa Clara factory, many of the people who trained him were Mexican immigrants who knew full well that Hadco's decision to open a plant in Asia would mean fewer openings for other Mexican immigrants in California. Jagau's supervisor, a Mexican immigrant, ultimately joined him in Kuching.

In the new corporate ethos, employees are entitled to their differences— no, they should revel in them. By pouring their authentic identities into their jobs, employees are believed to be more creative and effective. Corporations are discarding the old assumption that employees must think and act the same. They do not have to bring the same tools, attitudes, values and even language to work.

A modem factory in Morton Grove, Illinois, is typical. The factory's 1,200 workers speak twenty different languages in "an industrial Tower of Babel."[11] It's a miracle the plant runs at all. Pragmatism rules. The owner of the plant, a high-tech company named 3Com, takes a simple approach. "Managers don't even try to accommodate cultural quirks—probably an impossibility anyway," notes one observer. "They just make it clear they expect newcomers to adapt to the factory's methods." On the plant floor they must mingle and cooperate, but in the lunch room they can cluster in their ethnic and linguistic groups if they wish.

Routine procedures neutralize prejudices. A Burger King I frequent with my kids in London illustrates this. The place is in London's racially and ethnically mixed Lewisham neighborhood. Here the very structure of fast-food operations reduces the chance of diversity turning against itself. The hamburger cooker from Nigeria or Cyprus must follow the same procedures as the one from Bristol or Hong Kong. They are all judged by the same metric. The experience of this level playing field—which a young immigrant or native may not experience in any other aspect of daily life, not in school, on the bus and certainly not in encounters with police or courts—can have a profound effect. Value springs from performance. This performance, while modest, arises from achievement, not group affiliation.

Often, corporations require such specialized talents that a team can be assembled only virtually, or by drawing on members in various locations around the world. Speed is another factor. By scattering members of a team across time zones, round-the-clock progress is possible. One part of the team can write code during the day, and while those workers sleep, colleagues on the other side of the planet can test the code. When members of the first group arrive at work the next morning, they are greeted by a list of their mistakes, thus hastening the process of improvement.

Such global teams are on the rise, and not only because of time pressures and skill shortages. Corporations find that the line between local and global blurs when they are designing many products and services. No master recipe controls the balance between local and global elements. Since the balance constantly shifts, many companies hybridize their teams.

Consider Philips, the world's largest consumer-electronics company outside of Japan. The Amsterdam-based company makes everything from toasters to televisions, lightbulbs to computer chips, electric toothbrushes to traffic-management systems. Its broad product line puts pressure on its industrial designers. In the 1990s, Philips transformed its approach to design under the leadership of Stefan Marzano, an Italian who put diversity at the center of design on the premise that creativity is stimulated by unusual combinations of people. He hybridized a Dutch-heavy team, ending up with offices in twenty countries, including Taiwan, Singapore, India, France and the United States. Among his staff of 500, he counted thirty-three nationalities. And they weren't in all the obvious places either. In Holland, about half of the designers were Dutch. Elsewhere, the mix was more radical. Only three of the eight designers in Hong Kong were Chinese; the others were from Belgium, England, Ethiopia, Germany and Singapore.

Marzano didn't look only for an ethnic and national mix. Trained in architecture and a professor at a design school in Milan, he also expanded the definition of a designer, pushing outside of the traditional boundaries of industrial engineering. He hired anthropologists, psychologists, sociologists and architects. He loaded up on young people, another means of achieving fresh thinking, driving down to thirty-three years the median age of the people in his division. Finally, he attracted more women, adding another creative dimension by sharply increasing their number to 40 percent of his total staff.

By the late 1990s, Marzano's retooling had turned Philips into a trendsetter for consumer design. The company introduced splashy colors and aerodynamic stylings to traditionally black, boxy products. Philips didn't stop at aesthetics: Relying on original field research on how people around the world brush their teeth, take their coffee and even chop up their vegetables, company designers influence how appliances work—and how consumers behave.

Such innovations confirm, at least for Philips, the value of hybrid teams, especially in the design of products or services that connect with a person's intimate habits or feelings. "You get a richer environment, you have more insights, because people reason from their own background," says Grant Davidson, one of Marzano's lieutenants. "The result will be richer than if you don't have that multicultural environment. I'm sure of this because we've reaped the rewards. We have an absolute advantage from having many cultures."

Davidson explains that the team not only arrives at better answers but also asks better questions. The idea of tailoring a blender to different societies around the world—giving certain additional blending speeds, beyond the basic set, to Chinese consumers—arose from having employees from different parts of the world tackle the task. "These are daily objects that everyone has an opinion of," Davidson says. "People go to a diversity of places when they go home and they return with richer experiences. They bring their tastes with them." In other words, even as people adopt universal products like toasters or coffeemakers, "you don't want to cut out the possibility that they can take along their national traits with them into this new realm." Thus, one-size-fits-all designs sometimes don't make sense, which is why hybrid teams are needed in the first place. Some experiences are novel enough to sustain a global approach. Others are too specific. "It's no longer desirable to make a global blender," Davidson says, "because the habits of how people use it are so diverse."

McMONGREL

As the Philips example suggests, diverse companies can better connect with diverse consumers. The best multinationals sell in scores of countries around the world, so their sympathy for ethnic, national and racial groups grows in value over time. They market the mongrel way, which differs from the simpler ethnic approach, described earlier, in which a black salesman handles black customers or a Hispanic ad agency designs a Spanish-language ad campaign in Los Angeles. In the ethnic approach, markets are treated as nations, and staff and techniques grow separately; a product or service that catches on with, say, Colombians or Vietnamese isn't likely to leech into the company's broader business. Mongrel marketing builds on the interaction between different groups and the realization that outsiders often penetrate a group's defenses better than insiders because they take less for granted.

Big corporations are champions of diversity, not just in their hiring practices, but in what they sell. They revel in differences because, more so than any other institution, they suspend judgment about quality, or the distinctive attributes of a thing or activity. To multinationals, all qualities are equal. The only attributes that matter are the size of markets and the prospects for profit. The attitude can seem cold-blooded, as if a multinational doesn't care what it sells or to whom. But it's also refreshing in a world where other leading institutions—from churches to governments—too quickly condemn differences in behavior. Multinationals are, if anything, too willing to create astonishing amalgams by mixing seemingly contradictory qualities from different parts of the world.

A remarkable case of such corporate hybridity occurred during NATO's war against Serbia in spring 1999.

As the leader of the attacking forces, the United States came under intense criticism from the Serbian government. Ordinary Serbs vilified symbols of American power. For McDonald's, the war presented a delicate problem. The company directly owned fifteen restaurants in eight Serbian cities. And there was no mistaking its American connections. In the words of one reporter in Belgrade, Serbia's capital, "McDonald's is a pervasive symbol of Western pop culture, Yankee know-how and American corporate cunning."

Soon after NATO's seventy-eight-day air war began, Serbian mobs vandalized McDonald's outlets in four cities, including Belgrade. The attacks forced the restaurants to close. With the air assault accelerating—and the world media demonizing Serbia's government and people—McDonald's could easily have abandoned the country.

Instead, the company's Serbian managing director, Dragoljub Jakic, decided to keep the restaurants open. He had always tried to associate McDonald's with the Serbian community since opening the company's first outlet in 1988. McDonald's sponsored schools, sports clubs and children's hospitals, building goodwill. But its image and products were generic, essentially the same as in the United States.

Jakic realized this policy would not work during the middle of a war—even a war that pitted his bosses' country against his own. He decided to hybridize his McDonald's restaurants. *The Wall Street Journal* described how: "To help overcome animosity toward a quintessential American landmark, local restaurants promoted a domestic pork burger with paprika garnish called McCountry. They put a traditional Serbian cap on the Golden Arches in posters and lapel buttons—national flourish to evoke Serbian identity and pride. They handed out free cheeseburgers at anti-NATO rallies. The basement of [a McDonald's in Belgrade] even served as a bomb shelter."[12]

The moves worked—so well that when the war ended, McDonald's sales equaled its prewar business (this, despite the battering Serbia took and the continuing anger of its people toward the United States). The fifteen restaurants were "thronged with Serbs" because the company succeeded in localizing its global content. "After all, I don't associate McDonald's with America," said one customer. "Mac is ours."

McDonald's says none of its American employees directed the response by its Serbian restaurants. But the company was clearly proud of the tactics. McDonald's Serbian manager "was functioning as a hamburger guy and not as a politician," said a McDonald's spokesman. "He demonstrated how adaptive he could be under the circumstances."

Indeed, this was a textbook case of how a multinational goes beyond value-free marketing and actively mixes cultural elements in fresh ways. So much for the notion that no two countries with a McDonald's franchise would ever go to war. Not only did they go to war, but McDonald's took both sides. Simple nostrums don't describe cosmopolitan corporations. They revel in contradictory cultural elements, wedding yin and yang. This is how the world looks, viewed through the prism of hybridity. McDonald's flair for adopting Serbian traits illustrates the power of multinational corporations as agents of a special brand of diversity. That it occurs on corporate terms makes it no less real.

And no less confusing for those who long for a simpler time when people more easily chose sides. In France, McDonald's faced withering criticism in 1999, despite its status as the country's number-one restaurant chain with 800 outlets (annual sales of $2.5 billion). Angry farmers staged a series of protests at the company's restaurants; one became a national hero after being jailed for vandalizing a partially finished restaurant. McDonald's responded the mongrel way: by launching a nationwide ad campaign in which the company insisted that the Big Mac was a native French food. In one ad a cowboy stood under an American flag and said, "What I don't like about French McDonald's is they don't buy American beef." The text of the ad asserts that in France McDonald's buys only French beef, a move aimed at placating farmers and those French consumers who mistrust hormone-fed American cattle.

McDonald's approach exposes the perplexing tensions between roots and wings. Consider the French actor who in October 1999 made a donation to a farm group protesting McDonald's. The actor said that he "hoped by this symbolic gesture to support the fight against globalization and the power of money." But as a newspaper revealed, the actor earned the donated funds by appearing in a McDonald's commercial.[13]

SCHERING

The benefits of hybridization can be great, but conversion takes practice. It isn't easy for a mature corporation, with scant diversity, to go hybrid quickly. This is why so many important global corporations still seem monocultural. The departure of American executives from Chrysler, after its purchase by Daimler, and from Bankers Trust, after its takeover by Deutsche Bank, show that even when a corporation knows it may be financially rewarded for exploiting diversity, it may fail to do so. Certainly, it can't do so overnight, if only because it takes time to absorb new faces. The web of nationality ensnares many companies, shaping simple procedures like job titles and pay scales to more complex ideas about what makes for good performance, proper etiquette and feasible goals.

One British financial officer at a Japanese securities company once spent months seeking a suitable title because headquarters in Tokyo kept rejecting his suggestions. The Londoner finally let the Japanese choose a title for him from an approved list. The CEO at a leading European company once told me privately that he would surely benefit from having more diversity among his top fifty managers. Nearly all hailed from the same country as he did, which produced a kind of tunnel vision at the company. Still, the CEO insisted, "You can't expect me to dump a planeload of North Americans on this place."

Because national identification seeps into the crevices of corporations, many behave more like "national champions" than global competitors. Headquarters retains its national character and is largely cut off from outsiders. Such corporations don't even realize the need to hybridize. Some leaders of American-based companies, because they rely on such a diverse workforce or because their founders are foreign, organically hybridize. Others, like the managers at McDonald's or McKinsey, pragmatically pursue this end, gearing their training, tactics and strategies toward it. But many corporate leaders, like the European CEO I spoke with, believe it's too daunting to mongrelize their talent.

It is not. A company can consciously strive to raise the level of mixing among its employees and in such a way that creates not more opportunities for assimilation into the dominant style but a kaleidoscope of styles and interests under a common banner. This hybridity ideal, however, has been misunderstood even by people who decry the limits of a national approach to business culture. Kenichi Ohmae, the longtime chief of McKinsey's Japanese consulting practice, provides the classic example of the failure to grasp that the opposite of national identity isn't a hollow corporate cosmopolitanism. In his influential 1990 book, *The Borderless World,* Ohmae advised companies to "create a system of values shared by company managers around the globe to replace the glue a nation-based orientation once provided." He added: "The customers you care about are the people who love your products everywhere in the world. Your mission is to provide them with exceptional value. When you think of your colleagues, you think of people who share that mission. Country of origin does not matter. Location of headquarters does not matter. The products for which you are responsible and the company you serve have become denationalized."[14]

Ohmae's advice is conventional wisdom, but if naively followed, it diminishes people. A person's origins matter. Rather than promote creativity, a complete identification of an employee with his employer's transnational network robs him of valuable local identities. It leaves him bereft of meaning and motivation. This is why many executives are leery about abandoning national identity, because the alternative seems worse: an empty globalization that produces a workforce without soul. Surely it is better to embrace both roots and wings and to craft ways for both the local and the global to drive performance together. But how?

The German pharmaceutical company Schering is wrestling with this very question. Schering employs 56 percent of its 22,000 workers outside of its home country, chiefly in the United States and Japan, where its subsidiaries traditionally operated quite independently of each other. In the past, when pharmaceutical markets varied greatly by country because of different government regulations, this independence made sense. But with governments standardizing their drug rules, Schering must gain more bang from collaboration between its country units.

A major difficulty is that few Japanese or Americans work in Schering's sprawling Berlin headquarters, and just a handful of non-Germans rank among its top 100 executives. By contrast, hundreds of Germans work in foreign units. To be sure, some Americans and Japanese visit Berlin frequently, but the company's core remains dominated by Germans who shape the company's priorities, from research to marketing. Top managers want to change this, but aren't sure how to do so.

Enter Dieter Schmeier, a twenty-nine-year veteran of Schering and a native German. As top managers wrestled with the company's lack of diversity in its main operations, Schmeier, an organizational psychologist, stepped back from the problem. He enrolled in a management program at Harvard University in Cambridge, Massachusetts. For four months, he lived in a dorm with eight other executives. Two were from the United States, and one each came from South Africa, Australia, Canada, India, China and the Philippines.

Schmeier had never been part of such a diverse team and was skeptical of the value of mixing people so thoroughly. Five other Germans (none from Schering) were in the same program, and Schmeier wondered why he didn't get to room with them. The living situation was important because the Harvard instructors expected each resident group to tackle class assignments together, coming up with a single "answer" for the four or five case studies assigned as homework each day.

This routine seemed hard to Schmeier, not only because he had to work in English, the native language of nearly everyone in his group. He also found the Americans—and to a surprising degree the Canadian, Australian and Indian participants—reached decisions very quickly—even too quickly. "They are hip shooters," he says. "We [meaning Germans] are more analytical. We're more logical and systematic. Before the Germans try to make a decision, they would like to try to have all of the facts. This means we are slower on the one hand but more correct on the other hand."

Schmeier realized that speed mattered more than ever before and that some problems were so poorly understood or so short-lived that an exhaustive answer was either impossible or pointless. Even though he wanted to make faster decisions himself, the group's pace bothered him. But he had to keep up. "I have no alternative but to go with the residential group," he says. "I was obliged and compelled to go as fast as possible."

Besides joining his group members in classroom work and case studies, Schmeier shared outdoor activities with them. These included rafting and climbing—ventures that required members to rely on each other for aid. The experiences "help to create trust and a 'we' feeling," he says.

As the months went by, Schmeier began to realize why Harvard was "very clever to bring together people with very different backgrounds." His whole outlook about mixing began to shift, from disbelief that mere cohabitation could do so much to promote understanding to a positive attraction to the ideal of mixing. He suddenly realized what many Americans take for granted: the power of diversity.

"It's possible to form a team with people from different backgrounds," Schmeier realized. "The backgrounds—religious, cultural, national—don't make any difference. We overcame these differences very quickly, and everybody learned from the others."

Schmeier's insight fired his imagination. Could Schering do the same? He was not talking about the sort of universal brotherhood that make some Germans grow rapturous. His bond with his Harvard mates didn't erase their differences; in fact, he seemed all the more aware of the differences between Indians and Filipinos, Australians and Americans, South Africans and Canadians. What made mixing work was that the group had a common goal along with different approaches.

When Schmeier returned to Schering, he was a man possessed with what he saw as the truth. Mixing matters, he told people.

They started to listen. It helped that he could give examples of competitors in the pharmaceutical industry that had begun to fill jobs, anywhere in the world, not based on a candidate's passport but on the person's suitability for the job.

Schering's board asked him to draw up a plan for hybridizing the company. He made a radical proposal that boiled down to this: "Getting the best people wherever they are, and it doesn't make a difference what country they are from. That's the idea. If there is a vacancy, we have to look around the whole world of our subsidiaries for the best candidate."

This idea represented a dramatic change from company practice. Schering limits job contests by country, so that when a marketing post in Berlin comes open, only Germans learn of it. Similarly, only Japanese employees would be up for a Tokyo job. The system effectively makes mixing impossible.

Schmeier wanted the old system scrapped. Besides advocating the opening up of job competition, he argued that Schering must circulate more of its foreign talent. Nearly 95 percent of its executives working outside of their home country were German. This meant that Americans not only couldn't win rotations into Germany—they couldn't win them anywhere. "We have to change this imbalance," he urged. "It's absolutely necessary."

Schmeier made one more key point. Employees should circulate more frequently, despite the extra costs. Drawing on his Harvard experience, he insisted that it was through a critical mass of associations with strangers that people really grow, that reaching a threshold of experiences of other places is more important than simply getting to know one new place. "If they stay too long in one country," he said, "then the idea to make a person multicultural gets lost. Then we will be helping a German become an American or a Frenchman. That's not the idea."

THE BOARD HAS approved Schmeier's plan, agreeing that mixing managers is important. But the endorsement is only a start. Schmeier knows many barriers exist to achieving his vision of a mongrel corporation. Employees must be encouraged to move. Help must be given to spouses. New jobs must be attractive. Middle-level managers around the world also must grow enthusiastic about Schmeier's vision because, in the end, they make most hiring decisions. They are the ones who must work alongside strangers after decades of working only with their own kind. Schmeier cannot predict how quickly they will change, but he believes that his company's success depends on this.

"If we can overcome the obstacles," he says, "then maybe we will have much more success than in the past." But he wants more than the business success that mixing may bring: He wants the feeling he had back in the dorm at Harvard. Just a few days before I met him, one of his mates from the American program turned up in Berlin for a visit. The meeting reminded him of what he'd felt in that Harvard dorm: a sense of connection to strangers, a bond that affirms difference without erasing it. "I must say I found eight friends over there," he says. "Everyone knows the older you get the more difficult it is to make friends." And yet he found the proof in the bond he felt toward his visitor. "The effect isn't just on the surface," he says.

So Schmeier holds a vision of tomorrow that is caught in the stubborn present. "Today if we have a vacancy," he says, "we maybe think of three names: Muller, Schmidt, Lagenstein. What we have in mind in future is to have a different set of names: Smith, Lee Ping, Rodriguez. That is the idea."

SHADOWS

The chameleon quality of the multinational corporation makes it a natural promoter of hybridity but a strange one nonetheless. McDonald's embrace of Serbian symbols and its pandering to French pride reflect the company's drive for profits, not its zest for diverse cultures. As Gupta of McKinsey says, the corporation seeks diversity as a means to an end, not an end in itself. And therein lies a source of great tension: The multinational corporations that promote a new cosmopolitanism may be the very force to undermine the social and cultural structures that are essential to holding together pluralistic nations.

When merit is master, performance obliterates distinctions between people based on color, family background, religion, gender, place of birth and myriad other inherited or elected characteristics. This principle is good. The workplace becomes a hothouse of hybridity, a meeting ground for all sorts. But this same process separates winners from losers and accentuates inequality. With the market as arbiter, new inequalities arise, notably in terms of distribution of wealth and opportunity. Multinationals pay huge salaries to their top talent—talent harvested from all over the world, drawn in part by elevated wages and the hodgepodge community they join. Citizens of the world, armed with the best techniques, these corporate cosmopolitans are pampered. They live in exclusive, polyglot neighborhoods with other elite knowledge workers, forming an informal global aristocracy. They can, if they wish, cut their ties with both the ordinary and more privileged people of their native land. Highly mobile and plugged into hybrid networks, the new elite depends little on a larger public. Its members look after their own. If they do not like a society's schools, hospitals and parks, they can afford to build their own.

Although achievement is based on talent and performance, the elite—despite its ethnoracial diversity—can seem a more worrisome group than those spawned by older forms of hierarchies based on status, class, color and creed. Traditional elites were tied to place, their power and status arising from specific national or regional communities, so that they had a stake in the health of the entire community. Not so the new elite. Consider the mind-set of Mark Mobius, a celebrated money manager who runs $12 billion worth of assets and seems to personify, as *The Economist* put it, "the global footloose force called 'international capital.'" Mobius owns apartments in Germany, Singapore and elsewhere, though mainly as investments. He essentially lives on a private jet, traveling upward of 250 days a year. Born on Long Island, he is the son of a white American father and a Puerto Rican mother. In the mid-1980s, he swapped his American passport for a German one in order to smooth relations with business contacts in developing countries. Still, his fluid nationality fools few. Once on a visit to Russia, a former manager of a Soviet enterprise greeted him with the quip, "Are your capitalist plans to destroy the Russian economy proceeding on schedule?" Mobius think it's unfair for poor countries to blame their problems on Western financiers, but he does little to dispel suspicions that he lacks sympathy for those tied to a place. The flight of talented people from mismanaged nations—and the withdrawal of money by foreign investors—

is to be welcomed, Mobius thinks. "I want these countries to sink, so that they get cheap," he once said.[15]

All wings and no roots, Mobius epitomizes what social critic Christopher Lasch described as "the revolt of the elites." Writing before his death in 1994, Lasch found that "the chief threat [to the social order] seems to come from those at the top of the social hierarchy."[16] To critics like Lasch, the global business elite destroys local practices and threatens the survival of distinct cultures. *Star Wars* supplants local myths and tales. Genetically modified food supplants local varieties. Chain stores and generic products crowd the landscape. Slowly, every place starts to look the same, courtesy of multinationals and their internationally minded leaders.

Multinationals often promote more than mere blandness. Some spread new skills and reward employees for merit and performance in ways that combat xenophobia, bigotry and tribalism. These are the "knowledge" multinationals whose workers are valued at least in part for their ideas and morale. But other multinationals profit from low wages and exploitation of raw materials: forest products, oil, minerals, cash crops and the like. In these cases, multinationals usually do more harm than good, but even when they do good, the challenges of diversity remain. Nations—whether they tame multinationals or are tamed by them—must still balance the contending demands of their ethnic and national minorities. Whether these nations defend the sort of generous social-welfare benefits favored by Germany or adopt a system of American-style self-reliance, they must still expand their sense of national identity in order to accommodate diversity. Whether India and China gain ground against rich nations with the help of multinationals—or lose ground because of them—many of their best and brightest people will live, learn and work in rich nations courtesy of foreign capitalists. Whether multinationals reach limits or continue to expand their power over global markets, the same logic of hybridization will shape the competitive contests among nations, communities and individuals. Hybridity is a friend to both free-marketeers and those who want to tightly control capitalism. Mongrelization cuts across ideology, but by no means marks the end of it.

A JAPANESE TRADER REVIVES GOOSE-DOWN INDUSTRY...IN POLAND

WROBEL, POLAND—Kotaro Tatsuma first fell in love with a Polish girl and then fell in love with Polish geese, which is why on a warm summer day he is entering a stinking barn in Wrobel, in Poland's goose-breeding heartland. Holding his breath, Kotaro roots through a chest-high bag of freshly plucked feathers, then spreads two handfuls on the floor.

"Look at this," he says, holding aloft a flowerlike plume. "This is very special."

Kotaro is thrilled by a single piece of the furry undercoating of an egg-laying "mother" goose. The choicest fluff from a Polish goose—used in high-end comforters and sleeping bags—sells for more than ten times the price of ordinary feather and is considered the most valuable down in the world (far pricier than down from China, the world's largest supplier by bulk). Kotaro, a thirty-four-year-old native of Japan, never meant to become the down king of Poland, but now that he is, he thinks of almost nothing else. He schemes of ways to improve Poland's output of down, its quality and its reputation. He woos top farmers of down, trying to encourage them to stock more egg-layers. He has persuaded the Polish government to certify domestic down for the first time, planting a seal of approval on all exports. He sells "organic" down, from the bellies of geese whose feed contains no dietary additives or antibiotics.

Kotaro even imagines automating the grueling task of plucking down and feathers, a manual process that is so exacting that one false tug can ruin a swatch. To this end, he once bought a ladies' electric razor to demonstrate how he thought it could remove down from a goose—by shaving his own leg. "The experiment wasn't a success," he says.

Kotaro's wild goose chase began in 1989, when, having just graduated from university, he took a vacation to Poland. He met a student, Kinga, a young woman who adored the movie star Bruce Lee. Watching Lee in films had inspired Kinga to learn martial arts and the Japanese language, which she thought had been Bruce Lee's native tongue.

Kotaro fell in love with Kinga and then couldn't bear to tell her that Bruce Lee had not been Japanese. Kinga didn't learn the truth until a year later when she visited Kotaro in Japan, on the same trip in which she accepted his marriage proposal.

The couple spent four years in Japan. Kotaro worked first for a bank and then for a trading company, enduring the jibes of coworkers who said that having a Polish wife would hurt his career. Kinga liked Tokyo, however. She decided to leave only after she got pregnant. "I wanted to deliver my baby in Poland," she says. "The feeling was stronger than me." Kotaro returned with her to Poland, knowing no Polish but thinking he could use his Japanese connections to set up a trading business.

After a few false starts, he found goose down. Japanese consumers love it, paying as much as $2,000 for comforters filled with the finest Polish stuff. Some Japanese hotels even advertise that their beds are decked out with comforters filled with Polish down.

The Japanese are attached to Polish down for sound reasons. Scientists (and not only Polish scientists) say that down from Poland is the world's finest because of the quality of its geese, its benign climate and its low, lush, marshy terrain, which is ideal for geese if not humans. Under communist rule, however, the government's goose monopoly sold down feathers as a commodity, dispatched by weight and unbranded. In time, many consumer products weren't even labeled as containing down from Poland. When Poland threw off its Soviet yoke a decade ago, the shift to private ownership created disarray among feather producers, because previously the state-owned monopolist had bought all feathers at set prices.

It took a foreigner, Kotaro, to identify the potential of seeking premium prices for the best Polish down and to spread the word about Poland's superior geese . Kotaro's plant, in the city of Dobczyce, is cherished by locals who before Kotaro's arrival had only a condom plant—one of Poland's biggest—to boast about.

Many Poles are grateful for Kotaro's efforts. "His activities have been very positive for the industry and the country," says Zbigniew Kossowski, director of the Central Animal Breeding Office.

Yet as an outsider Kotaro ruffles rival feathers in the goose trade. Poland is one of the most homogeneous countries in the world, virtually entirely Catholic and ethnically Polish as a result of border shifts and resettlements of non-Polish people after the upheavals of World War II. For many Poles, Kotaro is the only Asian they've ever met.

"Of course I am and will be a foreigner here, but I am not a guest any more," Kotaro says. "Because of the success I've had, some people have to listen to what I say—no matter how maniac it sounds to them." Indeed, some rivals dismiss Kotaro as too crazy about goose down for Poland's good (or his own).

Adam Kluzniak, chief of the country's feather-and-down trade group, says Kotaro can't possibly succeed at selling Polish-branded down as a premium-priced filling because Chinese producers are "flooding the world with junk." Kluzniak opposes the government's certification plan and says he won't invite Kotaro to join his trade group. He says this isn't because Kotaro is Japanese but because the two men fought over buying the same idle factory equipment from the government. Kotaro ended up outbidding Kluzniak in a public auction. Kotaro says he'd like to join the feather group, but he won't beg for an invitation.

Kluzniak says he is uncomfortable having a foreigner as a member and adds that perhaps "it is the same for the Poles and the Japanese today as it was for Jews and Poles years ago." The association of Kotaro with Jews is not meant as a slur, but rather a historical allusion: before the Holocaust Jews dominated Poland's goose business. They were not only traders but also feather pluckers and down buyers, says Jerzy Halbersztadt, a historian of Jewish life in Poland.

While Poland now forbids the export of live geese, in the 1930s such trade flourished with Germany. Jews frequently *walked* flocks of geese across the border to German buyers. Feather brokers also were usually Jews—indeed, so many were Jews that even decades after the Holocaust, and the virtual disappearance of Jews from Poland, Poles still saw the task as a Jewish occupation.

Kotaro's rise to the top of the down trade exposes a sensitive subject: Polish intolerance. This does not surprise Kinga's father who was born in Italy and moved to Poland as a child in the 1960s. A short burly man who is shop steward in Kotaro's down factory, Kinga's father sympathizes with his daughter's husband. "It will take a long time for people to realize that Poland isn't a closed country," he says. To be sure, it would help if Kotaro spoke Polish better. Kotaro's daughter corrects his Polish grammar and even his wife prefers to speak English with him. So when he walks into a barn, Polish farmers can be excused for misunderstanding him. Still, his respect for farmers—and their geese—is undeniable. One day he crawls on his hands and knees through a pile of down on a stinking barn floor and he tells one of his best goose breeders that her latest plucking contains 38 percent pure down.

"No, 45 percent," the breeder shoots back, knowing that the higher the percentage of down, the more money he pays. The breeder says she plucked a bit later this year, so that her down is thicker than usual. "Look deeper into the bag," she says. "There's no cheating."

Kotaro feels around some more, even holding a piece of down next to his ear to listen to the sound it makes when he crunches it.

The sound is good. "Forty percent," he offers. This percentage means he will pay about $1.50 a kilo for the down.

The breeder accepts and says, softly, "You little Jew."

CHAPTER 8

MONGREL LEADERSHIP IN FRANCE, GERMANY, AND SINGAPORE

*The principle on which this country was founded and by which it has
always been governed is that Americanism is a matter of mind and heart.
Americanism is not, and never was, a matter of race or ancestry.*

—FRANKLIN D. ROOSEVELT[1]

*Political resistance to intermingling of peoples and skills across state
boundaries is therefore far from negligible, and may well increase in time
to come as the difficulties of living in polyethnic societies become more
widely apparent. . . . Nothing assures that the assortment of migrants
and their skills will fit smoothly into the host society.*

—WILLIAM H. MCNEILL[2]

*Many people, of all political stripes, have hoped and assumed that ethnic
and national identities were a transient phase of human history. These
parochial allegiances were supposed to fade as the world became increasingly integrated both economically and politically. In reality, "globalization"
has often created more room for minorities to maintain a distinct identity
and group life. Globalization has made the myth of a culturally homogenous
state even more unrealistic, and has forced the majority within each state to
be more open to pluralism and diversity. The nature of ethnic and national
identities is changing in a world of free trade and global communications,
but the challenge of multiculturalism is here to stay.*

—WILL KYMLICKA[3]

*Diversity is, increasingly, the fate of the modern world. The capacity to
live with difference is . . . the coming question of the twenty-first century.*

—STUART HALL[4]

SIT ACROSS from Zoo Station, a busy Berlin underground stop near the
swank boulevard of Kurfurstendamm. As I sip a Pilsner, I talk with Ilka
Schroder, the youngest member of the European Parliament. Schroder's
blond hair is ultrashort, and she carries her entire Rolodex in her backpack.

She is small, and her baby face makes her look like a teenager. Having grown up in Kreuzberg, the neighborhood with perhaps the highest proportion of foreigners in Berlin, she enjoys diversity.

If some diversity is good, more ought to be better, she concludes. Then she asks a logical question that only an idealistic youth can earnestly pose: To create as much diversity as possible, why not erase all borders and citizenship requirements?

"This is my radical vision," she says. "To open the borders of the whole world."

Her vision, of course, sounds noble and romantic, and Berlin is a good place to voice it. The city, after all, was split arbitrarily for a half century. The Berlin Wall became a metaphor for senseless divisions between people. Schroder's vision of a borderless world, though inspired by the removal of the Wall, is whimsical and even sophomoric. Still, the mere possibility of a borderless world challenges those who argue, as I do, that greater diversity will strengthen rich nations. Why, then, won't these same nations benefit from an unlimited amount of diversity? Why not tear down all the walls?

There are good reasons not to. Perhaps all rich nations could allow reciprocal work and residency arrangements. Rich nations aren't ready for unrestricted movement; not even the fourteen-member-nation European Union allows it. The disparity in wealth and opportunity is so great between rich nations and more populous poor ones that migration controls must be a feature of life for a long time. Indeed, fair and consistent immigration and citizenship laws sustain diversity and are the soil out of which successful hybridity springs. Diversity demands balance. A nation needs enough diversity—and enough respect and freedom for its diverse peoples—in order to unleash the "hybridity factor." But just as a nation can realize this dividend only by achieving a threshold of diversity—or a critical mass of "strangers" in its midst—so too can a nation suffer from admitting too many outsiders. Biologists talk about a similar principle in nature. Too little diversity and an ecosystem stagnates. A critical level of diversity brings forth new innovations. Too much diversity, however, "will be toxic to members of the ecosystem." As the evolutionary biologist Stuart Kauffman notes, "each ecosystem must somehow rein in this explosive tendency."[5]

Consider the analogous situation for a nation. Say 5 million Indians, a mere 0.5 percent of India's population, were to move to Ireland, population 3.7 million. That doesn't create diversity but a new India, with an Irish minority. There can, in short, be too much of a good thing. However, by admitting 250,000 Indians—and 25,000 people from each of ten other countries—Ireland isn't swamped by newcomers but rather is positioned to harvest their talents. This kind of diversification of diversity lays the conditions for a vital society that supports innovation, wealth creation and social cohesion. In short, Ireland gains larger wings while retaining strong roots.

The example looks different if we hypothesize that of 5 million newcomers to Ireland, no single country sends more than one-twentieth of the total. Thus, the potential for virtuous mixtures is enhanced, and Ireland's national character becomes more varied but is not erased. This is how it should be. Newcomers should not eradicate the existing culture. They alter it, supplement it, but not bury it.

This, then, is the paradox of diversity. It is not either-or. The central question is how to control the degree of diversity and to achieve the kind of mixing that promotes happiness, liberty and prosperity. For some nations, the answer might be more legal immigration and more freedom to pursue diverse identities and communities. For others, it might be fewer opportunities for newcomers and a pause in the diversification of diversity. Nations must decide how best to balance the needs of natives and newcomers, hybrids and one-dimensionals. In the decades ahead, many rich countries will find themselves compelled to import people simply to stave off stagnation. How many people do they let in? To whom do they open the door, and to whom do they close? And what are the best ways for natives to reap the benefits of newcomers and for both "us" and "them" to discover new ways of being?

These questions are urgent. In every wealthy nation, minority groups already seek recognition for their differences and an unprecedented level of participation in mainstream life. In the United States and Canada, the great campaigns for minority rights and hybrid identities are largely in the past. But in the rich nations of Europe and Asia, the great struggles over minority rights and hybridity lie ahead. Leaders will be made and broken by these struggles. Their success, in large measure, depends on how they are able to exploit the hybridity factor for political, economic and cultural gain.

THE ENTREPRENEUR

Marc Lassus, his employee badge "001" swinging from his neck, bursts unannounced onto the floor of a factory in the south of France. With an entourage of managers in tow, he views row after row of machines spitting out "smart cards," a type of computer chip used in cellular phones and credit cards and to store medical data, among other things. Along the way, he waves, winks and congratulates machine operators. It is nearing midnight, a time when most other French executives are in bed. Lassus's eyes are bloodshot, but he's winding up, not down.

Lassus (second syllable rhymes with Zeus) declares a surprise break for about forty factory hands and ushers them into a conference room. He likes to meet with night-shift workers because he feels they are isolated and "we need to show them we care." He then presents his version of tough love: For the next hour he opines on the future of his company, Gemplus, and rails against the habits of French workers and managers. The machine operators, at first skeptical, warm to his tirade. Lassus, after all, is one of France's most successful entrepreneurs, and his performance—capped by his answering questions—is typical. He constantly goads his French employees to broaden their perspective, flying into a rage when he sees a fellow countryman behaving in characteristically French fashion.

"They are good people," he says later of the factory workers, "but they need to be pushed. It is good for them." Then he adds, slyly: "Even though they are French, they want to improve. You need to coach them."

Lassus, sixty-one years old, uses his same blunt coaching style with university-educated employees. He tells an engineer who asks him for career advice, "Please learn English. It's like not having a driver's license." To a manager proposing a new business venture, Lassus complains that his plan is too cautious. The manager sees the chance to use smart cards as payment for bus fare in many French cities. But after seeing sales projections, Lassus says, "I was dreaming of more revenues" and tells the manager to concoct a plan that extends beyond France.

Lassus leads by example. Angered by French socialists, he turned down a medal of honor from the government. He flies coach and drives his own car, almost unheard of in elite French management circles. He won't allow reserved parking spaces at Gemplus, so executives who arrive at work late face a long walk to their desk. He banned smoking in meetings because he thought the French penchant for puffing away at work was unhealthy.

He sent a serious message when he moved to London in order to escape what he considers France's stultifying formality (and its high taxes on personal wealth). He has ordered his managers to speak English on the job and flouts a French law that requires all documents drawn up in France to be in the native language (he prefers them in English because it is more widely understood). One of his sons, also an executive with the company, lives in the United States. Lassus says that ultimately most top managers will live outside of France.

A native of France's Basque region, Lassus grew up alienated from the country's Parisian elite and with strong local ties. After gaining a doctorate in physics, he joined Motorola, the U.S. electronics giant, working in various countries for the company for fifteen years. Semiconductors, the brains behind computers, were his specialty. "In semiconductors, you forget about borders," he says. "All products go worldwide."

He returned to France in 1983 to run a computer-chip company and in 1990 started Gemplus. France was a natural home because the government-owned telephone company launched the world's first large effort to accept electronic payment, in the form of money stored on a smart card, for telephone calls from public booths. From a base in France, the smart card later spread to Europe and then Asia. France now accounts for a tiny fraction of Gemplus's sales, and roughly half the company's employees work outside the country.

Informal and unpretentious, Lassus has a flair for mischief. Handsome and powerfully built, he looks like a French actor whose name doesn't immediately come to mind. He thinks like an outsider, losing no chance to tell the nationalistic French that they must relentlessly look beyond their borders even as they cherish their own traditions. "Be open, don't be too Frenchy," he told one graduating class at a university near Gemplus's headquarters. "Go abroad, learn something and come back and help your country."

Lassus wars against the formality of French business. "Bureaucratic culture is the genius of the French people," he says. "I have to fight against it everyday." And he heaps scorn on the country's brittle educational establishment, which, he sniffs, selects students for its top universities based "on how a seventeen- or eighteen-year-old does on a math test."

His chief weapon against Franco-sclerosis is to reward performance. "The good-old-boy network you find at so many French companies is almost absent here," says one foreigner.

Humility also lets in fresh air. Lassus once declared on French television that he values the janitors at his company as much as anyone else. His mother told him he sounded silly, but he wants to instill pride in ordinary tasks. Whenever he visits a company office, he ducks into the bathroom for a quick inspection. Pity the employee who visits at the same time. On one visit to the company's Paris office, he exploded at the sight of an empty paper-towel dispenser. He complained to a lawyer who happened to be present at the time. The lawyer volunteered to fill the dispenser and did so, while Lassus looked on smiling.

In another clear message, Lassus counts a janitor, Paul Castlerot, as among his closest friends at the company. "I respect him as much as any top engineer," he says. They originally struck up their friendship after Lassus visited one factory bathroom and, so impressed with its cleanliness, wrote an ode to menial labor and taped it to a toilet. The janitor assigned to the bathroom found the poem and sent Lassus one in reply. Impressed, Lassus sent him another poem. The two men traded lyrics for months.

Besides jolting French people into an awareness of their national limitations, Lassus tries to bring more outsiders into his company's home operation. But he meets resistance. It took him nearly ten years to fill a top-management post in France with an outsider. He finally landed an American as chief financial officer, but only after he agreed to a demand by his French managers that the newcomer speak fluent French. The requirement—even though the company presents its financial data in English—lengthened the search and partly explained why Lassus's first pick for the job backed out.

Importing technical talent from Asia is difficult, too, because of French prejudices. Lassus hired a Singaporean for a senior position and found his work superb. But he had a habit of working over weekends, which bothered his French colleagues. They called a meeting to discuss their concerns, pointedly keeping it a secret from Lassus. At the gathering they shared their suspicions about the Singaporean. The group, consisting of all French men, agreed that the Singaporean was probably an industrial spy and that he should be banned from the office outside of "normal" (read French) work hours. When Lassus heard about the decision, he defended the Singaporean and overturned his managers. He was so ashamed of his colleagues that he kept the episode a secret from his Singporean protégé.

The man, Thian Yee Chua, still works closely with Lassus and only learned of the accusations of disloyalty much later. He of course knew of tensions over his work hours, but "it made me sad to learn of their suspicions," Chua says of his French colleagues. He never gave a thought to leaving Gemplus because of Lassus's backing. "He gives opportunities to anyone who believes something will work," Chua says. "He doesn't care if you're a black cat or a white cat, only that you can catch a mouse."

Lassus doesn't see his penchant for diversity as an abandonment of his French roots, but as a way of giving his countrymen wings. In any case, he tells workers that adding new rooms to their French "house" is unavoidable. "We have no choice: Either we achieve this hybridization or we die."

THE ACTIVIST

Like Marc Lassus, Cem Ozdemir is also caught between two worlds, bent on crafting the means for others to live in both. The first person of Turkish descent to win a seat in Germany's Bundestag, or parliament, Ozdemir is the darling of liberals who insist Turks can adopt German ways and so need not be feared. Ozdemir, age thirty-four, is Germany's poster boy for assimilation, the country's favorite Turk. One prominent observer goes so far as to declare that for Germans, Ozdemir is "the Turkish-German of their dreams."

Outwardly, Ozdemir agrees. His life goal is to be accepted as a German and to have other Turks emulate his buttoned-down, nonthreatening style of advocacy. "There are going to be Ozdemirs at every level, local state and federal," he has said, predicting: "One day it will be very normal for a non-German like myself to be a member of the government."[6]

Ozdemir speaks flawless German (as well as excellent English). He revels in his outward signs of assimilation. He boasts that ordinary Germans see him as a curiosity, wanting to see firsthand that he does not kneel on a prayer rug or smoke hashish from a water pipe. "I was born in this country, grew up in it, and people still are amazed that I can speak German," he says.

As if to underscore the way he confounds stereotypes, he tells me straight off—when we meet in his jam-packed Bundestag office—of a recent visit to Washington, D.C., where he met with a senior official at the U.S. Immigration and Naturalization Service. Knowing only that Ozdemir was a member of the German parliament, the official tried to strike an immediate bond in that chummy American way. "I know all about your immigration problems," he said. "You've got the Turks and we've got the Mexicans. Both people just want to get on our welfare systems and milk them."

As the American dug a deeper and deeper hole for himself, Ozdemir never said a word. He thanked the man for his time and left, knowing that an aide would soon tell him of his blunder.

In the same sly way, Ozdemir must play both ends against the middle in Germany. He must convince Germans that Turks are just like them, while at the same time persuade assimilationist Turks that they need not abandon their foreign identity. His are the politics of hybridity, European style. Painfully aware of the second-class status of Turks in Germany, he is obsessed with reminding people of his own Turkishness lest they mistake this slender, black-haired man for a "pure" German.

Both of Ozdemir's parents hail from Turkey, and he only gained German citizenship—a requirement to hold an elected office—after an exhausting six-teen-year process in which he was ultimately forced to surrender his Turkish passport. Such difficulties in winning a seat at Germany's table have alienated many people of Turkish descent. Some belong to separatist organizations, which often have an Islamic flavor. These groups tend to spit in the eye of Germans, spurning assimilation in favor of supporting their own media, businesses and neighborhoods. They also hold out Turkey as a kind of Promised Land, which strikes Ozdemir as absurd. Still, he connects with alienated Turks.

"What we're watching is a self-fulfilling prophecy," he has said. "Because Germany hasn't embraced the Turks, the Turks are becoming the types of people Germany doesn't want to embrace. This begins the vicious circle. Because they aren't included, Turks go their own way. Germans and Turks distrust each other, communicate with each other less and live beside each other instead of with each other."[7]

Ozdemir wants to break this vicious cycle. He wants to teach both Germans and Turks alike a lesson in hybridity. He wants to be the Jackie Robinson of Germany, a "model" minority leader who nonetheless remains faithful to his roots because of the stigma attached to them.

He has so far to go he can't measure the journey. No single organization represents Turkish interests throughout Germany, and few local groups lobby effectively. Many Turkish activists remain more interested in events in their parents' homeland than in their own. The German government, meanwhile, ignores the Turks. Not one Turk (or anyone from other minorities, for that matter) serves as a government minister. Germany has a foreigners commission, which is responsible for ethnic issues, but its chairwoman and all of its members are Germans. A reform of citizenship laws has made it easier for Turks to gain a German passport, but still requires them to renounce their Turkish citizenship.

Ozdemir argues that many Germans and Turks fail to grasp that multiculturalism is about adding, not subtracting. It is not a choice between integration or disintegration. It is not about Turks becoming Germans or seceding from Germany. It is about shared processes, not practices. "There are some rules that we have to share in common," Ozdemir says. "It's really the [German] constitution and the official [German] language. But besides this, people are free. They are free to dress the way they wish, to choose their 'mother' language, to believe in what they wish to believe in. Beyond that, nothing. This is what we have to tell the Germans. They mix up integration and disintegration. A lot of Turks mix it up too."

Both sides must do more, in Ozdemir's view. Turks must build media for Turks living in Germany, not for those back in Turkey. And the few German experiments in minority media, such as Radio Multikulti in Berlin, must be expanded nationwide. Turks must try harder to master German, especially written German. But Germans must offer the Turkish language and history as standard fare in schools and universities. Antidiscrimination laws are also needed. Ethnic Germans can still get away with barring blacks from discos or placing advertisements that prevent Turks from renting certain apartments.

Ozdemir thinks Germans will listen to him because he plays by German rules. He takes the moral high ground—and holds a trump card. If the Germans don't embrace him and other "good" Turks, separatist Turks will only become more influential and more likely polarize Germany. Can Germans really afford not to make Ozdemir happy?

Just as Jackie Robinson triumphed on the baseball field because he demanded no special favors, even when insulted on the field and underpaid off it, Ozdemir asks for nothing not offered a German. "I can be as German as you" is his implied message. But like Robinson, whose outward assimilation belied his revolutionary political awareness, Ozdemir wants to lead a transformation in German society. Robinson changed the way baseball was played, and thus what it meant to blacks and whites both. Ozdemir wants all Germans to view themselves in new ways. "It must be easier to say I belong to this country," he says. "There's still a problem with saying that in this country, as you can say in America. No matter your background, where you are from, you can say, 'I'm an American.' It's much harder to say, 'I'm a German.' Call me whatever you want, but I belong to this country."

Treating Turks and other minorities as full participants in German life, he says, "is the best way to fight against nationalism, religious fundamentalism and separatism. To make it easier to be accepted by the majority, this is what we need."

Ozdemir hardly sounds like a firebrand, yet his views seem radical to German politicians frozen in time, still debating whether non-Germans really belong in their country. "The conservative policy is that immigrants are worse than you think and the Left says they are not as bad as you think," Ozdemir says. "This is not enough any longer." Without issuing threats, he points out that the clock is ticking. "We've lost a lot of time," he says. "Now we must catch up."

THE PATRIOT

George Yeo disagrees with people who say that successful polyethnic societies such as the United States are an accident of history and cannot be replicated. His opinion isn't merely academic. As a veteran minister in the government of Singapore, Yeo is part of an ambitious experiment aimed at managing diversity for economic benefit and national advantage. Using the tools of public policy, Yeo tries to increase the diversity of people in his Southeast Asian city-state while at the same time maintaining ethnic harmony and supporting Singapore's authoritarian and communal concept of government.

Racial and ethnic diversity is one of the pillars of Singaporean society, and Yeo understands better than most of the world's political leaders that diverse societies aren't static. Ordinary people now invent and reinvent their identities, moving to the places that most attract them and reflect their values. "Human talent is mobile," he says. "You don't have to be an American if you don't want to be an American. You can go to Europe. You can come to Singapore. You can go to Israel. You can go back to India. Talent is mobile. Capital is mobile. Knowledge is mobile. So unlike the industrial world where you are trapped within a jurisdiction at the mercy of a monopoly government, in the coming world the government will have to compete for that same talent and knowledge and capital."[8]

Without an infusion of talented newcomers—from elsewhere in Asia, Europe and North America—Singapore will stagnate and shrivel, Yeo insists, explaining the logic: "If you look at the demographic profile of any city, it cannot replicate itself with its own population. You can't replicate San Francisco or New York or London by depending on the talent pool available by native San Franciscans or New Yorkers or Londoners.

"If someone said from today Wall Street will be reserved only for native New Yorkers, you might as well close Wall Street. So if a city becomes a state and puts a fence around itself, it faces a critical dilemma of how it reproduces itself. So it needs selective in-migration."

How to attract talented foreigners? The lure, Yeo says, is to provide what he calls "brain food," the environment that talented people want and need. Supply this artistic, technical and intellectual environment, he says, "and the brains will come. Starve them of this food and they will leave for somewhere else."[9]

Selectivity is crucial. At 225 square miles, Singapore is larger than most major cities, but still has little room to spare. "Every foreigner we bring to Singapore must be a net asset," he says.

Singapore has actively pursued a pro-immigration strategy for decades, but it's now more important than ever. "In a post-modern economy, you need much more talent," Yeo says, referring to the armies of brain-workers who produce the intellectual property, or "software," that has replaced raw materials and manufacturing as the main source of new wealth. "In the future you've got to have talent from a wide geographical area. A country can't hope to achieve its goals without that."

To be sure, newcomers can't be allowed to overwhelm Singaporean society. This is a real danger. Talented newcomers may be more individualistic or dissident than Singapore's controlled society is willing to accept. Or they may destroy the country's finely tuned ethnoracial balance if, for instance, an overwhelming number of the newcomers were Chinese or Indian. Yeo concedes that diversity breeds creativity but only "when the combination is right," he says. "It can also lead to conflict and kinds of friction. So if you have a culture which somehow enables you to absorb talent and fit them in, and allow them to nourish in a creative way, then you succeed. [If] you can't accommodate the tensions, then [diversity] is destructive."

Singapore, a former British colony that gained independence in 1965, gives permanent residency to about 20,000 newcomers annually, adding to a base of about 3.5 million citizens. Relative to Singapore's size, this is a large number of immigrants, and Yeo finds that he must explain to existing residents why they benefit from an inflow of talented foreigners. On the surface, these additions intensify competition for good jobs. "Every talented foreigner who comes here creates insecurities among Singaporeans who are in competition with them," Yeo admits. "So we have to manage it politically."

This becomes more difficult during a slow economy. In a parliamentary debate in the late 1990s, when Singapore's growth rate slumped following the Asian crisis, one immigration critic urged the government to "think Singaporeans first," claiming that at a time "when many [Singaporeans] feel threatened, a call for foreign talent may be misplaced." Yeo replied that Singapore needed immigrants even more during an economic slowdown: "Precisely at a time like this, when we need many foreigners to help us take our economy to the next phase, we must not send the wrong signal."[10]

Yeo doesn't favor opening the floodgates to foreign talent, however. Another senior official in Singapore told me that he favors importing annually as many as 10,000 engineers, mainly from India and China. Even though this would throw some Singaporean engineers out of their jobs, the official thinks it would force them to improve their skills, thus benefiting Singapore's economy in the long run. When I recounted this to Yeo, he dismissed the idea as too radical, even though bringing in vast numbers of foreign engineers would indeed expand Singapore's knowledge pool. Instead, he favors maintaining traditional levels of immigration out of the conviction that Singapore has traditionally forged a good balance between natives and newcomers.

Since Singapore's founding in 1819, diverse peoples have fueled its vitality and creativity. The British colonialist Stamford Raffles conceived of Singapore as a polyglot port, nurtured by a reliable administrative and legal system and by education offered to people of all races. On the strength of diversity, "Singapore rose from a small settlement as it attracted Chinese, Malays and Europeans," notes Robert Brenner, a business professor at McGill University. "Trade and security brought prosperity to immigrants who had arrived penniless from China and Indonesia."[11]

In facing critics of diversity, Yeo has tough tools at his disposal. Unlike other rich nations, Singapore can jail people without trial, crush political critics through lawsuits, control the media through censors and ban speeches or rallies that offend minority groups. Unfairly dubbed "Disneyland with a death penalty" by one Western critic, Singapore nonetheless combines Western consumerism and technology with Asian-style authoritarianism and rigid rules over even trivial behavioral (chewing gum, for instance, is a crime). The country's elite also places much faith in social engineering, backing campaigns to promote everything from more creativity to better manners among its citizens. Immigration thus becomes another "engineering" project, with Yeo calibrating the inflow—of skill types and points of origin—in order to maximize what the ruling elite believes will promote Singapore's best interests.

This kind of hybrid leadership can seem chilling in its precision. "For every two babies we deliver, we bring in one foreigner," says Yeo. "I don't think we can scale it up very much more. But if you maintain the quality of immigrants, in another 10 to 20 years they will have a profound effect on the nature of Singapore. These newcomers are bound to send Singapore in a different direction. To a certain extent, we welcome it."

But the influence of outsiders must be weighed against the need to maintain harmony among the country's chief ethnic groups. Singapore is home to three main groups: the majority Chinese (75 percent), Islamic Malays (15 percent) and Hindu Indians (7 percent). It also has sizable Japanese and Anglo-American communities. Mixing is widespread. One in four Singaporeans marries a foreigner, and interracial weddings are common. But the groups retain distinctive features, in part because the government reinforces ethnic pride through what it calls "ethnic self-advancement institutions." The government considers economic strength a key part of ethnic vitality. Although it doesn't practice formal affirmative action programs, the government tries to maintain a balance among its main groups. For example, it puts limits on ethnic concentration in housing estates so that they don't become inhabited solely by one group or another. It also seeks a balanced level of home ownership. In 1980, only half of the nation's Malays lived in homes their families owned, whereas nearly two-thirds of all Chinese did. By 1990, nine out of ten Malays lived in homes they owned, an even higher percentage than the Chinese.

Interference within ethnic groups is limited. Schools insist that a student whose parents are of Indian descent study Tamil or another Indian language; it won't allow them to choose, say, Chinese. The government also won't permit anyone to encourage religious conversion. It allows Islamic courts, for instance, to discourage Malays from marrying outside of their faith. It encourages involvement in ancestral countries—such as the practice by ethnic Indians of taking a spouse from India, or the custom of ethnic Chinese of doing business in mainland China—out of a sense that such connections strengthen traditional identities against the inevitable dilution that occurs within multiethnic societies.

These steps limit hybridity, but without them the government fears the loss of roots and a backlash by those who feel the loss most intensely. As a result, political representation reflects a belief that groups—not just individuals—have rights. Yeo, for instance, is critical of the notion of one man, one vote: the ideal of direct democracy that animates U.S. politics. He thinks that often the masses get it wrong, and that a whole range of problems are better resolved by technical experts who are insulated from voters. This idea, while surprisingly popular in Europe (where many political officeholders aren't directly elected), is generally shunned by Americans, so it represents another of Singapore's interesting departures. The suspicion of direct democracy reflects in part an unwillingness of the ruling People's Action Party, of which Yeo is a prominent member, to cede power to opponents. But it also reflects an enlightened paternalism that has often benefited the country. Consider the extraordinary political intervention in 1999 by Lee Kwan Yew, the nation's founding father and still influential leader. Lee felt so strongly that an Indian ought to gain the ceremonial post of president that he convinced the government to ban all the Chinese candidates and permit only his favored man, an Indian, to run in what then became a staged election. "It's time to remind Singaporeans to have a symbol of a multiracial community, an expression of our national identity," Lee explained.

Singapore's government also bans criticism of its different ethnic groups on the grounds that this might inflame tensions and lead to tribal violence. Under the banner of multiculturalism, Singapore has shut down Web sites, silenced dissident politicians and censored publications and movies. Critics of this practice say it goes too far and is partly aimed at insulating the wealthy Chinese elite from scrutiny. But Yeo argues that ordinary people can't be trusted to hold a reasoned, constructive debate about ethnicity. Were it not for government paternalism, he adds, Singapore might rip apart. The almost daily communal violence in nearby neighbors India and Indonesia "reminds us that things can go desperately wrong very quickly" in a multiethnic nation, he says.

Yeo credits Singapore's respect for diversity for its phenomenal economic growth over the past quarter century. "Cosmopolitanism has become part of the local culture," he says. "We grew up with foreigners in our midst." Extensive mingling made Singaporeans into a people that "accepts change and adaptation as a way of life," he says. "We've always adjusted from British days, never overly committing to any product or service. So in the 19th century, it might have been opium or spices. Then during World War II it became tin. Then with the auto industry it became rubber. Then manufacturing. Now it is Asian currency units and financial instruments and brain work. So we have no emotional attachment to any product or service. Whatever is the most interesting game in town, we want to be part of that game and we will make the necessary internal adjustments. We treat them almost as technical adjustments. So the large culture is one which is accepting of foreigners, that is cosmopolitan and adaptable." Although the benefits of this approach are clear to Yeo, he won't go so far as to call cosmopolitanism a prescription for the new century. "History is a long time," he says. "The pendulum swings one way, it swings the other way. What is now an advantage may become a disadvantage. There may be times, again, when the world gets divided into tribes or into geographical areas and where prejudices are required to unify human beings. We are not infinitely flexible. History plays tricks with us."[12]

Yeo's preoccupation with history is consistent with Singapore's hybrid reality. The country's deft management of national symbols reinforces the cosmopolitan ideal while affirming specific ethnic loyalties. As an approach to promoting roots and wings, it can be heavy-handed, but it works. In official histories, presented in children's texts and museum exhibitions, Singapore is depicted as a tiny but brave trading post that was propelled into a lonely independence by political forces beyond its control. According to the myth, Singapore overcame race riots and ethnic divisions by respecting local differences and forging shrewd ties with all the world's major peoples. The government gives life to this hybrid tradition by encouraging people to travel, study and live abroad. It lures multinational corporations with tax breaks, then encourages them to place Singaporeans on foreign assignments. Some of the nation's best artists, technologists and executives have made their reputations abroad, underscoring the belief that Singaporeans must win on a world stage, not only on their small island.

But at the same time, Yeo wants Singaporeans to show loyalty to their home, reasoning that national identity still matters and that transnationalism isn't enough. "Almost everyone here has roots in a diaspora, either Chinese, Indian or Malay," Yeo says. "They all got here by the British empire. But if we are just diasporic peoples, then Singapore is no more than a hotel, a way station, for everyone to come and to refresh themselves before moving on."

Yeo worries that hybridity may come to mean precisely that: Singapore as the means to reconnect with roots or reinvent oneself by drawing on a kaleidoscope of cultural elements. What endures for Singapore? "This is a problem we're confronting all the time," he says. "So on the one hand we welcome foreign talent, and on the other hand we encourage Singaporeans to see the world as their oyster. But at some level people must take national service seriously and be prepared to die here."

The violent image is a reminder that Yeo is also a high-ranking officer in Singapore's military establishment who worries about national security. Surrounded by far larger countries, Singapore is defined by its perceived vulnerabilities. "Deep insecurities drive us on," Yeo says. "They are never resolved. They can never go away. The insecurity of being a tiny speck of land . . . this insecurity is permanent."

It also makes Yeo search for reasons why hybridized Singaporeans should retain a strong link to their national land. This is Yeo's great puzzle, which— as he is still in his forties—may engage him for the rest of his public career. "Unlike Israel, where there's a sacredness, a holy history, we don't have that here," he says. "Yet we've got to make Singapore sacred. It will take a long time."

COSMOPOLITICS

Leaders face greater stresses than ever. There are no cheat sheets on managing diversity. The International Monetary Fund doesn't issue a formula for the correct level of ethnic and racial mixing within a given nation. The right balance is discovered. Finding and keeping this balance requires a new style of leadership suited to the special demands of diverse nations. The same holds true for corporations and community organizations, artistic movements and political parties. Even groups that promote the interests of racial and ethnic groups are awakening to their internal diversity and the limits of homogeneity.

All of these public and private institutions need hybrid leaders—leaders who will tackle three difficult tasks.

First, they will strive for social cohesion but not homogeneity.

Second, they will argue for the value of flexible identities, but not seduce their followers into abandoning traditions.

Third, they will resist the temptation simply to substitute one badge of membership for another. Hybrid leaders can impose no single test for inclusion. Rather, they insist that the meaning of "belonging" will reveal itself over time.

In short, hybrid leaders celebrate multiplicity. Their central task is neither to eliminate identity differences, nor only to cheer them. Each hybrid leader sees these differences as a foundation on which to enlarge his or her nation's house. New rooms get added to accommodate border jumpers and category smashers. Other new rooms provide a meeting place where differences matter.

Hybrid leaders promote union, not unity. They instill the desire for promiscuity, not fidelity. But this does not mean, to paraphrase Abraham Lincoln, that they want a house divided. Nor do they wish to freeze the power and number of each ethnic and racial group. They fight against ossification and the natural drift toward rigid classifications. They promote further diversity in the knowledge that (absent more newcomers, or new identities and affiliations forged by current citizens) their own nation will grow stale, inbred, infertile.

Hybrid leaders presume that identities are more flexible than many think. They cheer the reinvention of self, of ethnicity, of nation. They argue for a societal commitment to individual freedom, personal responsibility and fair play. They accept that people have different aspirations, values and lifestyles and may share little save for the willingness to respect their differences and cooperate when necessary. But they also believe that even deeply entrenched differences aren't permanent. As Ernest Gellner once observed, "Cultural traits, though often experienced as given, can be under deliberate control." The leader's task is to control and transform these traits.[13]

Past leaders certainly imposed imperial identities on their followers by constructing a unity where none existed. They standardized languages, erasing dialects. They supplanted national identities, where local ties predominated. They installed new rituals, traditions, holidays and celebrations, all in the service of a dominant identity. Indeed, leaders from time immemorial have been masters of igniting identity makeovers.

Hybrid leaders draw on this tradition. Like past leaders, they are saddled with followers whose identities are not wholly plastic, so that they are in a sense working with flawed material. Great leaders realize that many people won't change, but somehow they must be conned into changing. They must be tricked into making sacrifices that are only seen as sacrifices after the fact. They must be seduced into tearing down the walls of their existence and rebuilding new ones before they fully grasp the disappearance of the old ones. This was of course one tactic tried by Martin Luther King Jr. He knew many whites would never shake their deeply held prejudices, but he asked that they pretend to. He told Americans that they would be a lot better if they did—that somehow by pretending they would plant the seeds of respect and lead, some-day, to a finer form of nation.

Hybrid leadership carries this tradition of asking more of people than they actually have to give, but it represents a fundamental break too. In the twen-tieth century, leaders wanted to promote a common identity. *E pluribus unum.* Out of many, one. The job of a leader was to jam the clay of diverse human-ity into a single mold, and then to protect and preserve this mold out of a belief that thereafter ordinary people would wish to avoid revising their goals.

The ideal of unity possesses a beguiling simplicity, but has proved hard to realize in practice, as the contrasting experiences of Germany and the United States illustrate.

In 1908, at the height of the first great wave of non-English-speaking immigrants to the United States, a Jewish playwright named Israel Zangwill coined the term "melting pot" to describe the American process of integration. The term gained great currency and is still often invoked as an explanation for the assimilative power of the American experience. Yet the melting-pot ideal came under fire almost from its first expression, when Randolph Bourne attacked it in a 1916 *Atlantic Monthly* article in which he repudiated the xeno-phobia sparked by America's entry into World War I:

> The foreign cultures [in the United States] have not been melted down or run together, made into some homogeneous Americanism, but have remained distinct but cooperating to the greater glory and benefit, not only of themselves but of all the native "Americanism" around them.
>
> What we emphatically do not want is that these distinctive qualities should be washed out into a tasteless, colorless fluid of uniformity. Already we have far too much of this insipidity—masses of people who are cultural half-breeds, neither assimilated Anglo-Saxons nor nationals of another culture.[14]

The melting-pot ideal survived Bourne's attack mainly because the United States shut off immigration after World War I. The civil rights movement, however, ignited a new ethnic consciousness among Americans, who turned against assimilation. In *Beyond the Melting Pot,* Nathan Glazer and Daniel Moynihan reprised Bourne's view of a "trans-national America," defined by distinct ethnic groups. The two scholars argued that sharp ethnic and racial differences persisted in the United States, even in the grandchildren of immigrants, because "as the groups were transformed by influences in American society, stripped of their original attributes, they were recreated as something new, but still as identifiable groups."[15] Glazer and Moynihan essentially accepted the old homogeneous notion of the American, only positing a half dozen molds instead of one. These molds, which were essentially Bourne's national colonies dressed up as ethnic groups, jostled for power and status. The grand story of America, from this perspective, became the fight for a balance among groups whose members could not change teams, only help their team get ahead.

This simplistic model of America faced immediate stresses, not the least from rising levels of intermarriage. By the 1990s, the notion of "beyond the melting pot" was replaced by the model of hybridity as Americans increasingly crossed familiar boundaries. As noted earlier, the U.S. Census Bureau in 2000 allowed people for the first time to pick more than one race and ethnic category to describe themselves. This landmark shift—a final repudiation of the Glazer-Moynihan thesis—resulted from pressure by biracial and multiethnic parents who did not want their children to elevate one aspect of themselves over another.[16]

Paradoxically, it was only at the end of the 1990s that people could see the true meaning of the civil rights movement. In the 1960s, of course, integrationist and separatist leaders battled for supremacy within minority communities. Mainly, they differed over style rather than substance. They differed in emphasis, not fundamentals. This has long been poorly understood. Cultural separatists don't wish to secede from the mainstream, forging a distinct colony; they want power in their adopted country. Separatist agitation is a means to power, and it is the power to shape relations with the mainstream that separatists usually seek. Integrationists, meanwhile, also want more power. They just put more emphasis on gaining control of established institutions rather than creating new ones under their sway.

The classic polarities facing minority leaders are embodied in the lives of Martin Luther King Jr. and Malcolm X. In the late 1960s, Martin and Malcolm vied for influence among Americans. Martin preached integration and interracial harmony. Malcolm stressed black nationalism and self-reliance and openly questioned the capacity for whites to rid themselves of racism and coexist with blacks. But before both were killed by assassins, they showed an increasing attraction to each other's polar positions. Martin grew frustrated with white intransigence, especially after campaigning in the North, and recognized that blacks helping blacks was crucial to any program of racial equality. Malcolm understood that the definition of blackness flowed from white mentalities and that black advancement was inextricably linked to white reform.

In the end, hybrid leaders must affirm the value of acceptance and the reality of difference. They must praise universality and particularism. They must mix and match elements from the songs of Martin and Malcolm, not choose one or the other.

Purists find this eclectic approach difficult to accept. Even Randolph Bourne, a patron saint of multiculturalism today, could not abide the specter of the mixing of ethnic groups, for he wished to celebrate difference, not the freedom of people to shuffle the deck and create still more diversity. Mixing seemed vile. The logic of his view, however, leads to notions of "separate but equal" and apartheid-type walls between groups in the name of preserving and protecting their "integrity."

To be sure, Bourne criticized the hegemony of Anglo-Saxon culture in America, chastising English immigrants to the United States for imposing their culture on "minority peoples" when they themselves were "the descendants of foreign-born." How could Anglo-Saxons scold minorities "for not being melted in a pot" when that pot "never existed," he wondered? But in place of the mythical melting pot, Bourne sought to freeze a constellation of ethnic groups—with each functioning as a "national colony" that would "retain in its foreign press, its vernacular literature, its schools, its intellectual and patriotic leaders, a central cultural nucleus." This core must be protected, for the alternative, in Bourne's limited perspective, was unwanted deracination. He wrote: "Just as surely as we tend to disintegrate these nuclei of nationalistic [read "ethnic"] culture do we tend to create hordes of men and women without a spiritual country, cultural outlaws, without taste, without standards but those of the mob."[17]

LEADERS ARE RARELY poets or saints. Bereft of inspiration and ideals, they fall back on stark options. Bourne's notion of national colonies is one that, perversely, resonated with Adolph Hitler. He saw Jews as a colony within Germany and denied them the capacity for assimilation into the German mainstream. It was a short step from colony to ghetto. Enraged that Jews had indeed assimilated, Hitler stigmatized them as mongrels and half-breeds, seeing in their eviction and extermination a great relief for Germany.

The notion that minorities are colonies persists in Germany, among not only nativists but also centrists and leftists who conceive of multiculturalism in the same terms as Bourne. This is why the melting-pot myth, by contrast, seems so benign to some Germans. They are seduced by this chimera, unaware that it doesn't apply even to so-called ethnic Germans who emigrate from other countries. The costs of the melting-pot myth are high. Not only does it blind Germans to the possibilities of hybridity, but it also fails as social policy.

In the early 1990s, Helmut Kohl blithely undertook the reunification of his country on the assumption that, since Germanness was fixed and obvious, it would not be very hard to "melt" the ethnic Germans who lived outside of Germany's post-1945 borders. On this assumption, Kohl accepted the return to his country of millions of ethnic Germans from the former Soviet bloc. Many neither spoke German nor knew much about the society they were entering. The result has been an unwanted and misunderstood diversity. Kohl's dream of a German melting pot imploded; differences between East and West Germans remained large.

Both the melting-pot and the national-colony ideals retain a residual attraction for leaders in search of bold ways of organizing experience. In an era of rapid change, the idea that all people either are members of profoundly different groups or share essential features eases the anxiety over diversity. Choices become simpler: Either accept that good fences make good neighbors, or demand that everyone hew to the same standard.

In this dichotomy, a nation becomes either a confederacy of groups or a megagroup, a bland superethnicity. The roles of leaders become predictable. The national-colony ideal exalts the local and discourages cultural exchanges beyond the level of the colony. Colony leaders thus are essentially conservative, pinning their legitimacy on their ability to preserve difference, not to change and grow. The melting-pot leader, by contrast, all too easily leaps into the realm of the universal, confident that group differences will vanish in a sea of brotherhood. The melting-pot leader struggles to craft a definition of common humanity acceptable to all, but inevitably falls short and must impose a single mold on a diverse people. At best, the melting-pot leader may inspire hope that new collective identities will emerge on a national, regional or global scale. But he can't see that these proposed mega-identities are shaped by an old, exhausted, imperial nationalism.

Both the national-colony and the melting-pot ideals are fantasies. That they survive seems rather sad. Perhaps future thinkers will show more daring, more courage to break free from tired dichotomies. Individuals do not harbor the soul of humanity. Nor are they colonists without free will. Nations are not cults. Ideals are crutches, not altars. The sole path to harmony in a world of difference is a shared commitment to respect those differences and to allow their logic to unfold. This common faith has replaced shared views and practices as the basis for a workable society.

Even this faith must be provisional, however. Liberty demands flexibility. Neither countries nor ethnic groups nor individuals make lifetime guarantees. They can revise their goals and loyalties. Such revisions are accelerating with technological change and greater mobility. Shrinking time, shrinking space, shrinking borders, shrinking certainty—these are the soil out of which hybridity springs. Leaders large and small show glimpses of the new way, yet it is too soon to derive from their tentative steps a primer on hybrid leadership. Experiments still overshadow sure-fire methods. For the foreseeable future, earnest efforts will count for more than expert techniques. But the target is clear.

MALAY NATIONALISTS WHO LOVE. . .SINATRA AND AMERICAN WRESTLING

BANGKOK—The woman sitting across from me in the swank Dusit Thani hotel is one of Thailand's best and brightest. Educated in the United States, she's a computer whiz at a local company. She wears a bland business suit and peppers her conversation with "TCP/IP" and other cybervocabulary. When talk turns to romance, her fiancé—a New Yorker seated next to her—beams. She's proud of being part of a Thai-American marriage, she says, adding, "Many Thai woman dream of having an American's baby."

My jaw drops. I expect her to reassure her boyfriend immediately—to tell him she isn't one of those women. Yet she goes right on talking, saying, "Thai people think these babies are more beautiful, better endowed."[1]

The Thai passion for Americana goes beyond babies. Thailand's largest private employer is an American maker of computer diskdrives. The country's program for restoring to health its battered financial system, which collapsed in the summer of 1997, was taken whole cloth from the way the United States handled its savings-and-loan crisis in the 1980s. And the new Thai constitution contains another American invention: a bill of rights.

The Americanization of Thailand raises a thorny question: Does valuing another culture necessarily mean devaluing your own? There's no pat answer. Some in Thailand welcome American values and practices; others complain that their autonomy and distinctiveness are being violated. "We're being praised, cajoled and bullied into liberalization," says Sura Sanittanont, a Bangkok investment banker and sometime government adviser. "But look at the terms we're offered. They're outrageous," reducing Thailand, he says, "to a fiefdom. This is depressing—for the Thai economy, the Thai people."

A sense of invasion is widespread. From Moscow to Montreal, Kuala Lumpur to Kiev, Caracas to Capetown, many critics object to the Americanization of the world. To them, the American model consists of this: a preference for private profit over public good; winner-take-all rules that reward the rich and penalize the poor, widening the gulf between the two; and the substitution of a generic pop culture—defined by English, Hollywood, the Internet and even American conceptions of beauty and bravery—for local alternatives. A haven for diversity at home, America abroad seems imperialistic, imposing a rigid culture on others.

I am painfully reminded of this when one evening I visit a Malaysian journalist whom I consider a close friend. On greeting me, he calls me "Al," ignoring my reminder that my name isn't Al. For the next hour, however, I am only "Al" to him. I finally realize he is mocking me, reducing me to a caricature of Al Gore, the then U.S. vice president who was vilified in Malaysia in 1999 after he visited the country and lectured its prime minister, Mahathir Mohamad, on the need to respect the rights of his citizens. Though Gore's outburst was prompted by Mahathir's jailing of his deputy, Anwar, on trumped-up charges of sexual misconduct, it made no difference to loyal Malaysians who joined Mahathir in accusing Americans of meddling. Gore personified this ugly trait. To my friend, I was suddenly "Al," an arrogant outsider all too willing to judge him by my standards.

The encounter leaves me angry, but also wondering how much I impose my American values on others. I bring this up with Chandra Muzzafar, one of the world's leading Islamic intellectuals and a Malaysian dissident who was once thrown in jail in a government crackdown. Muzzafar favors more dissent and individual rights. "One of our biggest problems," he says of his country's Islamic culture, "is that we don't question or challenge the ruler. We should ask questions. We can do so without being brash. This is where I see a big dichotomy between our actual traditions and our precepts. In Islam, it is our duty to right wrongs." Then, quoting an Islamic prophet, he says, "A word of justice uttered before a ruler is the greatest jihad."

Muzzafar is no Islamic Thomas Jefferson. He thinks the upswing in U.S. power gives the impression that America's polyglot society sustains innovation, but he warns against a rush to judgment. "A certain creativity emerges from individual freedom, but that same individual freedom sometimes degenerates into a crass individualism with all its dire consequences," he says. He sees these effects threatening Malaysia, challenging "the core values that hold a society together." Still, Malaysians don't adopt American ways, but adapt them to suit their needs and traditional practices. Perhaps the best example of this comes from Mahathir himself, a frequent critic of the United States who—alone among leaders of Asian countries hit by financial calamities in the late 1990s—openly defied American advisers by adopting a fixed exchange rate and other government controls on capital. The moves were supposed to scare away foreign investors and doom Malaysia's economy, but they actually seemed to spur the country's recovery. For his re-election campaign in November 1999, Mahathir chose as his campaign motto "My Way," taking the words (and meaning) from the famous Frank Sinatra song. "We have achieved whatever we have achieved according to the Sinatra principle," Mahathir said before his victory. "We have done it our own way." Indeed, the Malaysian took special glee from invoking an American icon to underscore his successful disregard for the United States.

The paradoxical nature of Americanization is driven home to me one steamy afternoon when I take a high-speed riverboat up the Baram River, which runs deep into the jungles of Borneo. I am heading toward Marudi, a logging town that's the lifeline for various indigenous tribes in the Baram region. Some of the natives still make their livelihood off the jungle's bounty, live in wooden longhouses and follow many old customs. Inside the boat, seated across the aisle from me, is a woman from the Orang Ulu group. Her body is covered with brightly colored tattoos, and her ears are elongated, the result of attaching heavy weights to her lobes. I imagine that I am a complete alien to her, so immersed is she in her native mores. My little fantasy does not survive for long, however. When the boat hits cruising speed, the skipper puts on a video for the passengers in the cabin. The screen fills up with two big white guys. They toss themselves around a ring. They are American professional wrestlers. I am bored until I notice the Orang Ulu woman next to me. Her eyes are fixed on the screen, and she is howling with laughter, her face exploding each time a big hulk falls to the canvas.

Her taste for wrestling isn't a quirk. That evening, I dine with a militant antilogging activist: a Kayan tribe member considered so radical by the Malaysian government that it has seized his passport. After dinner, he invites me to his house and, with geckos running up and down his walls, he plays a traditional Kayan guitar. His brother sings folk songs in their native language, while he smiles approvingly. When I tell him about the Orang Ulu and her passion for wrestling, he confesses that he too loves American wrestling. So does every Kayan he knows.

CHAPTER 9

THE DIVERSITY ADVANTAGE AND ITS CRITICS

Plural dimensions of human identity often don't rest easily with each other, and sometimes not at all.

—MITCHELL COHEN[2]

It is a peculiar sensation, this double consciousness, this sense of always looking at one's self through the eyes of others, of measuring one's soul by the tape of a world that looks on in amused contempt and pity.

—W.E.B. DU BOIS[3]

National identity is in any case a matter not only of how we see ourselves, but also of how others choose to see us.

—IAN BURUMA[4]

A global order does not imply converging cultural identities. The current rage to make customs and practices uniform will be self-defeating if it leads to identical societies that harbor deep resentments towards each other. Being different can be an asset in complementary cooperation. Being identical can lead to fratricidal conflict.

—FRANCOIS GODEMENT[5]

Why can't we all just get along?

—RODNEY KING[6]

THE ARGUMENT in favor of hybridity ranges so widely over so many topics that it is bound to spark disagreements and challenges. Just how nations can best achieve the harmonious mixture of different groups is a subject of enormous controversy. Facts can help only so much in this task. Facts make sense in the context of a set of beliefs, values, and a vision of what a particular community or nation aspires to. Without such a vision, facts have little meaning, and different visions will inevitably lend different meanings to the same set of facts.

This is worth keeping in mind when evaluating criticisms of *The Global Me*. Critics basically fall into two camps. Some critics are illiberal and reject pluralism. They essentially argue that radical mixing is a mistake and that group identities are easily identifiable and fixed. Nothing good can come from mixing black and white, Asian and Hispanic, Jew and Gentile. These critics insist that people of different races, religions and ethnicities are best kept apart. While the iron-clad strictures of apartheid might seem anachronistic to them, they would not object to prohibitions against, say, interracial marriage or the allowance of, say, all-white or all-black schools for those parents who prefer them. If such separation can't be done legally, they would like it accomplished through informal means: by discouraging intermarriages, restricting immigration and promoting a race- or ethnic-based norm for schools, corporations and even government. Believers in purity, real or imagined, these critics dismiss as illusory the social vitality and economic competitiveness garnered by mongrel nations such as the United States, Canada or Singapore. In short, they see the world as divided between the pure and the impure. This view is at odds with reality, however, and thus creates its own crises. Highly diverse societies exist all over the world, and no manner of ethnic cleansing, separatist machinations or "random" violence can readily reverse this diversity. Racialists cannot easily dispute this. Nor can they easily imagine that in any rich nation a majority of people share their views. The very untenability of their position increases their isolation and thus compounds the irrationality of their views.

I disagree with racial purists on many points. But I find them hard to argue with because no set of facts will convince them of the benefits of impurity. Racialists should not be ignored, however. They pose serious threats to mongrel societies. The siren song of racialists—separate states for separate "people"—is a dangerous illusion that can provoke ethnic strife. This illusion led to the foundation of Jim Crow laws in the United States, which from the 1890s to the 1960s made a pretense of providing "separate but equal" facilities for whites and blacks in the South. This same perverse reasoning informed South Africa's apartheid system. It informed the breakup of Yugoslavia in 1991, the genocide against the Jews in World War II, the assault on Turkish Armenians in 1915 and the slaughter of Rwanda's Tutsis in 1994. Even now this logic infuses anti-Semitism in Poland with a sense of manifest destiny. It fuels racists in the United States and immigrant-bashers in Europe.

Critics of the second type favor diversity but worry that a nation can have too much of it. They oppose legal or informal ways of keeping groups separate and realize that a member of one group must have the means to take on the characteristics or join another group (say, through intermarriage or choice). But these critics insist that a commitment to diversity must not undermine the shared values that hold a nation together. They worry about the costs of diversity, especially when faced with large numbers of people who make the sort of multiple attachments—to different countries, languages, ethnicities, races and cultural styles—that increasingly serve as the motor of political, social and economic vitality. Well-meaning, these critics are often liberal and pluralist: They are opponents of discrimination and advocates of multiculturalism in schools, workplaces and society at large. But they fret that the strain of accommodating real differences among inhabitants of a nation may cause the common culture to buckle and the nation to break. They worry about the tendency for at least some members of ethnic and racial groups to prefer their own kind, for instance. They also worry that, despite the evident achievements of immigrants, many newcomers to a society are left out of the dominant scene and that even their children and children's children may be left out too.

What follows are eight common questions about hybridity. Each is an invitation to further debate. Such debate is healthy; balancing personal and communal identities with the imperative of achieving social and economic vitality is a conversation without end.

1. With all this diversity, can the center hold?

Europeans have long wondered how the United States gains leverage from its breathtaking diversity. The peerless French observer of the American scene, Alexis de Tocqueville, once mused about the "society which comprises all the nations of the world—English, French, German: people differing from one another in language, in beliefs, in opinions; in a word a society possessing no roots, no memories, no prejudices, no routine, no common ideas, no national character, yet with a happiness a hundred times more than our own." Then de Tocqueville asked, "What is the connecting link between these so different elements? How are they welded into one people?"

This puzzle, of how the United States stays whole, lies at the core of the insecurity over mongrelization. The simple therapy for this anxiety is to accept that national unity isn't predicated on the creation of a single people. Diverse peoples can subscribe to a core set of values, thus ensuring national unity. This process is so banal that many Americans take it for granted. National symbols and practices, meanwhile, tend to get adopted more enthusiastically by newcomers or minorities, perhaps because they have more to prove. Think of the children of interned Japanese immigrants—indeed, the children of immigrants from Italy and Germany too—who in World War II joined the U.S. Armed Forces. To be sure, in the decades following the civil rights movement, both minorities and ethnic groups (even second- and third-generation ethnics) held more tightly to their roots, or what they took to be their roots. By the 1990s, millions of Americans held another passport or had the right to do so. Yet despite this heightened sense of difference, hallmarks of American life and values remain: the hegemony of English, self-reliance, limited government and tolerance for difference. While the traditional symbols of American nationalism are indeed in retreat—I am thinking here of the flag, military service and an unquestioning pride in American accomplishments—national unity seems as high as ever because the country is prosperous and virtually all indicators of social well-being—from declining poverty and teen pregnancy to decreased rates of divorce and violent crime—are improving.

Of course, national unity is hard to measure, and ideological differences make it especially hard to separate exaggerated fears from reasonable concerns. Some political conservatives in the United States fear the collapse of a common national culture, seeing in the proliferating loyalties of immigrants and natives alike the specter of what Arthur Schlesinger Jr. calls the "disuniting of America." Much of this concern seems fueled by the rising numbers of poor and uneducated immigrants, from Mexico especially, and the new tolerance toward the use of Spanish at home and in public. But it is also fueled by a growing impatience with the venerable ideal of hyphenated Americans. Some people to the left of political center insist that new Americans need not assimilate into a mainstream culture that they see as coercive and arbitrary. Both sides of the political spectrum, however, often fail to recognize that many ordinary people want it every which way: engagement with their heritage, selected associations and dedication to some elements of a common culture.

The popularity of multiple identities, coupled with a view of America as a big tent rather than a tapestry or mosaic, makes fruitful discussions between the Left and the Right nearly impossible. A third-generation Korean in the United States is more likely to see himself as both Korean and American, rather than Korean-American. To the Left, this duality suggests a certain unwillingness to whole-heartedly affirm Koreanness, whereas to conservatives it suggests an opposition to a shared American way of life. This latter objection, meanwhile, begs the question of whether it is even possible to identify core values that all Americans ought to hold dear. While this seems a reasonable aspiration, just how do Americans identify the core values that constitute Americanism? After all, the United States remains deeply polarized over gun control, its impoverished underclass, the role of religion in public institutions, reproductive rights and the utility of bilingual education. Is English an essential value, for example? Is there a list of ten values, out of which an American must assent to, say, seven in order to endorse national unity?

The very difficulty of identifying shared values that aren't merely an expression of empty slogans (or the recitation of "universal" values such as those embodied in the Ten Commandments) prompts some people to look elsewhere for a civic nationalism. Perhaps values aren't critical to unity; perhaps unity requires only participation in shared institutions, such as courts, schools, government and the like. These are what Anthony Appiah calls "the conditions necessary for a common life." But this approach won't satisfy many political conservatives, since it leaves plenty of room for differences. After all, Appiah thinks it is a mistake to presume that Americans (or the citizens of any nation, for that matter) "really need . . . shared core values." Participation in shared institutions, Appiah insists, is enough. "To live together in a nation," he writes, "what is required is that we all share a commitment to the organization of the state—the institutions that provide the overarching order of our common life. But this does not require that we have the same commitment to those institutions, in the sense that the institutions must carry the same meaning for all of us."[7] There is a common life, then, but no common standard, no ruler against which all are measured.

Appiah's "solution" brings us full circle: In a hybrid nation, a shared commitment to institutions still means citizens can take opposing views on vital questions of identity—about the language, symbols, processes and ideology demanded of public life. Moreover, residential patterns are highly ethnic- and racial-specific. In many U.S. cities, one-third of all blacks live in chiefly black neighborhoods, and Hispanics and some Asian groups are heavily concentrated too.[8] These patterns raise the question of whether the United States is a multiethnic society or a collection of ethnic groups that share a big tent. An exhaustive study of southern California, which tracked residential patterns by country of origin in an area in which fully half of the state's population lives, suggested that the latter is the case. The study, published in 1997, found that southern California was "a set of separate societies rather than a single society of varied ethnic identities," citing the high concentrations of ethnic and racial separatism in the region. This separatism is worrisome because it means that some Americans experience much less diversity than they might. It also means that conflicts can take on a racial or ethnic character, as when during the Los Angeles riots of 1992 blacks and Latinos turned on Korean shopkeepers.

The problems in Los Angeles don't support the view that hybridity endangers social cohesion. For all the legitimate fears about the growth of separate subcultures in the United States, the degree of interpenetration, cooperation and substitution among group members remains remarkable. "For every episode of ethnic discord and conflict," notes ethnicity scholar Lawrence Fuchs, "there are thousands of examples of cooperation and sharing."[9]

Most Americans know it's unrealistic for scores of ethnic groups to live together without tension. Besides, the litmus test of a good society isn't whether it eradicates tensions between people but in how it resolves these tensions, or contains them. As the philosopher John Kekes showed in *The Morality of Pluralism*, a society only really knows that it's free enough to express contending values when conflicts over values break out. This means that people often mistake strains on national unity as signs of weakness when they are indeed signs of strength.

This paradox can be seen through the prism of African-American experience. Given their history of oppression and exclusion, blacks in the United States have understandably responded to feelings of not being wanted by showing feelings of not wanting to be in America. At times, this rejectionism expressed itself as (in the nineteenth century) a Back-to-Africa movement or (in the 1930s) in the form of a Communist Party campaign to create a "black" state in the deep South. But these separatist drives were always a minor note in African-American life. The major note always sought to mix racial pride with the realization that blacks were shaped by America and were shaping it even in the face of a rigid social hierarchy. In short, blacks had no exit from America, even when America didn't want them.

W.E.B. Du Bois, the great African-American scholar, perhaps best expressed the poignancy of this situation. Born in 1868, while the embers of the Civil War still burned, Du Bois lived into the early 1960s, just as the civil rights movement kicked into full swing. Du Bois keenly felt what he called the "double consciousness" of the American Negro, and his classic work, *The Souls of Black Folk,* written in 1903, gives a stunning description of multiple identities:

> One ever feels his two-ness. An American, a Negro; two souls, two thoughts, two unreconciled strivings; two warring ideals in one dark body, whose dogged strength alone keeps it from being torn asunder.
>
> The history of the American Negro is the history of this strife—this longing to attain self-conscious manhood, to merge his double self into a better and truer self. *In this merging he wishes neither of the older selves to be lost.* He would not Africanize America, for America has too much to teach the world and Africa. He would not bleach his Negro soul in a flood of white Americanism, for he knows that Negro blood has a message for the world. He simply wishes to make it possible for a man to be both a Negro and an American, without being cursed and spit upon by his fellows, without having the doors of opportunity closed roughly in his face.[10]

Du Bois has much to teach people of color—and whites too—about the practice and pain inherent in balancing a double, triple or even quadruple consciousness. The dominant people and culture of every society have many ways of imposing, softly and strongly, their ways of thinking and acting on those who favor one or more different (read minority) styles. Hybridity is an invitation to attempt to disentangle these colliding styles. This disentanglement is hard work. Nothing should suggest that mongrelization is a panacea. Du Bois's insight is an elegant reminder of why radical mixing puts stress on the center of a society and indeed must do so. Differences erased or forgotten are more dangerous than differences affirmed or revealed. In seeing these differences, however, do not mistake the bending of the social order for its breaking. The center will hold as long as most people in a nation-state want it to, and see it in their self-interest, or group interest, to work toward common ends. These ends can be as ordinary as building a new road or water system or as complex as hiring police officers or defining a new school curriculum. These ends can be shifting, fluid, contradictory, accepted by some and not by others. They bring to mind Lincoln's famous saying that the duty of a leader is only to please some of the people some of the time. If this seems an insecure foundation for a nation, bear in mind that this insecurity pervades the entire U.S. experience. As the historian Perry Miller once wrote, being "an American is not something to be inherited so much as something to be achieved." And achieved it must be, again and again.[11]

2. Isn't hybridity contributing to the decline of national sovereignty and the importance of nation-states?

Nations are indeed in decline, but the culprit isn't hybridity. Pin the blame for the eroding sovereignty of nations on a complex interplay of the following factors: technology; trade and financial integration; the end of the Cold War and the concomitant rise of American hegemony in matters of international security; the growing role in global civic affairs of multilateral organizations such as the International Monetary Fund and the World Trade Organization. These factors both encourage and reflect the reality that small and large nations interpenetrate one another more deeply now than during any prior period in modern history. This interpenetration has benefits, but among the costs are a perceived loss of independence and a growing pressure to collaborate with other nations in crafting common responses to what some national leaders still view as unique problems.

The European Union offers many examples of the way transnational alliances create tensions for national governments seeking to respond honestly and openly to local conditions. Consider the Republic of Ireland's fight against price inflation. With the fastest-growing economy in Europe, real wages and business profits are rising faster than ever before in Irish history. Yet property prices are soaring, and demand for goods and services has never been higher. Acting independently, the Irish government would surely raise interest rates sharply in order to dampen demand and relieve inflationary pressures. The power to do so, one might argue, goes to the heart of national sovereignty, since nothing is more central to Ireland's transformation from impoverished backwater to postindustrial juggernaut than the maintenance of material prosperity. Yet the Irish government has little power to fight inflation because its central bank no longer has any real power. As an original member of the EU nations that launched the common currency known as the "euro," high-growth Ireland has the same interest rate as Germany, France and Italy—slow-growth countries with little inflationary pressures. These large, sluggish countries need ultralow interest rates to spur economic growth, so a central banker in Frankfurt obliges. Ireland gets low interest rates, even though monetary stimulus is the last thing it needs. To grasp the difficulty of this, imagine the chair of the Federal Reserve, which sets U.S. interest rates, a Brazilian living in Mexico City who's preoccupied not with U.S. economic growth but with the peso's depreciation.

The affront to Irish sovereignty is actually worse than this, though. Because the euro is dominated by slow-growth countries, this currency—introduced with great fanfare in January 1999—lost about 15 percent of its value in its first year of trading. Thus the Irish economy is stimulated not only by low interest rates but also by a depreciating currency. To people with dollars or yen or British pounds, Irish assets seem to be getting cheaper—and thus more desirable because of the country's robust growth. The depreciated euro, then, draws still more foreign investment into Ireland, which in turn raises demand and puts even more pressure on prices. All policymakers can do is to raise taxes (not politically acceptable) and jawbone unions and unorganized employees to accept modest wage gains.

Clearly, the Irish government has less sovereignty (defined as independent power for action) than formerly, but would anyone return to the days when Ireland was unfettered by the EU? Hardly. In the Irish context, the sovereign power to set interest rates meant little when an economy stagnated, so just who mourns this loss? On the other hand, the citizens of Ireland and their elected representatives now depend for their macroeconomic stability largely on people who live in Brussels and Frankfurt. That some of these very transnational technocrats hold an Irish passport makes the situation no less insecure according to the traditional metric of national power.

The Irish example reveals the complexities of the so-called decline of the nation-state. Obviously, hybridity has nothing to do with this source of decline. Consider another area where it seemingly does. In brief, this might be called the problem of the disappearance of patriotism. The German political writer Josef Joffe has neatly laid this problem at the door of identity politics: "When the individual is king, societies don't easily rise to the bugle call of war." This has its good aspects, of course. To quote Joffe: "Individuals matter more than collectives, and groups—defined by ethnicity, race or economic interest—matter more than the nation. The flag has frayed, so to speak, and power has shifted from the state to its citizens." Again, it is hard to argue that this trend is unwelcome, at least in wealthy nations of Europe, North America and Asia, where central governments hogged power, often to the detriment of their citizens, for much of the twentieth century.[12]

But individualism isn't tantamount to disloyalty. Citizens who share their affections with other tribes and places may actually show more loyalty to their adopted countries and more enthusiasm about their countries' values than do natives. There is a certain logic to this: People who flaunt their love for the Other are indeed more likely to draw complaints of disloyalty so, thinking ahead, they are careful to be able to prove otherwise. Such gut feelings are supported by scholarship. One exhaustive study of the tendency of immigrants to represent mainstream U.S. interests both in America and abroad criticizes "the alarmist vision of multicultural critics who see a balkanization of American culture and society" because of "ethnic groups' affinity with homeland cultures and the advocacy of home country political causes."[13] For example, the children of immigrants are well represented in the armed forces. No less a celebrated military leader than Colin Powell, the son of Jamaican immigrants to New York, can attest to the enduring tendency of immigrants and minorities to show loyalty to American national interests.

So it is possible that hybridity brings out the patriot in people. What about their lives outside of the political arena? Consider language, probably the most sensitive of all the cultural issues. Do people count as having assimilated if they don't chiefly speak English? Most consensus-oriented Americans insist that speaking English well is a defining characteristic of Americanization. Without a common language, the tower-of-Babel effect will unfold in the United States, leading to all sorts of fragmentation as communities follow their tongues, not their mutual economic, social or political interests. This specter of the Babelization of the United States seems far-fetched, especially at a time when English is more popular than ever around the world and when a critical competitive advantage held by ordinary Americans is their sheer ability to communicate well in English, the global language. But perhaps we should step back for a moment and ask the most radical question first: Would it be so terrible if the United States became a bilingual or trilingual nation, at least within certain cities or regions? Would this variance stoke separatist fires? Would it threaten the hegemony of English in the United States? Such effects seem hardly imaginable.

Given the high levels of immigration in the past two decades and the concentration of non-English speakers in certain cities and neighborhoods, it is natural that many languages seem to be thriving in the United States. It may even be natural to think that, in some places, an English speaker is actually disadvantaged. This impression may be reinforced, unwittingly, by government policies that encourage the use of secondary languages—and Spanish especially—on public signs and official documents. The real question, however, is how these languages will fare over time.

The evidence on the issue is not nearly so dramatic as English-language purists would like to believe. Indeed, there are reasons to think that some significant number of immigrants learn English well, lose touch with the languages of their original countries and do both roughly as fast as they've always done. One study by the research arm of the National Academy of Sciences found that nearly three-fifths of the immigrants who came to the United States in the 1980s said in 1990 that they spoke English well.[14] To be sure, the National Academy found that just one quarter of the 1980s immigrants from Mexico spoke English well by 1990. Some even think Spanish has reached a critical threshold that guarantees its survival in the United States even absent a continuing flow of newcomers from Mexico. But much evidence can be marshaled against the case that Spanish and other secondary languages are sinking roots in the United States, which in the words of sociologist Ruben Rumbaut is "a language graveyard." Rumbaut, who studies the language traits of immigrants across generations, believes English will remain dominant and that "the prospects of fluent bilingualism for the third and fourth generations are slim to none for the most part."

The debate over secondary languages in the United States will take many years to sort out. It does underscore, however, that the question of assimilation can be twisted many different ways. One person's healthy hybridity is another person's ghettoization. More sophisticated analysts, concerned about identifying nuances and not just scoring political points, realize that the dominant culture has no choice but to absorb or integrate newcomers whether or not they feel a strong tug toward other cultures and countries. More significant are the terms of integration, and these terms are historically conditioned: Each generation, in other words, defines what it means to be an American and just how acceptable are pre- or post-American affiliations. Sociologists bloodlessly call this dynamic process "segmented" assimilation. The term is unwieldy but the point well made. To paraphrase the Princeton University sociologist Alejandro Portes, the question is not whether newcomers will adapt to a society, but to what segment of that society will they adapt? In short, assimilation isn't an all-or-nothing gambit, or an instant transformation either. It is a long-term process that, as immigration researcher Gregory Rodriguez notes, "has never required the obliteration of ethnic identity." Nor does there exist any neat checklist of items that "qualify" someone as a bona fide American.[15]

If national identity is more about shades of gray than black or white, this doesn't mean hybrids can guarantee that multiple senses of belonging will never rip apart a nation. Canada has come close with its Quebec separatists. Britain—with its commitment to devolved political power in Scotland, Wales and North Ireland—could well come undone. Even in the United States, where the attraction of belonging to the world's lone superpower appears overwhelming, fragmentation is conceivable. The American Southwest, with its historical affinities to Mexico, might someday hive off. And today independence movements exist in Puerto Rico, Hawaii and the American territories in the Pacific. Still, the point isn't to predict the future, but to gauge the threats to national cohesion. On its own, the presence of strangers does not raise the risk of disunity, nor does the attachment of the children of strangers to their parents' roots.

3. What about poor nations? Why aren't they going hybrid?

Every broad explanation can be stretched only so far. In this book I seek to explain the central rhythms within rich nations and the wider environment in which they compete for economic and cultural advantage. Poor nations are excluded from my analysis except to the extent that they produce global hybrids. The reason is straightforward. In poor nations, diversity is overwhelmed by other forces, notably deprivation, inequality of wealth, poor education and health care, and weak commitment to rule by law. Until poverty and inequality are substantially reduced, poor nations can't capitalize on the potential benefits of diversity in the same way that rich nations do. Before putting diversity into the service of hybridity, poor nations must improve the quality of education, health care and other public goods. To be sure, this is to some extent a chicken-and-egg problem. Ethnic strife can undermine efforts to raise the quality of life. Communal battles consume scarce resources. Efforts at power sharing distract attention from other concerns. But often poverty is the prime culprit. It gives rise to ethnic strife where it would otherwise not exist.

Many poor nations possess dazzling diversity, of course. Some countries, such as Brazil and India, boast a vast number of ethnic groups, religions and languages and even show a relatively high degree of social harmony given their diversity. But other poor nations, which possess a similar degree of social variety, suffer from a history of strife. A third group of countries—such as Poland and the Czech Republic—are nearly rich, but still haven't faced up to basic issues about minority rights and toleration. Postcommunist countries in Eastern Europe are attracting immigrants from poorer parts of the region, including the former Soviet Union, and have seen distressing eruptions of anti-Semitic, anti-Gypsy or antiforeigner feelings. South Africa is highly diverse racially and ethnically and is the wealthiest country in sub-Saharan Africa. But to sustain a multiracial society after decades of apartheid, South

Africa must discard the racial hierarchies of the past and elevate the needs of black South Africans over other groups in such a way as to reinforce ethnoracial distinctions and undercut hybridity, at least in the near future. In Argentina and Chile, the two Latin American countries perhaps nearest to the rich club, hybridity is limited by widespread corruption, income inequalities and historical intolerance for political dissent.

The outlook for hybridity is also murky in China, the world's largest official monoculture. China's communist government enforces an unbending homogeneity that essentially denies the existence of the country's staggering ethnic, religious and linguistic diversity. China's treatment of national minorities—from Tibetans to Taiwanese—is appalling. So is its treatment of religious minorities, from fervent Muslims to the Falun Gong sect. It requires only a small leap to conclude that government limits on the expression of difference impede creativity and reduce the chances that China can reap the bounty of its diversity at home and abroad (via its diaspora communities). It seems fair to think that China's government will someday pay a steep price for imposing a uniform identity on its people. But the government shows few signs of encouraging regional and ethnic identities, and no less so the sorts of constructed identities that underpin the Falun Gong spiritualism. Instead, China's government upholds the myth of Chinese oneness. Like other poor nations, China may ultimately receive a wealth boost from its diversity, but probably only after many years and much internal change. Like other countries that don't qualify as rich, China is beset by too many internal problems for the hybridity factor to kick in. The many diverse communities in China can only hope that the country achieves the elusive threshold development that will enable it to reap the benefits of diversity.[16]

By far, poverty is the greatest single barrier to hybridity. Grinding poverty makes life hard to bear and inspires utopian longings among the dispossessed. As Michael Ignatieff has eloquently noted, "What could be more like paradise on earth than to live in a community without enemies? To create a world with no more need for borders, for watch-posts, a world freed from fear in the night and war by day? A world safe from the deadly contaminations and temptations of the other tribe? What could be more beautiful than to live in a community with people who resemble each other in every particular?"[17]

To denizens of rich nations, the deadening sameness of the societies spawned by this utopian dream renders them abhorrent. But inspired by deprivation, these other-worldly stirrings are a reminder that the social harmony achieved by wealthy nations reflects not a superior culture but more advantageous material circumstances. Indeed, the value of the culture of poor nations isn't at issue. It is their capacity to transcend their respective cultures and to mix and match alien cultural elements. In many rich countries, and especially the United States, this capacity is highly developed; in poor countries, it generally isn't.

This distinction reflects a common-sense notion about national development. Paradoxically, a capacity for mixing and matching features from different racial, ethnic and national identities may arise only after a nation imposes a monolithic mentality on its people (who may be quite diverse or not). A nation may have to assert a uniform identity—and exclude those who don't adhere to it—before this monolithic identity can be transcended. In this stage of development, policies of cultural preservation, which dictate that contending groups willfully stay apart or suffer penalties for deviating from "national" traits, may actually better serve all the groups of a nation on the presumption that "a person can profit most from other cultures if he is first relieved of the worry that his own culture is about to disappear."[18]

In crude form, this belief is the logic behind power-sharing arrangements in Bosnia and Macedonia, affirmative-action programs in Malaysia and South Africa or the Quebec language law that forbids people of French descent to send their children to a non-French-speaking school. This same urge for "ethnic cleansing" led Serbia to murder its Kosovar minority in 1999, Indonesia to attack ethnic Chinese in the late 1990s and Uganda to expel its Indians in the 1970s. That these actions undermined the economies of these countries mattered not to elites, who put (rightly or wrongly) a higher value on homogeneity.

In short, beneficial forms of diversity require a political, social and economic maturity that poor nations don't possess. To put it another way, diversity can be harnessed only by countries with a high level of education and sophistication, rule by law and a commitment to tolerance and respect for ethnic minorities and immigrants. Again, this premise suggests the seeming paradox that nations require a high degree of "social capital" in order to increase diversity noticeably.

Yet the situation isn't hopeless. Many poor nations already contain pockets of great diversity, where hybrid people and organizations flourish. The largest, most sophisticated cities in the developing world—Bombay, Bangkok, Buenos Aires—resemble the cities of industrialized countries in their degree of social mixing. And elites in poor countries, often because of their ability to travel and attend school abroad, are increasingly linked to a diverse international society. They are frequently among the high-skilled immigrants—the physicians, engineers, and executives—who are sought by wealthy countries. Indeed, to a surprising extent, elites from poor nations actually redefine their local roots after achieving a measure of international success. It is after they return home, armed with more experience and savings, that they feel their national origins more intensely.

This tendency suggests that a developmental theory of diversity is plausible. Broadly, it amounts to this: As nations cross a wealth threshold, their capacity for dealing with difference takes a quantum leap, and they become poised to harness diversity for national advantage, rather than simply seek to keep the lid on or, worse, foment communal strife. Why should wealth matter so much? That it does should hardly surprise people. It is well known that wealth affords nations with advantages in many fields: from military contests to scientific achievement, from art to sport. Wealth shapes more ordinary aspects of life too. Consider population change. Demographers long ago established what they call the "demographic transition": the way birthrates alter as societies grow richer. "First comes a decline in mortality, leading to a short population explosion," says one writer, describing the consensus view. "Then, after an interval of variable length, a steep decline in the birthrate [occurs], which slows, halts or may even reverse the rise in numbers."[19] Nearly everywhere, "demographic transition" roughly describes the forces behind the decline in population growth. Certainly, this decline is not universal. Some poor countries—like China—curtail birthrates through discipline. And some rich countries, after sharp declines in birthrates, see modest upturns. But generally as countries grow richer, birthrates decline. This same sort of transition may apply to hybridity. Greater hybridity may be a dynamic of rich countries that is as inexorable as population stability—and for poor countries may become a signal right of passage.

4. Does the existence of holy lands and sacred ground make harmonious mixing and hybridization undesirable or impossible in many places?

For some people, identity and territory are synonymous. Self and land are linked. In ancient times, exile was among the most painful of penalties. Nothing was worse than expulsion from one's homeland. The self thrived in symbiosis with the land. Battles over control and ownership of land shaped the collective consciousness of many peoples. From Mexico to Ireland, from the Great Plains of North America to the savannas of southern Africa, people defined themselves in relation to land. Loss of land often meant, if not loss of identity, a severe trauma.

Some stretches of land fuel conflicts to this day, seemingly possessing a malevolent logic of their own. Jerusalem is perhaps the ultimate case of holy land—to which Jews, Christians and Muslims claim a special bond. For thousands of years, all three groups have struggled to gain an edge in the contest for control over this venerable city. Even today the Palestinian claim on Jerusalem remains a sticking point in the Arab-Israeli peace process. Land conflicts also arise when once-evicted people return from exile, as in Kosovo or Rwanda. Who gets what? Boundaries, drawn arbitrarily ages ago, can cause conflicts too. Bitter disputes also arise over which people came first and which came later to a territory. Whose claims carry more weight? The question is deceptively difficult, since delving further and further into the past often reveals that many "original" inhabitants of a territory came from somewhere else. To be sure, special issues arise over whether later settlers were welcomed into a community, or whether they forced their way in. If people always found new homes peacefully, this question might not loom so large, but in history newcomers often resorted to violence to carve open space for themselves. When power relations shift—as in South Africa—the once-oppressed group can exact its revenge on the descendants of invaders by trying to expel them or, nearly as painful, seeking the recovery of stolen lands.

Though many land disputes lead to violence, not all do. There are a surprising number of examples of one group giving up land to another in order to promote ethnic and racial harmony, or at least a reduction in strains. In 1999, the Republic of Ireland renounced its claim to Northern Ireland as part of a power-sharing plan for the British province that brought Catholic nationalists into a multiethnic government for the first time. Canada gave wide-ranging authority over its huge northern territory to the Inuit tribes in the late 1990s. Though imposing various conditions, Israel agreed to give Palestinians land under Israeli control out of which to form their own state.

Land partition doesn't always ease ethnic tensions, however. The classic case is Britain's partition of the Indian subcontinent between Muslims and Hindus, a decision that led to millions of deaths in 1947. Today, India is a multiethnic nation, yet tensions with Pakistan remain high. When both countries openly tested nuclear weapons and fought a border war in the late 1990s, these tensions underscored the limits of ethnic partition.

Even in cases where rival parties accept partition, this may only raise the puzzle of access: Are outsiders allowed to visit a sacred land and even settle there? And if outsiders are allowed to settle, how does the dominant group avoid being swamped by outsiders who might spoil the sacredness of the land?

This problem sometimes leads to violence; the original British decision to allow Jews to begin settling in Palestine early in the twentieth century well illustrates this. But the access question also lends itself to a variety of peaceful solutions too. Quebec is a good example. To be sure, the Canadian province could attempt to enforce a law forbidding any outsiders to move in, thus protecting the hegemony of its Francophile culture and French language. But to do so would surely mean economic stagnation, which in turn would ultimately enervate Quebec culture. So Quebec's answer is to court immigrants but to require them to adopt Quebecois ways by learning French, sending their children to French-speaking schools and obeying the various rules aimed at ensuring that Quebecois culture continues to dominate the province. Malaysia's state of Sarawak, on the island of Borneo, offers another preservation model. Unlike more densely populated parts of western Malaysia, Sarawak is home to a majority of indigenous people who live in relative harmony with Malay and Chinese ethnic groups. To maintain this balance, the Sarawak state government restricts the inward movement of people from elsewhere within Malaysia. While surely an abridgment on the freedom of other Malaysians, the restriction helps to ensure that indigenous people aren't swamped by outsiders. In Switzerland, foreigners can't own land, making it more difficult for them to sink roots in the country.

Another policy approach is to make life difficult for people who are different, thus encouraging them to leave. Many new nations formed out of the breakup of the Soviet Union passed language laws that discriminated against Russian speakers by, say, requiring all government workers to know Latvian, Romanian or another local language. In Ireland, the numbers of Jews and Protestants declined steadily from the 1920s to the 1970s partly because of a whole range of social laws that reflected the dominance of the country's Catholic majority. When Germany's need for "guest workers" fell sharply in the 1970s, the government offered to return them home; those who stayed were denied full rights.

These examples suggest that conflicts over how to share space take many forms and that people who feel a special bond to a place can justify excluding strangers, especially if their own culture is rare or endangered. Some argue that particular ethnic groups have an absolute value, and should be protected against threats from outsiders. If land is critical to a group's identity, then land must be protected. This may limit the freedom of nongroup members, but it can be justified on practical grounds. The economist Stephen Marglin has argued that "cultural diversity may be the key to the survival of the human species" by keeping alive lifestyle alternatives, not only in their present condition but also for the possibility of future developments from these alternatives. For example, what if the world needs the skills of hunter-gatherers at some point, but all of them are gone? Or it turns out that a folk-healing tradition once practiced by an Amazon tribe combats some future disease, but nobody is left who knows the remedy? What then? Spawned by anthropology, this idea gained its greatest currency through the popularity of *Star Trek:* Captain Kirk was never to interfere in a distinct culture's trajectory for precisely these reasons.[20]

The belief that distinct cultures can be ruined by contact with strangers is a romantic one, based on an assumption that certain cultural traits can be preserved only by their original carriers—and without interference. The ideal of isolating cultures is rooted in the experience many indigenous peoples have had with modernity. Rather than providing opportunities for more satisfying lives, encounters with outsiders have harmed many isolated cultures. Such damage has given rise to a kind of ecological argument in favor of isolating indigenous people and even small or fragile minorities. This might be called an endangered-species thinking about humanity. Endangered societies should be protected, in this reasoning, much in the same way animals and plants are protected in order to preserve biodiversity.

Certainly, the biodiversity metaphor may make sense for the planet's ecology. But it is no argument against mixing of people. To start with, even if mixing leads to the decline of a pristine society, it may still be possible to record and then revive the society's cultural traditions before they disappear. The Swedish anthropologist Ulf Hannerz notes that it isn't fair to assume that alternatives, once lost, "will be lost forever." People can reconstruct the alternatives as they need them, he says, "without seeing them continuously modeled." It also is naive to assume that cultural diversity is "a shared reserve," which can be drawn on like savings in a bank account. Even if the constellation of traits that make up a distinct culture can be stockpiled somehow, there is no guarantee that a specific cultural practice—say, a kind of mediation practice among peasant farmers in northern Burundi—can be applied to a new setting—say, a farming community in rural France. Hannerz, for instance, questions the whole belief that "whatever seems to work in one culture can be predicted to be equally successful" in another, citing "the difficulty of transporting items of culture from one context to another."[21] There is also the possibility that ethnic groups, even when driven from their sacred lands by conquest or economic forces, can reconstruct their communities in new places. The success of widely dispersed communities (of Jews, Indians, Chinese and others) lends support for this option. More specific migrations certainly seem feasible. The breakdown of order in West Africa and the Congo, for instance, led many leading African musicians in the 1980s and 1990s to shift their base to Paris and London, expanding the reach of their music while at the same time gaining more stable support. When a measure of political stability returned to Nigeria, the Congo and elsewhere in the region in the late 1990s, musicians from the region retained their cosmopolitan connections.

Ethnic groups with their own territory are presumed to oppose contacts with strangers. To allow openness is to risk diluting their cultures. But openness is desirable precisely because it allows minority cultures to win support for their culture in the wider world, while at the same time drawing on the resources of outsiders. In a loose way, it makes sense to think of a world market in cultures, so that attractiveness of a particularly culture can be "measured" by how many nonmembers of this culture admire and perhaps adopt aspects of it. The "popularity" of a culture, then, influences its chances for survival. A strong culture will be adopted by others and proliferate, while weak cultures won't be emulated by outsiders. It matters little whether the groups or nations that stand behind these cultures are large or small. The writing of Ireland, the instrumental music of Mali, the vocal singing of Cape Verde, the pop music from Jamaica—these illustrate the way the cultural achievements of less numerous peoples can be amplified globally through contact with strangers. In the cultural marketplace, large countries (or tribes) don't carry an inherent advantage. Their bigness isn't all that important because, unlike markets in goods and services, the market for cultures can't be captured and monopolized. The cultural market isn't a zero-sum game. After all, consumers can adopt many cultural styles—different ones for different circumstances. Thus, in a sense, ethnic and national cultures live and die with the market, driven by taste and utility.

This kind of thinking about culture may seem bloodless, but it is this very realization that drives many land-based ethnic groups or nationalities to open up and mix with others. This mixing is a matter of freedom and pragmatism, wholly consistent with the sacred nature of land and identities arising from a sense of place and space. Enlightened minority groups see mixing as their lifeblood. Openness paradoxically promotes cultural survival. Closing off, by contrast, is a luxury that usually can be afforded only by a minority group that isn't endangered.

I am reminded of this paradox on a visit to the Gagauz people of southern Moldova. One of Europe's smallest minorities, the Gagauz are Turkish-speaking Christians who moved from Bulgaria 200 years ago and settled in what was then Russia's Pale of Settlement. Under the Soviet Union, the Gagauz retained their status as a distinct minority though the government gradually shut down Gagauz schools and cultural organizations. When Moldova become independent in 1991 and declared Romanian its national language, the Gagauz threatened to secede. To retain Gagauz loyalty in 1994, Moldova granted them regional autonomy. The Gagauz, who number about 150,000, now elect their own assembly and a chief, or *Bascan*, who also sits in Moldova's national parliament; pass local laws; have their own university and a Gagauz-language television station. A revived Gagauz identity reflects the ideal of a multiethnic nation. In a symbol of this, the Gagauz flag flies over public buildings but always alongside a Moldovan flag. That is the law: One flag can never be shown without the other.

Like many in the former Soviet Union, the Gagauz are dreadfully poor. Most are farmers whose output is still ruined a decade after the Soviet crackup. Official statistics show a staggering two-thirds decline in real income. Daily life is miserable. Some parts of Gagauzia have electricity only a few hours a day. Piped water is undrinkable in all but a few places. Heating is scarce. Salaries are a pittance and rarely paid on time. Yet few Gagauz yearn for a return to more prosperous Soviet days. Liberation has deepened poverty but revived the Gagauz cultural identity. This has not turned most Gagauz into bigots but has encouraged their hybrid tendencies. They are an obscure example of cosmopolitan patriotism.

The Gagauz have mixed easily with other groups for centuries, so their hybridity is deeply felt. Political and cultural autonomy is a welcome relief from the rigidities of communism, but not an invitation to wall themselves off from others. The attitudes of Constantine Popovich are typical. Popovich lives in Komrat, the capital of Gagauzia. Fifty-something, he manages a fruit-juice plant. He thinks of the Gagauz as an irreducible entity, a nation among nations. Still, he assimilated to Soviet life as a young man. His wife is a Russian, and he speaks Russian along with Gagauz. His children, meanwhile, reflect his multifaceted sense of belonging. His daughter is a doctor in Gagauzia who is actively reviving the culture. His son lives in Odessa, part of the Ukraine, and is removed from Gagauz life.

I meet Popovich at his juice workshop. In a small, chilly room outside of his bottling line, we chug tall glasses of apple, peach and carrot juice sold under the name Basarabia, which is a variant of the old Russian name for the Pale of Settlement. After we talk about his plans for turning Gagauzia into a regional center for fruit juices, I ask him about identity: What does it mean to be Gagauz? "I don't care about nationality," he says. "I care more about a person's personality.

"Nationality is artificial," he adds. "It's created." Mixing is better, and it won't threaten the survival of the Gagauz, who persevere by keeping alive their language, family traditions and a diasporic tie with the culture and practices of Turkey. Withdrawal of the Gagauz into an enclave is absurd, he thinks, and hardly the aim of autonomy. "It's impossible for a nation to be pure," he says. "It's impossible to prohibit intermarriages." Then he pauses and adds, "This is the world. Everything is in movement. You can't stop this amalgamation."

And he wouldn't stop it even if he could. "Let's say Gagauz were pure. No Russians. No Moldovans. Would this nation be richer, wiser, happier?" He shakes his head. "Cosmopolitanism is reality."

These philosophical reflections, coming from a juice maker on the margins of Europe, surprise me. His days and nights are consumed with finding cash-paying customers—mainly in Russia, Poland and Moldova itself—for his juice. Yet his thoughts about identity come pouring forth. This is in part because I've prodded him by expressing amazement that the Gagauz are surviving despite their history of intermingling with others. Turning the tables on me, he asks, "Doesn't the United States fear it will lose its identity because of its immigrants?" Before I can answer, he says: "It's not important to me who lives in a country. What's important is what that person does for the country." Then he displays his force of his reasoning, thinking about the poverty of his tribe and the wider world he gained sight of during Soviet times. "If the Gagauz become wealthy and powerful, our Gagauz identity won't get lost," he says firmly. "If Gagauzia becomes weak, so will our identity."

The connection seems obvious to him as a man whose livelihood depends on the fruits of the earth. "What about the flowers?" he asks. "When the pollen is carried from one flower to another, don't the flowers get better, sweeter, stronger?" He knows the answer, at least for the Gagauz. "Maybe," he says, "it's more important to have it better, not pure."

As I drive away from Komrat, I think of how Popovich reflects the classic tension between the assimilated and unassimilated, between Martin Luther King Jr. and Malcolm X. Critics of mixing have always insisted that authentic identities must be based on shared notions of purity. But with global connections spreading, and with people gaining the ability to possess both roots and wings, this age-old dilemma seems to be losing its force even in places such as poor Moldova, where the conditions for a violent racialism would seem to apply. Instead, I am struck by Popovich's dedication to the belief that openness strengthens. The rewards outweigh the risks.

I tell this to Yuri Novasadiuk, my companion in the car. Like me, Yuri is the child of a Jewish-Gentile intermarriage. His father (now deceased) was from Ukraine, and his mother is a Russian Jew. Only now can Yuri, who is forty-four, speak freely about his submerged Jewishness. After marrying outside of her group, his mother was shunned by her own parents, while the larger Soviet society stigmatized her for the very Jewishness of her parents. Even though Yuri's mother didn't practice Judaism (and certainly didn't encourage her children to do so), she had her limits. In the 1970s, when Jews began to stream out of the Soviet Union for Israel, she was asked by the KGB to denounce as traitors some fellow teachers who were petitioning to leave. She refused and was fired, never to work again.

Yuri recalls his peculiar shame over his mother's circumstances. "I was embarrassed by her Jewishness and ashamed that I felt this in her presence," he tells me. Only now, a decade after the Soviet breakup, is Yuri starting to examine his own shadowy roots. "Every person likes to know, who am I?" he says. This question of identity is personal and highly specific, but no less crucial for being so. After all the political and economic disappointments of Moldova's experiments with capitalism, Yuri is convinced that the big change involves how well he and others come to understand their hybrid backgrounds. This, after all, was what communism tried to eradicate. He says, "What I value most about democracy is that it lets people say who they are."

The freedom to speak about oneself leads many places, but a land of imagined purity—of a good life based on the eradication of the stranger—is not one of them. As Yuri has belatedly come to know, he carries both friend and stranger in his heart.

Yuri's experience is one kind of answer to the challenge of holy lands. There are others. I am struck by one as I sit inside a cold, brightly lit chapel on a large, wooded school campus in the market town of Ballinasloe. I am in the West of Ireland. It is the first day of the new millennium, January 1, 2000, and I am here to join my wife's family, the Currans, for a reunion. My wife's family is large: She has eleven brothers and sisters, and each is married and has children. One of her brothers teaches in this very school, and he arranged the gathering. Many in-laws like me are present; some are so deeply involved in the family that I can't imagine the Currans without them. I have never asked myself if I am a Curran, but at times like this I consider myself at least to possess some sort of family visitor's pass. I am an uncle to thirty-seven Curran children, ranging in age from eight to twenty-nine. I know many of my wife's siblings well and have stayed in their homes as they have in mine. We share many memories. This New Year's Day, about sixty Currans sit in this beautifully decorated chapel, their eyes on a young priest standing at the altar. He is giving mass. At some point, he breaks off from his religious script in order to acknowledge the purpose of this gathering. In the back of the chapel, my nine-year-old son Liam waits with seven other children, each holding a special object. Liam holds a piece of dark, dense turf in his hands. Symbol of the family's tie to its ancestral land, this turf literally gives warmth; it is fuel for the fire, dug up from an ancient bog and then dried until consumed in flames.

"A hunger to belong is at the heart of our nature," the priest declares, grabbing my attention. I am standing now, along with the others, who are quiet with expectation. "Family is the home of belonging," the priest goes on. "Our first sense of family is nurtured in the home. It is in the home that we find a sense of being wanted, of being part of something special, larger than ourselves."

I glance back at my son waiting his turn. "Mostly we take this sense of belonging for granted," the priest says. "Unless we lose it. Through the family we find intimacy, and if we do not feel we belong then we feel empty. We feel we have nothing. Each of us needs the anchor of the family to bend with the storms. This gathering reminds you of your rootedness to the land and to your family. In these times, the hunger to belong is intense. It rarely has been more urgent. So that for all of you the family is a blessing and privilege. You belong to something special, irreplaceable."

As the priest speaks, I think about what he says and how it applies to me, a non-Catholic, an adopted Curran. His words cut both ways. Families aren't only the fruit of roots, the pride of those born into them; families are nourished by those who join them too. Strong families are energized by the outsiders they take in. Even the natural-born Currans must decide how much energy to devote to their family; in a sense, they too choose to belong, choose how to define their family, choose how hard to work at maintaining ties. This sense in which family ties are achieved, not just inherited, explains the striking cohesion of the Currans. Their gathering—like so many others I have witnessed over the decades—is an act of will, not the expression of an ancient blood tie. Communion doesn't come automatically. Curran family members have invested with meaning gatherings such as this, so that whatever sacred ties they feel between one another, and the land they inhabit, are as much achieved as inherited. What manner of Curranness have I achieved in spite—or indeed perhaps because of—my otherness? Have I made this tie sacred for myself, or is it merely an accident of my marriage? As my son walks quickly up the aisle toward the altar, holding his piece of turf, I puzzle over my predicament. I feel that Liam's relationship to the Currans is no less complicated than mine even though his mother's blood flows through him.

The priest looks down at my son and speaks of the turf in his hands. "The symbol of energy," the priest says, as he takes the turf from Liam and holds it aloft. Liam seems sorry to let it go and hesitates, the priest's arms making a halo above his head. Then the priest calls out the name of another Curran child, and Liam turns and steps down from the altar. As he walks down the aisle past me, I realize he is surely of this family. If Liam is a Curran, would anyone deny that sometimes I am too?

5. In terms of hybridity, aren't the United States and Canada exceptions, not models for the rest of the world?

Advocates of multiculturalism in North America often are dismissed by critics elsewhere with the following argument: The United States and its northern neighbor, Canada, are just too different from the rest of the rich world to be copied. People can't expect Europe and Japan to build North American–style pluralistic societies. It's not fair or reasonable to expect this because Europe and Japan don't have traditions of mixing and can't change overnight.

This is the argument, at any rate, and the headlines often lend credence to it. Japan remains so aloof from outsiders that an acclaimed film, *Ichigensan* ("first-timer"), dramatized the way in which Japanese politeness toward foreigners is "the commonest form of rejection." The central character of this film, released in 2000, is a Swiss-born graduate student in Kyoto who speaks fluent Japanese, but can forge a bond only with a blind Japanese woman. Unable to see his non-Japanese features, she falls in love with his flawless Japanese accent. Her disability, in short, frees her from the national obsession of keeping at a distance those who look or act differently.[22]

In Europe, outsiders are more welcome than ten or twenty years ago , but immigrant-bashing persists—and is even rising in some countries. Spain has seen a rise in violence against immigrants—most illegals, seeking economic opportunity—from Africa. So has Italy and Ireland. Voters in the Netherlands, famous for their tolerance, rebelled in 2002 against what they saw as the too-easy embrace of immigrants, especially those who are not white. Surprising the Dutch political elite, they voted for a populist who made limits on immigration—and criticism of immigrant lifestyles, especially those that practice Islam—a key piece of his political platform. The populist agenda was lent more credibility because its leader was a homosexual and generally held liberal social views. Only his assassination in 2002 prevented him from becoming the Dutch prime minister—if not that year, then ultimately.

In France, immigrant-bashers also have gained ground. In the presidential election of 2002, Le Pen, a veteran opponent of French multiculturalism who traditionally wins support from 10 to 15 percent of the general electorate, scored enough votes to gain second place and a slot in a run-off election against incumbent Jacques Chirac. Le Pen's achievement set off a landslide of moaning in France, and around the world, about the shifting European attitudes towards diversity. But in the run-off, Le Pen failed to raise his vote-count, and Chirac won in a walk, with more than eight in ten voters choosing him. Le Pen's failure to move beyond a small (albeit significant) minority suggests that the backlash against immigration and people of color in Europe is not as worrisome as pundits insist. Just as the U.S. and Canada harbor a minority of people who reject multiculturalism, so does Europe.This minority should not be ignored—and policies can be put in place to allay the fears of some of these people (for instance, those who have lost jobs or seen wages fall because of immigration, which is a legitimate concern). But Europe's anti-immigrant minority, while vocal, cannot move into the political mainstream. Look what happened when the anti-immigrant party of Austria won a place in the governing coalition after winning one-quarter of the votes in an election in 2000. The European Union, of which Austria is a member, voiced objections and sanctioned the country. And within Austria, the anti-immigrant got no further and indeed went into retreat. The media attention and scrutiny from neighbors made Austrians more aware of how flimsy an issue immigration is in this wealthy country.

To be sure, much of the fuel for immigrant-bashing is provided by European elites who mouth pieties about tolerance and the value of multiculturalism but continue to support policies that guarantee a second-class status for non-white immigrants. In some parts of Switzerland, applicants for citizenship must submit to a humiliating beauty contest, in which their neighbors are asked to vote yea or nay on their candidacy. Besides circulating the applicant's picture, local governments also give out information on the person's job and salary. The process is grueling and seems aimed at intimidating people into not applying for citizenship—and settling for a second-class status. This is especially troubling since even those who are born in Switzerland aren't guaranteed a passport. When a twenty-year old secretary, born in the Swiss city of Emmen of immigrant parents from Bosnia, was turned down, she was bewildered and uncertain about whether she would try again. "The details they ask are so personal, so private," she said.[23]

Liberals and social democrats in Europe like to blame conservatives for stoking xenophobic feelings. They bemoan the periodic outbreaks of violence against immigrants (even in bastions of tolerance such as Sweden), but fail to link these outbursts to the unwillingness of Europe's political elite to accept immigration as a normal state of affairs rather than an unfortunate accident.

As Salman Rushdie has noted, the resistance to diversifying Europe's popula-tion "is invariably linked to failures" of liberal and social-democratic policies, not to any positive vision of the future put forth by right-wingers.[24] Rather than being seen as purely shameful, immigrant-bashing is a useful reminder that the terms of national identity shift only painfully, accompanied by a degree of social tension, even strife.

The key is to respond creatively to such tensions, which are present even in the United States, the prototypical immigration country. Indeed, U.S. open-ness isn't as rooted in tradition as many presume but is often a shrewd response to changing conditions. Contrary to the myth of America as haven, the United States hasn't always welcomed outsiders. In the nineteenth cen-tury, it expelled Asians, and in the twentieth century at times excluded Japa-nese, Chinese and Indian migrants from obtaining citizenship. After 1920, the United States shut the door on Europeans too, even turning away some Jews fleeing Nazi persecution in the 1940s. By the early 1960s, immigration "seemed a closed chapter in the American past," noted Harvard University professor Oscar Handlin.[25]

In short, America has blown hot and cold about strangers at its gates. Prior to 1914, the country was hot. From World War I to the late 1960s, it was cold. From 1970 to 1980, it was warmer. Since 1980, it has been very hot indeed, receiving at least 20 million immigrants.[26] In the 1980s, immigrants accounted for one-quarter of the increase in the workforce. In the 1990s, they accounted for one-half of the estimated 1.5 million workforce increase. In the first eight years of the decade, 8.6 million people immigrated to America, representing 42 percent of the country's population increase of 20.4 million. At the start of the new century, one in ten Americans was foreign-born. And because of the higher fertility rates of immigrant women, George Borjas, the immigration scholar and Harvard University professor, has concluded that immigrants now have "a near-record role . . . in determining" changes in American society and economy, virtually equal to the effect of immigration on the United States in 1910, when 15 percent of the population was foreign-born.[27]

Just as the American picture is distorted, so is the picture for Europe and Japan. If the hostility to immigrants is so great in Europe and Japan, then why are the ranks of their immigrants growing? Both Europe and Japan saw their share of foreigners and foreign-born residents rise sharply in the 1990s. Even countries with historically low numbers of nonnatives saw sharp increases. Migration into Spain, Italy, Portugal and Finland grew so fast that one migra-tion watcher dubbed them "the new immigration countries." Germany saw the percentage of nonnatives in its workforce more than triple from 1986 to 1996. Germany's foreign-born portion of its population rose to 9 percent from 7.5 percent during the same period. In Japan, "contemporary levels of immi-gration are historically unprecedented," one observer concluded in the late

1990s. The official count of foreigners in Japan grew to only 1.1 percent in 1996, up from 0.7 percent ten years earlier, but these figures don't reflect what one study called "substantial illegal immigration."[28]

The data suggest that the social dynamic within rich Europe is closer to the U.S. situation than many realize. And it is likely to get even closer. Population experts predict that European nations will have to allow high levels of immigration for the next few decades in order to prevent crippling labor shortages in the face of falling birthrates. Joseph Chamie, director of the United Nations population division, believes that the likely reaction to Europe's predicament will be pursuit of what he calls "replacement" migration. He predicts that for Italy to keep its population at 1995 levels, it will have to add about 9 million immigrants by 2025 (300,000 a year), Germany will need to import 14 million people (500,000 a year), France 2 million and the European Union as a whole about 35 million. To maintain its 1995 ratio of elderly to active working people, the European Union will need a staggering 135 million immigrants by 2025.[29]

The worker deficit doesn't mean, of course, that Europe or Japan will embrace hybridity out of necessity. But the opposite—a profound halt to immigration and a retreat into monoculture—isn't likely either. European nations and Japan will strive for some kind of balance between roots and wings. And that will inevitably mean a new deal for immigrants and minorities within those countries.

6. Isn't cultural diversity ultimately threatened by mixing and interpenetration on a global scale? Whatever diversity is spawned by mingling in the short term, won't a single, undivided homogeneous mass of humanity emerge in the long run unless something is done to keep people apart?

This paradox looks deceptively simple to unravel. Logic seems to dictate the conclusion that over a millennium, say, widespread mixing will slowly and inexorably erase human differences that took form over thousands of years. In my own travels, I frequently meet people—even those with a mongrel heritage—who see difference threatened by the very forces of intermixing that would seem to protect it.

Sitting one night in a London restaurant, a noisy overpriced place on Leicester Square, a group of women from Ghana, in West Africa, are talking about their lives in Britain. One woman, the youngest of the bunch, sticks out. She's twenty years old, tawny-skinned and with a Zorba-like face. Her name is Violet Alexis, which hints at her curious ancestry. Her mother is from Ghana, and her father is from Greece. The couple met in Europe and moved to Canada, where Violet was born. She attended schools in rural Canada—virtually all-white schools—and then enrolled in a university in Toronto, a mongrel city seemingly well suited to her. But after her first year of university, she visited Ghana, and her passion for her Africanness ignited. She recently transferred to a university in Britain, to be closer to relatives from Ghana, and when I met her she was dating a West African man. Still, while exploring different sides of herself, she was not trying to persuade me that she was African, or even black. "I don't think of myself as either white or black," she told me and then issued the prediction I hear so often. "Someday," she said, "everyone will be mixed."

That someday everyone may be mixed is no certainty. It is not the same as saying that everyone will be the same either. Social identities don't result from mathematical formulas. The metaphor of genetic diversity ultimately would seem to yield an undifferentiated humanity. Yet while useful to suggest the possibilities of a recombinant population, the genetic metaphor fails to describe humanity's fate. To be sure, one of the great dramas of this century—indeed of this millennium—is whether large-scale mixing will lead to greater variety in human types around the world or give rise to a single human race—Globo sapiens—with a common look (light brown) and a uniform sound (English).

The story of Violet Alexis, which is far more common than many people imagine, suggests a different and vastly more interesting future: one in which races and cultures proliferate and flourish within a global context. For even as a generic culture takes hold in airport lounges, corporate boardrooms and international media, an endless parade of new hybrid cultures will arise, clustering around communities of interest and practice and located in neighborhoods and cities, places and spaces. This tendency—proliferating local identities within a global context—may get diluted over hundreds of years as future generations find their differences wearing down, like smooth rocks on an ocean beach, under the weight of close and steady contact. Yet even over a millennium, hybridity may overwhelm homogeneity.

The experience of language offers insights into why this may be so. There are about 6,000 living languages spoken in the world, with an estimated 96 percent of them spoken by only 4 percent of the world's 6 billion people. Three thousand languages are spoken by less than 10,000 people; five out of six languages have less than 100,000 speakers. Half of these marginal languages are endangered. In scores of cases, only a handful of speakers remain alive. And one census taken in 1999 found that fifty-one languages had only one speaker left (twenty-eight of them in Australia). One leading linguist, David Crystal, predicts that over the next century as many as 3,000 of the world's languages will die out. The proximate cause: contact with strangers.

The disappearance of a language certainly represents the loss of distinct cultural traits. But the growing incidence of what Crystal calls "language death" isn't happening in isolation. In some sense people trade one language for another in order to forge a connection to a wider community and thus amplify their talents, increasing their value by making themselves more widely understood. For this reason, a higher percentage of people today are bilingual than ever before in history. This is mainly due to the spread of English, whose rapid acceptance around the world raises the specter of a single language taking over, emerging as a key marker for the dreaded Globo sapiens. But counterintuitively the spread of English isn't killing other languages; it is adding to the diversity of languages spoken by a community or nation. In short, the global stock of language "capital" seems to be growing, not shrinking. As Crystal reasons, "Even if one language does, through some process of linguistic evolution, become the world's lingua franca . . . it does not follow that this must be at the expense of other languages. A world in which everyone speaks at least two languages—their own ethnic language and an international lingua franca—is perfectly possible and (as I shall argue) highly desirable. Because the two languages have different purposes—one for identity, the other for intelligibility—they do not have to be in conflict."[30]

The evolution of language is only a rough analogy for the future of mongrel humanity. But it suggests that claims about the death of diversity are weaker than they may seem.

7. Does the argument in favor of hybridity apply to gender and sexual identity?

Most definitely. People are free to choose their identities. They are defined by their accomplishments as well as their inherited traits. And the more diverse a group—be it a corporation or a university faculty, a charity or a police force—the more likely it is to flourish. The criteria for diversity certainly cover women and homosexuals, and not only as a matter of fairness but also on utilitarian grounds. A society can't afford to squander the talents of its members (in the case of women, half its population). In any case, the odds are that given the increased opportunities for talented people to move to countries where they are really wanted, women and gays who are marginalized by the mainstream won't stick around for long. They will find a new home where they will realize more fully their aspirations, or they will change the mainstream society in ways that make it more attractive to them.

8. Isn't blood really thicker than water? Isn't human identity based on having an enemy?

Call this the "blood and belonging" argument, the idea that individuals hunger to be part of the panting herd and that the herd's strongest validation comes from crushing another herd. In this way of thinking, even educated people are subject to blood pangs. No matter how hard these people try to hybridize and accept the stranger within and without, when the going gets tough—say, the first time their Mercedes (or cow) is stolen—they will shed their multiple affiliations, strip down to their core identity and start attacking aliens. This argument makes for great copy, and journalists love it. It's even reassuring to many ordinary people because it implies a certain delicious fatalism to communal violence.

Large-scale communal violence always contains unfathomable mysteries. But studies of genocide, for instance, consistently isolate social, political and economic factors that, while neither excusing nor fully explaining vast violence, at least strip away some of the mystery. In the case of the at least 500,000 Tutsis slaughtered in Rwanda by neighboring Hutus in a mere 100 days in the spring and summer of 1994, scant evidence exists of an ancient blood feud between the two groups. The cause of the genocide seemed to be simmering tensions, exacerbated by social and political inequalities fostered by former colonial masters, rather than any differences of language, customs, religious beliefs or physical traits. Hutu and Tutsi had, after all, a long history of intermingling and comity that blurred their differences. Philip Gourevitch, in an exhaustive account of the Rwandan carnage, reported that Hutus and Tutsis, far from forging separate identities, had become indistinguishable through centuries of mixing. "We can't tell us apart," one Rwandan told Gourevitch, who noted that Hutu and Tutsis "spoke the same language, followed the same religion, intermarried, and lived intermingled, without territorial distinctions, on the same hills, sharing the same social and political culture in small chiefdoms." The violence by Hutus against Tutsis (and the later reprisals by Tutsi survivors) was linked to the Rwandan state's failures to cope with resentments spawned by Belgian colonialists, who favored the Tutsi, viewing the Hutu as inferior. Belgium, which ruled Rwanda until 1962, turned "relatively fluid" relations between the two groups into "something very rigid and hierarchical," one historian noted. By the late 1950s, as Belgium prepared to hand over the country to home rule, ethnic differences had sharpened, with Hutu attacks on the Tutsi elite coming in 1959. By the early 1960s, a cycle of ethnic violence set in; for the first time, people were killed simply for belonging to one group or another. But then as now, the fighting was about power—who gets it and how much. Although described in ethnic terms, the cleavage between Hutus and Tutsis has little to do with "blood" differences, but much to do with present-day fears and opportunities.[31]

The complexity of ethnic conflict comes home to me one evening as I sit in the corner of a darkened restaurant in Bujumbura, the capital of Burundi. The mirror image of Rwanda, its northern neighbor, Burundi has been dominated by its Tutsi minority, which has used control over the military and economic life to withhold power and prosperity from Hutus, who number an estimated 85 percent of the population. I am sharing a pizza and locally brewed Amstel beer with a tall, skinny man who sits with his back to the wall, his eyes scanning the restaurant every few seconds. He is a senior officer in military intelligence and a Tutsi well known for his commitment to the dream of a peaceful multiethnic Burundi. When the country's democratically elected Hutu president came under attack from the Tutsi army in 1993, this man followed the law. He protected the president, bringing him to a safe house. When the president was later killed anyway, he spoke out against the murder.

Tonight, he is here to tell me how he has suffered because of his actions. It is widely believed that those who conspired to assassinate the president have tried to kill him. As if to underscore the hazards he faces, he coolly draws a gun from his jacket and lays it on the table, his fingers brushing against the grip. This man has no regrets about helping the Hutus and talks forthrightly about how laws must protect both groups. He seems to represent a quiet kind of hero, unwilling to take sides even when many of those around him are doing only that. I expect him to talk easily about how Burundi can only free itself from communal violence—the country has been mired in a cycle of killing between Hutus and Tutsis that has cost 200,000 lives since 1993—through a round of forgiveness, respect and power sharing between the two groups. But then he staggers me by confessing his belief that the Hutus, if given power, will destroy the Tutsis. Even this night, he thinks, Hutus are planning an uprising.

Come morning, there is no uprising, but this man's fear remains. His fear destroys the power of mixing, but he is not bound to feel this fear. Poverty fans his fear. Corruption fans his fear. An absence of courts and justice fans his fear. Elites fan this fear in order to protect their status and ill-gotten gains. Change these factors, and this man's fear vanishes.

Such changes are not simple, by any means, but they do not require a revolution in human consciousness either. Members of one group are not hardwired to turn against members of another. This belief—that somehow people are incapable of forging successful mixed communities—is the grandest distortion to emerge from all the hand-wringing over world affairs since the end of the Cold War in 1991. My Burundian military officer—and many more in his country—are trapped by a madness of their own making. They are seduced by the logic of the pre-emptive strike, getting them before they get us. The appeal of this logic should concern all those who favor hybridity, who admire the mongrel and who strive to mount a new cosmopolitanism. But their concern should not give way to disillusionment. Peaceful intermixing of different peoples is no biological or historical impossibility. The bounty of fruitful mixing is harvested each day in New York City, Los Angeles, London, Berlin, Singapore and countless other hybrid spaces. As much as people talk about the primacy of blood ties—as much as they are moved by the disastrous bloodletting in such places as Burundi—what's more remarkable is the joy and discovery (of themselves and others) that people experience when thrown together with strangers. As it turns out, ordinary people are the first to say that diversity works whenever it's given a fair shot.

This stubborn fact makes me optimistic that growing ethnic and racial diversity will benefit mature nations and that those who say the world is going to hell in a handbasket will be proved spectacularly wrong. I am thus picking a fight with the prophets of doom. They need to be called into question. One of the most persistent dystopians, Michael Ignatieff, writes of how "the world is not run by skeptics and ironists but by gunmen and true believers, and the new world they are bequeathing to the century already seems a more violent and desperate place than I could ever have imagined."[32] To write these words, one must have an impoverished imagination, and a short memory. This is the language of scare tactics aimed at milking an audience. For all the frightful violence in the world, for all the cold-blooded warlords and the senseless killing, from Sierra Leone to Kosovo, from the inner cities of America to the suburbs of Johannesburg, who would turn the clock back to 1989, before the breakup of the Soviet Union and the emergence of Eastern Europe from totalitarianism? Or who would choose the early 1960s, when two power blocs— the American and the Soviet—stood ready to unleash a nuclear exchange almost certain to obliterate humankind? Surely, the ethnopolitical violence that inspires the journalist Robert Kaplan to envision "the coming anarchy" is not so widespread, relentless and severe that anyone would turn the clock back to 1945, when the world lay in ruins from a global war and Hitler, his defeat not inevitable, still stoked the gas chambers with Jewish, Gypsy and other "mongrel" blood.[33] Neither would anyone trade today's communal violence in Indonesia, India or Africa for the late 1930s when the Japanese raped Nanking and Stalin relentlessly slaughtered millions of Soviet citizens. Or would anyone long for the early 1930s, when the industrialized world lay in depression and colonialists still abused vast parts of Asia and Africa?

No, the dystopians are well-intended but wrong. The Bosnias and the Rwandas of the world, scenes of chilling brutality, are not preludes to a global inferno, precursors of what Ignatieff calls "the battle between the civic and the ethnic nation." The world will always have conflicts because, as John Kekes observes, "Making a good life unavoidably involves losing something valuable."[34] But that is no reason to believe it is impossible to strike a healthy, sustainable balance between roots and wings. For all its shortcomings and costs, the model of hybridity offers the best means of doing so.

To be sure, the terrorist attacks of September 11, 2001 have no precedent in the American past and so raise the specter of a dark and dangerous future. The attacks marked the end of an era of optimism about the forces knitting the world closer together. The forces of cosmopolitanism, either of old or the new variety, were also weaker than they seemed, but 9-11 shed a sobering light on the forces of reaction and tradition, revealing the full depth of the anger some feel towards a world of mixing and transcendence of tradition. But even if 9-11 stands as a reminder of the global limitations on diversity and tolerance, the events of that awful day underscore the importance of promoting the ideal of respect for other cultures and mutual understanding. What is the alternative? Who would choose, in the wake of 9-11, to seal borders, close off one nation from another, forbid intermarriage and retreat into islands of imagined purity and harmony? In the wake of 9-11, few have proposed a head-in-the-sand response. Instead, serious people have said 9-11 underscores the need for greater engagement between people of radically different views and social-cultural styles. The project of hybridizing the human community goes by different terms to different people, but 9-11—with its stunning sadness—has shown that there is only one way forward and that is by pursuing the diversity advantage.

So yes, we must listen to the pessimists. The world is a dangerous place. We must not fear defending ourselves. So the peddlers of negativism and insecurity have lessons to teach. But they do not have the entire answer. The dystopians, the peddlers of negativity and anxiety, are well-intended, but they only take us so far. We still need a positive vision of a world where different peoples not only co-exist but communicate through their differences. The World Trade Center bombing, while providing scenes of brutality and humiliation, is not a prelude to a global inferno arising from what Ignatieff calls "the battle between the civic and the ethnic nation." Quite the opposite. Osama bin-Laden is a child of transnationality, not an ethnic nation. He constructed a network out of disparate elements. He created a hybridized Islamic fundamentalism that sought to draw on disaffected peoples from a variety of nations and cultures. Even an American, John Walker, joined bin-Laden's mongrel tribe, illustrating the extent to which the enemies of tolerance and multiculturalism are themselves imbued with the presumptions of multiculturalisms, which in turn suggests that they are influences by cosmopolitan thinking. Walker had his roots—in suburban pop-culture—but also his wings. His ability to join bin-Laden through his creative (if misguided) act of re-invention draws on the same hybrid imagination that sustains so many other Americans today. The stench of 9-11 still fills our lungs so that the paradox of terror escape us: far from repudiating the mongrel, bin-Laden is no tribal warrior, but a malevolent hybridizer.

That even terror networks rely on the liberating mixture of roots and wings provides no balm for our anxieties, however. In the future we will not be free of conflict because conflict is inherent in a good society because, as the philosopher John Kekes observes, "Making a good life unavoidably involves losing something valuable." But that is why it is possible to balance roots and wings, tradition and freedom. Whatever its flaws, the hybridity model offers the best means of doing so.

A MONGREL WORLD

"On what wings dare he aspire."
—WILLIAM BLAKE[1]

"I see humanity as a family that has hardly met. . . . Even those who have never set foot outside the land of their birth are, in their imaginations, perpetual immigrants. To know someone in every country in the world, and someone in every walk of life, may soon be the minimum demand of people who want to experience fully what it means to be alive."
—THEODORE ZELDIN[2]

"To those who believe in race, the spaces in between are plugged tight with impurities: quadroons, octoroons, mulattos, morenas, mutts, mongrels, half-castes, half-breeds, halfies, hapas.
"To those who do not believe there is only this faith: the mixed shall inherit the earth."
—ERIC LIU[3]

THE AGE OF HYBRIDITY is only in its infancy. All over the world racial and ethnic mixing is on the rise. The people profiled in this book are the first wave of liberated hybrids. More are coming.

They face resistance, to be sure, but freedom is their great equalizer. Freedom unleashed the identity revolution. People choose the lives they lead and their range of choices too. Whereas they once had the freedom only to explore an inherited culture, or were relegated to living in enclaves or ghettos in a strange land, they can now build a life from the materials of any culture they know.

This kind of life is new. The old rules don't apply. A hybrid life—a *mongrel* life—will make for a long journey. People will preach apocalyptic disaster for those who embrace hybridity. Nations may muddle along for decades, uncertain whether they have shaken off the prejudices and discomfort that long have characterized mixture and cross-breeding. For these nations, and the world, there will be stops and starts, setbacks and disappointments. Big change won't come overnight. But the direction is clear.

Mixing is a reality. It can be tamed and exploited, not halted or reversed. Roots are not the enemy of wings, and wings can enhance roots, not destroy them. Those nations who fail to make the most of their diversity will shrink in stature, perhaps in size too. Those who deny their diversity by stigmatizing aliens and by branding their own people as traitors, will do worse. If those nations are not doomed, then surely they will be forgotten.

Individuals face less momentous choices. No one will be compelled to pursue a mongrel life. Many will choose to stick close by ancestors, guarding their imagined purity. But they are already a lonely lot. They will grow lonelier still.

Lonely, too, will be those people who tolerate strangers, indeed even welcome them, as long as they behave as guests and *stay in their place*. But advocates of this limited mixing will find to their distress that the best and brightest of their own tribes will lead an exodus to places where hybridity reigns. They will link up with like-minded others in lands near and far.

Happily, tommorrow's hybrids are not a select group. They are the scientist and the janitor, the artist and the house painter, the teacher and the traveler. They are the drum majors of difference.

Hybridity is open to all. Admission is free. It is the ultimate democratization of life. No more walls.

Build a better self. Build a better nation. Build a better way to build. Be all you can be, even if it's another race, religion, creed or color.

Mongrelization transcends toleration. It affirms the tension inside all of us between family and foreigner, native and exile, friend and foe. We can not quell this tension, only learn to harvest its bounties. Indeed, it is only through a collision of different values that we even realize that our differences are respected. So pluralistic tension is a touchstone of the good life.

MUCH IS UNCERTAIN. But the past and present suggest that, under the right conditions, diverse societies can thrive by realizing the promise of hybridity: of the wealth and happiness made possible through the wedding of roots and wings.

Just what are the conditions that enable a whole nation to possess both roots and wings? To respect and observe the stranger within and without? These are great questions, yet we may only know the answers after the fact.

I am reminded of this when I speak with the historian William McNeill as I finish this book. In his seminal study, *The Rise of the West: A History of the Human Community*, McNeill argued that contact with strangers was the motor of historical change. He would later say, in a series of lectures given at the University of Toronto in 1985, that the equation of ethnicity and nationality—and indeed the whole project of patriotism and defining identity through imagined blood lines—was a curious detour in the course of human affairs. "The special conditions supporting the ideal of national ethnic unity . . . were transitory," he said, "whereas the factors promoting ethnic mixing were enduring."

Yet while McNeill found ethnic mingling on the rise everywhere in the world in the 1980s, he told his audience, "Nothing assures that the assortment of migrants and their skills will fit smoothly into the host society." Indeed, a new combination of people "brings both gains and losses, as every important change inevitably does." One of the "losses," he added, was that societies "have almost always accepted and enforced inequality among the diverse ethnic groups of which they were composed."[4]

At the dawn of a new century, such inequalities are no longer accepted in liberal political nations and certainly are resisted more aggressively than ever before by migrants. This sets the stage for humanity to forge a new balance between novelty and comfort. "For the human race, change comes from the meeting of strangers," McNeill tells me. "Strangers upset you in some sense but they still bring new ideas and techniques, which make you pause and wonder and maybe change your ways. By accepting this multiplicity, you surrender a certain psychological comfort and social cohesion for innovation and novelty. This tends to weaken social cohesion and beyond a certain point it becomes counter productive. Exactly where that point is no one can tell in detail."

I say that in *The Diversity Advantage* I insist that nations can manage hybridity by striking a better balance between innovation and tradition. Isn't this possible, I ask McNeill?

He laughs and corrects me. "Politicians and you journalists act as if we can control this. We can't. Things happen. People react as best they can." I try to protest but he brushes me aside. "You expect us to run ourselves as if we know what we're doing. That's not the way human beings behave. They never have." He pauses, then adds solemnly, "Some societies will suffer Bosnia and some will have the stimulus of multiplicity and not break down." There's no way of telling in advance, he says, what's the best mix between comfort and novelty for any one nation. People—even patriots—must grope.

But we are not completely in the dark. "The optimal mix," McNeill says, "will tend to spread and the success of different countries will register what that mix is. Throughout history people in one country are struck again and again by the realization that other people can do things we can't. That's what history is: the recognition that something is rather superior to what you have. One people do something well and then they get imitated. These things spread. When there's something that's better than anything else it tends to spread. This is what people know. They know how to adjust, borrow and sometimes to improve on that. This is the whole history of mankind."

It is also humanity's future. For the billion people in the world's rich nations, and even more elsewhere, life will increasingly be lived the hybrid way: by people piling up a multiplicity of attachments, participating in many places at once. Aided by communications technology and travel, "the proportion of the human race doing this will be much greater than ever," McNeill agrees. "This is so new that it takes imagination to think what life will be like in another generation or two." The experience of diaspora, described in chapter two, points the way. "Now the home country won't disappear when you cross the ocean," McNeill says. "Assimilation will go more slowly in some ways. Human beings have always had a series of roles that they play at different times in their life cycle, but the variety of identities is going to increase. Because of this, I don't think we'll see a single human kind. There will be innumerable diasporas, each retaining a certain distinctiveness."

OTHERS ECHO McNeill's studied reflections. Demographers predict that over the next fifty years the number of people with mixed ancestry will soar. One respected forecast predicts that the percentage of Americans claiming mixed ancestry—meaning some combination of Black, White, Hispanic and Asian—will likely triple, to 21 percent by the year 2050. Within some groups the rates will be even higher. Among Asian Americans, the percentage could reach 36; for whites 21; for blacks 14; and for Hispanics 45.[5] The percentage rates in Europe, Japan, Australia and Canada will rise as well.

People are celebrating difference as never before. Can they all have it wrong? Are they misfits without a cause? No. They've got it right. Pure is passé. Original is out. The hybrid is hip.

Hybridity is a better way of thinking about diversity. Only hybridity promises to make diversity an advantage for communities, corporations, nations and their leaders. The melting-pot ideal won't do it. The separatist ideal of national colonies won't do it either. And refusing to recognize diversity won't do it either.

This last option is often the first option in poor countries. We know the horrors of ethnic cleansing. We know the disappointments. We know about the failures to halt the carnage. We know that ethnic conflicts will dominate this new century and mock the apostles of mixture. These certainties are etched in our minds along with the awful images from Kosovo and Timor, Rwanda and Bosnia—bloody rebukes to those who harbor the dream of a productive politics of difference.

Do not be confused by the failures of diversity in poor countries. Their problem is not diversity. Mixing doesn't cause social explosions. Poverty causes them. Joblessness causes them. Homelessness and hunger and ill-health cause them. Bad government does too. So does the distant thunder of colonialism. And the greed of dictators.

If rich nations have a special role, it is surely to show the rest of the world that mixing of peoples need not kill anyone. Rich nations can show that intermingling of peoples is practical, preferable and profitable. Because some day these poor nations will have to turn their diversity into a strength too.

Only hybridity will make it so. Only a new cosmopolitanism, imbued with an appreciation for both roots and wings, will satisfy the demands of liberty. Only a commitment to diversity that transcends the ideological traps of the past can survive.

This is a hard message but sometimes the hard way is the only way. After all, radical mixing is here. Its arrival is unmistakable. It is breaking down social categories, giving rise to new combinations, fueling creativity and forcing people to re-examine their habits and traditions. Radical mixing is reordering the wealth of nations and national identities. It is the most powerful social force on the planet, more powerful than the shifts in technology and economics that are causing more mixing of people. Technology and economics change the world, but mixing alters who we are. It turns us inside out.

Look in the mirror. Look, really look.

Does the box *they* put you in describe who you are?

See what I mean?

This is scary but exciting. This will add to rather than diminish our humanity.

Is this not our best hope?

NOTES

The following citations refer only to text drawn from other sources. All other direct quotes are based on the author's personal interviews and are not cited here.

INTRODUCTION

1. Whitman quote in R. Takaki, *A Different Mirror: A History of Multicultural America* (1993), 428.
2. R. Bourne, "Trans-National America," *Atlantic,* July 1916.
3. T. R. Gurr, *Minorities at Risk: A Global View of Ethnopolitical Conflicts* (1993), 5; *World Directory of Minorities* (1997).
4. J. Smith and B. Edmonston, *The New Americans: Economic, Demographic and Fiscal Effects of Immigration* (1997), 91; *USA Today,* "Blended Races Making True Melting Pot," September 7, 1999.
5. A. O'Connor, "Learning to Look Past Race: Walnut's Young People, Seeing Friends Rather Than Skin Color, May Offer a Glimpse into America's Future," *Los Angeles Times,* August 25, 1999.
6. Melville quote cited in R. Takaki, *A Different Mirror: A History of Multicultural America* (1993), 427.
7. Alternatively, Germans and Japanese—and notably many conservatives in the United States—essentially argued that the United States would never regain global economic dominance because its society was built on racial and ethnic mixing—that these presumed "impurities" simply were too big a burden on the American economy. Well, where are the advocates of this position now? After a decade of economic stagnation in Japan and Germany. They are keeping their heads down, and are embarrassed to be reminded of their chauvinism.
8. M. Kanabayashi, "Tokyo Is Urged Not to Ease Its Tight Immigration Laws," *Wall Street Journal,* April 29, 1999; "Japan Advised to Open Up," *International Herald Tribune,* January 19, 2000.
9. S. Castles and M. Miller, *The Age of Migration: International Population Movements in the Modern World* (1998), 203.
10. *Yomiuri Shimbun,* "Unveiling Religious Debate in German Schools," July 28, 1998; *The Guardian* (U.K.), "Germany to Deport Boy," November 14, 1998.
    The boy reportedly had a record of more than sixty offenses, but his appeal to Germany's supreme court failed even though his parents had lived legally in the country for thirty years.
11. D. Hollinger, "Nationalism, Cosmopolitanism, and the United States," in N. Pickus, ed., *Immigration and Citizenship in the 21st Century* (1998).
12. *Concise Oxford Dictionary,* 10th ed., 1999.

13. S. Rushdie, "In Good Faith," *The Independent on Sunday*, February 4, 1990, 18–20.
14. R. Cohen, *Global Diasporas: An Introduction* (1997), 30.
15. A. Appiah, "Cosmopolitan Patriots," in P. Cheah and B. Robbins, eds., *Cosmopolitics* (1998), 91–92, 111.

    Mitchell Cohen calls rooted cosmopolitanism "a dialectical concept . . . which accepts a multiplicity of roots and branches and that rests on the legitimacy of plural loyalties, of standing in many circles, but with common ground." See Cohen, "Rooted Cosmopolitanism," *Dissent*, Fall 1992.

    I wish to thank David Hollinger for bringing to my attention his use of the word "wings" as a *yin* to the *yang* of "roots."
16. United Nations, *Human Development Report* (1999); World Bank, *World Development Indicators* (1999); Merrill Lynch, *Global Reference Statistics* (1999).

    Excluded from my list of rich nations are the following: (1) overseas territories of major powers such as Bermuda, the Faroe Islands, French Polynesia, Guam, the Virgin Islands and the Dutch Antilles; (2) oil kingdoms Kuwait, Brunei and the United Arab Emirates; (3) microstates such as Monaco and Liechtenstein; (4) the religious state of Israel, where the potential for hybridity collides with the national charter.
17. M. Ignatieff, *Blood and Belonging: Journeys into the New Nationalism* (1993), 13.

CHAPTER ONE: THE IDENTITY TOOLBOX

1. E. Liu, *The Accidental Asian: Notes of a Native Speaker* (1998), 82–83.
2. S. Kauffman, *At Home in the Universe* (1995), 114.
3. R. Lifton, *The Protean Self* (1993), 136.
4. When it comes to tracking ethnic and racial mixing, and its relation to national identity, demographers are plagued by poor data. This drawback may be inherent in building a statistical portrait of the makeup of a society by age, race, gender and ethnicity. The data on race, ethnicity, religion or any other identity attribute ultimately arise from one of two sources: self-reports or observations by others. Both have shortcomings. First, self-reports: The offspring of a mixed marriage, for instance, may lack the language or tools to adequately describe himself. He may choose one category in one setting and a different one in another. This may strike him as perfectly sensible: In the home of his Mexican father, he is Mexican, but when visiting his child's school he may present himself as white or Hispanic or just an American. An Australian whose grandparents hailed from Britain, Scotland and Ireland may decided to emphasize his Scottishness when that seems in fashion or celebrate his Irishness later in life. Because self-reports vary so greatly, observers are sometimes asked to classify people. But outsiders often impose labels on people that don't fit snugly, ignoring the mixed backgrounds in favor of clear descriptions.

    All this labeling creates a thicket of problems for demographers, whose statistical results can dramatically shift because of what they call "exogamy assumptions." Some simple examples show why assumptions matter and how hard it is to craft useful ones. As one demographer explains, "Conventional population projections make a simple assumption that children will eventually report their ethnicity to be the same as their mothers." But look what happens if they don't. "Suppose that the population consists only of Italians and Norwegians. Suppose further that each couple has two children. If Italians marry only Italians, then the future size of the Italian population will be a function only of the demography of Italians. All progeny of Italian parents would presumably report themselves as of Italian ancestry. But the two children of an Italian and Norwegian couple may report themselves as" Norwegian, Italian or both. Assumptions about exogamy, therefore, matter a great deal to a society's statistical self-portrait.

To be sure, demographers have tried to mitigate the effects of the unfathomable variety of self-perceptions and attributed affiliations and the mixing that underlies them. In a benchmark 1997 analysis of American social identities commissioned by the National Academy of Sciences, demographers gained greater accuracy by assuming (as is fair to do) that native-born people have a greater tendency to intermarry than foreign-born people and that the propensity for intermarriage grows with each successive generation born on U.S. soil. Different groups also out-marry at different rates, so that greater clarity can be gained by building these rates into a population model. Moreover, people with multiple affiliations tend to emphasize one affiliation over another, at least in some ethnoracial combinations (many offspring of black-Latino intermarriages see themselves as black, for instance). When these factors are taken into account, a more sophisticated basis for statistical assumptions is possible (though it doesn't even begin to tackle the identity issues raised by voluntary affiliations illustrated by Barry Cox, in which someone "joins" an ethnic group not through marriage but sheer will). But problems with data still limit this more nuanced analysis. Data on mixing between *unmarried* couples is virtually nonexistent, for instance. Even intermarriages depend on the observer. For instance, a white person might identify an Asian in-marriage when the daughter of Cambodian immigrants marries the son of Chinese immigrants; yet these families might dissent. African Americans might view the marriage of a white man and white woman as completely unlike the marriage between themselves and a person of Mexican descent; yet if the white man is the offspring of German-born parents and the white woman's parents are Holocaust survivors, then surely this is a significant mixture.

The point of all these examples is not to suggest that attempts by demographers to capture radical mixing, or hybridity, are hopeless; only that the task is exceedingly difficult and that—because the basic data of analysis are historically conditioned—it may not get any easier for a long time. It will take at least a generation for today's heightened awareness of the Janus-faced nature of social identity to begin to shape the ethnic, racial and national breakdowns in population reports.

See J. Smith and B. Edmonston, *The New Americans: Economic, Demographic and Fiscal Effects of Immigration* (1997), 89–93.

5. "From Newcomers to New Americans," National Immigration Forum, July 1999; *USA Today*, "Blended Races Making True Melting Pot," September 7, 1999.

6. "Love on the Global Scale Can Be Bumpy," *Asiaweek*, March 10, 1995; "International Matchmaking Organizations: A Report to Congress," by Robert J. Scholes of the University of Florida, INS, 1999; "Love and the Law," *Newsday*, February 23, 1999; "Divorce, Custody and International Battle," *Chicago Sun-Times*, November 21, 1996.

Such marriages were once viewed chiefly as a ruse for one of the mates to obtain a U.S. residency permit, but the INS estimates that only 6 percent are phony. The U.S. government still gives international newlyweds a hard time, on the basis of a 1986 law that makes a foreign spouse wait at least two years before gaining the right to permanent residency in the United States. Often, the wait is much longer. "Many couples face unwanted separations, financial hardship and shattered dreams," one newspaper reported, when they try to enter the United States as a couple. Then there is the problem of breakups. Stories abound of foreign-born men spiriting their children off to their homeland to take advantage of favorable custody laws. American women have done the same in the United States.

Paradoxically, international unions are often seen, at least by the American men who procure wives through matchmaking services, as a means to validate their "traditional values." Thus, they are opening themselves to a cosmopolitan experience out of a belief that "American women are thought not content to be wives and mothers but seek personal satisfaction through their own careers and interests, while the foreign woman is happy to be the homemaker and asks for nothing more than husband, home and family. Again, true or not, this is the perception."

7. D. Hollinger, "Postethnic Nationality and the Separatism of the Rich," *Public Historian,* Winter 1997.
8. "What Color Is Black," *Newsweek,* February 13, 1995.
9. W. Sollors, ed., *The Invention of Ethnicity* (1989), xix.
10. P. Collier, "Doing Well Out of War: An Economic Perspective," in *Greed and Grievance: Economic Agendas in Civil Wars* (2000).
11. E. Hobsbawm, *The Invention of Tradition* (1983), 1–14.
12. Sollors, *The Invention of Ethnicity,* xiii–xiv.
13. J. Eller and R. Coughlan, "The Poverty of Primordialism," reprinted in Sollors, *The Invention of Ethnicity,* 45–50.
14. D. Hollinger, *Postethnic America* (1995), 39.
15. Phone statistic cited in P. Iyer, "The New Business Class," *New York Times Magazine,* March 8, 1998.
16. For a fuller treatment of these possibilities, see F. Cairncross, *The Death of Distance* (1997), 242–245.
17. Sinead is a pseudonym.
18. Thanks to David Hollinger for suggesting this phrase.
19. Cited in R. Cohen, "Memory Goes to War," review of M. Dobbs, *Madeleine Albright: A Twentieth-Century Odyssey* (1999), in *New Republic,* July 12, 1999.
20. R. Solomon, *Continental Philosophy Since 1750: Rise and Fall of the Self* (1988), 187.
21. Lifton, *The Protean Self,* 50.
22. C. Taylor, "Politics of Recognition," in D. Goldberg, ed., *Multiculturalism: A Critical Reader* (1994), 79.

CHAPTER TWO: ROOTS AND WINGS

1. "The New Immigrant Tide: A Shuttle Between Worlds," *New York Times,* July 19, 1998.
2. W. McNeill, *Polyethnicity and National Unity in World History* (1986), in A. D. Smith and J. Hutchinson, eds., *Nationalism* (1994), 304.

3. The mobility statistic credited to Stephen Moore of the Cato Institute: *The Economist,* March 11, 2000.

4. R. Cohen, *Global Diasporas: An Introduction* (1997), 93.

5. "The New Immigrant Tide: A Shuttle Between Worlds," *New York Times,* July 19, 1998.

6. Yanni is a pseudonym.

7. C. Dugger, "In India, an Arranged Marriage of 2 Worlds," *New York Times,* July 20, 1998.

8. Ibid. This *New York Times* account is also based on author's interview with Shahshi Sethi.

9. D. Held, A. McGrew, D. Goldblatt, and J. Perraton, *Global Transformations: Politics, Economics and Culture* (1999), 311–312.

10. L. Fuchs, *The American Kaleidoscope: Race, Ethnicity and the Civic Culture* (1995), 283–285; O. Handlin, "The Newest Newcomers," in J. Miller, ed., *Strangers at Our Gate: Immigration in the 1990s* (1994, Manhattan Institute), 12–17; "The New Americans," *The Economist,* March 11, 2000.

11. N. Harris, *The New Untouchables* (1995), 15.

12. S. Castles and M. Miller, *The Age of Migration: International Population Movements in the Modern World* (1998), 294.

13. "Constructing a Typology of Ethnic Conflict," in *Ethnic Conflict and Migration in Europe* (Ethnobarometer Program, 1999), 40.

14. Held et al., *Global Transformations,* 283.

15. G. Borjas, *Heaven's Door: Immigration Policy and the American Economy* (1999), 8.

16. F. Fernandez-Armesto, *Millennium: A History of the Last Thousand Years* (1995), 409.

17. Harris, *The New Untouchables,* 36, 137.

18. N. Templin, "Menial Labor: North of the Border, Doctors and Lawyers Are Picking Broccoli," *Wall Street Journal,* March 4, 1996.

19. Cited in J. Crisp, "Policy Challenges of the New Diasporas," paper delivered at a conference on migrant diasporas, London, April 22, 1999.

20. Harris, *The New Untouchables,* 133, 136.

21. S. Sassen, *Guests and Aliens* (1999), 6.

22. Cohen, *Global Diasporas,* 3–4.

23. K. Tololyan, "Rethinking Diaspora(s): Stateless Power in the Transnational Moment," *Diaspora,* 5:1 (1996), 3.

24. Cohen, *Global Diasporas,* 21, 26.

25. K. Tololyan, "The Nation-State and Its Others," *Diaspora,* Spring 1991, 5.

26. F. Ng, "My Father's American Journey," *New Republic,* July 19, 1996.

27. Author interview with Aihwa Ong. See also A. Ong, "Flexible Citizenship Among Chinese Cosmopolitans," in P. Cheah and B. Robbins, eds., *Cosmopolitics* (1998).

28. Author interview with T. Alexander Aleinikoff.

29. P. Spiro, "Dual Nationality and the Meaning of Citizenship," *Emory Law Journal,* Fall 1997, 1444.

30. P. Iyer, "The New Business Class," *New York Times Magazine,* March 8, 1998.

31. Cohen, *Global Diasporas,* 89; T. P. Coogan, *De Valera* (1993); Ho and Gandhi entries in H. Gates Jr. and A. Appiah, eds., *The Dictionary of Global Culture* (1996).

32. B. Parekh, "Integrating Minorities in a Multicultural Society," in *European Citizenship, Multiculturalism, and the State* (1998), 68.

33. W. Kymlicka, *Multicultural Citizenship* (1995), 193.

34. Held et al., *Global Transformations*, 312.
35. E. Hobsbawm, *Nations and Nationalism Since 1780* (1990), 11.
36. Kymlicka, *Multicultural Citizenship*, 90; author interview with Kymlicka.
37. Kymlicka, *Multicultural Citizenship*, 103.

CHAPTER THREE: MONGRELIZE OR DIE!

1. Rushdie quote from ABC News, "The Century," April 10, 1999.
2. A. Storr, "Maladjust Your Mindset," *Times Literary Supplement*, July 23, 1999.
3. Seidenberg quote in *Fortune*, July 19, 1999. At the time, Seidenberg was chief executive officer of Bell Atlantic.
4. D. Landes, *The Wealth and Poverty of Nations* (1998).
5. Storr, "Maladjust Your Mindset."
    "Creativity" is hard to define. I agree with Storr's assertion that "the fundamental definition of creativity is blurred and a matter of dispute."
6. Gardner's views in P. Hall, *Cities in Civilization* (1998), 10–12.
7. L. Galambos and J. Sturchio, "Science, Leadership, and Business: The Multinational Gives Way to the Global Firm in Pharmaceuticals," unpublished paper, March 2000.
8. Naipaul cited in U. Hannerz, *Transnational Connections* (1996), 127.
9. F. Fukuyama, *Trust* (1995), 21.
10. Ibid., 27.
11. "Arsene Wenger, a Football Coach for Europe," *Economist*, February 27, 1999.
12. Hannerz, *Transnational Connections*, 62; I. Lubart, "Creativity Across Cultures," in R. Sternberg, ed., *Handbook of Creativity* (1999), 344–345; C. K. Bradshaw, "Beauty and the Beast: On Racial Ambiguity," in M. Root, ed., *Racially Mixed People in America* (1992), 79.
13. Author interview with Karim Rashid; L. Hales, "A Populist Designer Takes America by Storm," *Washington Post*, in *International Herald Tribune*, August 10, 1999; P. Patton, "Sensuous Minimalism Makes Trash Can a Star," *New York Times*, in *Chicago Tribune*, November 29, 1998; J. Pryweller, "Plastics Sitting Pretty—and Chic," *Plastics News*, April 26, 1999; "How Many Industrial Designers Does It Take to Make a Cup of Tea?" *New Yorker*, December 27, 1999.
14. Eschoo quote in V. Loeb, "Top Chinese-American Scientists Feel Victimized," *Washington Post*, in *International Herald Tribune*, November 26, 1999.
15. A. Saxenian, "Silicon Valley's New Immigrant Entrepreneurs" (Public Policy Institute of California, 1999).
16. G. Zachary, "Foreign Dependency: Silicon Valley Relying on Immigrant Engineers," *San Jose Mercury News*, May 15, 1988.
17. S. Castles and M. Miller, *The Age of Migration: International Population Movements in the Modern World* (1998), 214; Fuentes quote in R. Takaki, *A Different Mirror: A History of Multicultural America* (1993), 426; McWilliams quote in Saxenian, "Silicon Valley's New Immigrant Entrepreneurs," iii.
18. "How Real Is the New Economy?" *Economist*, July 24, 1999, 17.
19. Landes, *The Wealth and Poverty of Nations*, 278.
20. For a fuller account of research and World War II, see G. Zachary, *Endless Frontier: Vannevar Bush, Engineer of the American Century* (1997); T. Hughes, *American Genesis: A Century of Invention and Technological Enthusiasm* (1989).

21. T. Sowell, *Migrations and Cultures* (1996), 38.
22. A. Richie, *Faust's Metropolis: A History of Berlin* (1998), 53–55; S. Sassen, *Guests and Aliens* (1999), 8.
23. Landes, *The Wealth and Poverty of Nations*, 276–281.
24. C. James, *Fame in the 20th Century* (1993), 62.
25. Saxenian, "Silicon Valley's New Immigrant Entrepreneurs," 2–3, 56–62; J. M. Johnson and M. C. Regets, "International Mobility of Scientists and Engineers to the United States—Brain Drain or Brain Circulation?" National Science Foundation (U.S.), November 10, 1998; A. M. Findlay, "New Technology, High-Level Labor Movements and the Concept of the Brain Drain," Organization for Economic Cooperation and Development.
26. N. Harris, *The New Untouchables* (1995), 139.
27. W. McNeill, *Polyethnicity and National Unity in World History* (1986), excerpted in J. Hutchinson and A. Smith, eds., *Ethnicity* (1996), 107–111.
28. Sassen, *Guests and Aliens*, 9–11; Robert Brenner, "The Makings of an Economic Miracle," *Wall Street Journal*, June 5, 1997.
29. Brenner, "The Makings of an Economic Miracle."
30. Sowell, *Migrations and Cultures*, 105, 251.
31. Hall, *Cities in Civilization*, 285–286.
32. A. Smith and J. Hutchinson, eds., *Nationalism* (1994), 287.
33. Sowell, *Migrations and Cultures*, 313–323.
34. R. Cohen, *Global Diasporas: An Introduction* (1997), 16–17.
35. C. Safina, *Song for the Blue Ocean: Encounters Along the World's Coasts and Beneath the Seas* (1998), 218–219.
36. S. Kauffman, *At Home in the Universe* (1995), 292.

CHAPTER FOUR: THE HYBRIDITY FACTOR

1. E. Renan, "What Is a Nation?" (1882), reprinted in G. Eley and R. Suny, eds., *Becoming National: A Reader* (1996).
2. N. Malcolm, *Kosovo: A Short History* (1998), 23.
3. Clinton quote from address to American Society of Newspaper Editors, April 15, 1999.
4. Rock quote from his "Bigger and Blacker" performance.
5. Associated Press, "Ignatz Bubis, 72, Jewish Leader, Dies," *International Herald Tribune*, August 14, 1999.
6. In an August 1999 ruling, for instance, the California Supreme Court said that judges who prohibit in advance the use of racial slurs in the workplace do not violate First Amendment rights. In his opinion the state's chief justice found that such speech constitutes employment discrimination and that a ban on slurs against racial groups "does not violate the right to freedom of speech." *Los Angeles Times*, in *International Herald Tribune*, August 4, 1999.
7. Malcolm, *Kosovo*, 58–80.
8. R. Cohen, *Global Diasporas: An Introduction* (1997), 13.
9. B. Kimmerling and J. Migdal, *Palestinians: The Making of a People* (1994), 96–123, 127–156; also author interview with Migdal.
10. E. Bronner, "Rewriting Israeli History: Textbooks Focus on Facts," *New York Times*, in *International Herald Tribune*, August 16, 1999.

11. W. Kymlicka, *Multicultural Citizenship* (1995), 28–29.

12. M. Lind, "Why There Will Be No Revolution in the U.S.," *New Left Review*, January-February 1999, 233; quote from Alexis de Tocqueville in W. Sollors, *Beyond Ethnicity: Consent and Descent in American Culture* (1986), 3.

13. C. Kolker, "Spanish Becomes the Language of Government in a Texas Town," *Los Angeles Times*, in *International Herald Tribune*, August 14, 1999.

14. J. Herbst, "Global Change and the Future of Existing Nation-States," in W. Danspeckgruber, ed., *Self-Determination and Self-Administration: A Sourcebook* (1997).

15. T. Sowell, *Migrations and Cultures* (1996), 177.

16. E. Liu, *The Accidental Asian: Notes of a Native Speaker* (1998), 82–83.

17. J. Kaufman, "Help Wanted: Immigrants' Businesses Often Refuse to Hire Blacks in Inner City," *Wall Street Journal*, June 6, 1995.

18. M. Valbrun, "New Blood: A Wave of Refugees Lubricates Economy of Rusty Utica, N.Y.," *Wall Street Journal*, March 8, 1999; M. Coeyman, "New Home, New School: Utica, N.Y., Adjusts to Thousands of New Immigrants and Their Children," *Christian Science Monitor*, August 31, 1999.

19. M. L. King, *I Have a Dream: Writing and Speeches That Changed the World* (1992), 180–192.

CHAPTER FIVE: MONGREL NATION

1. B. Brandt, "Agents of Change: Young Berliners of Turkish Origin and the Politics of Citizenship," paper delivered at conference "Nationalism, Identity, Minority Rights," University of Bristol (UK), September 16–19, 1999.

2. OECD, *Trends in International Migration* (1998); R. Munz and R. Ohliger, "Long Distance Citizens: Ethnic Germans and Their Immigration to Germany," undated manuscript, Humboldt University; S. Castles and M. Miller, *The Age of Migration: International Population Movements in the Modern World* (1998), 193.

3. J. Ardagh, *Germany and the Germans* (1995), 16.

4. *The Economist*, August 7, 1999, 105.

5. Ardagh, *Germany and the Germans*, 9; W. Drozdiak, "A Decade Later, Hopes Fade for East Germans," *Washington Post*, in *International Herald Tribune*, September 27, 1999.

6. John Ardagh has observed: "Easterners in their turn, today, still resent the way that the west has simply taken over the east as a kind of colony, imposing its own systems and standards, without much regard for local feelings." Ardagh, *Germany and the Germans*, 9.

7. G. Zachary, "Letter from Magdeburg," *Washington Quarterly*, Spring 1999; "In Germany, West Gains As More Lose Jobs in East," *International Herald Tribune*, November 10, 1999.

8. T. Sowell, *Migrations and Cultures* (1996), 50–55.

CHAPTER SIX: DIVERSITY BY DESIGN

1. In P. Smith, *Japan: A Reinterpretation* (1997), 41.
2. Excerpted with permission of author, from K. Singh, *Catwalking and the Games We Play* (1998).
3. In T. Derricotte, *The Black Notebooks* (1997), 10.
4. Following American style, I use the word "nation" to refer to national governments and the life of a country. Europeans prefer the word "state" for this and reserve "nation" for ethnic groups within a state. European scholars thus speak of a single state as containing many nations. Though a fine distinction, it confuses Americans, who think of the "state" as referring to one of the fifty constituent parts of the American nation. They also consider this nation as unitary and the peoples within it free to associate and identify themselves in any forms they wish, including racial and ethnic groups.
5. FitzGerald's quote from his Williamson Memorial Lecture, University of Stirling (Scotland), 1989.
6. C. Townsend, *Ireland: The 20th Century* (1998), 222–223.
7. *Irish Independent*, August 21, 1999.
8. "Ireland: Honey Pot," *Economist*, August 28, 1999.
9. *Irish Independent*, March 20, 2000.
10. Scannell quote in D. Scannell and S. Champion, eds., *Shenanigans: An Anthology of Fresh Irish Fiction* (1999), ix; Toibin quote in "The Shock of the New," *Independent* (London), September 18, 1999.
11. J. Herbst, "Global Change and the Future of Existing Nation-States," in W. Danspeckgruber, ed., *Self-Determination and Self-Administration: A Sourcebook* (1997), 83; T. Karl, *The Paradox of Plenty* (1997).
12. No widely accepted definition exists of what makes a nation "small." As Jeffrey Herbst notes in a review of the literature, scholars range in defining "small" as those countries with anywhere from 1 million to 10 million people. Some economists even qualify as "small" all countries whose domestic policies can't significantly affect the world economy, which could certainly include even Turkey or Canada. Because definitions vary so widely, Herbst concludes that "the demarcation between 'small' and 'not small' is usually arbitrary." See Herbst, "Global Change," 80.
13. "Little Countries: Small but Perfectly Formed," *Economist*, January 3, 1998.
14. E. Gellner, *Nationalism* (1997), 48.
15. T. Inglis, *Moral Monopoly: The Rise and Fall of the Catholic Church in Modern Ireland* (1998), 18–19.
16. For a scholarly account of official Irish attitudes toward Jews, see D. Keogh, *Jews in Twentieth-Century Ireland* (1998).

    Keogh observes that anti-Semitism remained prevalent in Ireland into the 1970s and that the Jewish community, never large, has seen its ranks steadily depleted. According to Keogh, the Jewish census in Ireland fell from 3,907 in 1946 to 2,633 in 1971. The official figure in 1991 was 1,581, but Keogh estimates that by the mid-1990s no more than 1,200 Jews remained in Ireland.
17. F. O'Toole, *The Lie of the Land: Irish Identities* (1999), xvii, 5.
18. In C. Honore, "Along with Wealth, Irish Gain Xenophobia," *National Post* (Canada), April 16, 1999.
19. *Irish Independent*, March 20, 2000.

20. In K. Holmquist, "Strangers in Their Own Land," *Irish Times*, August 17, 1999.

21. P. MacÉinrí, "How Does It Feel? Migrants and the Postmodern Condition," *Chimera* 9, 1994, 87–94.

22. P. MacÉinrí, "States of Becoming: Is There a 'Here' Here and a 'There' There?" *Chimera* 13, 1998, 24–34.

23. B. Spindle, "In Kanazawa, Japan, There Is a Fireman Unable to Fight Fires," *Wall Street Journal*, July 28, 1998.

24. P. Smith, *Japan*, 274; author interview with Florian Coulmas.

25. N. Kristof, "For Japan, Signs of Diminished Influence in Next Century," *New York Times*, in *International Herald Tribune*, August 2, 1999.

26. B. Wysocki, "Where Will All the Babies Go?" *Wall Street Journal*, January 1, 2000; "Japan Advised to Open Up," *International Herald Tribune*, January 19, 2000; H. French, "Demographics Pushing Japan to Open Up to Immigrants," *New York Times*, in *International Herald Tribune*, March 15, 2000.

27. T. Sowell, *Migrations and Cultures* (1996), 125–137; OECD, *Trends in International Migration* (1998), 253; H. French, "Demographics Pushing Japan to Open Up to Immigrants," *New York Times*, in *International Herald Tribune*, March 15, 2000.

28. In S. Romero, "An Exodus of Emigrants: Brazil's Japanese Community Submits to the Pull of the Homeland," *New York Times*, in *International Herald Tribune*, October 18, 1999.

29. J. Rauch, *The Outnation: A Search for the Soul of Japan* (1992), 79.

30. Y. Ono, "The Big Yawn, or How the Pill Made Its Way to Japan," *Wall Street Journal*, July 1, 1999; *Irish Times*, "Japan's Doctors Finally Accept the Pill," September 3, 1999.

31. "A Small Victory for Women at Japan Inc.," Associated Press, in *International Herald Tribune*, August 6, 1999.

32. W. McNeill, *Polyethnicity and National Unity in World History* (1986), excerpted in J. Hutchison and A. Smith, eds., *Ethnicity* (1996), 108–109; W. Morton, *Japan: Its History and Culture* (1994), 141–143.

33. Morton, *Japan*, 272–275.

34. T. Berger, "International Migration and Japan: Between the Irresistible Force and the Immovable Object," unpublished presentation at the University of Virginia, January 19, 1999.

35. Ibid.; F. Coulmas, "Japan's Minorities, Old and New," unpublished paper presented at "Nationalism, Identity, Minority Rights" conference, University of Bristol (UK), September 16–19, 1999.

36. D. Struck, "Navigating the Bases the Japanese Way," *Washington Post*, in *International Herald Tribune*, September 6, 1999.

37. Kristeva quote in P. Smith, *Japan*, 269–270.

CHAPTER SEVEN: THE COSMOPOLITAN CORPORATION

1. McGinn quote in "Where Diversity Really Works," *Fortune*, July 19, 1999. McGinn is CEO of Lucent.

2. Dahrendorf quote in "The Third Way and Liberty," *Foreign Affairs*, September-October 1999.

3. Yeo is chair of the Economic Development Board, Singapore (author interview).

4. Lindahl quote in *International Herald Tribune*, July 17, 1999.
5. Author interview with Elizabeth Marx.
6. D. Lyons, "CEO Export-Import Trade Flourishes," unpublished paper, July 1999. Lyons is a senior director in the New York office of executive recruitment firm Spencer Stuart.
7. *Baffler* 12, 1999, 82; "Retooling," *Marketing Tools*, April 1998.
8. P. Harris and R. Moran, *Managing Cultural Differences* (1996), 12–15.
9. S. Stecklow and J. Karp, "Borrower Beware: Citibank in India Used Collectors Accused of Strong-Arm Tactics," *Wall Street Journal*, May 25, 1999.
10. T. Buerkle, "In Corporate Europe, Homegrown Talent Starts Calling Shots," *International Herald Tribune*, July 27, 1999.
11. T. Aeppel, "Babel at Work," *Wall Street Journal*, March 30, 1998.
12. R. Block, "Target Marketing: How McDonald's Survived in Belgrade," *Wall Street Journal Europe*, September 3, 1999.
13. A. Barrett, "Hey, Why Do You Think We Call Them French Fries," *Wall Street Journal Europe*, December 9, 1999.
14. Ohmae quotes in U. Hannerz, *Transnational Connections* (1996), 85–86.
15. "The Face of Mammon," *Economist*, December 4, 1999.
16. C. Lasch, *The Revolt of the Elites* (1995), 25.

CHAPTER EIGHT: MONGREL LEADERSHIP

1. Roosevelt quote in R. Takaki, *A Different Mirror: A History of Multicultural America* (1993), 374.
2. W. McNeill, *Polyethnicity and National Unity in World History* (1986), 81.
3. W. Kymlicka, *Multicultural Citizenship* (1995), 7.
4. Cited in S. Vertovec, "Multi-Multiculturalisms," in M. Martiniello, ed., *Multicultural Policies and the State: A Comparison of Two European Societies* (1998), 37.
5. S. Kauffman, *At Home in the Universe* (1995), 113–114, 128.
6. *Time International*, January 25, 1999.
7. F. Kempe, *Father/Land* (1999), 237–238.
8. "Talking with Tomorrow: George Yeo," *Wall Street Journal*, January 1, 2000.
9. Ibid.
10. Associated Press, "Singapore's Yeo Defends Efforts to Lure Foreign Talent," March 11, 1999.
11. R. Brenner, "The Makings of an Economic Miracle," *Wall Street Journal*, June 5, 1997.
12. "Talking with Tomorrow: George Yeo," *Wall Street Journal*, January 1, 2000.
13. E. Gellner, *Nationalism* (1997), 2–3.
14. R. Bourne, "Trans-National America," *Atlantic Monthly*, July 1916.
15. Quote in J. Hutchison and A. Smith, eds., *Ethnicity* (1996), 135.
16. J. Spencer, *The New Colored People: The Mixed Race Movement in America* (1997), 2–4.
17. Bourne, "Trans-National America."

CHAPTER NINE: THE NEW COSMOPOLITANS AND THEIR CRITICS

1. G. Zachary, "The World Gets in Touch with Its Inner American," *Mother Jones,* January 1999.
2. M. Cohen, "Rooted Cosmopolitanism," *Dissent,* Fall 1992.
3. W.E.B. Du Bois, *The Souls of Black Folk* (1903; Penguin ed. 1996), 5.
4. I. Buruma, "Churchill's Cigar," *Granta* 65, 1999.
5. F. Godement, *The Downsizing of Asia* (1999), 115.
6. The beating of Rodney King by the Los Angeles police in the early 1990s sparked rioting in that city and King's own plea for calm.
7. A. Appiah, "Cosmopolitan Patriots," in P. Cheah and B. Robbins, *Cosmopolitics* (1998), 101–103.
8. L. Funderburg, "Integration Anxiety," *New York Times Magazine,* November 7, 1999.
9. L. Fuchs, *The American Kaleidoscope: Race, Ethnicity, and the Civic Culture* (1995), xx.
10. Du Bois, *The Souls of Black Folk* , 5 (Penguin ed. 1996).
11. Miller quote in W. Sollors, *Beyond Ethnicity: Consent and Descent in American Culture* (1986), 3.
12. J. Joffe, *The Future of Great Powers* (1998), 43–47.
13. Y. Shain, *Marketing the American Creed Abroad: Diasporas in the U.S. and Their Homelands* (1999), 31.
14. J. Smith and B. Edmonston, *The New Americans: Economic, Demographic and Fiscal Effects of Immigration* (1997), 376.
15. Rumbaut cited in D. Miller, "Scholars of Immigration Focus on Children," *Chronicle of Higher Education,* February 5, 1999; G. Rodriguez, "From Newcomers to New Americans: Successful Integration of Immigrants into American Society," National Immigration Forum, July 1999.
16. For a more optimistic view of minorities in China, see M. Pei, "From Nominal Autonomy to Genuine Self-Administration: A Strategy for Improving Minority Rights in China," in W. Danspeckgruber, ed., *Self-Determination and Self-Administration: A Sourcebook* (1997).
17. M. Ignatieff, "The Scene of the Crime," *Granta* 63, Autumn 1998.
18. A. Lamey, "Francophonia Forever," *Times Literary Supplement,* July 23, 1999.
19. "Population: Like Herrings in a Barrel," *Economist,* December 31, 1999.
20. Marglin quote in U. Hannerz, *Transnational Connections* (1996), 62–64.
21. Hannerz, *Transnational Connections,* 62–64.
22. S. Kaori, "Inside and Outside, a Foreigner in Japan," *International Herald Tribune,* February 1, 2000.
23. E. Olson, "Swiss Town Puts Brake on Hopes for Citizenship," *International Herald Tribune,* March 13, 2000.
24. S. Rushdie, "Europe Must Blame Itself," *Independent on Sunday* (London), February 6, 2000.
25. O. Handlin, "The Newest Newcomers," in J. Miller, ed., *Strangers at Our Gate: Immigration in the 1990s* (1994, Manhattan Institute), 12–17.
26. Center for Immigration Studies, "Immigrants in the United States: A Snapshot of America's Foreign-Born Population" (January 1999); D. Held, A. McGrew, D. Goldblatt and J. Perraton, *Global Transformations: Politics, Economics and Culture* (1999), 292.
    The number of immigrants in the United States totaled 13.6 million in 1910

and barely rose over the next twenty years. After 1930, the number of immigrants steadily declined, falling below 10 million, or just 4.8 percent of the total population in 1970. In 1980, the absolute number of immigrants in the United States exceeded the number in 1920 for the first time in sixty years. In 1990, the number reached 20 million.

27. R. Judy and C. D'Amico, *Workforce 2020: Work and Workers in the 21st Century* (1997), 98; G. Borjas, *Heaven's Door: Immigration Policy and the American Economy* (1999), 7–8.

28. Organization for Economic Cooperation and Development, *Trends in International Migration* (1998), 30–33; Held et al., *Global Transformations*, 315–316.

29. B. Crossette, "The World: It's the American Way, Europe Stares at a Future Built by Immigrants," *New York Times*, January 2, 2000.

30. D. Crystal, "The Death of Language," *Prospect*, November 1999; D. Crystal, *Language Death* (2000), 24.

31. P. Gourevitch, *We Wish to Inform You That Tomorrow We Will Be Killed with Our Families*: *Stories from Rwanda* (1998), 47–50; I. Fisher, "The Recent Roots of Hutu-Tutsi Hate," *New York Times*, in *International Herald Tribune*, January 4, 2000.

32. M. Ignatieff, *Blood and Belonging: Journeys into the New Nationalism* (1993), 248.

33. R. Kaplan, *The Coming Anarchy* (2000).

34. J. Kekes, *The Morality of Pluralism* (1993), 23–24.

This means, Kekes notes, that people come to realize "first, that, the conflict we are facing is usually not a crisis produced by our adversary's stupidity, wickedness, or perversity but merely another manifestation of the unavoidable conflicts that will continually occur if values are plural, conditional, incommensurable, and incompatible."

CONCLUSION: A MONGREL WORLD

1. W. Blake, "The Tiger."

2. T. Zeldin, *An Intimate History of Humanity* (1994), 465–467.

3. E. Liu, *The Accidental Asian: Notes of a Native Speaker* (1988), 75.

4. W. McNeill, *Polyethnicity and National Unity in World History* (1986), 59–60, 80–85.

5. M.Puente and M. Kasindorf, "Blended races making true melting pot," *USA Today*, September 7, 1999.

ACKNOWLEDGMENTS

ANY BOOK THAT ranges over so wide an area invites major misunderstandings. Broad generalizations naturally prompt skepticism, especially when they address questions of "national character" or group attributes. Individual variety is immense, yet people and their societies do often share more in common than most in this ego-mad world will admit. To be sure, some of my analyses may seem ill-advised or inapplicable to some places, but I hope they are correct in the main. The specialization of knowledge only grows, and the intellectual trends run counter to broad judgments. But important questions still animate people, and still must be answered. I faced down the fear of synthesis on a massive scale by reminding myself that although my truths are partial, partial truths are better than none at all.

I did not write this book as a neutral observer. I have a point of view: I am a humanist and a mongrel lover. I am convinced by my own evidence and arguments, but I also am a creature of my past. I am committed to hybridity because I've lived it. My parents are in an intercultural marriage. When they wed secretly in the early 1950s, it was rare for the son of southern Italian immigrants to marry the daughter of Jewish immigrants from Poland and Russia. As a child, I visited my Italian grandparents on most Catholic holidays and marked Jewish occasions with my mother's relatives. As my father renounced Catholicism in order to marry, I never stepped inside a Catholic church in order to worship. At the age of nine, I asked for religious instruction, having tired of seeing all the children in my class leave school early in order to be with their own kind. My parents joined a synagogue, and I received a bar mitzvah at the age of thirteen. While I sang from the Torah, I saw my father—seated in the first row of the synagogue—fall asleep. This was an odd reminder that maybe I didn't have my own kind.

I can't recall the Italian and Eastern European sides of my family ever meeting. My father's father, Pasquale, called Jews "Christ killers," though he seemed to treat me no worse than a Catholic Italian. He was a highly local person, trusting only those he had known for many years. My father joked that Pasquale, who was from a village outside of Bari near the Adriatic coast, spoke a dialect of Italian that only two people understood: Pasquale and his wife. They had a habit of seeing something new in Brooklyn (which could be almost anything) and then making up a word for it that at least sounded Italian. He first delivered ice to people (in days before electric refrigerators) and then home heating oil. As a present to my father, when he dropped out of high school in the 1940s, Patsy gave him the ice business, which was on its last legs.

Bubbie, my mother's mother, congratulated me on escaping the clutches of Catholicism. She wasn't big on compliments. Her favorite saying was "a knock is as good as a boost." If she didn't bring you to tears, you considered it an achievement. To Bubbie, there were three types of people: Jews; non-Jews; and Super Jews, who nobody could believe were Jews but actually were, such as the baseball star Sandy Koufax and the countless number of entertainers who *really* were Jewish. Was I *really* Jewish? Though in terms of the faith, I was bona fide through the lineage of my mother, I always felt Jewish-plus. This sometimes was nice, but sometimes not. It left me with a triple consciousness: Italian, Eastern European and white American. Sometimes, I felt like a bystander in a war between my ethnic selves: I was an insider and outsider at the same time, never entirely comfortable with other whites, Jews or Italians notwithstanding. I was always wondering whether the fabric knitting us together would rip open, exposing our differences.

My relations with my wife and children are shaped by the protean nature of ethnicity. My wife, Honorah Curran, was the ultimate stranger to me: I was a New York mutt; she was a virginal Irish Catholic from a farm in Tipperary County. The youngest of twelve children, she grew up in a thatch-roofed cottage whose only water source was a well down the boreen. She milked goats, kept racing dogs, hens, geese and cows. Her first school was a one-room house warmed by a single turf fire. It was a short walk from the "Kickham Tree," a memorial to one of the country's staunchest Republican writers. Honorah left Ireland in the mid-1970s, traveling first to Italy, then to Germany and finally to the United States. She came to San Francisco out of curiosity, and stayed, though in the course of twenty years she's visited Ireland about twenty times. Our two children, to whom I have dedicated this book, are dual citizens: American and Irish. Their surname is my American invention ("Zachary" was chosen by my father so that he could sound less Italian), and their first names, Liam and Oona, are Gaelic.

I am not living in the United States as I write this. Though living abroad reminds me of my Americanness, I can't say what specifically makes me American beyond a belief in merit and the possibilities open to those who work hard and welcome change. For me, being American resists any norms, definitions or a priori obligations. No metric exists against which strangers or minorities or migrants or whoever can be judged and found wanting. This is not the same as saying there is no good or evil, right or wrong, only that an American's national inheritance—first language, skin color or group affiliation—does not define our possibilities. Out of the freedom to make and remake ourselves and our societies, our ideals grow, our moral nature shows.

I HAVE MANY PEOPLE to thank for their help in the course of writing this book. First and foremost, my wife Honorah Curran, and my two children. Honorah held together our family, accepted with understanding my frequent research trips and shared my enthusiasm for diversity. Liam, age nine, urged me to write as short a book as possible, applying the same principle of brevity to his own homework assignments. Oona, six, often wished that she could write as fast as I could on my computer and settled for doing wicked imitations of me hunched over the keyboard.

Colleagues at *The Wall Street Journal*, where I've worked since 1989, provided much help for which I am deeply grateful. Paul Steiger, the paper's managing editor, allowed me to relocate from San Francisco to London and then take time off from the paper in order to write this book. Dan Hertzberg and Mike Miller, two senior editors at the paper, supported my quixotic interests and encouraged me to pursue articles that furthered my understanding of the way the forces of identity, diversity and national competitiveness affect a globalizing world. Greg Hill, a dear friend and an editor in San Francisco, helped me to organize several international trips from which the seeds of this book sprang. John Bussey, the *Journal's* foreign editor, and Greg Steinmetz, the former London bureau chief, let me roam over a wide range of topics and geographies. Page One editor John Brecher asked me to report a detailed piece on how America contains its social strife. Marcus Brauchli, the paper's national editor and former China bureau chief, tipped me off to the existence of the Canto-pop singer Barry Cox. Tom Petzinger, formerly a columnist with *The Wall Street Journal*, discussed ideas, read over draft chapters and suggested additional sources; I am most grateful for his help. Bill Spindle, of the *Journal's* Tokyo bureau, shared contacts. Also, portions of *The Global Me* have appeared in the *Journal*, though in different form.

My association with other publications helped too. Jeff Klein, formerly the editor of *Mother Jones*, prodded me to think more deeply about the ways in which the whole world is Americanizing. Michael Mazarr and Nick Koukopoulos, editors at *Washington Quarterly*, published extended articles on Germany and Ireland, on which I draw from here. Joel Bleifus and Craig Aaron, editors at the radical newsweekly *In These Times*, offered a forum for reportage and views that fall outside the mainstream.

IN MY RESEARCH I was greatly aided by the scholarly literature on the subjects of identity, diversity, ethnicity, pluralism, cosmopolitanism, migration, multinational corporations, finance, economic competitiveness, nationalism and international security. Conversations and exchanges with sociologists, historians, anthropologists, cultural-studies scholars and economists proved especially helpful. David Hollinger, an intellectual historian at the University of California at Berkeley, drew on his erudition and judicious spirit to answer my questions about ethnicity, diversity and multiculturalism in the American experience. Annalee Saxenian, a regional economist at Berkeley, shared with me her research and thinking on the relationship among diversity, creativity and economic vitality. Aihwa Ong, a Malaysian-born anthropologist at Berkeley, helped me to better understand transnationality, hybridity and new forms of citizenship. Robin Cohen, a sociologist at the University of Warwick, England, shared his thinking about global diasporas and invited me to an invaluable meeting of leading thinkers on migration at London's Chatham House. Wolfgang Danspeckgruber, director of the Liechtenstein Research Program on Self-Determination at Princeton University, provided inspiration and ideas at the start of my research. Louis Galambos, an eminent historian of business at Johns Hopkins University, invited me to lead a seminar on diversity, creativity and the multinational corporation, where he and colleagues critiqued my ideas. Thomas Berger, a political scientist at Hopkins, shared unpublished research on Japan and Germany. John Kekes, a philosopher at the State University of New York at Albany and my academic adviser during my undergraduate studies there, raised important criticisms of my handling of key philosophical concepts. Will Kymlicka, a philosopher at Queen's University in Ontario, Canada, advised me on the varieties of multiculturalism and let me attend his lectures at the Central University in Budapest. Mark Krikorian, director of the Center for Immigration Studies in Washington, D.C., shared his daily electronic bulletin on global migration, providing me with an unparalleled source of current reports on this broad, fast-moving field. Steve Vertovec, an anthropologist and director of the University of Oxford's Transnational Communities project, suggested readings and contacts. Larry Elliot, economics editor of *The Guardian* newspaper in London, helped me hone my views on multinational corporations and the world economy.

Many people (beyond those credited in the text) helped me arrange interviews and gather materials in various countries. The generosity of strangers always amazes me. Without their aid, this book would be much poorer. I received special help from Martin Jaehn, Kathleen Brown, Almut Schoenfeld, Christina Cziscek, Katrin Gilwald, Johann Goldammer (Germany); Walter Coles, Susan Collin Marks, Andrea Durbin (Washington, D.C.); Annie Bailey, Doug Bibby, Cathy Cook, Harry Grunert, Jack Prizmich, Orville Schell (Berkeley, California); Corey Dubin (Santa Barbara, California); Kristin Njalsdottir (Iceland); Denis Lyons, Hwee Hwee Tan (New York); Kirpal Singh (Singapore); Dindall Rahoon (Malaysia); Chellis Glendinning (New Mexico); Visar

Didar (Macedonia); Liudmila Turculet, Dima Sandu (Chisinau, Moldova); Jean-Marc Giry (France); the Curran family and the Mullinahone chapter of the Gaelic Athletic Association (Republic of Ireland); Birgit Brandt, Nicholas Brealey, Philip Dodd, Mary Hickman (Britain); Johann and Patricia Hengelmon (Holland); and Alexis Sinduhije and Shamill Idriss (Burundi).

In the course of researching this book, I spoke with hundreds of people around the world, interviewing dozens of them many times. In organizing this material, I was aided by my close friend Mark Kavanagh, whose job as a teacher of English to immigrants in Los Angeles gives him a special empathy for the topics handled in this book. Mark's wit, intelligence and sanity were a boon. Wendy Lustbader, a social worker and author in Seattle, closely read the manuscript and made many valuable suggestions. Sarah Ellison doggedly tracked down articles, facts, books and phone numbers.

Finally, my thanks to Geoff Shandler, my editor at PublicAffairs, and Joel Fishman, my agent. Both had the courage to support my vision for this book, helping me to refine my words and thinking over time. In a publishing scene where business values are ever rising and the space to produce thoughtful books is narrowing, Shandler and Fishman had the generosity to share my dream. In a world wedded to Internet-time, where images and data overwhelm our capacities for careful selection and reflection, we leave too little room for childish dreams of tolerance, mutual respect and brotherhood. We should not lose these dreams. If we can make and remake ourselves and our communities—in ways hybrid and not, across continents and cultures, races and ethnicities—then surely we can dream of a better future in which the finest things of yesterday and tomorrow commingle in this moment in time.

G. P. Z.
London, March 2000

INDEX

INDEX